CRUCIB

SURVIVAL

CRUCIBLE FOR SURVIVAL

Environmental Security and

Justice in the Indian Ocean Region

EDITED BY TIMOTHY DOYLE
AND MELISSA RISELY

RUTGERS UNIVERSITY PRESS

New Brunswick, New Jersey, and London

Library of Congress Cataloging-in-Publication Data

Crucible for survival: environmental security and justice in the Indian Ocean region / edited by Timothy Doyle and Melissa Risely.

    p. cm.

Includes bibliographical references and index.

ISBN 978-0-8135-4313-0 (hardcover : alk. paper)—ISBN 978-0-8135-4314-7 (pbk. : alk. paper)

  1. Environmental policy—Indian Ocean Region.   2. Environmental protection—Indian Ocean Region.   3. Environmental justice—Indian Ocean Region. I. Doyle, Timothy, 1960–   II. Risely, Melissa, 1972–

GE190.I43C78   2008

363.7009182'4—dc22

2007039081

A British Cataloging-in-Publication record for this book is available from the British Library.

The publication of this book has been made possible, in part, by a gift from Robert Mortensen.

Visit our Web site: http://rutgerspress.rutgers.edu

Manufactured in the United States of America

Contents

Preface

In 1998, one of this volume's editors, Timothy Doyle, published an article in a special edition of the *Third World Quarterly* dedicated to exploring North-South political geographies. This edition, put together by David Simon and Klaus Dodds, included an array of articles from scholars across the globe, most of whom adopted a critical geopolitical stance. One of the contributors, unbeknownst to Doyle at the time, was an Indian scholar by the name of Sanjay Chaturvedi. Chaturvedi is that most unusual of academics, one who actually *reads* journal articles and then attempts to construct networks of scholars with like-minded interests to himself. So, with this in mind, Doyle received an email from his fellow contributor, inviting him to come to India to further his research at the Centre for the Study of Geopolitics at Panjab University. So began a close personal and professional relationship with Sanjay Chaturvedi. In one of many meetings in both India and Australia, he explained his decision, along with Dennis Rumley of the University of Western Australia (another remarkable man), to set-up an Indian Ocean Research Group (IORG), whose key objective was to initiate a policy-oriented dialogue, in the true spirit of partnership, among governments, industries, NGOs, and communities, toward realizing a shared, peaceful, stable, and prosperous future for the Indian Ocean Region. The objectives were grandiose, but Chaturvedi and Rumley are the sort of people that make one believe that such a thing could happen and, more importantly, that such a group could make a real contribution to the lives of the many people across the Indian Ocean Region. And so, the cat, as it were, was out of the bag.

Chaturvedi and Rumley argue that the Indian Ocean—and the states that exist on its periphery—possesses enormous geopolitical significance, if only in terms of trade. Given its relative location and the fact that it provides a relatively short and economical link between the Pacific and the Atlantic, it is perhaps not surprising that, not only does the Indian account for the transportation of the highest tonnage of commodities in the world, but that more than three-quarters of this is extra-regional trade (IORG 2006). Due to these enormous economic stresses (among others) on the region, environmental factors become extremely important, and will increase in their level of significance in the near future. The Indian Ocean is known to contain an enormous wealth of natural resources, the implications of which is yet to be fully determined. The Indian Ocean Marine Affairs Cooperation (IOMAC) grouping, for example, has already been involved for several years in issues associated with the management of the Indian Ocean tuna fishery. The utilization of these resources, among others, in the context of the delimitation of exclusive economic zones requires careful monitoring and inter-state collaboration.

Finally, the Indian Ocean Region is home to over one-third of the earth's population, many of these comprising the poorest communities on the planet.

As a consequence of these initial negotiations, in 2001 Doyle was offered the position of Founding Convenor of Human and Environmental Security in the newly established Indian Ocean Research Group. At first, despite understanding the commitment of the newly formed IORG to environmental concerns, Doyle had reservations about accepting this post, as it had become widely understood that much of the environmental security rhetoric had been co-opted already by interests pursuing *business-as-usual,* with nation-states, multi-national corporations, and national elites using green language as an additional means of *securitizing* the environment and further disciplining poorer populations to conform to their development projects. But Chaturvedi and Rumley were unshakeable in their commitment to the environment portfolio, allowing Doyle to interpret environmental security in a style that suited his intentions. These specific understandings and interpretations of human and environmental security shape this book, and are essential to achieving the grander goals of the IORG. Its charter reads: "For the maintenance of the peace and stability of the Indian Ocean Region, it is of the utmost importance that regional, coastal, island, and landlocked states become aware of the geopolitical orientations of one another and of Indian Ocean neighbors. The description, collation and analysis of such orientations will assist greatly in the maximization of regional transparency regarding regional state goals and intentions."

The IORG Human and Environmental Security Project is based, therefore, on the assumption that all nation-states within the Indian Ocean Region share a common interest in ascertaining and maintaining a secure environmental future. This project aims to provide a workable concept of a regionally shared, basic and secure environmental future, as well as to identify and research appropriate mechanisms and management strategies that can be employed in problem-solving capacities.

Research leading to environmental security has now moved through two major stages. The first stage was to collate baseline social and environmental data that identified the key environmental security issues within the region. This was done by collating existing data, as well as pursuing fieldwork within different parts of the region. Notions of environmental security within the region are multitudinous, differing greatly at times, from country to country, subculture to subculture. Common appreciation of these diverse understandings and interpretations has been essential to ascertain during the initial stages of the research. This situation makes "on-the-ground" research essential in the context of environmental security issues, as the problems/issues must be valued and understood at the community level, where most of the shared solutions lie.

The second part of the research now moves beyond the definitional stage. Building on the data base, problem-solving strategies are then to be identified and analyzed. Ultimately the environmental security component of the IORG seeks to produce issue identification and problem-solving techniques that can be used by a variety of nongovernmental, governmental, and industrial partners in their implementation of solutions ascertaining and maintaining environmental security in the region.

The other important relationship that must be honored here has ultimately shaped this book: that which has formed between the two editors. Risely completed a Ph.D. with Doyle at the University of Adelaide in 2003. Much of her research has focused on the rapidly emerging biotechnology industry, with its enormous impacts upon food production across the globe. With deep-seated environmental justice concerns, Risely has become very much involved in the IORG Human and Environmental Security Project, and for the past three years has worked tirelessly on pursuing its objectives.

Much of the work of the IORG is about building networks of trust and collaboration across the region between scholars, policy practitioners, non-government groups, and community organizations. In many ways, this often comes in the form of *academic diplomacy.* Academics have a certain freedom of movement, allowing them to move beyond political borders during difficult times, and within restrictive circumstances. Their objectives are often more inclusive of broader and longer-term concerns than those of nation-states, and not as profit-oriented nor as self-interested as those of the corporate world. With all their faults, universities are still *universe-cities,* with their scholar-citizens well-practiced in developing and nourishing transnational networks well before this current fashion of globalization seized the world in the 1990s.

Building these networks has been enormously time-consuming, but equally rewarding, with the fruits of many of these relationships revealed in the pages that follow. For this is not just an edited collection, but the early rewards of the IORG process. Since the inception of the group, we have held symposia on water security in India, energy security in Iran, seaways security in Malaysia, and fisheries security in Oman. In each of these places, we have constructed working relationships between governments, corporations, NGOs, and communities, as well as scholars. Using these symposia as network-building and agenda-setting exercises, further research teams have been developed for particular purposes, spawning new theoretical and on-the-ground projects. So, the contributors to this volume, apart from presenting papers to one or many of these symposia, are now all part of the IORG Human and Environmental Security Project.

Issues of human and environmental justice, security, and emancipation in the IOR are complex and immense, and most of the projects we have embarked upon cannot be measured within scales of human lifetimes, but in a time frame more suited to understanding the life and death of oceans.

This book is just one small part of one small beginning.

Timothy Doyle
Melissa Risely
www.iorgroup.org

Acknowledgments

The efforts of many people go into making such a book, and despite our best intentions, only a number can be mentioned here. First, thanks must go to Professors Sanjay Chaturvedi and Dennis Rumley for reasons fully elucidated in the preface to this book. Praise, also, must go out to all members of the Indian Ocean Research Group (IORG) who have shared this journey since 2001.

Specific thanks to Dr. Brian Doherty of Keele University for allowing us to reproduce certain arguments in the final chapter, made in earlier works by Doherty and Doyle (2006) which featured as a special edition of the Routledge journal *Environmental Politics* 15 (5) entitled "Beyond Borders: Environmental Movements and Transnational Politics." Also, in chapter 1, discussions relating to different definitions of environmental security were first published by Doyle (2004) in "An Agenda for Environmental Security in the Indian Ocean Region," eds Chaturvedi and Rumley, *Geopolitical Orientations and Security in the Indian Ocean,* Mew Delhi, South Asia Publications, 154–171.

Research for chapter 12 first appeared in another Rutgers publication by Doyle (2005) *Environmental Movements in Majority and Minority Worlds: A Global Perspective.* Finally, the bulk of chapter 16 by Rumley and Doyle first appeared as a work in progress presented to the 3rd IORG symposium in Kuala Lumpur in 2005.

On the editorial side, credit but no blame must be accorded to our editor Doreen Valentine, our production manager Suzanne Kellam, and our hard-working and incredibly thorough copy editor Derik Shelor. We would also like to acknowledge Linda Christensen for her work in preparing the index and proofreading.

The editors wish to provide tribute to the contributors of this book, spread as they are across this vast, under-resourced region, for their scholarship, compassion, and patience. In many ways, bringing this book together is a validation and, indeed, a celebration of the region itself.

Finally, this book is written in a spirit of both admiration and solidarity for the people of the Indian Ocean Region, many of whom struggle on a daily basis to access the basic needs necessary for their survival.

PART I

INTRODUCTION

1 Crucible for Survival

EARTH, RAIN, FIRE, AND WIND

TIMOTHY DOYLE

In pre-colonial times the Indian Ocean was a crucible for the first global economy. . . .

(Ghosh and Muecke 2004)

Introduction

In February 2007, we were in Muscat, Oman, for the Fourth Meeting of the Indian Ocean Research Group (IORG), focusing on issues of marine biodiversity and fisheries security. Fish is the most earth's most traded commodity, and in many ways the successful management of global fish stocks will determine human survival in the long term. Muscat was a very appropriate place to host such a conference. It is from here that stories of Sinbad the Sailor first emerged, telling epic tales of a man sailing the seven seas, with the Indian Ocean as the fulcrum of such adventures. It is also most appropriate in the context of the 21st century, for to describe the environmental security of Oman is to provide a snapshot for the whole region. In many ways, telling the story of modern Oman touches on most of the major themes of environmental security and justice which emerge from this compendium.

First, and most obviously, providing an environment which is secure for the majority of the people living in Oman is a question that haunts policy makers in that country. Oman's natural terrestrial environment has been devastated. Particularly since the 1960s, the nation has relied almost exclusively on oil exports to support the local economy. As is suggested in later chapters in this collection, oil—or black gold—can be simultaneously a curse as well as a gift. Its absolute dominance of the local economy and ecology of a country often means neglect in a whole range of competing management spheres. Water, for example, is a real problem in Oman. Groundwater has been so heavily drawn down that now the sea invades the underground aquifers, the land becoming too rich in salt. Soil, as a consequence, is often imported into Oman for the purposes of growing foodstuffs. This incredibly expensive practice is offset by revenue gained from oil production. Unfortunately for Omanis, their oil reserves are dangerously low, and are predicted to run out within the next fifteen years.

As a means of providing an environmentally secure future for Oman, the Sultanate is looking to diversify its economy, and sees the expansion of its fisheries as a logical step in this direction. It was within this context that the IORG was invited to Oman, hosted by the Sultanate and the Ministry for Fisheries and Agriculture. In an opening address, Dr. Hamad bin Said Al A'ufi, Undersecretary of the Ministry, stated that the fisheries sector is considered "one of the most important non-hydrocarbon sectors being relied on to boost the national economy" (*Times of Oman* 2007). He went on to say that he saw the IORG as a partner in helping Oman preserve fisheries resources for future generations by developing wise polices to achieve food security under sustainable development. The language of sustainable development is something that the countries of the Indian Ocean have inherited, in recent times, from the more wealthy global North: the more affluent *minority world*. Indeed, these words are wise, but it must be understood at the outset of this work that the levels of environmental *in*security across the Indian Ocean Region are far higher and more critical than in the more affluent world. The absolute decimation of environments is commonplace. Thus, the direct transporting of environmental management concepts from the minority world to the majority world are not always relevant, appropriate, or sufficient.

One example of the emptiness of the sustainable development rhetoric in the context of Oman was imparted on us during a visit to a local beach to witness local fisheries practices. Along one particular stretch of beach, for hundreds of yards, was a mass of shark carcasses rotting in the intense sunlight. Each shark was whole except for its fins, which had been cut out of the bodies, and then these fins were collected on a single large blanket at one end of the beach. After some discussion, we learned that the fins would be exported to lucrative Chinese markets, while the rest of the carcasses would be discarded. This is reminiscent of the ivory trade in Africa, and in no way can it be considered sustainable development. What was learned over the next week was that Oman suffers from a problem that is endemic across this great ocean, one which excludes effective environmental management. It operates from a position of ecological ignorance. In short, scientific baseline data is almost nonexistent: knowledge about fish stock numbers, breeding patterns, and ecosystems is minimal. Shark numbers are currently being decimated, but there is rarely understanding about absolute numbers, or species-type. Without baseline data, sustainable development simply cannot take place. How can regulation and policing take place without numbers of cull to enforce? To Oman's credit, the government is desperately trying to embark on new scientific programs, but economic pressures to double the size of the fishery in the immediate future may hamper these programs, however honorable these intentions. In an ocean of poverty, science is usually considered a luxury.

The next theme that emerges from the Omani experience is human and environmental justice. Today, deterioration of air, water, energy, and biodiversity, for example, are causing increasing degradation of the environment and human health. It is widely recognized that these problems disproportionately burden poor communities, raising the issue of *environmental justice* for the peoples of Indian

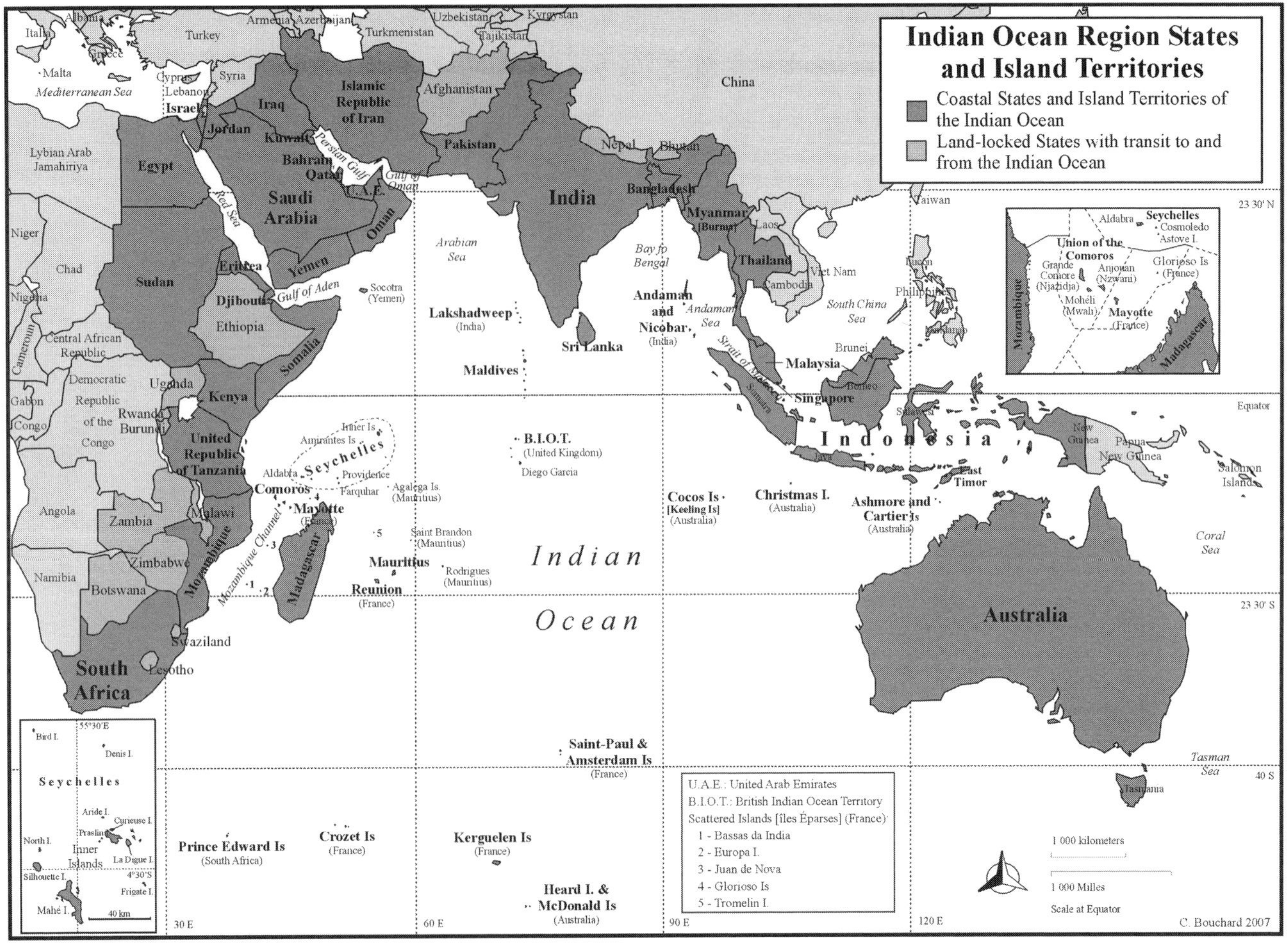

Map 1.1 Map of the Indian Ocean Region.
Source: Christian Bouchard.

Ocean. This book affirms the right of all people inhabiting in the region to live and work in a peaceful environment with clean air, fertile land, healthy and abundant water, and sufficient food, along with the right for the region's people to have their voices heard and, ultimately, to influence decision-making that impacts upon their existence. Calls for *environmental justice* include: equity in the distribution of environmental goods, ills, and risks; recognition of the diversity of the participants and experiences in affected communities; the protection of community capabilities and functioning; and participation in the political processes that create and manage environmental policy (Schlosberg 2007, 517–40). Much of the literature on environmental justice is about environmental equity, but also there are concerns about giving voice to people to *determine* their own environmental futures, to participate in the environmental management of their earth, their resources. Much of the literature on environmental justice, however, is again written within first-world contexts, imagining that liberal democracies are the norm and that "deliberative democratic" citizen participation can easily be achieved. In Oman's case, as with many nations across the Indian Ocean Region (IOR), liberal democracy has not been embraced. A sultanate is built on a model of absolute power, however benign. In fact, in many parts of the IOR, authoritarian and hybrid-authoritarian states are the norm, and many are still in transition from colonial rule.

There are a number of points to be made here. First, there is no doubt that increasing the participative role of citizens in government is a good thing, and that authoritarian regimes are less capable of allowing these increased levels of participation than democratic systems of governance. Models of environmental management, however, which do not incorporate the complexities of divergent forms of governance, are found sorely wanting and often have little to offer non-western systems of governance. Second, the model of democracy which is often offered as part of the minority world's sustainable development and environmental justice packages is not democracy in the traditional sense of the word, but rather more closely aligned with market principles (Doyle 1998). Notions of liberal and social democracy, such as responsible government dispensing its mandated powers to legislate, regulate, and moderate against the excesses of an anti-social minority in efforts to protect the will of the majority, are often jettisoned in favor of free market rhetoric, and short-term profiteering. So when this market-driven version of democracy is sold and then utilized in the global South, rather than empowering local peoples, it is usually seen as a means of diminishing the role of states as environmental managers, and handing over this role to the private sector to regulate their own activities. There is no doubt that environmental justice necessitates increased participation in good governance, but as the following chapters of this book are testament to, human and environmental justice for the people in the IOR is most often fought outside the state, outside of large corporations, and very often directly *against* these entities. In fact, often liberal democracy is seen as *westernization* rather than evidence of "freedom."

But at an even more basic level, the concept of justice in the context of the IOR—the Ocean of the South—can be understood as ensuring that basic needs for survival are satisfied. Access to, for example, shelter, clean water, and food are, in fact universal human rights, reflected in the International Human Rights Covenants (Barnett and Dovers 2001). So, in many ways, academic treatments of environmental justice in a predominantly third world context do not have to be overly complex in their interpretations of the term. Rather, justice can be seen in the light of providing greater equity among the people of the IOR, regardless of which nation- state they abide in. In Jonathan Barnett's excellent treatment of environmental security from a critical perspective, he writes: "Neither skepticism about the possibility of absolute equity, nor the postmodern unmasking of the way universal claims about justice are a means by which some groups advance power over others, should compromise the validity of the goal of justice. Best seen as intellectual checks against the replacement of one undesirable state with another, these concerns should not impede progress towards a more just world, for there are clear disparities in life chances among people which are morally indefensible and demand action" (Barnett and Dovers 2001, 4).

This book investigates the problems and the struggles of peoples across the region to attain basic levels of justice and security. Much of the book has really devoted itself to listing the basic issues that people confront in their daily lives across the region. At times, this resembles a litany of woe. But, in defense of this approach, most people in the minority world are unaware of the nature of the threats to livelihood that confront most people in the IOR. In many ways, this book is really only the beginning: recording the issues that make up an initial agenda for environmental security in the region. What remains to be done (and this is tackled in the final chapter) is to begin to understand how change can be brought about that emancipates people within this oceanic frame from their continual backbreaking and life-taking struggle to survive. Although several of the contributors argue from a critical realist perspective, outlining the means in which nation-states within the region can better address environmental problems, the vast majority of the contributors depict the key movers for change as existing in the third sector: non-government organizations (NGOs) and new social movements (NSMs). In may ways, it is easier to refer to these diverse players as occupying a green public sphere (GPS). It is within this sphere where hope predominantly lies.

Because environmental issues straddle nation-state boundaries, these disparate actors seem more able and more inclined to focus on environmental issues at a regional and oceanic level. Indeed, they match the corporate form in their abilities to cross transnational borders and, in the case of the IOR, seem more likely to have a capacity to think *regionally*. But unlike transnational corporations, with their primary focus being profit, most calls for global environmental justice and security come from new social movements involved in *environmental emancipation*. These movements are radical challengers to business and politics-as-usual across the earth. The IOR, including its littoral states, has been correctly described as the "Heart of the Third World," or the "Ocean of the South" (Chaturvedi 1998). This book seeks to address key issues that are vital to determining the region's human and environmental justice and security. The ramifications of environmental security in the Indian Ocean Region, if not achieved, would be dire on a global scale, not purely on a regional one.

Research in the more affluent and powerful *minority world* (Doyle 2005) has been heavily biased toward the Atlantic and Pacific Ocean regions. This book sets out to define a tangible identity for this neglected geopolitical sphere, seeking a workable concept, while recognizing the immense diversity of the region. The region is defined not simply on the basis of geographical factors, but more importantly as a series of complex organic and human relations and conditions that bind it. For example, biological factors such as the Blue Fin tuna migrations and meteorological phenomena such as the monsoons are examples of these unique and dynamic relations. Human trade and migration routes provide additional levels of palimpsests, drawn over ecological maps.

The IOR has suffered, therefore, within a void of cultural interpretation, pre- and post-colonization. The IOR has been correctly recognized by some researchers, such as Chaudhuri (1990), Subrahmanyam (1990), Frank (1998), and Ghosh and Muecke, eds. (2004), as a communication hub for civilizations established well before the rise of Europe. In pre-colonial times the Indian Ocean was a "crucible" for the first global economy involving Chinese, South Asian, and Middle Eastern trade (Frank 1998). Nature was dominant and sacred. It was with colonization and technological mastery that nature disappeared from view (Muecke 2003). There is a growing recognition from within the IOR of the need to again listen to the arguments of nature to expand our "oceanic knowledge" (Muecke 2003).

Structure of the Book

The book is divided into five parts, each with four chapters, and then a final conclusion. It is imperative that certain introductory discussions are pursued before the book *proper* is presented. Part One, therefore, attempts four major tasks. First, in the latter part of this chapter, the concept of environmental security is more fully developed. The idea of environmental security that informs the authors is based on the assumption that all nation-states within the IOR share a common interest in ascertaining and maintaining a secure environmental future.

Environmental security is one of the most important shared interests of the region, and thus a policy-oriented dialogue is essential, creating partnerships among governments, industry, NGOs, and the broader communities. This work seeks to establish a heightened level of regional transparency of goals, improving regional and global relations. It recognizes the benefits of regional cooperation and collaboration within the IOR. Many of the risks associated with securing environments cannot be addressed as issues within the limited frame of the *nation-state*. Instead, they are *oceanic*. This specific chapter then seeks to explore the concept of environmental security within the Indian Ocean Region. Depending on the disciplinary paradigm, whether it be international relations, critical geopolitics, military security, or environmental politics, definitions of environmental security are as numerous as definitions of what constitutes the "environment" itself. In the recent environmental security literature, issues that fall under its rubric are multifarious and diverse. Some of these include: biological and ecological security, the greening of military operations, climate change, desertification, biodiversity, human population and migration, fisheries, forests, energy, water, nutrition, shelter, and poverty.

Two categories can be used to order this cacophony of issues in the first instance. First, most environmental security issues are still cast around the "security" of the nation-state. Second, a more inclusive definition, one that transcends nation-states' boundaries, relates to conditions that secure individual access to a basic infrastructure for survival in a geopolitical region defined by shared environmental boundaries. Environmental security, in this vein, is reliant on shared understandings of ecological conditions leading to potential and real conflicts, as well as developing a more sustained, peaceful, and resource-secure regional future.

In Chapter Two, Dennis Rumley first investigates the concept of the Indian Ocean as a concrete *regional* geopolitical entity before he moves on to outline what is meant by *security* in the broadest sense of the word, exploring both traditional and alternative interpretations within the region. Chapter Three, by Sanjay Chaturvedi, forms an integral cog of Part One, as it relates to the single most important "event" to shake the region during this work's compilation. Any book that seeks to address environmental security within the IOR cannot ignore the shock, devastation, and loss of the 2004 tsunami. Chaturvedi also further develops the concept of environmental justice within this oceanic frame, arguing that "disaster" management in the region will remain meaningless unless local people are empowered to take part in the "risk management" exercises that effectively govern their lives, rather than leaving it to a top-down approach, dominated by donor organizations, insurance companies, and Northern governments, however well-intentioned. The answer, as Chaturvedi most eloquently puts it, is not to be found in the creation of centralized mega and multi-state early warning systems of seismic events, but through the genuine emergence of movements for human and environmental justice across the South.

Marcus Haward contributes the fourth and final chapter to this introductory part. Although this book includes discussions of both littoral and non-littoral states of the Indian Ocean, the very nexus of the book is the ocean itself. Haward paints a picture of the region from this oceanic perspective, highlighting the key points of pressure: the coastal areas. Haward tells of the importance of international conventions, and an integrated regional governance approach, while stressing the continued importance of national regimes.

After the completion of Part One, each new part in this collection focuses on the four fundamental elements needed to provide human beings with the most basic forms of environmental security: Earth (land, biodiversity), Rain (water, marine issues), Fire (energy), and Wind (air, climate), and as such, these four elements provide the book with its conceptual structure. In a sense, these elements are thrown into this book's crucible, and hopefully the alchemy that ensues will begin to go some way in articulating the key environmental issues confronting this region, which makes up approximately one-third of the globe's population.

The theory that these four elements form the basis of all things has existed since ancient times. This holds true today and serves to highlight the interconnectedness of humans and nature. That is, humans are a part of nature, with all things necessarily made up of the same basic elements.

Parts Two to Five, then—delineated by each of the four elements—begin with a chapter-length regional overview of the specific issues in question. Only then can detailed case studies be adequately investigated and contextualized.

In relation to these specific and detailed case studies, this volume give voice to contributors from nation-states on the Indian Ocean rim. Rather than providing another body of work involving the prescription of solutions to environmental ills from *outside,* this volume explores environmental issues and problem-solving strategies from *within.* This is central to the volume's regional response. Each contributor is briefed with the overall goal of establishing a workable concept of a regionally shared environmental future, building problem-solving capacities, and suggesting solutions to regionally shared problems. It is hoped that through the presentation of case studies on the specific examples of human-created hazards confronting these basic elements for survival, avenues for collaboration and improved regional dialogue and cooperation will be identified. Ultimately, in this work's conclusion, we argue that the most successful initiatives emerging to alleviate human and environmental insecurity in the region will emerge from a public space that is led by non-governmental and new social movement actors who genuinely represent the needs of the ocean's citizens.

For the remainder of this chapter, let us now fully investigate divergent concepts of environmental security at a theoretical level, as well as touching upon some of the key environmental justice and security issues as they confront the region today.

What Is Environmental Security?

The environment has often been used as a tool of war, from the salting of Carthage to the Russians' scorched earth retreats before the armies of Napoleon and Hitler. Plato, mocking the notion of a republic of leisure, argued that such a regime would soon resort to a war to satisfy its taste for more space and natural resources. But sustained thinking about the environment-conflict connection is a product only of the last few decades. While clashes over non-renewable resources such as oil or gold are as familiar as the Persian Gulf war, the question now is about the role of renewable resources such as water, fish, forests, and arable land (Dabelko 1999, 2).

Although there have been conflicts over resources since the earliest human societies, interest in both renewable and non-renewable resources within environmental security frameworks has dramatically increased since the end of the Cold War. Security is usually understood in state-centric terms, "concerned with intentional physical (mainly military) threats to the integrity and independence of the nation-state" (Scrivener 2002, 184). Immediately after the so-called victory of capitalism and the breakup of the communist-inspired U.S.S.R. in the late 1980s, world orders that had existed since World War II were called into question. During this time of uncertainly, there emerged a global, almost post-modern, policy-shaping concept embracing a shared plurality of interests that crossed nation-state borders, commonly referred to as *multilateralism*. The multilateralist decade of the 1990s, which ended as the current phase of American unilateralism emerged forcefully in the new millennium, was an era when new boundaries and borders were drawn in the sand, as alternative concepts of identity and collectivity were imagined. One such idea which evolved at this time was that of *environmental security*.

This trend was reinforced and supported by military establishments who sought means by which they could continue to justify Cold War levels of military expenditure during an apparent time of peace and prosperity for the West. As a result, both the United States and Russia formed high-level units of environmental security within established security institutional infrastructure, such as the Pentagon's Center for Environmental Security.[1] Paradoxically, some peace advocates also championed the concept. In a book appropriately entitled *Green Security or Militarized Environment,* Jyrki Kakonen writes:

> Peace researchers have argued for environmental security in order to show that . . . national defense resources could be used for civilian purposes in the field of environmental problems. The aim is to convert military resources . . . to do the environmental protection in order to transform the military into a paramilitary and further into a non-military organization. This is an option after the Cold War, but there is a danger that the militarist approach to deal with environmental issues leads to the militarization of the society. (Kakonen 1994, 4).

As with the now dominant concept of *terrorism,* the *environment* is an extremely powerful multilateral concept that crosses nation-state borders relatively easily. In this vein, a new enemy is imagined, one that is not a human terrorist, but nature itself. This interest in a *combative environment* is not new. In western terms it has been aptly recorded in the 18th-century works of Thomas Hobbes. In his most famous work—*Leviathan*—Hobbes depicts nature as being in a state of perpetual war with itself: "and the blood-dimmed stains shall be loosed upon the world and all anarchy will prevail" (Hobbes 1651). This conservative view of nature was used by Hobbes to justify his call to create an all-powerful authoritarian "machine" that would be the only means to avert global environmental catastrophe. Of course, in this understanding of nature, humanity is also in a perpetual "state of warre" (Hobbes). This western understanding of the "state of nature" is not just restricted to neo-Hobbesians, but has substantial populist credence, as most western imaginings comprehend peace to be the aberration while war is construed as the "natural state."

This interest in Gaia as the common enemy (as well as a pathway to common salvation) was further heightened in the West due to increasing, but rather late, understandings that the minority world (the more affluent world) had to share its basic survival systems with the majority world (the less affluent world). This concept of a shared Spaceship Earth had been vociferously pushed by the western environmentalists since the late 1960s, but due to the characteristic conservatism of the disciplines of international relations and security studies, this green rhetoric was only picked up in the academic literature and the governmental gray documentation in the late 1980s and early 1990s.

This interest in environmental security emerged forcefully in the Brundtland Report in 1987, and increased at the first Earth Summit in Rio de Janeiro in 1992. The nexus between environment, development, and security was never stronger than at the recent "Earth Summit Plus Ten" in Johannesburg in 2002. The notion of environmental security, however, is hotly contested. Its most common variation is concerned with the impact of environmental stress on societies, which may lead to situations of war within and between societies. In this manner, environmental security agendas are about seeking issues that, if not addressed, may provide the basis for increasing human conflicts. In this sense, environmental security is understood in somewhat negative terms.

The advantage of this redeclared enemy—nature itself—was, or so it was believed in the Westphalian mindset, that it constituted a "common" security issue for all humankind, or in the words of Gro Harlem Brundtland, "Our Common Future." Of course, the symbol "environment" is not commonly understood at all; rather, the issues which gather under its umbrella are culturally diverse. Concepts of environment are far from apolitical; rather, they are the exact opposite (Doyle 2002). They are intensely politicized categories utilized to redraw boundaries of collective identity, behavior, political activity, security, and, most importantly, power and resource distribution. Elsewhere I write: "So environmental politics is not just about 'goodies' versus 'baddies.' This symbol environment has such power that numerous cultures, and the powerful and powerless within them, invoke its name for disparate purposes" (Doyle and McEachern 1998, 2001, 2008, 4).

That the "environment" flag means many different things to different people, does not make it a charlatan. Rather, it is a symbol almost as broad as nature itself. It is perfectly chosen for the infinity of possible responses that gather under and around it. Just when its appears that a safe net of definition can be cast over it, it wriggles out and takes on a new guise, in a separate context (Doyle 2002; Chaturvedi 1998). Therefore, the list of issues that make up an environmental security agenda is an important list, but an extremely subjective and culturally determined one. Such an agenda must be cognizant of these different meanings and issues, and respectful of these differences and variations if practical solutions are to be uncovered that make sense to the people who are most affected by these forms of environmental degradation.

At the end of the 1980s, when these agendas for common futures were first being drawn up, predominantly *western* issues were being recast as *global* ones. The minority world, in this light, portrayed the major problems of the globe as species extinction, global climate change, desertification, and overpopulation.[2] Needless to say, at the end of the 1980s these were not issues high on the environmental agenda as defined by most people living in the majority world. Other issues of more immediate survival dominated (and still do), such as health, shelter, food, and water security. In a provocative book entitled *Tears of the Crocodile,* Middleton et al. argue that the developed world has managed to divest itself of its responsibility to the global environment by moving the arena "away from people and onto things, forces." They write: "In short the developing world, for the first time, is being asked to be an equal partner in a worldwide endeavour precisely because the emphasis has shifted away from the needs of the poor. By advancing an environmental agenda the North has once more concentrated on its own interests and has called them globalism" (Middleton et al. 1993, 5).

Within this western framework, when people are seen as part of an "environmental security" agenda, they are not perceived as part of the environment—they are simply users or, in the case of the poor, degraders (Doyle 1998). In 1990 the United Nations Human Development Report argued that poverty is one of the greatest threats to the environment, and in 1993 the International Monetary Fund (IMF) announced: "Poverty and the environment are linked in that the poor are more likely to resort to activities that can degrade the environment" (International Monetary Fund, cited in R. Broad 1994, 812–22). There are two key problems with this line of argument. First, all poor people are regarded in an homogenous fashion. An important distinction must be made on the connections between of *types* of poverty and environmental degradation. For example, those still operating subsistence lifestyles (though under threat), those who have been recently removed from this lifestyle, and those who have long ago been driven to the precipice of survival (the "landless and rootless") have very different relationships with their environments. The latter have no security of tenure and little connectedness to place. This category includes those peasants and squatters who survive by cutting forest cover, by consuming wildlife, and by planting crops on soils that will erode.

Second, many western environmental security theorists fail to weigh the costs of advanced industrialism on a global scale, not just within the boundaries of nation-states. Issues of overconsumption in the minority world—and by the minority world—cannot be underestimated. The fact that the United States and Japan together represent 40 percent of the world's gross national product cannot be denied (Imura 1994). In the Indian Ocean Region, the consumption patterns of Australians far outweigh most of their Indian and South-East African neighbors.

Obviously, this agenda for this kind of common environmental security was greeted with some skepticism in parts of the majority world. Dabelko writes:

> In less developed countries of the world, these ideas have elicited mixed emotions. Obtaining food and water is a daily struggle for the world's 800 million malnourished people, and according their problems the high priority of a security issue obviously has great appeal. But leaders in . . . Cairo, and Kuala Lumpar also fear that such an approach will invite violations of their national sovereignty as outside powers intervene to "help." They gave a frosty reception, for example, to Gorbachev's 1988 proposal to complement the blue-helmeted armed forces serving under the United Nations with a "Green Helmet" force to react to natural catastrophes and environmental crises (Dabelko 1999, 14–18).

A concept of environmental security that is more inclusive of the interests of the majority of people in the Indian Ocean states, both littoral and non-littoral, is one that moves away "from viewing environmental stress as an additional threat within the (traditional) conflictual, statist framework, to placing environmental change at the centre of cooperative models of global security" (Dabelko and Dabelko 1995, 4). But to do this, there must be increased understanding of the environment, not as an external enemy force, but as a diverse nature that is inclusive of people, a nature that has the potential to provide to individual citizens of all countries in the Indian Ocean Region secure access to basic nutrition, adequate access to healthy environments, appropriate shelter, and a security to practice a diverse range of livelihoods that are both culturally and ecologically determined.

Environmental Security Issues in the Indian Ocean Region

While many parts of the minority world are currently seeking technological solutions to environmental problems, for many researchers in the Indian Ocean Region the major task is still documenting the list of environmental problems, attempting to collate baseline data that is sadly missing.

There is an enormous gap in the literature on environmental security and the Indian Ocean Region. There have been substantial academic works completed in recent years on the broad subject of environmental security (see, for example, Deudney 1990; Myers 1989, 1995; Dabelko and Dabelko 1995; Broda-Bahm 1999; Lowi and Shaw 2000; Redclift 2000; Cheremisinoff 2002). Some of these works move from theory into empirical research, but when this occurs, most of this scholarship is based in and around the Atlantic, Pacific, and Southern Oceans (see Kakonen 1994; Barnet and Dovers 2001; Dokken 2001; Foster 2001). It has been very rare that researchers have utilized the concept of environmental security in the Indian Ocean Region.

This lack of research literature reflects a broader neglect by the more affluent, minority world in addressing social science policy issues confronting the South. There have been some articles addressing a particular environmental security issue in a specific country, such as water wars in the Jordan Basin (see Shaheen 2000) or environmental degradation leading to human displacement in South Africa (Singh 1996). In a search of the electronic version of *Expanded Academic Index,* only one reference emerges which includes environmental security insights into the Indian Ocean Region as a whole (Chaturvedi 1998).

Obviously, establishing an environmental security agenda for the Indian Ocean Region is also significant in that it addresses basic survival issues that affect the inhabitants of the region, approximately one-third of the globe's population. Chaturvedi writes: "The Indian Ocean has been rightly described as the 'Heart of the Third World' or the 'Ocean of the South,' with low per capita income and low levels of development in the majority of countries. The overwhelming mass of these peoples struggle to survive under the conditions characterized by chronic poverty, precarious political systems, stagnating and struggling economies, fragmented political systems guided by the considerations of ethnic identities" (Chaturvedi 1998, 712).

The concept of environmental security must be brought to life by reference to some of the most pressing environmental issues confronting the Indian Ocean

Region. Just seven broad areas are identified here, each one ecologically interlocking with the other, snowballing in magnitude, creating desperate realities for billions of people, culminating in abject poverty, both in terms of biodiversity (or lack thereof) and in terms of human existence: land degradation; water; fisheries; climate change; nuclear waste; environmental refugees; and urban explosion and deterioration.

Land Degradation/Deforestation

As Graeme Hugo writes, "contemporary environmental degradation in Less Developed Countries has its real roots in historical processes such as colonial exploitation which produced different modes of agricultural and pastoral activity to meet the needs of the colonial power and different patterns of population growth and distribution from those which prevailed in precolonial times" (Hugo 1996, 124). Land degradation is a very broad environmental security issue, and its causes are many. Obviously, an important contributor is deforestation. In the Indian Ocean Region vast areas of forest have been eradicated. The size of these areas simply defy the limits of our imaginations, they are literally beyond quantification. Even in the more affluent parts of the Indian Ocean Region, this decimation has continued unabated despite the concentrated efforts of the Australian environmental movement which, for thirty years, has had a principal focus on forest conservation, sometimes to the detriment of other pressing environmental issues (Doyle 2000). Australia is currently fourth on the list of so-called third world deforesters of hardwoods, after IOR partner Indonesia, Brazil, and the African Republic of Congo. Also, satellite imagery has revealed that less than 15 percent of South Asia is currently forested (Hassan 1991, 13). Deforestation, coupled with poor agricultural practices, and continuing tectonic movements have led to floods, soil erosion, and siltation. In his work on environmental issues and security in South Asia, Shaukat Hassan writes in direct relation to the Ganges riverbed, which has risen by over 0.5 meters since the early 1990s: "The result has been increasingly disastrous floods, as well as the heavy siltation of tanks and reservoirs, whose life expectancy has been reduced by a third because several times more sediment flows into them than was calculated at the time of their construction. Among the downstream consequences of soil erosion are the choking of estuaries and harbours, and land formations in the Bay of Bengal, both of which have created conflict between India and Bangladesh" (Hassan: 16).

In Africa, land degradation is severe. Commercial deforestation, logging, and grazing have been massive, leading to a loss in biodiversity and increased run-off, which removes topsoil and increases siltation. In research dedicated to environmental security and displaced people in southern Africa, Meena Singh explains: "Soil loss in Southern Africa has been estimated to be approximately 400 million tonnes per annum, and soil erosion has been cited as one of the greatest environmental problems facing Southern Africa. Refugees and internally displaced people in Mozambique, Malawi, Zimbabwe, Zambia and Ethiopia, who are forced by their desperate situation to seek shelter and energy, have removed trees. This has resulted in increased soil erosion, which produces an almost moonscape environment" (Singh 1996, 3).

Also, of course, there are many Indian examples, such as those cases which have emerged in the eastern states of Assam and Tripura. Bangladeshi immigrants, fleeing from famine and other environmentally related occurrences particular to their low-lying homelands, have "altered the local balances in landownership, political power, ethnicity, and religion, stirring local resentments, riots, and an anti-immigrant movement" (Dabelko 1999). The resultant violence claimed thousands of lives in the early 1980s and has flared up again in recent times.

Water

Land degradation is closely associated with the critical issue of water, and water is an issue that crosses national and state borders with relative ease, reflecting the geophysical reality of rivers and waterways. Of all the oceans, apart from being the poorest, the IOR possesses some of the driest areas on the planet, with Australia widely known by the title of "the driest continent on earth." In relation to the Middle East, Naeff and Matson produced a relatively early work entitled *Water in the Middle East: Conflict or Cooperation?* In 1984, they wrote: "Few regions of the planet offer a more varied physiography or richer mix of ethnicities [and] religions. . . . Out of this compound, one issue emerges as the most conspicuous, cross-cutting and problematic: water—or rather its scarcity" (Naff and Matson 1984, 1).

Water was a major contributing factor in the Arab-Israeli conflict in 1967. During this period Israel was attempting to develop a nation-wide water supply and distribution system: the National Water Carrier (Shaheen 2000, 139). The Arab League responded by making known its intentions to divert the river systems of the upper Jordan to Syria and Lebanon. Military attacks on Arab sites ended attempts at riparian diversion. Obviously, environmental security issues are not always the fundamental cause of wars, but there is no doubt that in this case, where there are long-standing ethnic and cultural divisions, a resource issue can be the "straw that breaks the camel's back."

In South Asia, there have already been intense disputes over the utilization of the Cauvery River between the states of Karnataka and Tamil Nadu. In 1991 several people were left dead and there was a temporary exodus of 100,000 Tamils from Karnataka.

In Australia, currently in the grip of a nation-wide drought, the water issue, or lack of it, is now critical, straining relationships between several states with political boundaries traversed by the country's major river: the Murray. The World Health Organization released a report in 2000 stating that unless profound changes are made to water management along the Murray, then cities like Adelaide, the capital of South Australia, which includes the Murray's mouth, will be unfit for habitation by the year 2050.

Obviously water issues include scarcity, as well as pollution, land degradation, and displacement concerns. Pollution of streams and water tables from waste from manufacturing industries, intensive agriculture, and imperfect engineering feats such as mega dams and mass irrigation systems is currently having dramatic effects on the quality of potable water sources. Many who live in the IOR live beyond the safety net of bottled "mineral water," with women experiencing the brunt of carrying safe water long distances on a daily basis.

There is no doubt that the Green Revolution of the 1970s and 1980s increased crop productivity. But its medium- to long-term impacts are just being felt. For example, the system of Bangladeshi subterranean wells, hailed as a savior of agriculture during the 1980s, is now contributing to the arsenic poisoning of millions of people.

In India, the food bowl of the nation, the Punjab, is now in danger of over-irrigation, with three crops often being harvested per year since the Green Revolution. Pumps now run 24 hours a day on fully subsidized electricity, and for the first time salinity is rearing its head as the water table rises to dangerous levels. One can only imagine South Asia's plight if the remarkably fertile Punjab becomes an ecological disaster zone.

Unfortunately, the future of water management in the poorer regions of the IOR has been vested in a faith in mega-technological solutions. Just when the more affluent world is lamenting the failure of mega dams, the South is investing heavily in this outdated technology. The construction of these dams has led to the displacement of millions of people across the region. A famous case, of course, is the Narmada project in Gujarat and Maharastra. The mass displacement of peoples in the Narmada Valley has led to vital disconnections within and between communities and their place (Doyle 2004).

In a rather sensationalist book entitled *Water Wars,* John Bulloch and Adil Darwish write: "when next it [war] comes, as come it will, . . . every confrontation in the future will be affected by hydrography of the region. Water wars are on the way" (Bulloch and Darwish 1993, 198–99).

Fisheries

The Indian Ocean contributes 6 million tonnes of marine fish production per annum. Most of the fishworkers live in coastal communities that are often considered risk communities due to "their isolation, fragile resource base and, often, poorer levels of education and health," Chaturvedi writes. "The traditional and customary rights of coastal fishing communities have been eroded by the expansion of large-scale coastal tourism and industrial development. . . . In their eagerness to secure valuable external earnings, states such as Indonesia and Thailand have frequently ignored the basic needs of local coastal communities and local women workers have subsequently migrated from, for instance, Sri Lanka to the Maldives in search of work in the fish processing plants" (Chaturvedi 1998, 713).

Aquaculture, a multi-national industry, is also changing the fabric of lives in these coastal communities, converting and destroying the ecological security of coastal farmlands and mangrove systems that sustain life, and replacing them with globalizing monocultures. The power of aquaculture industries is immense, as they have been allowed to develop almost unchecked. Even in more affluent parts of the IOR, such as Australia, there are few regulations with teeth to effectively guide these industries. In some ways, this reflects the offshore nature of these activities, which are largely away from the critical or regulatory eye. In a hallmark case of the Environment, Resource and Development Court (ERD) in 1999, the Conservation Council of South Australia (CCSA) challenged the state government in conjunction with the powerful tuna fishing industry over tuna feed-lots in Louth Bay on the Indian Ocean. Despite a successful outcome, with the CCSA proving that the industry did not adhere to the principles of environmentally sustainable development (ESD), the state government overrode the court ruling, in favor of continued questionable aquacultural practices.

Obviously, coastal and low-lying island communities are also most at risk from climate change.

Climate Change

Originally, climate change was considered a classic environmental security issue in Northern terms. As aforesaid, the North came to comprehend that it had to share the same atmosphere and oceans with the South, and a continued policy of laissez-faire would be detrimental for the more affluent world. Also, climate change was a classic environmental issue portrayed as a natural "force," rather than one which directly related to people. Consequently, climate change has not traditionally been seen as a key issue in the majority world. In recent times, however it has assumed greater prominence among majority world environmentalists, due to the fact that some of the world's biggest polluters and/or reliers on fossil fuels have not signed the climate change protocols in Kyoto and Johannesburg. Further tensions have emerged due to the fact that both island states in the Indian Ocean and poorer dwellers and coastal fishworkers on coastlines will be the principal victims in global climate change. In this manner, climate change has metamorphosized from an elite, scientific, Northern issue into one which can usefully fit into the environmental justice agenda of the South.

At the end of October 2002, 5,000 people from communities in India, including international NGOs, gathered in a Rally for Climate Justice in New Delhi. This rally was organized to coincide with the United Nations meeting on climate change (Conference of Parties 8—COP8), and was organized by the India Climate Justice Forum, including the National Alliance of People's Movements, the National Fishworkers Forum, Third World Network, and CorpWatch. In a press release, Friends of the Earth International (FoEI) wrote of the current frustration with climate change negotiations: "But climate negotiations show no progress and communities are calling for urgent action to address climate change and to protect their livelihoods in a manner that is consistent with human rights, workers' rights, and environmental justice. . . . Given the entrenched opposition to action from the fossil fuel industry and governments like the US and Saudi Arabia, environmental organisations joined forces with social movements in order to progress this most urgent agenda. The window of opportunity to prevent dangerous climate change is closing fast and, for many communities, the impacts are already alarmingly present" (FoEI 2002).

Nuclear

Mention must be made of the nuclear issue as an environmental security issue. Obviously, nuclear war is a major environmental disaster, and the nuclear fuel cycle, from uranium mining to weapons testing, can have devastating impacts upon our environments. Australia at the moment is one of the world's biggest uranium producers. It is also one of the proposed dumping grounds for the world's nuclear waste. Pangea, a transnational waste company, has targeted Australia over recent years, most particularly the Indian Ocean rim states of South and Western Australia, which it sees as likely fuel dumps, due to geological and political security.

Obviously, tensions have increased in the region due to recent nuclear brinkmanship between India and Pakistan. But let me limit most comments here to the potential for an accidental release from a nuclear reactor in the region. Jon Barnett and Steven Dovers from ANU explore this possibility within an environmental security framework in relation to Indonesia: "According to the framework, the most difficult environmental problems are those with the most widespread impact (spatial scale), particularly if the impacts are spread across political boundaries. One study of the likely impacts of a release of radioactive material from Indonesia's proposed nuclear power programme shows that released gases could travel as far as Australia, Brunei, Malaysia, Papua New Guinea, Singapore, Thailand, and of course, through Indonesia itself" (Barnett and Dovers 2001, 164).

At Chernobyl, radioisotopes were spread over a 100,000 square kilometer area, and "in terms of security, the magnitude of the clean-up after Chernobyl has been likened to the task of rebuilding after the German-Soviet war" (Barnett and Dovers: 164). With the higher levels of rainfall in the tropics of Southeast Asia, a leak would produce higher levels of radioactivity delivered by rainfall.

As with the case of mega dams, in the poorer parts of the globe such as the IOR, much faith and limited finances are being invested in technological solutions to environmental and resource issues—outmoded and dangerous solutions. Many of these have now been effectively discarded by the more affluent minority world within their own national jurisdictions but which are vociferously hawked in the markets of the South.

Population Movements/Environmental Refugees

Human overpopulation is an obvious and much quoted environmental security issue. The issue of environmentally enforced population movements—environmental refugees—is of more relevance here due to its complex connectedness to all environmental issues I have previously touched upon in this chapter. Deforestation contributes to climate change, which exacerbates flooding in, for example, Bangladesh, which causes increased land degradation; leading to clean water shortages (the impact of arsenic in wells). The flooding also further exacerbates the siltation of rivers, decimating coastal fishing grounds, and leads to enforced population movements into northeastern India, which contributes to conflicts highlighting ethnic, religious, and cultural differences. Kaplan imagines a not-too-distant-future: "As the Maldive Islands, off the coast of India, sink into oblivion, and the shorelines of Egypt, Bangladesh, and Southeast Asia recede, tens of millions of people (are driven) inland where there is no room for them" (Kaplan, quoted in Curtis 1998, 32).

The fact remains, however, that one does not have to imagine some hypothetical future scenario to realize the magnitude of this problem. The Indian Ocean Region is at once home to the generators of the most refugees and the area with, by far, the top refugee-hosting countries. Particularly Afghanistan, Rwanda, Iraq, Somalia, Eritrea, Sudan, Bangladesh, and Burundi produce the bulk of the world's refugee movements. Interestingly, it is many of these same countries, with the inclusion of Iran, Pakistan, Tanzania, and Ethiopia, that are these refugees' new hosts. In the mid-1970s they added up to about 3 million refugees, and by 1995 this number had escalated to 27 million, and this does not count those displaced within their own countries. It also does not include those displaced by development projects, such as large dams, within their own countries (Renner 1996, 101).

Traditionally, refugees were defined in a manner that was appropriate to describe them after World War II: as people with "a well-founded fear of persecution for reasons of race, religion, nationality, membership of a particular social group or political opinion" (Harrell-Bond, quoted in Singh 1996, 128). But now, the reality has forced a new definition, one that includes the concept of "an environmental refugee." Environmental refugees have now been defined as "people who fear that for environmental reasons they may not remain alive unless they migrate" (Zaba, quoted in Myers 1995, 28).

As touched upon, internal migrants *within* nation-states are often not recorded as environmental refugees, despite the fact that they often are even greater in number than those involved in transnational cross-border population movements. In the South African context, Singh states: "People moving from rural areas in the Cape to the outskirts of Cape Town make up one of the fastest growing internally displaced groups in South Africa. Many of the displaced people were made redundant from white farms and were faced with the daunting choice of returning to impoverished homelands or trying to find a better life in the city. Since this phenomenon has only really started exploding in the 1990s, there is an absence of data and very few studies on the topic" (Singh 1996, 125–34.)

Urban Explosion and Environmental Decline

Much of the stress on cities in the majority world nations of the IOR comes from the huge migration of environmental refugees from rural into urban areas. This migration, in "western" terms, is akin to the agrarian and industrial revolutions in its magnitude. These cities are increasing in population between 80,000 and 200,000 people per annum (Douglas et al. 1994). Of course, one of the additional causational factors of this migration is the globalization of trade, which has contributed to a decrease in the opportunities of small landholders and workers to make a subsistence living.

Multi- and transnational corporations can produce commodities far more "efficiently," utilizing cheap labor markets and the less stringent environmental demands of local legislation. Furthermore, urban environmental "damage is partly the result of local industries necessarily producing 'dirty' products in a bid to maintain competitiveness in the 'new global economy" (Doyle and McEachern 1998, 79).

And in many cities in the Indian Ocean Region (like Bandung in Indonesia, Mumbai in India, or Bangkok in Thailand), where there are massive population explosions, entire cities are forming outside of the established infrastructures of "city limits" to accommodate these environmental refugees. In the urban context, environmental security issues include the provision of clean water; the physical labor of cleaning up refuse and the disposal of solid wastes; the building of shelter and the provision of sewerage systems; treating people directly for disease and malnutrition; direct provision of food and other basic essentials for living; and co-ordinating many other "hands-on" tasks and activities (Doyle and McEachern 1998, 94). Ultimately, environmental insecurity leads to poverty: poverty in terms of a lack of biodiversity and poverty in terms of the incapacity of human beings to meet their most basic needs for survival.

Conclusion

These brief synopses of some of the major environmental security issues should not simply be read as a "litany of woes." All of these issues impact upon all nation-states in the Indian Ocean Region. In traditional, or "hard" security terms, environmental security issues, if not addressed, will lead to increases in human conflict and, ultimately, wide-scale disease, poverty, and death. But also, due to these problems' regionally shared nature, they are issues that invite cooperation between nation-states; a shared agenda can emerge, with the potential for promoting a peaceful and extremely necessary dialogue. The long-term outcomes of such multilateral dialogues are immeasurable in positive terms.

Ultimately, if solutions are to be pursued successfully, we must move away from the concept that environmental security uniquely concerns nation-states withstanding threats *from* the environment, and move to a position in which, in the words of David Scrivener, we "see environmental security as shifting the focus from state security to societal and individual well- being" (Scrivener 2002, 184), advocating the concept of environmental security as security *for* the environment (of which humanity is a part).

NOTES

1. Interestingly, since the events of September 11, 2001, environmental security in the U.S. context is often considered one and the same as "homeland security." (Cheremisinoff 2002).

2. For an excellent example of this line of reasoning, read Hartshorn 1991.

REFERENCES

Africa News Service. 2001. "US About-Face on Climate Change: A Threat to Global Environmental Security." March 15, 2001.

Barnett, Jon, and Stephen Dovers. 2001. "Environmental Security, Sustainability and Policy." *Pacifica Review* 13 (2) (June): 157–69.

Barry, J., and G. Frankland. 2002. *International Encyclopedia of Environmental Politics.* London: Routledge.

Beck, U. 1995. *Ecological Enlightenment: Essays on the Politics of the Risk Society.* Trans. M. A. Ritter. N.J.: Humanities Press.

Broda-Bahm, K. T. 1999. "Finding Protection in Definitions: The Quest for Environment Security." *Argumentation and Advocacy* 35 (4) (spring): 159.

Bulloch, J., and A. Darwish. 1993. *Water Wars: Coming Conflicts in the Middle East.* London: Victor Gollancz.

Chaturvedi, S. 1998. "Common Security? Geopolitics, Development, South Asia and the Indian Ocean." *Third World Quarterly* 19 (4): 701–24.

Chaudhuri, K. N. 1990. *Asia before Europe: Economy and Civilisation of the Indian Ocean from the Rise of Islam to 1750.* Cambridge: Cambridge Univ. Press.

Cheremisinoff, N. P. 2002. "Environmental Security: The Need for International Policies." *Pollution Engineering* (May).

Curtis, J. 1998. "The Challenge of Environmental Security." *Habitat Australia* 26 (6) (December): 32.

Dabelko, G. D. 1999. "The Environmental Factor." *The Wilson Quarterley* 23 (4) (Autumn): 14.

Dabelko, G. D., and D. D. Dabelko. 1995. "Environmental Security: Issues of Conflict and Redefinition." *Woodrow Wilson Environmental Change and Security Project Report* 1:3–12.

Department of Politics and Public Administration, University of Madras, and Foundation for Sustainable Development (India) at the Indian Institute of Technology, Madras, Report. 2002. "Citizen Action, Water Pollution and Public Health: An Analysis of Administrative and Implementation Dimensions." September.

Deudney, D. 1990. "The Case Against Linking Environmental Degradation and National Security." *Millennium* 19 (3) (winter): 461–76.

Dokken, K. 2001. "Environment, Security and Regionalism in the Asia-Pacific: Is Environemental Security a Useful Concept?" *The Pacific Review* 14 (4): 509–30.

Douglas, M., Y. S. F. Lee, and K. Lowry. 1994. "Introduction to the Special Issue on Community Based Urban Environmental Management in Asia." *Asian Journal of Environmental Management* 2 (1): ix–xv.

Doyle, T. 1998. "Sustainable Development and Agenda 21: The Secular Bible of Global Free Markets and Pluralist Democracy." *Third World Quarterly* 19 (4): 771–86.

———. 2000. *Green Power: The Environment Movement in Australia.* Sydney: Univ. of New South Wales Press.

———. 2002. "Dam Disputes in Australia and India: Appreciating Differences in Struggles for Sustainable Development." Paper presented at seminar on "India-Australia Relations: Emerging Trends," in Working Session III—"Sustainable Development: Emerging Issues," Indira Gandhi National Open University, in collaboration with Australia-India Council, Australia High Commission, New Delhi, November 25.

———. 2004. "Dam Disputes in Australia and India: Appreciating Differences in Struggles for Sustainable Development." In *India and Australia: Issues and Opportunities,* ed. D. Gopal and D. Rumley, 365–84. New Delhi: Authorspress.

———. 2005. *Environmental Movements in Majority and Minority Worlds: A Global Perspective.* New Brunswick, N.J.: Rutgers Univ. Press.

Doyle, T., and D. McEachern. 1998, 2001, 2008. *Environment and Politics,* 2nd ed., London: Routledge.

Foster, G. D. 2001. "Environmental Security: The Search for Strategic Legitimacy." *Armed Forces and Society* 27 (3) (spring): 373.

FoEI (Friends of the Earth). 2002. "Urgent Action Needed to Address Climate Change," press release. October 29.

Frank, A. G. 1998. *ReORIENT: Global Economy in the Asian Age.* Berkeley: Univ. of California Press.

Ghosh, D., and S. Muecke. "Commerce and Culture in the Pre-Colonial Ocean." In *Rogue Flows: Trans-Asia Cultural Traffic,* ed, K. Iwabuchi, S. Muecke, and M. Thomas. Hong Kong: Hong Kong Univ. Press.

Hartshorn, G. S. 1991. "Key Environmental Issues for Developing Countries." *Journal of International Affairs* 7:393–401.

Hassan, S. 1991. "Environmental Issues and Security in South Asia." *Adelphi Papers,* 262. London: International Institute for Strategic Studies.

Hobbes, T. 1651. *Leviathan.* London: Andrew Crook Publishers.

Hugo, G. 1996. "Environmental Concerns and International Migration." *International Migration Review* 30 (spring): 105–31.

Imura, H. 1994 "Japan's Environmental Balancing Act." *Asian Survey* 34 (4): 355–68.

International Monetary Fund, cited in R. Broad. 1994. "The Poor and the Environment: Friends or Foes?" *World Development* 22 (6): 811–22.

Kakonen, J. 1994. *Green Security or Militarized Environment.* Aldershot and Brookfield: Dartmouth Publishing Company.

Levy, M. A. 1999. "Exploring Environment-Security Connections" (World Wide Web sites on the relationship between environment and security). *Environment* 41 (1) (January): 3.

Lowi, Miriam R., and Brian R. Shaw. 2000. *Environment and Security Discourses and Practices.* London: Macmillan.

Lukong, P. F. 2002. "Dealing with HIV / AIDS in Sub Saharan Africa: Benefits and Challenges of a Spatial Approach in Cameroon." Paper presented at the Joint AURISA and Institution of Surveyors Conference, Adelaide, South Australia, November 25–30.

Madsen, Stig Toft. 1999. *State, Society and the Environment in South Asia.* Surrey: Curzon.

Middleton, N., P. O'Keefe, and S. Moyo. 1993. *The Tears of the Crocodile: From Rio to Reality in the Developing World.* London: Pluto Press.

Moench, Marcus, Elisabeth Caspari, and Ajaya Dixit. 1999. *Rethinking the Mosaic: Investigations into Local Water Management.* Kathmandu: Nepal Water Conservation Foundation and the Institute for Social and Environmental Transition, Boulder, Colo.

Myers, N. 1989. "Our Endangered Earth: Environment and Security." *Foreign Policy* 74 (spring): 23–41.

———. 1995. *Environmental Exodus: An Emergent Crisis in the Global Arena.* Washington, D.C.: Climate Institute.

Naff, T., and R. Matson. 1984. *Water in the Middle East: Conflict or Cooperation.* Boulder, Colo.: Westview Press.

Pettiford, Lloyd, and Melissa Curley. 1999. *Changing Security Agendas and the Third World.* London: Pinter.

Redclift, M. 2000. "Addressing the Causes of Conflict: Human Security and Environmental Responsibilities." *Reciel* 9 (1): 44–51.

Renner, M. 1996. *Fighting for Survival: Environmental Decline, Social Conflict, and the New Age of Insecurity.* Worldwatch Environmental Alert series. New York: Norton.

Schlosberg, D. 2007. *Defining Environmental Justice: Movements, Theories and Nature.* London: Oxford Univ. Press.

Schultz, Richard H., Roy Godson, and George Quester. 1997. *Security Studies for the 21st Century,* Washington, D.C.: Brasseys.

Scrivener, D. 2002. "Environmental Security." In *International Encyclopaedia of Environmental Politics,* ed. J. Barry and E. G. Frankland, 184. London: Routledge.

Shaheen, M. 2000. "Questioning the Water-War Phenomenon in the Jordan Basin." *Middle East Policy* 7 (3) (June): 137–50.

Singh, M. 1996. "Environmental Security and Displaced People in Southern Africa." *Social Justice* 23 (4) (winter): 125–33.

Soroos, M. S. 1995. "Environmental Security: Choices for the Twenty-First Century." *National Forum* 75 (1) (winter): 20–25.

Subrahmanyam, S. 1990. *Merchants, Markets and the State in Early Modern India*. Delhi, Oxford Univ. Press.

Thompson, M. 1997. "Security and Solidarity: An Anti-Reductionist Framework for Thinking About the Relationship Between Us and the Rest of Nature." *The Geographical Journal* 163 (2) (July): 141–49.

Times of Oman. 2007. "Weekly Meeting in Muscat." February 8, page 7.

2

Securitizing the Indian Ocean Region

CONCRETE ENTITY AND GEOPOLITICAL IMAGINATIONS

DENNIS RUMLEY

Introduction

The main purpose of this chapter is to identify some of the central issues raised in this book within the three broadly defined themes of changing geopolitical orientations, regional cooperation, and security concerns. However, before doing this, a brief discussion is undertaken of the question of Indian Ocean regional definition.

The Indian Ocean as a Region

From an academic geographical perspective, one of the broadest definitions of the region is that it includes 47 littoral and land-locked states bordering on the Indian Ocean (IFIOR 1995). However, if all Association of Southeast Asian Nations (ASEAN) states are included, then this raises the total number of regional states to at least 50. Either way, such a definition results in a very large region of considerable ethnic, religious, economic, political, and cultural diversity with little apparent commonality. However, it has been argued that, prior to European colonial contact, the economies of the Indian Ocean Region comprised a self-conscious "world" (McPherson 1993, 5). While there is presently a relatively low level of functional cohesion among regional states, the orientation to the ocean creates a degree of common interest and forms the basis for a potentially greater degree of functional interaction in the future. Furthermore, apart from the colonial heritage, one critically important commonality of Indian Ocean states is that the majority are members of the developing world and few of them possess high human development indices. Common developmental problems (Kerr 1981; Appleyard and Ghosh 1988) and their implications for national and regional security, defined in the broadest sense, can also provide a basis for increased South-South cooperation.

The academic and the practical policy definition of the Indian Ocean as a region is an inevitably contested issue as a result. The principal reason for this is fairly obvious—all regions are constructed, and, depending on the primary purpose of this construction—academic, administrative, economic, or, whatever—different regional definitions result. In short, the Indian Ocean, as a constructed region, will be defined by those who are involved in the construction process and whose collective goals will determine the composition of regional states. From the perspective of various types of regionalisms—economic, security, and environmental— regional definition, of course, also depends on those states willing to join and remain with the group. This essentially "inclusive-exclusive" debate runs through all global regionalisms, and the Indian Ocean Region is no exception. For example, the Seychelles, which joined the Indian Ocean Association for Regional Cooperation (IOR-ARC) in 1999, decided to withdraw in 2003. Other states, including Pakistan, are currently excluded from IOR-ARC. Furthermore, in the case of the Asia-Pacific Economic Cooperation (APEC) grouping, contrary to some expectations, India was excluded from regional membership in 1997. What these examples clearly indicate is that regional construction is essentially a geopolitical exercise and that regional membership will be determined geopolitically. In the final analysis, the essential elements of regionalism and regional construction derive from the geopolitical orientations of member and nonmember states, as well as political actors from the private and the third sectors, in the context of global, regional, and national imperatives. Furthermore, regions will expand or contract in direct response to the dynamics of these imperatives.

Changing Geopolitical Orientations in the Indian Ocean

It is not uncommon for Western commentators to underestimate the geopolitical importance of the Indian Ocean Region. There are at least five interrelated reasons why this might be so. First, some observers see the region only as comprising the "Third" world, and thus, by implication, it is of lesser significance. Second, and following from this, some Western observers simply remain ignorant about the Indian Ocean and about the geopolitical orientation of regional states due to the existence of other ocean priorities, such as the Pacific or the Atlantic. Third, those commentators who underestimate the geopolitical importance of the Indian Ocean, to some degree, still exhibit a kind of "colonial" perspective, as if the region had been frozen in time prior to the decolonization of most regional states. Fourth, ignorance can also be as a result of the fact that more needs to be written about the geopolitical importance of the Indian Ocean, in general, and the geopolitical orientations of Indian Ocean states, in particular. The latter is especially problematic from the viewpoint of the limited number of available works on regional states written from an "inside" perspective—for example, for the "Indian Ocean triangle" states, Australia (Rumley 1999), India (Panikkar 1955; Chaturvedi 1998), and South Africa (Mills 1998). A fifth point is that few regional state governments provide any explicit public discussion of their Indian Ocean orientations, with the notable exceptions of India's "Look East" strategy and Australia's "Look West" policy. How many of them are actually oriented toward the Indian Ocean is itself a debatable issue.

As has been pointed out in the preface, the Indian Ocean possesses considerable geopolitical importance, if only because of its operation as a "highway"

(McPherson 1993, 5). Trade interactions among Europe, the Middle East, and East Asia, for example, all rely on uninterrupted access through the Indian Ocean. Furthermore, the Indian Ocean Region comprises a number of sub-systems of varying geopolitical significance. Bouchard argues that it is only through the application of multi-scale analysis that the complexity of Indian Ocean geopolitics can be grasped (Bouchard 2004). The Persian Gulf sub-system, which contains the greatest regional concentration of global oil reserves, also is a region of high internal fragmentation while possessing above average GNP per capita. Social, economic, and political stability within these regional states and freedom of access through the Indian Ocean and contiguous seas by large oil consumers in the North is of inestimable importance to global economic stability.

The changing geopolitical significance of the Indian Ocean can be conveniently envisaged as comprising four principal stages—a pre-colonial phase, a colonial phase, a Cold War phase, and the present post–Cold War "globalized" phase. Jackson discusses the relevance of British colonial interests in the Indian Ocean from the 18th century until the 20th century, focusing on the region's strategic significance (Jackson 2005). While the Indian Ocean Pax Britannica, which was established after the Revolutionary and Napoleonic Wars, was shattered in 1941 by Japan, the region continued to be one of British hegemony until the 1960s, albeit as part of a reconfigured global order underwritten by United States' power.

To a considerable degree, the geopolitical importance of Indian Ocean states increased considerably during the Cold War phase. Superpower rivalry, especially from the late 1960s, propelled the search for regional client states in strategic locations, and especially those which were reaching independence and had access to or proximity to important regional resources. At about the same time that the superpowers were "invading" the British Lake, the British themselves decided to vacate it, and, by implication, Western strategic interests were left in the hands of the United States. To some extent, the historical legacy of the structure of Cold War linkages in the Indian Ocean Region still inhibits regional cohesion.

There are yet others who would discount the prospect for a consideration of Indian Ocean geopolitics due to the impacts of the processes of globalization. However, as Houbert (2005) argues, the global system of states remains as important today as the transnational capitalist economy. Furthermore, he suggests that, as far as the Indian Ocean Region is concerned, the configuration of land and sea still remains highly significant geopolitically. With decolonization on land, power at sea actually became more important.

In the post–Cold War period, some commentators argue that the Indian Ocean Region has entered a new geopolitical era; Bouchard refers to it as the "Indianoceanic order" (Bouchard 2005). The structure and dynamics of this new "order" are seen to be articulated around five principal characteristics—regional heterogeneity, a system of Indian Ocean sub-regional sub-systems, the emergent IOR-ARC, a subordination to large foreign powers, and the geopolitical importance of the ocean itself.

Regional Cooperation in the Indian Ocean

With the end of the Cold War, ideological regionalism eventually began to give way to economic regionalism, and this "new regionalism" took less note of former ideological divides and incorporated states at different levels of economic development. In part, such a development was a response to difficulties with multilateral arrangements, but it was also a response to concerns over some of the negative impacts of globalization. Furthermore, states felt that there was a direct correlation between economic regionalism and national economic growth, and that by being part of a regional arrangement they would ensure that they would not be "left out," and that they might be able to influence the behavior of other regional states in ways that would not be possible outside of regional arrangements. For states of the South, all of these reasons had particular resonance. However, the Indian Ocean faced a particular contextual problem because it did not possess a strong regionalism tradition. Furthermore, in many other cases around the world, regionalism was built on relatively strong bilateral linkages. In the Indian Ocean, however, relatively weak bilateral relations implied a relatively weak regionalism from the outset. On the one hand, the creation of the Indian Ocean Association for Regional Cooperation (IOR-ARC) in 1997 was a significant development. On the other hand, by dint of IOR-ARC membership, only 18 states around the Indian Ocean rim currently explicitly possess some degree of pan–Indian Ocean regional commitment.

Furthermore, there has been a reduced level of interest in IOR-ARC in recent years due mainly to its primary emphasis on the bureaucratic control of trade and investment issues (McPherson 2005). This has had two principal outcomes: first, other non-government "second track" groups have become essentially irrelevant to the operation of the regional organization, and second, many other important regional matters, ranging from HIV/AIDS to comprehensive security, are unable to be discussed. In short, for most Indian Ocean inhabitants, IOR-ARC is likely to have little relevance, unless and until regional state governments are prepared to refurbish IOR-ARC with a new vision and are willing to commit sufficient resources to ensure a positive and proactive commitment on the part of regional business and academic groups.

Thus, it seems that sub-regional groupings—ASEAN, GCC, BIMST-EC—rather than a pan–Indian Ocean regionalism, are more important in dealing with regional problems (Rao 2003).

Let us now move to the principal purpose of this chapter: to evaluate the nature of security threats that exist within the Indian Ocean Region (IOR). It is argued that many security threats are geopolitical constructions and that an attempt to objectively measure traditional security threats indicates that the region contains no "real" threat. Rather, the IOR is increasingly subject to a range of so-called nontraditional threats, all of which need to become the basis of a new regional security agenda. In order to elaborate this argument, this chapter is divided into five main sections. First, the overall question of "What is a security threat?" will be discussed. Second, some of the characteristics of regional geopolitically constructed threats will be examined. Third is a discussion and analysis of conventional security threats in the IOR. The fourth section highlights the potential regional implications of economic insecurity. Finally, due to constraints of space, the last section stresses the overriding importance of human security out of the myriad of regional nontraditional security threats.

What Is a Security Threat?

Constructing Security

It is well-known that security is both a contested and a multidimensional concept—it can embody traditional concerns over military security that are generally evident at the scale of the state, and it can also encompass concerns over other aspects of security, such as economic and environmental security. In addition, a broad definition of security would include other nonstate forms of nontraditional security, such as terrorism, money laundering, and drug trafficking. Thus, security threats can take many forms—from armed conflict to sexual violence against women (Commission on Human Security 2003, 49). Policies designed to meet traditional security concerns have generally been enacted at the state scale, but, with increasing globalization and technological change, policies associated with economic and environmental security and with all forms of nontraditional security increasingly necessitate inter-state cooperation (Rumley and Gopal 2007). This is a significant policy concern for most Indian Ocean regional states since the nature of nontraditional security threats is becoming increasingly more important, and since, in a globalizing world, states will wish to portray themselves both as being secure and as being of no threat. Constructing Indian Ocean security in the broadest sense in the 21st century requires regional cooperation.

Manufacturing Threats: Imaginings and Warnings

Among other factors, threat perceptions are a product of structural, geopolitical, historical, socio-cultural, and economic considerations (Tilman 1984). While a fundamental consideration in the formulation of security policy is a threat assessment, threat perceptions and assessments will vary over time both in terms of content and in terms of accuracy (Dupont 1991). However, threats may not be "real"; they may be manufactured. Many in the West possess a range of fears about the world and especially about Asia and the developing world. In addition, many Westerners are God-fearing and have a fear of the other. Western perceptions of the developing world, in particular, have been heavily influenced by "orientalism"—a Western concept that sees Asia, for example, as comprising a mixture of savagery, exotica, and despotism—descriptions that would be considered by most Westerners to be the very opposite of those attributable to themselves (Said 1991). The East is thus invariably demonized and marginalized in the West. Perhaps this is a function of the uncertain environment, or perhaps it is an innate characteristic of Western society.

In Australia, there has been a long-standing "red scare" and a "fear of the north." India, too, has felt regionally vulnerable. In Australia's case, a "sense of vulnerability" has characterized much of its modern history (Dalrymple 2003, 4).

Fear has also been a key feature of Australian domestic politics in recent years. Perhaps we all share some imagined fear and a fear of the unknown. Some might even fear freedom itself. The UN Secretary-General, however, has argued strongly for the global realization of a fundamentally different goal, "freedom from fear," as part of a broader vision of collective security. However, as Kofi Annan has recently pointed out: "Collective security today depends on accepting that the threats which each region of the world perceives as most urgent are in fact equally so for all" (Annan 2005, 24–5). Prioritizing and securing the strategic agenda of the North compared to the South is not part of this vision. There is therefore an urgent need to "democratize security."

The imaginings of fear can also be both constructed and manipulated. They can be constructed by governments, by intelligence agencies, by the media, and by education systems. Indeed, fear is often a function of a lack of knowledge. Fear can also be manipulated by governments—at election times, for example. In addition, government warnings about other states can reinforce fear based on inadequate knowledge. In this sense, "real" security threats are invariably seen to be those that are officially sanctioned by states and not those that are perceived by its citizenry. Thus, HIV / AIDS was declared a security threat by the UN Security Council in 2000 (Commission on Human Security 2003, 99). As the recent UN Commission has shown, if intelligence agencies and governments wish to find a threat, they will, irrespective of the data (Davis 2005).

However, perhaps not surprisingly, various facets of security can be in conflict and result in contradictions. In potentially conflictual environments between states, the involvement of other states in security matters—for example, in arms supply—can potentially exacerbate the situation. The extent to which such involvement is seen to be acceptable can produce what might be regarded as a kind of security hypocrisy. Some commentators might therefore be forgiven for perceiving a double standard in the U.S. condemnation of possible European arms sales to China while itself being in the process of deciding to supply F-16 fighter planes to Pakistan. The latter decision naturally led to "great disappointment" in India and perhaps contributed to the timing of an announcement of a significant upgrading in its military hardware (Agence France-Presse 2005). However, from an Indian perspective, such a decision must also be interpreted in the context of India's approach to security matters, which has been characterized as "modified structuralism"— that is, on the one hand, India seeks to maximize its own conception of power based on military strength, economic development, and internal order, while, on the other hand, being willing to yield concessions to rival interests (Bajpai 1998).

Even in "non-threatening" state-state relations, fear of reprisal often governs the nature of inter-state interaction. Unspoken threats can therefore arise due to asymmetrical relations between more powerful states and those wishing to guarantee their own economic security. Guaranteeing a state's economic security (or even a politician's re-election) in these circumstances may result in states' jettisoning principles related to human security. Particular dilemmas can arise when there is a contradiction between maximizing traditional security and maximizing a state's economic security.

Geopolitically Constructed Security Threats

In the 21st century, geopolitically constructed security threats have been ascribed by the West both to states and to regions. Thus, both "rogue states" and "failed states" have been portrayed by the West as being located outside of the civilized world in a way that echoes the Cold War good-versus-evil rhetoric of the conflict with the Soviet Union (Rumley 2003, 321). There is a tendency for international crises to be centered around weak or failing states (Fukuyama 2004, 93). The characterization of Iran, Iraq, and North Korea as being part of an "axis of evil" was based not only on the belief that such states were developing weapons of mass destruction (WMD), but that they were intending to use these weapons against Western interests.

Geopolitically constructed security threats are inevitably contested. The term Cold War, for example, which was popularized in the United States, has been interpreted as comprising four different but related conflicts—U.S.A. versus European states, economic center versus economic periphery, freedom versus totalitarianism, and U.S.A. versus U.S.S.R. (Rumley et al. 1996, 3).

Another well-known global geopolitical construction, of course, is the clash of civilizations hypothesis (Huntington 1996). For the IOR, this construction predicts an ongoing set of conflicts among African, Islamic, Hindu, Buddhist, Sinic, and Western "civilizations," with permanent "fault lines" being located where these six civilizations connect. However, Huntington would have us believe that Australia will be in permanent conflict with most of its Indian Ocean neighbors since the primary dimension of conflict is seen as between so-called Western civilization and the rest. As has been pointed out, not only is Huntington's concept of "civilization" conceptually and operationally flawed, but his analysis seems to ignore the fact that, in recent years, most violent conflicts have actually occurred within civilizations and more particularly within states (Rumley 1999, 27).

An alternative construction of a primary dimension of conflict that has implications for the IOR sees the main source of global conflict as being a "clash of fundamentalisms," especially between Islamic fundamentalism and what he characterizes as "the mother of all fundamentalisms: American imperialism" (Ali 2002, 281). Clearly, this characterization has some fundamental implications for real and perceived security threats within the IOR, given the locations of the land- and sea-based presence of the United States.

Most of the West Asian portion of the IOR has been characterized as "the global zone of percolating violence" and "is likely to be a major battlefield, both for wars among nation-states and, more likely, for protracted ethnic and religious violence" (Brzezinski 1997, 52–53). In addition, most of the Northern half of the IOR has been incorporated into a U.S.-designated "Southern Belt of Strategic Instability," which stretches from southern Japan in the east to northern Italy in the west (Flanagan, Frost and Kugler 2001, 17). Not only do such constructions tend to be self-reinforcing and self-fulfilling, they also become used as rigid templates for policy making.

From an Australian perspective, much of the eastern portion of the IOR has been characterized as an "arc of instability." This arc of instability, which is located within Australia's region of primary strategic interest, has emerged since the end of the Cold War in response to globalization, a history of colonialism, problems of social and political viability, poor governance, economic instability, aid dependency, ethnic tension, and religious fundamentalism (Rumley, Forbes, and Griffin 2006). The most recent government White Paper points out that, in Southeast Asia, for example, "extremists . . . target not only Westerners, but also seek to destabilize the region's secular governments" (Commonwealth of Australia 2003, 40). On the other hand, the contested nature of the "arc of instability" appellation has prompted one influential Australian commentator to refer to this region as an "alleged 'arc of crisis'" and to argue that its characterization is being used as a mechanism for increasing Australian government military spending or as a rational for an outdated regional strategic orientation (Dupont 2003).

While threats can be geopolitically constructed, the opposite can also be true—that is, security can potentially be enhanced by geopolitical constructions. In this sense, Indian Ocean economic regionalism, in the form of IOR-ARC, though still relatively weak, is potentially an extremely important mechanism for enhancing regional security (Bajpai 1998, 172). One of the more obvious reasons for this is based on an interaction-stability thesis—that is, the greater the degree of social, economic, and political interaction among states, the lower the probability of inter-state conflict. However, the current status of Indian Ocean regionalism, as expressed through IOR-ARC, is something of a self-defeating vicious circle, since the principal reason for its weakness lies in relatively weak bilateral socio-economic linkages within the IOR. Furthermore, such weak bilateral linkages militate against Indian Ocean regionalism from being fully inclusive and ensure a preoccupation with matters other than a very narrowly defined form of economic security.

Conventional Security Threats in the Indian Ocean Region: Measuring Security

Attempts to objectively measure security and to precisely define security threats are fraught with difficulty compared with, for example, the measurement of insecurity outcomes—such as the number of deaths in battle, or the number of piracy attacks. Threat assessment, at best, is an imprecise science, and, dependent on its policy impact, runs the risk of exacerbating insecurity, especially between states.

In terms of the most basic indicator of traditional security—defense expenditure—the Indian Ocean Region contains two of the world's top ten spenders—Saudi Arabia (US$21 billion) and India (US$13 billion) (Commonwealth of Australia 2003, 20). In addition, both Australia (US$7.5 billion) and Indonesia (US$6.2 billion) possess very substantial defense budgets, as do Iran (US$4.9 billion), Kuwait (US$3.3 billion), Malaysia (US$3.3 billion), Burma (US$2.8 billion), Oman (US$2.7 billion), United Arab Emirates (US$2.7 billion), Pakistan (US$2.5 billion), and South Africa (US$1.7 billion). As a proportion of GDP, however, it seems that few states have increased their defense expenditures (see Table 2.1 for 1990–2000).

While the Indian Ocean Region contains considerable variation by state in terms of the size of the armed forces, the level of militarization does not necessarily

Table 2.1   Some Conventional Security Indicators in the Indian Ocean Rim

	Armed Forces (total force)	Militarization (force as % pop)	Arms Imports US$M 2001	Defense as % GDP 1990	Defense as % GDP 2000
India	1,303,000	0.1	1,064	2.7	2.4
Pakistan (L)	612,000	0.5	759	5.8	4.5*#
Iran	513,000	0.8	335	2.7	3.8#
Egypt	448,000	0.7	486	3.5	2.3
Burma	344,000	0.8	na	3.4	1.7*#
Thailand	301,000	0.5	162	2.2	1.6
Indonesia	297,000	0.1	38	1.3	1.1#
Saudi Arabia	202,000	1.0	143	12.8	11.6*
Bangladesh (L)	137,000	0.1	180	1.0	1.3
Sri Lanka	115,000	0.6	40	2.1	4.5*#
Malaysia	96,000	0.4	20	2.6	1.9#
Yemen (L)	66,000	0.4	33	8.5	5.2
UAE (H)	65,000	1.7	288	na	na
South Africa	63,000	0.2	17	3.8	1.5
Singapore (H)	60,000	2.0	141	4.8	4.8*#
Australia (H)	51,000	0.3	687	2.2	1.7
Oman	44,000	1.8	30	18.3	9.7*#
Tanzania (L)	34,000	0.1	na	2.0	1.3
Kuwait (H)	15,000	0.6	34	48.5	8.2*#
Mozambique (L)	6,000	0.04	na	10.1	2.5
Average		0.6	262.2	7.3	3.8

All states have medium human development levels unless otherwise noted (H or L).

*military expenditure higher than on health

military expenditure higher than on education

Source: Rumley and Chaturvedi, 2004, p. 28.

correspond. Thus, while India has the region's largest armed forces, with more than 1.3 million in uniform, its militarization index is well below the regional average at 0.1. Kuwait, on the other hand, with armed forces numbering 15,000, has a much higher level of militarization. However, the regional arms trade is significant and there are considerable regional arms imports, especially to India, Pakistan, Australia, Egypt, Iran, and United Arab Emirates, which, to a considerable degree, reflect internal regional conflict and/or instability.

Unfortunately, given the developmental context of many Indian Ocean states, international as well as domestic realities ensure that often human development takes second place to military development. There are at least six regional states—Burma, Kuwait, Oman, Pakistan, Singapore, and Sri Lanka—in which government military expenditure exceeds combined government expenditure on health and on education.

Regional Nuclear Proliferation

Clearly, the extent of regional nuclear proliferation can be seen both as a regional security threat and as a guarantor of peace, depending on your perception and point of view. The standard arguments can be opposed—that is, the "more will be better" school of William Waltz and others versus the "more will be worse" perspective of François Sagan and others. On the one hand, while Waltz has argued that nuclear proliferation will lead to greater stability through deterrence, Sagan has argued that proliferation induces greater instability because of the potential for deliberate or accidental conflict and thus there is a need to enhance the global nonproliferation regime (Howlett 2001, 428–29).

Others have argued that the inevitability of nuclear proliferation has resulted in a fundamental shift in global geopolitics as a result of the onset of the "second nuclear age" (Bracken 2000). While the "first nuclear age" began on July 16, 1945, with the U.S. testing of the atomic bomb in the New Mexico desert, the "second nuclear age"—an "Asian nuclear age"—arguably began with Chinese nuclear tests in 1964, with India's nuclear test of 1974 being the first example of an "outlaw bomb" (Bracken 2000, 95–124).

While some regional states, such as South Africa, had nuclear weapons but gave them up, and others, such as Iran, may have them but say they do not, yet others, like Australia, seek shelter under a nuclear umbrella. Australia is comfortable with not having any nuclear weapons of its own while simultaneously exporting substantial quantities of uranium (admittedly under treaty safeguards). Furthermore, when Australia chastised India when the latter tested a nuclear device in 1998, this had an almost immediate negative impact on the economic security of both states, since the relative importance of trade declined.

Many Western commentators find it difficult to conceive of a state like Iran, with such enormous fossil fuel reserves, taking the pathway to nuclear energy. One obvious interpretation of Iranian nuclear behavior is that it is in direct response to that of Israel, and, earlier, to an Iraq that did possess WMDs. In the case of the latter, this same rationale lay behind the U.S. invasion, now aimed in part, it seems, to construct a new democratic map for the Middle East, the basic structure of which is yet to be determined. In the meantime, traditional security in Iraq is to be guaranteed by a U.S.-led coalition, although the United States, with in excess of 150,000 troops in country, is clearly the dominant force. Australia is the only Indian Ocean state which is a part of that coalition, and its original 400 troops are now bolstered by a further 450 in Al-Muthanna Province in southern Iraq to guard "Japanese engineers" (Kerin and Bita 2005). However, the planned exodus of other members of the coalition—for example, Italy, The Netherlands, and Ukraine—is likely to place greater strain on the Australian Defense Force, and, consequently, on Australian public opinion.

If we were to accept the argument that more is better, then India, Israel, Pakistan, and potentially Iran are no regional nuclear threat. Accepting the alternative argument, on the other hand, results in the opposite conclusion. Equality of nuclear security would necessitate that all regional states or that no regional state should possess nuclear weapons. Inequality of state access to nuclear weapons is arguably the "real" security threat.

Security Dilemmas and "Real Threats"

There is still a certain degree of resistance to the removal of Cold War conceptions of security that led to a spatial structuring of global space into a set of regions that were to be feared. What this helped to facilitate was a self-perpetuating "security dilemma"—that is, the production of a security threatening situation for one state or region that arises as a result of the perceived consequences of another state's or region's behavior in attempting to guarantee its own security (Rumley 1999, 16). The security dilemma possesses three essential characteristics—benign intent (actions are defensively motivated), uncertainty of intent (they did not know that the others were acting for defensive reasons), and paradoxical outcome (their actions only made matters worse) (Collins 2000, 24–25). State policy responses designed to meet potential threats can fall into a similar category.

Uncertainty of intent, of course, may also be a reflection of a lack of understanding over a state's regional geopolitical orientation. As has been noted, for the IOR, there is a general dearth of published material concerning the geopolitical orientation of regional states (Rumley and Chaturvedi 2004, 24). This lack of information means that regional states have to rely on perceptions of actions and their intentions, and it may well be that these intentions change or are perceived to change. Thus, some regional states might be forgiven for perceiving some ambiguity in how Australia sees its regional role—is it "honest broker" or is it "deputy sheriff"? Clearly, in the case of the latter, some commentators might thus perceive Australia to be potentially threatening, especially if it is seen to be associated with a doctrine of "pre-emption," which itself is an offensive posture based on perceived threat.

For the Indian Ocean Region, one could develop a simple hypothetical Indian Ocean state threat index (HIOSTI) based on conventional security data. For example, we would expect that for any regional state to pose a "real threat" it would have to be above average on all of these indicators—that is, we would expect a "real" state threat to be above average on militarization, on arms imports, and on the percentage expended on defense in 1990 and in 2000. When we examine the data we find, in fact, that no such "real threat" exists. Several states are above average on one or more of these categories, but no state is above average on all four. Indeed, only one state is above average on three of the categories (militarization and above average spent on defense in 1990 and in 2000), and that is Oman. Most strategists would not regard the state of Oman as an Indian Ocean regional threat, however. On the other hand, the apparent U.S. military build-up in Oman could be seen as a possible security threat to Iran (Johnson 2004, 252). However, in general terms, "real" security threats in the traditional sense of the term are intra-state and invariably do not emanate from other states (UN 2004, 24), and war data since the Second World War clearly demonstrate this.

Economic Insecurity in the Indian Ocean Region

It has often been said that a post–Cold War global North-South division is replacing the former East-West division as one of the principal dimensions of global conflict. In this new paradigm there is a danger of prioritizing the security agenda of the North at the expense of the South. Regional security threats can arise because of the instability of states with problems of economic, social, and political viability. In addition, resources scarcity and resources competition constitute threats, especially when they are linked to food and energy insecurity. Indeed, it has been argued that, in the years ahead, "resource wars" will become "the most distinctive feature of the global security environment" (Klare 2002, 212). Furthermore, states that "fail" due to basic problems of good governance and corruption are incapable of asserting authority within their own territories, and are seen to be "troubling to world order" since they may become sources of instability, mass migration, and terrorism (Rotberg 2002).

One of the important common characteristics of Indian Ocean states is that the majority are members of the developing world—indeed, some regard the Indian Ocean Region as the heart of the developing world. By far the highest proportion of regional states (48 percent) has a low human development index (HDI), concentrated principally in the North and East African and the South Asian Association for Regional Cooperation (SAARC) sub-regions. On the other hand, only 11 states of the IOR possess a high HDI—Australia, Bahrain, Brunei, Kuwait, Malaysia, Mauritius, Qatar, Seychelles, Singapore, Thailand, and the United Arab Emirates. In this sense, the Indian Ocean Region is a global focus not only for North-South conflict, but also for external intervention and potentially for South-South cooperation. Problems of underdevelopment, poor governance, internal political instability and conflict are thus common to many regional states (Rumley 1999, 228).

Africa is the continent that is the hardest hit by poverty, and, while life expectancy has been decreasing, there has also been an increase in food and energy insecurity. The annual HIV/AIDS deaths in Africa exceed the total number of battle deaths in all civil wars fought in the 1990s (United Nations 2004). If we take, for example, the eight states that constitute the Western Indian Ocean littoral (WIOL)—Kenya, Madagascar, Mozambique, Oman, Somalia, South Africa, Tanzania, and Yemen—only two, the northern and southern "anchors" of Oman and South Africa, do not possess low human development indices, and one, Somalia, has been classified as a "failed state." Furthermore, of these WIOL states, only the latter is not a member of IOR-ARC.

Addressing the problems of WIOL states necessitates confronting the causes of economic insecurity and also requires the implementation of a "shared vision of development" (Annan 2005, 8–23). The eight goals outlined in the 2001 UN Millennium Declaration—to eradicate extreme poverty and hunger, achieve universal primary education, promote gender equality and empower women, reduce child mortality, improve maternal health, combat HIV/AIDS, malaria, and other diseases, ensure environmental sustainability, and initiate a global partnership for development—are clearly central components of this shared vision. The "special needs" of Africa were referred to in the Millennium Declaration, and the UN Secretary-General has recently called for a green revolution in Africa and a new global partnership for Africa's development (Annan 2005). Among other things, this means that richer Indian Ocean states have a special regional developmental responsibility in order to enhance regional security. An analysis of the bilateral disbursement of official development assistance (ODA) to the 21 Indian Ocean littoral states is instructive in this regard (see Table 2.2).

The only significant Indian Ocean ODA donor contribution in 2002 was Australia to Indonesia. Furthermore, Japan was the largest ODA donor to eight regional states; France was the largest donor to an additional five states; the United States was the largest donor to three states; the Arab states were the largest donors to two states, and the EC, Germany, and the UK each donate the most to one regional state. Donor state ODA priorities are fairly well-defined, with Japan giving the largest amount to Indonesia; France gives the largest amount to Mozambique; the United States gives the largest amount to Pakistan; the Arab states give the largest amount to Yemen; Japan, the UK and Germany give the largest amounts to India; and the EC gives the largest amount to Tanzania.

Donor states appear to have fairly well-defined sub-regional priorities, with Japan giving the largest amount of ODA to every state surrounding the Bay of Bengal. France has concentrated its ODA mainly in the southwestern Indian Ocean, the United States in the Horn of Africa and Pakistan, and Arab states in Oman and Yemen.

Regional Non-Conventional Security Threats

In the world of the 21st century, however, what is becoming clear is that the traditional realist model of security—principally embodied in the view that threats emanate from one state, are aimed at another state, and are of a military nature—has increasingly come into question (Commonwealth of Australia 2003). Furthermore, the specific nature of these nontraditional security threats—for example, people smuggling, drug trafficking, piracy, and terrorism—require nontraditional responses by state security agencies (Dupont 2003). At the Indian Ocean regional scale, these new security threats essentially require a new approach to regional security cooperation at various levels.

Overall, there exists a fundamentally different mindset when comparing traditional and nontraditional security from the perspective of policy planning for potential threats. In the case of the former, there tends to exist a mindset of planning for conflict. In the case of the latter, on the other hand, there is more likely to

Table 2.2   Indian Ocean Littoral States: Bilateral ODA Recipients 2002 (US$M)

	Three Largest State Donors	Indian Ocean Donors in the Top 10
Bangladesh	Japan (262), UK (188), USA (95)	–
Burma	Japan (54), EC (10), UK (9)	–
India	Japan (768), UK (346), Germany (159)	–
Indonesia	Japan (891), USA (219), Germany (120)	Australia (79)
Iran	Germany (35), Japan (32), France (9)	–
Kenya	USA (108), UK (70), Japan (54)	–
Madagascar	France (99), EC (69), USA (42)	–
Malaysia	Japan (187), Denmark (18), Germany (6)	Australia (1)
Maldives	Japan (8), Norway (1)	Australia (1.3)
Mauritius	France (19), EC (16), Japan (3)	–
Mozambique	France (240), Italy (231), USA (148)	–
Oman	Arab states (53), Belgium (6), Japan (3)	Australia (0.1)
Pakistan	USA (656), Japan (284), France (250)	–
Seychelles	France (4), EC (3), Japan (1)'	–
Singapore	France (3), Japan (2), Germany (2)	Australia (0.2)
Somalia	USA (35), Norway (33), EC (32)	–
South Africa	EC (125), USA (98), UK (87)	–
Sri Lanka	Japan (249), Germany (25), Norway (25)	–
Tanzania	UK (208), EC (136), Netherlands (117)	–
Thailand	Japan (651), USA (36), Germany (20)	Australia (9)
Yemen	Arab states (188), Netherlands (35), Germany (31)	–

Source: Development Assistance Committee Web site.

be a view toward "planning for cooperation." Both, of course, can be self-fulfilling. In this sense, there is good reason to believe that Indian Ocean cooperation to meet a range of nonconventional security threats will actually lead to a minimization of traditional security threats. For the sake of the present discussion, only one type of nontraditional security threat—human security—will be considered here.

Human Security

The Commission on Human Security has argued that the current global war on terror is deficient in at least two ways. First, much state-sponsored terrorism is not addressed. Second, some legitimate groups have been labeled as terrorist organization in order to stifle any opposition to authoritarian government policies (Commission on Human Security 2003, 23). Clearly, the state still remains the central purveyor of security, yet it often fails to properly discharge its security obligations and at times can even be a threat to its own citizens. As a result, attention must now shift from the security of the state to the security of the people—that is, there is a need to shift the focus to human security (Commission on Human Security 2003, 2). This shift will involve greater attention being given to human rights and to assure the "freedom to live in dignity" (Annan 2005, 34).

One can examine this in another way by attempting to differentiate between threats to the state and threats to people. One of the changes consequent upon the end of the Cold War is that there was an important change of scale and differentiation in threat reality and threat perception. In the 21st century, while threats to the economy and the natural environment of states tend to be global, "real" threats to people are more likely to be intra-state and even intra-urban. In short, "real" threats to the state are global and "real" threats to people emanate from the state. The "democratization of security" is thus essential to address "real" needs.

The existence of authoritarian regimes in the Indian Ocean Region is not uncommon. Authoritarian regimes not only threaten their own people, they also threaten regional and even global resources security given their general coincidence with the distribution of hydrocarbons. Over the past thirty years, states that are classified as "free" in the Indian Ocean Region are in a small minority (consistently less than 20 percent), although it is clear that the overall pattern of states which Freedom House classifies as "not free" and "partly free" has changed since 1972. Nonetheless, at 2002, states in the "not free" category comprised the highest percentage, with several new states being placed in this category compared with 1992 (for example, Egypt, Maldives, Oman, Pakistan, Swaziland, UAE, Yemen, and Zimbabwe).

In its 2004 global survey, the state ranking of press freedoms, provided by the organization Reporters Without Borders, shows that the worst offenders are to be found in East Asia (especially Burma, China, Vietnam, and Laos) and in the Middle East (particularly Saudi Arabia, Iran, Syria, and Iraq). Of all of the Indian Ocean states, only two (South Africa and Australia) were in the ranking's upper quartile, and the largest group of states was located in the ranking's lowest quartile.

Former UN Secretary-General Kofi Annan has talked of the global need to strive for "larger freedom"—that is, a view of freedom which "encapsulates the idea that development, security, and human rights go hand in hand" (Annan 2005, 5). Among other things, international and regional pressure and public and private dialogue are needed to encourage larger freedom and to enhance the process of democratization.

In March 2005, Malaysia pressured Burma to implement democratic reforms. Parliamentarians from the ruling Barisan Nasional coalition tabled a resolution calling for Burma to be stripped of its chair of top regional grouping, ASEAN in 2006, unless its military regime rights its dismal human rights record.

Conclusion

In a very real sense, there is no necessity for regional states to devise a security regime during a period when the Indian Ocean is dominated by outside powers. The combination of colonialism and the Cold War ensured that regional states were insufficiently emancipated to collectively decide their mutual destinies. In any event, internal interaction was relatively weak and this ensured a weak regionalism. Just as security threats and insecurity are constructed, so security itself also needs to be constructed. As it stands at present, apart from the role of the United Nations and a few second track groups, much of the responsibility for constructing security in the Indian Ocean Region lies in the hands of regional states, whether they like it or not.

There are at least four implications of this security environment. First, there is no regional security regime for the Indian Ocean. Second, sub-regional security regimes are relatively weak. Third, security arrangements are essentially Western-oriented and are orchestrated by the United States. Fourth, there is an emphasis on stronger bilateral rather than multilateral security relationships in the Indian Ocean Region.

There is considerable scope to construct security regimes around areas of common interest—for example, the environment, sea lanes of communication (SLOCs), piracy, and so on—the majority of which are nontraditional (and perhaps less threatening) security concerns. Minimizing insecurity requires greater mutual knowledge, education, and understanding among Indian Ocean governments and peoples. Indeed, it has been argued that civil society will likely be a primary location for political struggle and political change during the current century (for example, Schecter 2000). Such struggles will be an outcome of the refusal by social movements to accept the taken-for-granted communication boundaries of established systems of domination such as states and because social movements will also offer resistance in opposition to neoliberal globalization (Routledge 2000). On the other hand, while another common assumption of the emergence of a global civil society is that new political organizations structurally converge around a common global agenda, in reality it seems that the convergence of world views is highly fragmentary (Heins 2000). Regional opportunities currently exist around the Indian Ocean for "second track" actors to make an important contribution to regional security. Other areas of concern, such as environmental security and many other nontraditional security threats, such as those noted above, might well form the basis of an increasingly strong civil relationship among people living around the Indian Ocean Region in the future.

REFERENCES

Agence France-Presse. 2005. "India Goes on Weapons Spree." *West Australian*, March 31, p. 31.

Alagappa, M., ed. 1998. *Asian Security Practice: Material and Ideational Influences*. Stanford, Calif.: Stanford Univ. Press.

Ali, T. 2002. *The Clash of Fundamentalisms: Crusades, Jihads and Modernity*. London: Verso.

Appleyard, R. T., and R. N. Ghosh. 1988. *Indian Ocean Islands Development*. Canberra: Australian National University.

Annan, K. 2005. *In Larger Freedom: Towards Development, Security and Human Rights For All*. New York: United Nations.

Australian Government. 2005. *Malaysia: An Economy Transformed*. DFAT, Economic Analytical Unit: Canberra.

Baginda, A. R. 2002. "Malaysian Perceptions of China: From Hostility to Cordiality." In *The China Threat: Perceptions, Myths and Reality*, ed. H. Yee and I. Storey, 227–47. London: RoutledgeCurzon.

Bajpai, K. 1998. "India: Modified Structuralism." In Alagappa, op. cit., 157–97.

Bergin, A. 2004. "The Proliferation Security Initiative—Implications for the Indian Ocean Region." Paper delivered to the second IORG conference on "Energy Security and the Indian Ocean," Tehran, February.

Blackwill, R. D., and P. Dibb, eds. 2000. *America's Asian Alliances,* Cambridge, Mass.: MIT Press.

Bouchard, C. 2004. "Emergence of a New Geopolitical Era in the Indian Ocean: Characteristics, Issues and Limitations of the Indianoceanic Order." In Rumley and Chaturvedi, op. cit., 84–109.

Bracken, P. 2000. *Fire in the East: The Rise of Asian Military Power and the Second Nuclear Age*. Perennial: New York.

Brzezinski, Z. 1997. *The Grand Chessboard: American Primacy and Its Geostrategic Imperatives*. New York: Basic Books.

Buzan, B., O. Wæver, and J. de Wilde. 1998. *Security: A New Framework for Analysis*. Boulder: Lynne Reinner.

Castells, M. 1997. *The Information Age: Economy, Society and Culture,* vol. 2, *The Power of Identity*. Oxford: Blackwell.

Chaturvedi, S. 1998. "Common Security? Geopolitics, Development, South Asia and the Indian Ocean." *Third World Quarterly* 19 (4): 201–72.

CIA. 2005. *The World Factbook*. Washington, D.C.: GPO.

Club de Madrid. 2005. http://www.clubmadrid.org (accessed December 2005).

Collins, A. 2000. *The Security Dilemmas of Southeast Asia*. Singapore: ISEAS.

Commission on Human Security. 2003. *Human Security Now*. New York: Commission on Human Security.

Commonwealth of Australia. 2003. *Advancing the National Interest: Australia's Foreign and Trade Policy White Paper*. Canberra: DFAT.

Cook, I. 2005. *Australians Speak 2005*: Public Opinion and Foreign Policy. Sydney: Lowy Institute.

Council for Security Cooperation in the Asia-Pacific (CSCAP). 2004. http://www.cscap.org/ (accessed January 2005).

Dalrymple, R. 2003. *Continental Drift: Australia's Search for a Regional Identity,* Aldershot: Ashgate.

Davis, J. H. 2005. "Report Faults US Spy Community, Challenges Strategy for Overhaul." *Baltimore Sun,* 1 April.

Development Assistance Committee (DAC). 2005. http://www.oecd.org.countrylist (accessed December 2005).

Doty, Roxanne Lynn. 2003. *Anti-Immigrantism in Western Democracies: Statecraft, Desire and the Politics of Exclusion,* London: Routledge.

Downer, A. 2005. "Securing Australia's Interests—Australian Foreign Policy Priorities." *Australian Journal of International Affairs* 59 (1): 7–12.

Doyle, T. 2004. "An Agenda for Environmental Security in the Indian Ocean Region." In Rumley and Chaturvedi, op. cit., 154–71.

Dupont, A. 1991. "Australia's Threat Perceptions: A Search for Security." Strategic and Defence Studies Centre, ANU, Canberra Papers on Strategy and Defence, No. 82.

———. 2001. *East Asia Imperilled: Transnational Challenges to Security*. Cambridge: Cambridge Univ. Press.

————. 2003. "Transformation or Stagnation? Rethinking Australia's Defence." *Australian Journal of International Affairs* 57 (1): 55–76.

————. 2005. "Neighbours Back on Track." *Australian Financial Review,* March 31, p. 63.

Eizenstat, S., J. E. Porter, and J. Weinstein. 2005. "Rebuilding Weak States." *Foreign Affairs* 84 (1): 134–46.

Flanagan, S. J., E. L. Frost, and R. L. Kugler. 2001. *Challenges of the Global Century: Report of the Project on Globalization and National Security.* Washington, D.C.: National Defense University.

Freedom House. 2005. *Freedom in the World Country Ratings: 1972* through 2003. http:// www.freedomhouse.org/ (accessed December 2005).

Fukuyama, F. 2004. *State-Building: Governance and World Order in the 21st* Century. Ithaca: Cornell Univ. Press.

Gopal, D., and D. Rumley. 2004. *India and Australia: Issues and Opportunities.* New Delhi: Authors Press.

Gordon, S., et al. 1996. *Security and Security Building in the Indian Ocean Region.* Canberra: Strategic and Defence Studies Centre, ANU.

Heins, V. 2000. "From New Political Organisations to Changing Moral Geographies: Unpacking Global Civil Society." *GeoJournal* 52 (1): 37–44.

Houbert, J. 2005. *The West in the Geopolitics of the Indian Ocean and India.* In Rumley and Chaturvedi, op. cit., 46–64.

House, J. W. 1984. "War, Peace and Conflict Resolution: Towards an Indian Ocean Model." *Transactions.* Institute of British Geographers, New Series, 9: 3–21.

Howard, J. 2005. "Australia in the World." Address to the Lowy Institute, Sydney, March 31.

Howlett, D. 2001. "Nuclear Proliferation." In The Globalization of World Politics, ed. J. Baylis and S. Smith, 415–39. Oxford: Oxford Univ. Press.

Huntington, S. 1996. *The Clash of Civilizations and the Remaking of the New World Order.* New York: Simon and Schuster.

IFIOR (Instructional Forum on Indian Ocean Region). 1995. *Current Economic Characteristics and Indian Ocean Linkage.* Instructional Forum on Indian Ocean Region, Working Paper, no. 2. Perth.

Jackson, A. 2005. "The British Empire in the Indian Ocean." In S. Chaturvedi and D. Rumley *Geopolitical Orientations in the Indian Ocean.* New Delhi, 30–45.

Johnson, C. 2004. *The Sorrows of Empire: Militarism, Secrecy, and the End of the Republic.* New York: Metropolitan Books.

Kerin, J., and N. Bita. 2005. "Diggers Could Go In as Italy Quits Iraq: PM." *The Australian,* March 17.

Kerr, A., ed. 1981. *The Indian Ocean Region.* Perth: Univ. of Western Australia Press.

Klare, M. T. 2002. *Resource Wars: The New Landscape of Global Conflict.* New York: Henry Holt.

McPherson, K. 1993. *The Indian Ocean: A History of People and the Sea.* Delhi: Oxford Univ. Press.

Mills, G. 1998. "South Africa and Security Building." Conference Papers, 127, Australian National University.

Mistry, R. 1997. *A Fine Balance.* Vintage International: New York.

Mohan, C. R. 2003. *Crossing the Rubicon: The Shaping of India's New Foreign Policy.* New Delhi: Viking.

Nyman, P. N., and J. S. Morrison. 2004. "The Terrorist Threat in Africa." *Foreign Affairs* 83 (1): 75–86

Panikkor, K. H. 1945. *India and the Indian Ocean.* London: Allen and Unwin.

Pickford, A. 2005. "Australia-PRC Relationship Hampered by Contradictions and Lack of Contextual View." Future Directions International, *Weekly Global Report* 1 (5): 1–5.

Proliferation Security Initiative (PSI). http:// www.state.gov/t/np/c10390.htm (accessed December 2005).

Rao, P. V., ed. 2003. *India and the Indian Ocean in the Twilight of the Millennium.* New Delhi: South Asian Publishers.

Reporters Without Borders. 2005. http://www.rsf.org (accessed December 2005).

Rotberg, R. I. 2002. "Failed States in a World of Terror." *Foreign Affairs* 81 (2): 91–103.

Routledge, P. 2000. "Our Resistance Will Be as Transnational as Capital." *GeoJournal* 52 (1): 25–33.

Rumley, D. 1999. *The Geopolitics of Australia's Regional Relations.* Dordrecht: Kluwer.

———. 2003. "The Asia-Pacific Region and the New World Order." *Ekistics* 70 (422/423): 321–26.

Rumley, D., and S. Chaturvedi, eds. 2004. *Geopolitical Orientations, Regionalism and Security in the Indian Ocean.* New Delhi: South Asian Publishers.

———, eds. 2005. *Energy Security and the Indian Ocean Region.* New Delhi: South Asian Publishers.

Rumley, D., T. Chiba, A. Takagi, and Y. Fukushima, eds. 1996. *Global Geopolitical Change and the Asia-Pacific: A Regional Perspective.* London, Avebury.

Rumley, D., V. L. Forbes, and C. Griffin, eds. 2006. *Australia's Arc of Instability.* Dordrecht: Springer.

Rumley, D., and D. Gopal, eds. 2007. *Globalisation and Regional Security: India and Australia.* New Delhi: Shipra.

Sachs, J. 2005. "The Development Challenge." *Foreign Affairs* 84 (2): 78–90.

Said, E. 1991. *Orientalism.* Harmondsworth: Penguin.

Schechter, D. 2000. *Sovereign States or Political Communities?* Manchester: Manchester Univ. Press.

Shiva, V. 2002. *Water Wars: Privatization, Pollution, and Profit.* Cambridge, Mass.: South End Press.

Singh, S. 2005. "China's Expanding Energy Deficit: Security Implications for the Indian Ocean Region." in Rumley and Chaturvedi, op. cit., 95–106.

Taylor, J. 2005. "China's Anti-Secession Law 'Empty': Experts." Australian Broadcasting Corporation (ABC) online, March 9.

Tilman, R. O. 1984. "The Enemy Beyond: External Threat Perceptions in the ASEAN Region." ISEAS, Research Notes and Discussions Paper, No. 42. ISEAS: Singapore.

United Nations. 2004. *A More Secure World: Our Shared Responsibility.* Report of the Secretary-General's High-Level Panel on Threats, Challenges and Change. New York: United Nations.

United Nations Economic and Social Commission for Asia and the Pacific (UNESCAP). http://www.unescap.org/ (accessed December 2005).

U.S. Defense Report. 2001. *U.S. Department of Defense Quadrennial Defense Review Report.* 30 September. Washington, D.C.: GPO.

Yee, H. and I. Storey, eds. 2002. *The China Threat: Perceptions, Myths and Reality.* London: RoutledgeCurzon.

3

The Post-Tsunami Indian Ocean Region

EMERGING PERSPECTIVES ON
ENVIRONMENTAL SECURITY

SANJAY CHATURVEDI

On December 26, 2004, an earthquake-induced tsunami disaster struck the coastal regions and communities on the Indian Ocean rim, killing more than 300,000 people and displacing 5 million. The coastal zones accounted for nearly 96 percent of the total human loss and sufferings and about 12 percent of the total economic damage recorded in Indonesia, Sri Lanka, India, Thailand, Myanmar, the Maldives, and Bangladesh. The fatalities were also reported in the Seychelles, and on the other side of the Indian Ocean in Somalia's Puntland region, Tanzania, and Kenya. While the then U.S. secretary of state, Colin Powell, compared the impact with a Hiroshima-sized nuclear explosion, the states that were most vocal and visible in offering assistance to tsunami-hit countries were those very powers (such as the U.S.A. and India) that are likely to act as the main military players in and around the Indian Ocean well into the 21st century (Huxley 2005).

In what ways has the Indian Ocean tsunami compelled and/or motivated both the national governments in the Indian Ocean Region and the concerned international organizations/NGOs to rethink the notion of "environmental security" with special reference to the mitigation and management of disasters? Is the post-tsunami Indian Ocean Region better equipped (both intellectually and institutionally) to anticipate, manage, and adapt to disasters? If yes, in what ways? If not, why not? Why has environmental justice, both as a concept and movement, not received the attention it deserves in the environmental security/policy discourse in the Indian Ocean Region?

"Environmental Security": Diverse Contexts,
Competing Texts, and Contested Readings

A systematic investigation of relatively under-researched links between environmental security and devolution of power to the grass roots should begin by acknowledging, at the very outset, that the realm of "environmental security" is marked by remarkably diverse contexts, competing texts, and contested readings. It is no doubt reassuring that vibrant, alternative political voices known as the environmental movements continue to demand environmental justice in different parts of the globe. Yet, there is a long way to go in this regard (Doyle 2000). One of the key challenges lies in turning the critical gaze of such alternative political voices to an understanding of linkages between "natural" disasters and democracy deficit on the one hand, and between "environmental security" and "environmental justice" on the other.

The 21st century has been described by some as the "Climate Century" (Glantz 2003). The latest report of the Inter-Governmental Panel on Climate Change (IPCC) mentions that the poorest of the poor in the world—and this includes poor people in prosperous societies as well—are going to be the worst hit. Those who are on the socio-economic margins will find it increasingly hard to adapt to climate change. Among the hardest-hit places will be parts of Africa, where arid climates will dry out further, resulting in starvation, and poorer regions of Asia that face threats of rising seas, diminishing freshwater supplies, and more virulent disease. Questions of equity, differential vulnerability within regions, and differing adaptive capacity are significant. The consequences of biophysical impacts can differ for different members of even the same community. Whereas some individuals or groups might perceive an opportunity with change, others might experience a loss, thereby altering group dynamics and making it difficult to arrive at a consensus on how to adapt and how the costs of adaptation should be equitably shared (O'Brien and Leichenko 2003).

Whether environmental security is compatible or in conflict with an exclusive focus on the security of the nation-state is a question on which different views have been expressed (Porter 1995, 218). Some analysts would prefer to approach environmental threats within the traditional, state-centric framework of "national" security. They would argue that the military qualifies to be a positive agent of environmental preservation not only because it is well organized but also because it can bring its organizational abilities to bear on local environmental problems (Butts 1994). Others would maintain that a part of the problem cannot be a part of the solution (Finger 1994, 169). There is a good deal of evidence to suggest that the military, implicated in the ideological geopolitics of the Cold War and shielded by the veil of secrecy and realist discourse of national security, continued to pollute at a large scale—both on land and at sea—for nearly half a century.

Having said that, the concept of security has been so closely linked to nation-states and armed forces that it is not easy to change its dominant essence. Those who question hegemonic discourses favoring "militarized environment" would argue that the notion of "environmental security" should be firmly anchored within the context of "human security." This alone, they believe, would ensure the pursuit of security resulting in the well-being of the people or environmental justice.

What Timothy Doyle (2000, 215) has to say on the environmental movement in Australia is equally valid and compelling elsewhere in the Indian Ocean Region. Doyle's plea to "repopulate the environment" is critically important for a region inhabited by what he describes as a "majority world" (Doyle 2005). Both a narrow definition of the term "environment" and eco-centric arguments privileging nature over communities are fundamentally flawed in the sense that they perceive the "environment" as "somewhere out there."

In view of the fact that since the early 1970s many environmental questions have been understood to be matters of largely "global" concern (such as ozone depletion, biodiversity loss, and global climate change), it has been argued by the proponents of a critical geopolitics that new forms of power/knowledge are now part of the 21st-century geopolitics. This is neither to question the validity of the climate change thesis nor to suggest that ecological degradation is simply a figment of imagination or does not in some sense "exist" in the real world. The key intention is to draw attention to the politics behind the productions of geographical knowledge of environmental crisis: how, for example, issues related to environmental degradation are framed and flagged, who is designated as the problem, and who is designated as the provider of the potential solution to the problem. How are the issues related to mitigation and management of natural disasters argued about and who decides what should be done, where, and by whom. What a critical geopolitical perspective on environment also does is show the power of the concept of "environment" and how it is deployed to moralize, to motive, and to include/exclude.

Yet another critical perspective on "environmental" security underlines the need for pluralization of environmental security into environmental securities. A critical understanding of how nature is constructed in different ways should enable us to appreciate better the diversity of "natures" and "environments" that we carry around in our heads, in our policies, and in our institutional structures (Eden 2001). As Doyle and McEachern (1998, 2) forcefully argue, "what counts as an environmental problem depends on varying ways of judging the ecological consequences of any particular act or development. It is important to understand that the term 'environment' is often constructed differently in different cultures and is used in different ways by different people. Not only is the word defined differently, but alternative clusters of issues are identified and a whole range of different kinds of politics can be generated on this basis." There are also local contingencies in the conditions under which environmental justice arguments are and can be evoked within strategies of resistance and activism. Having noted that, attempts at pluralization should be aware that too much emphasis on difference could isolate different understandings of environmental security, suppress recognition of what they have in common, and hinder coalitional activism.

Yet another insightful perspective on environmental security relates to what is now called the political ecology of disaster; a field that draws on the methodological fusion of Marxian political economy, human ecology, and development studies (Hewitt 1983; Maskrey 1989; Walker 1989; Hewitt 1997; Pelling 2003; Wisner, Blaikie, Cannon, and Davis 2004) and claims to be a catalyst for socio-environmental activism. This school of thought reminds us that invariably the root causes of people's vulnerability to hazards continue to be ignored. Whereas there is no dearth of rhetoric, or even effort to build institutions, a vast majority of countries in the world today lack effective implementation (Wisner and Walker 2005, 89). One of the key problems lies with the nature, scope, and impact of the global economy, especially the subsidy policies of the rich, industrialized countries that have undermined the livelihoods of small-scale farmers in the interior of affected countries. Violent conflicts, in Sri Lanka and Indonesia for example, have also pushed people from the hinterlands to the coastal regions.

While it is true that extreme natural events, such as the earthquake that generated the tsunami in December 2004, are "natural," the magnitude of the destruction and its impact on various social groups is determined by a number of factors. For example, why weren't people warned? Why were so many people unaware of tsunami risk? And now, after the event, why do national and local governments, by and large, continue to exclude local people from recovery planning? Why indeed are there reports of people returning to find that property speculators have occupied and claimed their house plots?

"Environmental Security" as "Environmental Justice"?

Questions such as the ones posed above are likely to remain partially answered unless the notion of environmental security itself is revisited in the light of "environmental justice," a concept (and movement) that has been rather slow in achieving the recognition it deserves in the context of environmental policy research and practice. Originating and framed in the United States, the concept of environmental justice is becoming broader in scope and more encompassing in the sites, forms, and processes of injustice with which it is concerned.

Environmental justice, at its core, is about incorporating environmental issues into the broader intellectual and institutional framework of human rights, democratic governance, and accountability (Wenz 1988; Capek 1993; Bryant 1995; Cutter 1995; Goldman 1996; Harvey 1996; Heiman 1996; Dobson 1998; Schlosberg 1999; Bowen and Haynes 2000). The normative thrust of the discourse of environmental justice relates to the issue of equity, with special reference to vulnerable groups and communities. In the context of the Indian Ocean Region, for example, such groups on the margins of various mainstreams would include indigenous peoples (the so-called tribal communities in India), the urban poor, migrant and landless communities, small and marginal farmers, and traditional fishing communities.

One important overarching question regarding environmental security is the issue of environmental justice for whom (Clayton 2000): how is the moral community defined in terms of inclusions and exclusions? Is it inevitable that individual concerns would automatically get overridden by the needs of a larger group or society, or are there certain ways and means of ensuring justice at both levels? Against the backdrop of globalization and regionalization of international relations, the environmental justice agenda is being broadened to include questions of distribution both between and across nation-states and extremely diverse political, cultural, and economic environments. Justice "to whom" is being cast in more inclusive terms to include, for example, differences of gender, age, and the rights of future generations (Dobson 1998).

What is "environmental" about justice? In linking environmental and social justice issues, the environmental justice approach seeks to question the abuse of power that results in poor people having to suffer the effects of environmental damage caused by the greed of others. The term necessarily encompasses the widest possible definition of what is considered "environmental" and insists on placing people, rather than flora and fauna, at the center of a complex web of social, economic, political, and environmental relationships. Most important, it concerns itself primarily with the environmental injustices of hierarchical and patriarchic socio- economic relationships, and the ways and means of questioning these wrongs and / or avoiding them in the future.

When the so-called natural disasters (such as the Indian Ocean tsunami) occur, they invariably divert the attention of both the governments and non-governmental organizations from manmade environmental disasters to which the poor and the marginalized have been long subjected on a daily basis. The example of the Sunderbans (the largest mangrove delta in the world, recognized as a World Heritage Site in 1989), forming the southernmost portion of the Gangetic delta, is most revealing in this regard. The Indian Sunderbans delta is home to about 4 million people, and its population is growing at an alarming rate of 27 percent every decade despite disasters that strike the delta and near nonexistent infrastructure. An increasing number of poor and disadvantaged Indians as well as thousands of illegal migrants from Bangladesh find it most convenient to make fragile river islands their homeland. The region is one of the most "backward" in the state of West Bengal, with literacy rates well below 35 percent and most communities lacking access to electricity, safe drinking water, and adequate infrastructure.

With a vast majority living below poverty line, about 38 percent of the Sunderban population comprises Scheduled Castes and Scheduled Tribes. It is important to note that mindless poaching and extraction of natural resources since the 1770s, combined with perennial vulnerability to natural disasters, has turned this ecological-heritage site into a dehumanized, disaster-prone zone. The landscape, once rich in biological diversity, has degenerated drastically over the last century, and the plantation and forest cover that provided natural resistance to tidal floods and other forms of calamities does not provide protection to communities anymore. Calamities, particularly tidal floods, happen on average 2.3 times a year.

The Sunderbans is an area traditionally well-known for its biodiversity but gradually succumbing to the mono-culture of shrimp cultivation. Shrimp cultivation is not only using up agriculture land but also khas, or government-owned lands, which by law are to be distributed by the local government to the landless. Another important deprivation is the loss of grazing land. Lack of fodder prevents poor people from raising goats and poultry as income generation activities. Those who are worst hit, needless to say, are the region's poor women (Guhathakurta and Begum 2005). Most women are either divorced or abandoned by their husbands. The husbands are forced to leave homes and families because of the lack of means of livelihood in the area. Shrimp cultivators are reluctant to use local labor for their farms; instead they bring them from other regions for this kind of seasonal work.

The case of the Sunderbans underlines the need to broaden the notions of the environment to include access to environmental goods and resources such as water, energy, and green space and the threat of "natural" as well as technologically produced risks, interfacing here with "vulnerability." Despite the growing concern about disasters, the impact on the ecology, and the effect on the communities, particularly their livelihoods, the only means adopted by the government to mitigate the effect of the disasters was embankment construction and repair. Embankments constructed in the past get breached every year and get re-laid. Few alternatives have been attempted in this area. As far as people's own initiatives to combat the effects of ongoing disasters in the delta are concerned, since these disasters are not as dramatic and devastating or life-threatening as earthquakes and tsunamis, neither communities nor the non- governmental organizations have exerted to take corrective or preparedness measures.

While opening up new pathways for activism, academic analysis, and institutional intervention, a dynamic and expansive environmental justice agenda, in conjunction with a critically conceived notion of environmental security, raises many challenges, especially in the post-tsunami Indian Ocean Region.

Governance, Environmental Justice, and "Natural" Disasters in India: Beyond the Institutional Landscape

The tsunami disaster affected almost 3 million people in India and left 12,000 dead. A total of 647,599 people had to move to safer places. The disaster affected women and children in particular: 75 percent of the fatalities were women and children. The state of Tamil Nadu (where 376 villages were affected) and the Union Territory of Andaman Nicobar islands suffered the highest human loss. The estimated total financial losses in India, according to official Indian sources, exceeded US$1.2 billion.

As of November 2006, 27,845 houses (28 percent) of the total 98,478 required across India have been completed, basically through the efforts of the state and NGOs, according to the report "Tsunami: India—Two Years After" (UN, the World Bank, and the Asian Development Bank 2006). The remaining homes are in various stages of construction, and a fairly large number of fishing communities are still in temporary shelters. In the state of Tamil Nadu, where about two-thirds of the destruction occurred, more than a third of the homes slated for construction have been completed and 20,128 have been handed over.

India, while refusing to accept any aid from outside powers and agencies for post-tsunami reconstruction and rehabilitation, was rather prompt in sending financial and material help to neighboring Sri Lanka. A key question in the development debate in contemporary India revolves around the relationship between growth, equality, and poverty. While it is true that India is too diverse to be represented in a meaningful way with singular development statistics (Grant and Nijman 2004), India's growth process during the last two decades seems to have polarized the economy, resulting in growth with inequality (Nagaraj 2000). The differential effects of liberalization and globalization are not confined to people according to socioeconomic characteristics, such as class, or to location in hierarchical caste-based social order. The differential effects also vary across space. Be it development or disaster (some would describe disaster as the unfinished task of development), it is important not only who you are but where you are. The majority of those affected on the coast by the tsunami were fisher-folk. And among them, the worst affected were the vulnerable groups as well as those living below the poverty line. According to certain estimates, as many as one-third of the people who bore the major brunt of tsunami are from the underprivileged and socially marginalized groups, such as the Dalits (the lowest caste in India) and tribal people (Nagaraj 2000).

Institutional Landscape: National Policy for Natural Disaster Reduction

As far as the institutional landscape dealing with disaster mitigation/management in India is concerned, it looks quite comprehensive and impressive on paper. For example, the high- powered committee for the preparation of disaster management plans, set up by the Indian government, comprises representatives from several ministries, including: Agriculture, Defense, Surface Transport, Power, Health and Family Welfare, Water Resources, Animal Husbandry, Urban Development and Poverty Alleviation, Planning and Program Implementation, Home Affairs, Rural Development, Information Technology, Information and Broadcasting, Communication, Heavy Industries, Social Justice and Empowerment, Civil Aviation, Non- Conventional Energy Resources, Petroleum and Natural Gas, Finance, External Affairs, Commerce and Industry, Science and Technology, Labor, and Consumer Affairs, Food and Public Distribution. It is to state the obvious perhaps that ensuring inter-ministerial, inter- departmental coordination itself is going to be a major challenge.

India's National Policy for Natural Disaster Reduction is aimed at ensuring reduction in (a) loss of lives, (b) property damage, and (c) economic disruption. The more specific goals have been identified as follows: creating public awareness about safety from disasters; amending/enacting legislation for safety from hazards; planning development areas with safety from hazards; protection of habitations from adverse hazard impacts; constructing new buildings safe from hazards; and retrofitting existing buildings for improving hazard resistance. Emphasis has also been placed on the adoption of certain legal measures. These include amendments to town/country planning acts and master plan area development rules; land use zoning in hazard-prone areas and establishing techno-legal regimes; incorporation of safety requirements in building bylaws of local bodies/panchayats—applicable to new buildings and extensions of old buildings; empowering local bodies to exercise control; legislation to upgrade hazard resistance of critical buildings for use and safety of large numbers of people—schools, hospitals, cinemas, congregation halls, water tanks, towers, telephone exchanges, fire stations, headquarters of police and administration.

The Disaster Management Bill of 2005 (as passed by the Houses of Parliament) has been described by many as a landmark for disaster risk mitigation in India. It defined disaster and disaster management in the following terms:

(a) "disaster" means a catastrophe, mishap, calamity or grave occurrence in any area, arising from natural or man made causes, or by accident or negligence which results in substantial loss of life or human suffering or damage to, and destruction of, property, or damage to, or degradation of, environment, and is of such a nature or magnitude as to be beyond the coping capacity of the community of the affected area;

(b) "disaster management" means a continuous and integrated process of planning, organizing, coordinating and implementing measures which are necessary or expedient for:

    (i) prevention of danger or threat of any disaster;

    (ii) mitigation or reduction of risk of any disaster or its severity or consequences;

    (iii) capacity-building;

    (iv) preparedness to deal with any disaster;

    (v) prompt response to any threatening disaster situation or disaster;

    (vi) assessing the severity or magnitude of effects of any disaster;

    (vii) evacuation, rescue and relief;

    (viii) rehabilitation and reconstruction.

The National Disaster Management Authority, with the prime minister as the chairperson, is given the responsibility for laying down the policies, plans, and guidelines for disaster management and for ensuring timely and effective response to disasters. However, the implementation has been entrusted to the "State Executive Committee," which is to be set up by the "State Disaster Management Authority." Each state government will then establish a District Disaster Management Authority for every district in the state. And subject to the directions of the District Authority, a local authority shall: (a) ensure that its officers and employees are trained for disaster management; (b) ensure that resources relating to disaster management are so maintained as to be readily available for use in the event of any threatening disaster situation or disaster; (c) ensure all construction projects under it, or within its jurisdiction, conform to the standards and specifications laid down for prevention of disasters and mitigation by the National Authority, State Authority and the District Authority; (d) carry out relief, rehabilitation and reconstruction activities in the affected area in accordance with the State Plan and the District Plan. The local authority may take such other measures as may be necessary for the disaster management.

The overall civil society response to the bill, which aims at promoting safer economic growth, especially in tribal and less developed areas, has been positive, but a number of critical concerns have been raised. First and foremost, it is not clear how state level disaster authorities will coordinate their efforts with the National Disaster Management Authority (NDMA), and what mechanisms will be proposed to increase flow of lateral relief and support between these authorities. The bill does not define victims or identify vulnerable populations. Although the bill is comprehensive, there is a possible pitfall in that it may restrict itself to relief and rehabilitation packages and may not execute effective operations for risk reduction, mitigation, and more importantly adaptation.

According to the bill, "local authority" includes Panchayati Raj Institutions (PRIs), municipalities, a district board, Cantonment Board [institutions that are entrusted with the responsibility to cater to the municipal needs and provide civic administration to the people residing in the cantonment], town planning authority, or Zila Parishad, or any other body or authority, by whatever name called, for the time being invested by law, for rendering essential services, or, with the control and management of civic services, within a specified local area. In contrast to the official construction of "local authority" at the grassroot levels, the civil society argument would be that Panchayati Raj Institutions (PRIs) at the village, block, and district level represent, but do not exhaust, the "community," which also includes user groups, self-help groups, traditional and self-initiated groups, and NGOs.

The community acts as a unit of management by virtue of the fact that water, forests, and uncultivated lands are held as common property resources. Ideally, community control over local government functionaries is likely to result in greater accountability. The problem of implementation in drinking water, watershed, irrigation, and forestry programs could also be answered by strengthening the participation of the local people and mounting the political pressure to ensure that the allocated resources are being properly utilized by a fixed deadline. It is equally important to ensure that unambiguous and impartial criteria are followed for selecting areas and villages for the purposes of relief and rehabilitation. The critics further point out that the bill must also redefine "reconstruction," since reconstruction is concerned with building much stronger lives and livelihoods and far more resilient adaptive strategies, and not merely replacing lost property.

In view of the fact that PRIs have been given a central and critical role by the Disaster Management Bill, the limitations of the legislation facing the PRIs need to be examined, even though briefly. One of the major inadequacies of the 73rd Amendment Act to the Indian Constitution is that the powers and functions of gram sabhas are not defined. Actual devolution of powers to panchayats are left to the discretion of the state governments. No autonomy has been granted to PRIs to function as institutions of self-government. Political reluctance to give up control over implementation and funds is another problem, and finances of PRIs leave much to be desired. The pace and progress of post-tsunami rehabilitation and reconstruction programs have shown that effective panchayats/user groups would require, in the first instance, an effective district and block level administration. This in turn might ensure greater coordination and better governance.

It has also been pointed out by some analysts that the bill needs to focus more on gender issues and on the special needs of women. The gender dimension of the devolution debate and its close link with disaster management is also extremely important. The different ways in which politics is understood locally and nationally also needs to be taken into account. The kinds of decisions that the gram panchayats make are often simultaneously economic, social, and political. They have to do with questions of land ownership, municipal facilities, marital disputes, and the distribution of power. This convergence of issues between public and private spheres encourages the panchayats to further expand the definition of the political to include issues that are normally considered private rather than public, social rather than political, and collective rather than individual.

Another challenge is to consider how some of the models of women's political engagement that have emerged at the local level can be reproduced nationally. This is one of the central questions that confront both states and women's movements in India. The ideal way would be not only the large-scale devolution of power to the local level, but also empowerment of women so that their voices and concerns find space due to them in decision making. However, what makes this so desirable is also what makes it so unlikely, namely the highly centralized character of the Indian state.

Disaster Management in Ethnic Conflict Zones: Lessons from Sri Lanka

When the tsunami disaster struck Sri Lanka on December 26, 2004, against the unsettling backdrop of a prolonged ethno-political crisis, many expressed the hope that the colossal tragedy might eventually prove to be a catalyst for reconciliation, confidence building, and geopolitical rehabilitation on a partitioned island. One of the key questions that emerged at the very outset, and in all its complexity, revolved around the issue of "representation." Who has the right to represent the victims of the tsunami on the island in both the national and international arena? Given the context, where an ethnic separatist insurgency has questioned the sovereignty of the state, the government cannot forego the claim to be the sole representative of the nation-state of Sri Lanka.

In the official Sri Lankan discourse, the state has to be the undisputed primary agency of the post-tsunami recovery process, responsible for the entire country; including the areas held by the Liberation Tigers of Tamil Elelam (LTTE). On the other hand, the LTTE, Sri Lanka's main Tamil nationalist movement (engaged in a prolonged armed struggle against the state with the objective of establishing a Tamil ethnic state in Sri Lanka's northern and eastern provinces) considers itself the "sole representative" of the Tamil nation. It also considers itself the sole political-military-administrative embodiment of the emerging regional Tamil ethnic state.

A number of civil society groups in Sri Lanka have forcefully argued that since the tsunami disaster struck Sri Lanka in a crucial phase of Sri Lanka's ethnic conflict and peace process, in which the cease-fire agreement was under severe strain and peace negotiations were in a continuing stalemate, it should not be seen as a mere "natural disaster." It is further emphasized that while planning various facets and phases of responses to tsunami, dimensions of both the ethnic conflict and peace process should be brought into consideration. All communities—Sinhalese, Tamil, and Muslim—should be approached and treated on the principles of equity and fairness.

According to Jayadeva Uyangoda (2005), political-administrative reforms are necessary to ensure popular participation as well as the widest possible political involvement in the reconstruction process. Otherwise, the present approach of "reconstruction from above" will generate popular resistance. The communities devastated by the tsunami have begun to protest against official and bureaucratic ineffectiveness in the provision of relief. The post-tsunami reconstruction in Sri Lanka, they argue, is not about constructing buildings, roads, and economic infrastructure. It involves rebuilding communities, community lives, and livelihoods and enabling nearly a million people who suddenly found themselves in absolute poverty and destitution. Neither the government nor the LTTE should approach this process, as they appear to do now, from a state-centric perspective. Unless the affected communities are active participants in the exercise of rebuilding their lives, livelihoods, and communities, the rebuilding process will be thoroughly undemocratic.

To ensure popular participation as well as participation of all actors in the political process in post-tsunami rebuilding, involvement and strengthening of the institutions of local governance is a better and workable option. Rebuilding local autonomy in the south as well in the north and east will also link the peace process with the tsunami recovery process. Regional autonomy with local autonomy, or "deep federalization" of the state in which local autonomy is guaranteed within a framework of regional autonomy, will provide better space for democratizing Sri Lanka's twin transition, from civil war to peace and from tsunami disaster to post-tsunami rebuilding (Uyangoda 2005, 351).

The case study of Sri Lanka is quite illustrative of what Joseph A. Camilleri and Jim Falk (1992, 185) have described as "the partitioning of environmental acts." The tension in post-tsunami Sri Lanka, and elsewhere in the Indian Ocean Region, is between a sovereignty discourse that is increasingly questioned by ecological degradation, natural disasters, and climate change, and the residual power of the discourse to constrain actions that appear to be inconsistent with the claim to sovereignty but are increasingly considered necessary to solve the problems. This tension is most palpable in relation to the manner in which the sovereignty discourse creates not only a spatial arrangement of political power, but also a corresponding partitioning of the biosphere.

What appears to be common to various disasters mentioned in this chapter so far, despite variation in terms of location, socio-political context, and geopolitical fallouts, is that hundreds of thousands of lives and livelihoods are destroyed and/or displaced. For those displaced, the proverbial billion-dollar question is this: What about the right to return home? Equally compelling are the housing, land, and property (HLP) rights, in the absence of which plans related to reconstruction, rebuilding, and regeneration cannot be successful.

It important to note that the tragic consequences of the Indian Ocean tsunami have indeed provided a pretext for evictions, land grabs, unjustifiable land-acquisition plans, and other measures designed to prevent homeless residents from returning to their homeland. Thailand, India, and other affected countries have restricted the right to return, but Sri Lanka stands out as the tsunami-affected country that has resorted to the most dramatic reshaping of its residential landscape through the reconstruction process.

The official understandings of "environmental security," however well-meaning they might be, often fail to understand the emotional-spiritual bond between communities and (home)land. Once humans are placed outside the perceived "environment," as referred to earlier in this chapter, a rather skewed understanding of environmental security ensues. The Sri Lankan government has prohibited new construction within 100 meters of the mean sea level (in some areas 200 meters), in order to pre-empt or minimize the disastrous impact of any future tsunami. It is important to note that the overwhelming majority of the more than 500,000 people displaced due to the tsunami lived within 100 meters of the coast. The government has promised to re- house those affected by the construction regulations and has undertaken to build a house for every affected house owner. While privately owned land within the 100-meter zone will remain the property of the original owners (and the government has stated that it will not claim ownership to such property), the 100-meter rule will permanently prevent hundreds of thousands of people in fishing communities and others who lived and worked on or near the shore from returning to their former lands. For those affected, the ground beneath their feet has collapsed beyond reclaim and recovery.

The official plea to protect the coastline and former residents from any future tsunami may appear entirely reasonable and consistent with human rights standards. However, these maneuvers to change the demographics of the Sri Lankan coastline can be criticized on several fronts. First, the people themselves do not want to move and generally long to return to their former lands. Second, there has effectively been no consultation on the 100-meter rule in Sri Lanka. And third, the exceptions to the 100-meter rule now being allowed—for hotels, wealthy property developers, and other privileged groups—raise serious concerns of favoritism.

It has been forcefully as well as insightfully argued by Scott Leckie, executive director of the Centre on Housing Rights and Evictions (COHRE, http://www.cohre.org/), who worked on housing, land, and property rights issues in Sri Lanka and the Maldives in the immediate aftermath of the tsunami, that the tsunami has underlined the need for a rights-based approach to post-disaster reconstruction. If housing, land, and property rights are put at the heart of a post- disaster plan—rather than dismissed outrightly as too complicated or expensive—the chances are that it will succeed. If these rights are brushed aside or systematically violated, not only will rights be abused but reconstruction efforts too will fail.

Lessons from the Indian Ocean Tsunami: Identified or Learned?

Let us take a closer look at the nature and extent of damage caused by the tsunami to coastal regions and coastal communities. According to the Food and Agriculture Organization (FAO), the damage to fisheries from the December 26 tsunami is worse than originally expected, with fishing families deprived of their former incomes as well as alternative jobs in local industries such as tourism. In Sri Lanka and parts of Thailand, even those fishermen who had not lost their equipment and were able to go back to work had problems selling their catch due to popular fears that the fish might have fed on dead bodies. In Sri Lanka, more than 7,500 fishers were killed by the tsunami, approximately 5,600 went missing, over 5,000 fishing families have been displaced, and nearly 80 percent of fishing boats destroyed. Ten of Sri Lanka's 12 main fishing harbors were devastated by the tidal waves. In Indonesia the tsunami killed two-thirds of the fishers in Banda Aceh, while in the surrounding area of northern Sumatra about 1,000 fish cage farms were destroyed.

In Indonesia, the disaster killed more than 115,000 people. Fishermen and their families were hit particularly hard. According to the official statistics, nearly 14,000 fishermen were among the dead, but some analysts estimate that the actual figure is larger. In the hardest-hit province of Aceh, a US$422 million industry was decimated in a matter of minutes, as the powerful walls of water flattened fishing villages, fish markets, and wharves, and smashed wooden boats into bits of wreckage (Nakashima 2005).

In its reports on the environmental impact of the tsunami in Sri Lanka and the Maldives (available at www.unep.org/tsunami), UNEP has noted that coastal areas where coral reefs, mangrove forests, and natural vegetation had been removed suffered the greatest damage. Although a large number of tourists were also killed by the tsunami waves, fishing communities were the worst hit. Looking ahead, the challenges that have been identified in general include not only the restoration of fishers' livelihoods and raising the income of coastal communities above pre-tsunami levels, but also capacity building to improve the skills of boat builders, enforcement of standards to reduce potential risks to fishermen, and revival of the tsunami-hit aquaculture industry. Both economic recovery and the generation of employment are among the top priorities. Many states and organizations are supporting reconstruction and rehabilitation efforts in the affected areas. While such efforts are much needed, they may not prove to be enough in both the medium and long term.

The post-tsunami forestry program of the FAO is based on the assumption that there is a need to help the victims of disasters in such a way that they can help themselves better (FAO 2005). It has been rightly emphasized that the sustainability of "reforested" areas critically depends on how communities sustain themselves until the trees themselves mature and provide livelihoods. In other words, it is necessary to invest in communities and their capacity building, particularly in the initial stages, in order to ensure that the reforestation efforts are maintained and further expanded.

In the aftermath of the tsunami, the transition from "environment as a symbol" to "environment as a movement" is critically important. It has been pointed out by some experts (see Standing 2005) that most assistance proposals made so far, in the wake of tsunami, have been predicated on depicting the disaster in terms of a job crisis. However, what is needed is a set of proposals that purport to recreate communities, and restore community networks and livelihoods. In other words, because the revival effort is mainly about recreating social entitlements, a right-based approach to social protection is absolutely necessary, especially for the poor and the marginalized.

It has also been argued that "the narrow focus of the media and most of civil society on the immediate human crisis has precluded other important discussions about the implications of this disaster that need to inform our thinking and actions" (Lorch 2005, 209). In the first instance, inadequate scientific information was provided to the world-wide audience who were keen to know more about the disaster. It also appears that the media failed to use the opportunity to initiate a wider awareness campaign on issues such as seasonality, climate change, and associated vulnerabilities in our lives. It also failed to capture and canvass the expert opinions on risk identification—its assessment and interpretation, innovation, and education strategies to create a culture of safety and resilience, reducing the underlying vulnerabilities and providing the preparedness capacity for effective response and adaptation. Lorch raises certain questions in regard to current tsunami reconstruction efforts and the appropriateness of the responses as well as their effectiveness over the short, medium, and long term that are worth citing: Are the right forms of temporary shelter being sent to the right places? How is increased vulnerability to disease being addressed? Are the temporary settlements being designed in harmony with the culture and social structures and built with the skills and capabilities of the affected? Is the reconstruction response being framed in a technological framework that is too narrow, when a wider engagement with local institutional and social aspects is required? How will improved resilience and sustainability be addressed?

Questions such as these highlight the importance of addressing various disasters and risks by combining bottom-up and top-down approaches to governance. It is to state the obvious perhaps that planning for mitigation of risks from natural (and other) hazards cannot be the sole preserve of governments and their various agencies. Individual organizations, such as insurance companies, too, have begun to realize their vulnerability and are responding by developing their own risk-management models to protect their services and people. Yet the notion of "good governance" continues to be addressed mostly in terms of vague generalities. It is now time to bring local initiatives and innovations to the fore and remove obstacles so that both civil society and local government can contribute toward disaster risk management. It is important to ensure, as the post-tsunami experiences from both India and Sri Lanka suggest, that the initiatives from below are empowered in such a way that they can effectively negotiate with provincial and national bureaucracies. The task is not easy since in many cases the dominant political elites have been quick to appropriate the language of "participation" and "people-centered planning," while proving to be reluctant in practice to devolve power to the grass roots.

Concluding the Inconclusive: Toward Environmental Justice Movements?

The vulnerability of a vast majority of states in the Indian Ocean Region to natural-social disasters is well recognized and recorded. It is equally well established, for example, that South Asia, both on land and at sea, is one of the most disaster-prone regions on the globe. As far as the Tsunami and associated "lessons" are concerned, the critical question is whether we have at best "identified" a few lessons or whether we have actually learned from them.

One of the key points made in this chapter is that both disaster management and environmental security should be seen as a continuum rather than as an outcome. The boundary between the "natural" and the "manmade" disasters, in reality, is much narrower than is often maintained by some analysts as well as policy makers. Both India and Sri Lanka are good examples to underscore the point that "environmental security" is not an end-category with settled understandings of either "environment" or "security." It is a highly contested site where the "official" and the "popular," the "formal" and the "informal," the "public" and the "private," the "national" and the "international" readings of disaster interact, compete, and sometimes even collide in pursuit of seeking grater legitimacy, authority, and effectiveness. Only a bottom-up and all-inclusive environmental movement can capture these diverse perspectives and bring them in the embrace of a dialogic mode. It is critically important that co-management and community-based approaches take into account social equity and ecological sustainability.

In the light of lessons identified (and hopefully learned as well) by both analysts and policy makers from the tsunami, the notions such as "environmental security" in general and "natural disasters" in particular should be approached and analyzed in their broader context of democratic "governance" and "representation," linking them to grassroot-level development initiatives and devolution of power. The tsunami has no doubt raised the level of awareness among the national governments, civil society, and the public at large. It has effectively questioned the existing disaster countermeasures in different parts of the Indian Ocean Region and underlined the need for better regional cooperation in terms of disaster reduction. Above all, the disaster has underscored the need to deepen the discourse as well as practices of democracy involving human rights (including the right to life with dignity) and humane governance.

The chapter has also shown that the impacts as well as implications of the Indian Ocean tsunami have been highly uneven in terms of both inter and intra state contexts in India, Indonesia, and Sri Lanka. It is equally obvious that certain actors and agencies have been quite forthcoming in making politics out of the tsunami disaster. Despite massive human and material costs, the tsunami disaster has not brought about any meaningful shift in the dominant realist paradigm of security even in the most affected states. As Huxley puts it:

> Separatist campaigns aimed at establishing independent states in Aceh and Tamil Elam will almost certainly continue, and will be resisted as staunchly as ever by Jakarta and Colombo respectively, though there is perhaps now a marginally greater chance of Tamil separatists in Sri Lanka coming to the negotiating table. The main extra-regional powers involved in the region's security may have temporarily gained slightly greater influence as a result of their relief efforts . . . . The tsunami's huge toll—which massively outweighed the likely casualties from any traditional security threat short of the use of nuclear weapons—should encourage South and South-eastern Asian states and their regional groupings to pay greater attention to human security issues. But

deep-rooted ways of looking at security and embedded inter-state rivalry suggests that security priorities and policies of regional states are no more likely to undergo sea-change than those of the industrial states which continue to dominate the region militarily, however desirable this might seem. (Huxley 2005, 130–31).

It is equally important to acknowledge that in "populated" environments of the majority world of the Indian Ocean Region, the notions of environmental "security" and environmental "justice" should go together. As shown by this chapter, there is a great deal of hierarchy in disasters, destruction, and even death. The category called "people" needs to be pluralized and the patterns of hierarchy and patriarchy exposed and questioned. It is vital to remember that different communities and groups are impacted differently when a sudden "natural" disaster strikes and contributes to further marginalization of those already on the periphery of a particular social order. It is unfortunate but true that centralization, in most of the Indian Ocean Region, is still a potent political agent, whereas decentralization is to be found more in rhetoric and less in practice (Siry 2006).

REFERENCES

Bowen, W. M., and K. E. Haynes. 2000. "The Debate over Environmental Justice." *Social Science Quarterly* 81 (3): 892–94.

Borgese, E. M. 1998. *The Oceanic Circle: Governing the Seas as a Global Resource.* Tokyo: United Nations Univ. Press.

Butts, K. H. 1994. "Why the Military Is Good for the Environment." In *Green Security or Militarized Environment,* ed. J. Kakonen, 83–111. Aldershot: Dartmouth.

Bryant, B. 1995. *Environmental Justice: Issues, Policies, and Solutions.* Washington, D.C.: Island Press.

Camilleri, J. A., and J. Falk. 1992. *The End of Sovereignty? The Politics of a Shrinking and Fragmenting World.* Aldershot: Edward Elgar.

Capek, S. 1993. "The 'Environmental Justice' Frame: A Conceptual Discussion and an Application." *Social Problems* 40 (1): 5–24.

Clayton, S. 2000. "Models of Justice in Environmental Debate." *Journal of Social Issues* 56 (3): 459–74.

Cutter, S. 1995. "Race, Class and Environmental Justice." *Progress in Human Geography* 19 (1): 111–22.

Dobson, A. 1998. *Justice and the Environment: Conceptions of Environmental Sustainability and Theories of Distributive Justice.* New York: Oxford Univ. Press.

Doyle, T. 2000. *Green Power: The Environmental Movement in Australia.* Sydney: Univ. of New South Wales Press.

———. 2005. *Environmental Movements in Majority and Minority Worlds: A Global Perspective.* New Brunswick: Rutgers Univ. Press.

Doyle, T., and D. McEachern. 1998. *Environment and Politics.* London and New York: Routledge.

Eden, S. 2001 "Environmental Issues: Nature versus the Environment." *Progress in Human Geography* 125 (1): 79–85.

FAO. 2005. *Rebuilding Livelihoods: Tsunami Response, Indonesia.* Rome: FAO.

Finger, M. 1994. "Global Environmental Degradation and the Military." In *Green Security or Militarized Environment,* ed. J. Kakonen, 169–91. Aldershot: Dartmouth.

Glantz, M. 2003. *Climate Affairs: A Primer.* Washington, D.C.: Island Press.

Grant, R., and J. Nijman. 2004. "Globalization and the Hyperdifferentiation of Space in the Less Developed World." In *Globalization and Its Outcomes,* ed. J. O' Loughlin, L. Staetheli, and E. Greenberg, 45–66. New York: Guildford Press.

Goldman, B. 1996. "What Is the Future of Environmental Justice?" *Antipode* 28 (2): 122–41.

Guhathakurta, M., and S. Begum. 2005. "Bangladesh: Displaced and Dispossessed." In *Internal Displacement in South Asia,* ed. P. Banerjee, S. Basu Ray Chaudhury, and S. K. Das, 175–212. New Delhi: Sage.

Harvey, D. 1996. *Justice, Nature and the Geography of Difference.* Oxford: Blackwell Publishers.

Heiman, M. 1996. "Race, Waste and Class: New Perspectives on Environmental Justice" (editorial introduction to special issue on environmental justice). *Antipode* 28 (2): 111–21.

Hewitt, K., ed. 1983. *Interpretations of Calamity.* Boston: Allen and Unwin.

———. 1997. *Regions of Risk.* Harlow, Essex, U.K.: Longman.

Huxley, T. 2005. "The Tsunami and Security: Asia 9/11?" *Survival* 47 (1): 123–32.

Lorch, R. 2005. "What Lessons Must Be Learnt from the Tsunami?" *Building Research and Information* 33 (3): 209–11.

Maskrey, A. 1989. *Disaster Mitigation: A Community Based Approach.* Development guidelines, no. 3. Oxford: Oxfam.

Nagaraj, R. 2000. "Indian Economy since 1980s: Virtuous Growth or Polarization"? *Economic and Political Weekly* (August 5): 2831–2838.

Nakashima, E. 2005. "For Now, Indonesian Fishermen Are Forced to Abandon the Sea: Officials Must Move Quickly to Revive Industry, Advocates Say." http://www.washingtonpost.com/wp-dyn/articles/A14326-2005Jan16.html.

O'Brien, K. L., and R. M. Leichenko. 2003. "Winners and Losers in the Context of Global Change." *Annals of the American Association of Geographers* 93 (1): 89–103

Pelling, M., ed. 2003. *Natural Hazard and Development in a Globalizing World.* London: Routledge.

Porter, G. 1995. "Environmental Security as a National Security Issue." *Current History* 94 (592): 218–22.

Schlosberg, D. 1999. *Environmental Justice and the New Pluralism: The Challenge of Difference for Environmentalism.* Oxford: Oxford Univ. Press.

Siry, H. Y. 2006. "Decentralized Costal Zone Management in Malaysia and Indonesia: A Comparative Perspective." *Coastal Management* 34:267–85.

Standing, G. 2005. "Tsunami Recovery Grants: Looking at Long-Term Sustainable Plans." *Economic and Political Weekly* 40 (6): 510–14.

Uyangoda, J. 2005. "Ethnic Conflict, the State and the Tsunami Disaster in Sri Lanka." *Inter-Asian Cultural Studies* 6 (3): 341–52.

UN, the World Bank, and the Asian Development Bank. 2006. "Tsunami—India: Two Years After, A Joint Report of the United Nations, the World Bank and the Asian Development Bank." http://www.adb.org/Documents/Reports/Tsunami-India/tsunami-india.pdf (accessed 8 November 2007).

Walker, P. 1989. *Famine Early Warning Systems: Victims and Destitution.* London: Earthscan.

Wenz, P. S. 1988. *Environmental Justice.* Albany: State Univ. of New York Press.

Wisner, B., and P. Walker. 2005. "The World Conference on Disaster Viewed through the Lens of Political Ecology: A Dozen Big Questions for Kobe and Beyond." *Capitalism Nature Socialism* 16 (2): 89–95.

Wisner, B., P. Blaikie, T. Cannon, and I. Davis. 2004. *At Risk: Natural Hazards, People's Vulnerability and Disasters,* 2nd ed. London: Routledge.

4   *Coasts Under Pressure*

MARINE AND COASTAL
ENVIRONMENTAL SECURITY
IN THE INDIAN OCEAN CONTEXT

MARCUS HAWARD

The tsunami of December 26, 2004, that struck coastal areas of Indian Ocean littoral states with such devastation and loss of life provided a graphic example of the forces of nature, and the effects of such forces on coastal communities. The tsunami and its aftermath were felt around the Indian Ocean Region, with coastal communities and environments destroyed in the area near the epicenter of the undersea earthquake off Aceh in Indonesia, in the southern parts of Thailand, the Maldives, and the Andaman Islands (Kay 2005). The tsunami also affected the east African coastline and was recorded at Australian stations in the Antarctic (Brolsma 2005, 13). The impacts of the tsunami—in destroying coastal areas and communities—provided clear evidence of the significance of the coastal zone to the economic and social fabric to the region.

The coast is the location of a vast majority of the Indian Ocean Region's population, industrial development, and communications infrastructure—ports, roads, railway systems, and airports. The coastal zone (including its marine and terrestrial components) has many uses and an equally diverse range of users. These activities have a number of impacts—direct and cumulative—on the coastal and marine environment. Management of this zone is directly related to environmental security—marine and coastal resources are critical to economic and community development underpinning such security. Institutional arrangements to address coastal management are important, yet understated elements in ensuring effective strategies to ensure security of coastal and marine environments and resources. This chapter surveys the development of response strategies to address pressure on marine and coastal environments in the Indian Ocean Region.

The Indian Ocean's Coastal and Marine Domain

The Indian Ocean occupies a basin of 73 million square kilometers, bordered by 38 coastal states on four continents (Kwiatowska 1994). The region contains diverse coastal and marine environments, vulnerable to development pressures. Mangrove areas are found around the region as well as seagrass beds, both critical habitats for a range of species. The region contains a range of coral reefs that provide an important source of food for local human populations and are of major commercial importance for fisheries and tourism (NOAA 1995). Destructive practices, such as excavations of coral and coral sand, sand mining, and illegal fishing practices, including the use of explosives and poisons, have damaged these reef systems. While there is little documentary evidence of the extent of this damage, it has been estimated that approximately 20 percent of coral reefs and 5 percent of sea-grass beds have been destroyed (NOAA 1995).

Environmental disturbances are "exacerbated by rapidly increasing coastal populations, widespread poverty that in turn promotes the unsustainable use of coastal resources, poorly planned economic development; under-resourced government institutions; and weak implementation of existing laws and policies" (Francis and Torrell 2004, 300). Coastal development poses challenges even for developed countries within the region, such as Australia, that have relatively effective governance arrangements (Haward 1995; Glazewski and Haward 2005). For other Indian Ocean states, coastal management is clearly even more of a challenge. The Maldives—an archipelago on the North Indian Ocean—comprises 1,190 islands and 26 atolls stretching over 870 kilometers in roughly a north-south orientation. The islands have a low elevation, many rising less than a meter above sea level, making them vulnerable to extreme events—as shown in the tsunami of December 2004. India, in contrast, has coastline of 8,129 kilometers and an exclusive economic zone (EEZ) (declared in 1976) of approximately 2 million square kilometers, with its coastal zone heavily populated and the location of major industry. On the Western Indian Ocean, Kenya has a coastline of 600 kilometers, with its coastal zone supporting 9 percent of the country's population (McClanahan et al. 2005). South Africa's coastline of 3,000 kilometers supports an estimated 30 percent of South Africa's population living within 60 kilometers of the coast (Glazewski and Haward 2005).

Fisheries

Fishing is a major activity in the region, with artisanal or small-scale commercial fisheries being important sources of food and protein for communities around the region. Fishing remains critical for both food security and export income for Indian Ocean states. In the case of the Maldives, for example, fishing is a mainstay of the economy, with 70 percent of export earnings derived from fishing and related activities. India, too, has seen considerable fisheries development from the mid-1980s. Fishing efforts are generally confined to inshore areas, with artisanal and traditional fishing operations comprising 93 percent of production. Deep sea fleets, operating to the edge of India's EEZ, only contribute 7 percent of production, mostly in prawn trawling. Despite this emphasis on coastal and inshore areas, production has increased by a factor of 6 in the last 50 years. While offshore fisheries provide some opportunities, there appears to be limited scope for further development of coastal and inshore fisheries around the Indian Ocean Region. In addition to these environmental limits, any increased development of fisheries for export to major world markets, such as to Europe and Japan, faces concerns from these markets over quality and safety of fisheries products.

The European Union (EU) banned seafood imports from India and Bangladesh in 1997 and demanded these countries improve seafood processing to meet EU-determined safety standards. While European and Japanese markets provide opportunities for Indian Ocean states, increasing support for eco-labeling and certification of fisheries by consumers, for example, through the Marine Stewardship Council (MSC) or similar processes (see Potts and Haward, 2007) is driven by demands for sustainable fisheries. The MSC has established a set of principles and criteria through which fisheries are certified and products from these fisheries provided with an eco-label. The MSC—independent of governments—is predicated on the assumption that eco-labeling provides benefits for fishers, processors, marketers, and retailers through premiums paid by consumers for certified fisheries. MSC has yet (as of 2007) to certify any Indian Ocean fisheries. The cost of MSC certification is high, and demands for such certification may have considerable impact on fisheries exports from the region as pressure from developed countries on food safety and certification of fisheries places increased costs on local producers.

Although the catch is relatively small in relation to other waters, the Indian Ocean has experienced significant growth in its offshore commercial fishery and has attracted vessels displaced from the Pacific and other regions, toward pelagic fisheries particularly in relation to tuna species. The Indian Ocean has witnessed an increasing build-up of vessels from the 1990s. This poses dilemmas for Indian Ocean coastal states. As in the South Pacific, commercial tuna fishing effort in the region is dominated by distant water fishing nations (DWFNs), who either fish in the high seas areas or negotiate access agreements to fish in coastal states' EEZs. Access agreements can provide opportunities for technology transfer and fisheries development assistance to the host country, but at the same time locks out opportunities for the host country. Uncontrolled exploitation of fisheries resources has significant resource and environmental security implications for Indian Ocean coast states.

Coastal Zone Management

Coastal zone management has increased in importance over the past 30 years, supported by initiatives at the international, regional, national, sub-national, and local government or community scales. These initiatives have centered on a shift from sectoral to integrated approaches to management of the coast, and increased recognition of the problem of cumulative impacts. Internationally the focus on integrated coastal zone management (ICZM) gained traction though the work of the World Commission on Environment and Development (WCED), also known as the Brundtland Commission, and its report *Our Common Future* (WCED 1987/1990). This report noted that the use of coastal areas for settlement, industry, energy facilities, and recreation will accelerate but that these areas would suffer increasing damage unless action was taken (WCED 1990).

Coastal and marine areas were also a focus of the United Nations Conference on Environment and Development (UNCED) held in Rio de Janerio, Brazil, in 1992. Chapter 17 of Agenda 21, the global action plan that was developed at UNCED, reinforced the need for more integrated approaches to coastal management. UNCED also served to initiate further action, with the World Coast Conference in 1993 held in Noordwijk in the Netherlands being an immediate and significant response (Haward and Hildebrand 1996). This conference, supported by the World Bank, helped develop the Noordwijk Guidelines for Integrated Coastal Zone Management that have provided a useful framework for development of coastal management programs and plans in the Indian Ocean Region (see Francis and Torell 2004). Translation of broad global objectives into feasible programs at regional, national, and provincial levels is not a simple matter, as even if effective programs are devised, implementation becomes a significant problem in itself (Davis and Haward 1994).

International, Regional, and National Instruments

The Law of the Sea Convention (LOSC) provides a key framework for ocean management. While it is less directly concerned with coastal management, the convention encourage states to cooperate in a range of areas, including marine environmental protection. The key areas of the LOSC provide the basis for delimitation of maritime zones, including the 12-mile territorial sea and 200-mile exclusive economic zone (EEZ), enhancing rights (and their concomitant obligation) of coastal states. All states in the Indian Ocean Region have declared territorial seas and 200-nautical-mile exclusive economic zones. The LOSC provides the legal basis for regimes for exploitation of both living and nonliving resources of the sea and below the seabed (with the resources outside national jurisdiction seen as the "common heritage of mankind"). This focus on exploitation is balanced by commitments toward protection of the marine environment, and urges states to collaborate over management and conservation of marine resources and the marine environment. The LOSC provides significant powers to coastal states in relation to their EEZs, and this has been an important factor in managing fisheries.

A number of other relevant international instruments can anchor coastal and marine environmental protection. The Convention on Biological Diversity (CBD), developed under the auspices of the United Nations Environment Program (UNEP) came into force in December 1993. This convention was developed in recognition of the present and future value of biological diversity, including marine biodiversity (Norse 1993), and its significant reduction around the world. Biological diversity is defined in the convention as "the variability among living organism from all sources including terrestrial, marine, and other aquatic ecosystems and the ecological complexes of which they are a part: this includes diversity within species, between species and of ecosystems." Each party to the convention has responsibility for the conservation and sustainable use of its own biological diversity, and is to cooperate in implementing the convention in areas beyond national jurisdiction such as the high seas. The CBD gave more explicit focus to marine and coastal issues through the Jakarta Mandate, negotiated at the second meeting of states party to the CBD in 1995, which provided a program of action that would focus on implementing the provisions of the convention as they related to marine and coastal environments.

Ship-sourced pollution has attracted considerable international attention—first, in response to the accidental discharge of pollutants, and second, from the dumping of wastes (including ballast water, plastics, and other material) from vessels. While shipping disasters such as groundings of or collision between oil tankers gains great publicity, these events comprise a very small proportion of marine pollution. Ship-sourced pollution is regulated under two international conventions, MARPOL 1973/78 (the International Convention for the Prevention of Pollution from Ships) and the London Dumping Convention (International Convention on Offshore Dumping 1975). The International Maritime Organization (IMO) is responsible for the administration of MARPOL, and has developed a Global Program for the Protection of the Marine Environment, addressing basic principles of "safer ships and cleaner seas." The Indian Ocean encompasses major shipping routes, with coastal states collaborating to ensure safe shipping and concomitant protection of marine and coastal environments. Annexes to MARPOL deal with different ship-sourced pollutants, with Annex V (governing garbage) totally prohibiting the disposal of plastics, including fishing gear, into the sea.

Other environmental instruments include the Convention on Migratory Species of Wild Animals (CMS, or the Bonn Convention) and the Convention on Trade in Endangered Species of Wild Fauna and Flora (CITES). While CMS has addressed issues related to the impacts of incidental catch of seabirds associated with fishing, CITES appears to provide opportunities to monitor and regulate trade for some fish species. This convention regulates trade in species that are threatened with extinction or may become so as a result of international trade driven by commercial demand (Kimball 2001). Article II of CITES provides for the inclusion in Appendix I of the convention species threatened with extinction that are or may be affected by trade. Listing on Appendix I prohibits international trade in wild specimens but does not prohibit the harvest of or domestic sale of fish caught by recreational or commercial fishers within a state's EEZ.

The Indian Ocean Region contains a number of regional initiatives directed at building capacity and supporting coastal and ocean management. These initiatives can link with, or are developed under the auspices of, international agencies such as the United Nations Environment Program (UNEP), the United Nations Food and Agriculture Organization, and the World Bank. The World Bank, for example, supports a number of regional programs, including the Coral Reef Degradation in the Indian Ocean (CORDIO) initiative to respond to the environmental damage to coral reefs in the region (World Bank 2004).

The UNEP Regional Seas program has been an important catalyst for ocean and coastal management in the Indian Ocean Region. UNEP, headquartered in Nairobi, Kenya, provides significant capacity for developing regional strategies and supporting national actions. The Regional Seas Program was established in 1974. It covers 13 marine regions, and for each region can include an action plan, an intergovernmental agreement, and detailed protocols dealing with particular environmental problems (Yearbook of International Cooperation on Environment and Development, 2004). There are two regional seas programs in the Indian Ocean

Region: first, the South Asian Seas program, and second, the East African Seas program. The South Asian Seas program is established under an Action Plan, while the East African Seas program is established under the Nairobi Convention for the Protection, Management and Development of the Marine and Coastal Environment of the Eastern African Region. Countries that are members of the Nairobi Convention are Somalia, Kenya, Tanzania, Mozambique, South Africa, Comoros, Madagascar, Mauritius, Reunion, and Seychelles.

The Bay of Bengal Program was established by FAO in the mid-1970s, with a range of projects being undertaken on marine resource management and marine environmental protection. In 1999, participating governments established a formal intergovernmental organization to replace the original FAO program, and at the same time enabled a broadening of the original aims (the development and management of small-scale fisheries). The Bay of Bengal Program has a central mission to ensure development based on responsible fishing practices and environmentally sound management programs (Bay of Bengal Programme 2005). Members of the Bay of Bengal Inter-Governmental Organization are Bangladesh, India, Sri Lanka, and the Maldives.

The Western Indian Ocean Marine Science Association (WIOMSA) promotes educational, scientific, and technological development of all aspects of marine science throughout the western Indian Ocean Region (WIOMSA 2005). The association holds conferences and workshops, and provides grants to support research activities as well as training activities.

In addition to these regional institutions there are a number of regional fisheries organizations within the Indian Ocean Region. These organizations include the Indian Ocean Tuna Commission (IOTC), responsible for management of tuna and tuna-like species in the Indian Ocean and adjacent seas, the Commission for the Conservation of Antarctic Marine Living Resources (CCAMLR), responsible for management of marine living resources in the Southern Ocean, approximately south of latitude 45_ South, and the Commission for the Conservation of Southern Bluefin Tuna (CCSBT), responsible for management of southern bluefin tuna throughout its range, which includes the Indian Ocean. A South West Indian Ocean Commission is under development. The Western Indian Ocean Tuna Organization (WIOTO) has no regulatory powers but aims to strengthen cooperation and coordination between coastal states in the western Indian Ocean.

States bordering the Indian Ocean vary considerably in the size and scale of marine and coastal management policies and practices. Despite these differences there is broad agreement on problems facing states, and responses needed. These responses include improving the integration of resource management with community development, incorporating local ecological knowledge into coastal zone planning, involving stakeholders, building partnerships, and integrating science into resource management (see Francis and Torell 2004; Clemett 2003). Initiatives that address these elements will also center on key dilemmas of environmental security as they affect the marine and coastal environment.

Sri Lanka established its first coastal zone legislation in 1981 and has pioneered a shift toward an integrated approach to coastal management. Revisions of the

Coastal Zone Management Policy in 1997 included increased attention to community participation. This policy attempts to identify local priorities but retains a focus on resource management rather than on local community needs (Clemett 2003).

India's amendment to its Environmental Protection Act in 1991 provided the basis for the regulation of various coastal zone activities (Subramanian, n.d). This led to the zoning of coastal areas and classification of these zones. The government of India constituted a National Coastal Zone Management Authority in 1998 and has begun a number of capacity-building and integrated coastal management projects under the auspices of the Department of Ocean Development (Subramanian, n.d).

Indonesia, a vast archipelago, has significant coastal management challenges, with important economic and social dependence on coastal resources (Patlis 2005). Governmental reform—devolving responsibility to the regional level for a large number of social, economic, and environmental issues—has posed further challenges. These challenges include gaps and overlaps in sector-based laws and regulations and between national and regional laws (Patlis 2005).

Broad features that can be identified at the national level in the North and North East Indian Ocean are replicated in the Western Indian Ocean. As noted by Francis and Torell, some eastern African countries, such as South Africa, Tanzania, Mozambique, and Kenya, have programs to address coastal issues at the national level (Francis and Torell 2004), but these programs vary considerably.

South Africa established a national integrated coastal management policy in 1999. This policy reflected broad government objectives in the post-apartheid era by the democratically elected government. The South African coast has become increasingly popular for business, commercial, tourism, and recreational activities, with a corresponding increase in the coast's proportionate contribution to total GNP (Glazewski and Haward 2005). The new government enacted a framework environmental act, the National Environmental Management Act, 1998 (NEMA), that partially repealed the previous Environmental Conservation Act. NEMA is underpinned by the tenet of cooperative governance by laying down a set of environmental management principles for decision-making on matters affecting the environment. One of these is devoted specifically to coastal areas that "require specific attention in management and planning procedures, especially where they are subject to significant human resource usage and development pressure" (Glazewski and Haward 2005).

Kenya's initial coastal management programs established in the early 1980s were within the UNEP Regional Seas program that provided training in integrated coastal management, but this early action was not supported by national-level legislation or effective institutional arrangements (McClanahan et al. 2005). Legislative reform in 2000, with the enactment of the Environmental Management and Co-ordination Act, provided necessary support for coastal management and reinforced institutional arrangements for coastal management and resource use. While the legislative base has been established, the institutional framework has yet to fully implement an integrated approach to management (McClanahan et al. 2005).

Australia, bordering the East Indian Ocean has a coastline of approximately 37,000 kilometers, the longest ice-free coast in the world. This coastline transcends a number of biogeographic regions, each containing a diversity of marine habitats. Management of the Australian coast reflects a similar diversity (Haward 2003), with the national, state, and local governments all having interests in Australian coastal zone policy. The Environment Protection and Biodiversity Conservation Act 1999 (EPBC Act) entered into force in July 2000 and provides legislative support to marine environmental protection in what are termed Commonwealth Marine Areas. Australia's Oceans Policy (launched in 1998) introduced regional marine planning by the Australian government (Bergin and Haward 1999; Haward 2001). While the state governments retain major responsibilities for current coastal management, there is formal intergovernmental interaction through different intergovernmental committees and meetings of relevant ministers. The Australian government has recently indicated that it is concerned with the problem of coastal development and has threatened to take a more activist role in this policy area.

The preceding survey reinforces the fact that while experience in national initiatives on coastal management varies markedly among coastal states within the region, it is clear that such initiatives are providing an important institutional framework for integrated coastal zone management. These frameworks and the ICZM processes and outcomes in turn address central issues related to marine and coastal environmental security. There is a need, however, to develop national-level integrated coastal management programs, moving from pilot projects that often stay focused on a specific area (Francis and Torell 2004).

Challenges: Improving Policy Capacity and Coordination

Local action is a necessary condition for effective coastal management, but it is not sufficient, as local action needs to be nested within national or sub-national programs. This "nesting" is important, as it provides a basis for integration of institutions and efforts, but also because locally based activities or programs may be limited in reach. Local programs can be effective in encouraging community action and can address direct impacts on coastal environments, but they may be less effective is dealing with the causes of downstream impacts. One key element in any discussion of institutional arrangements focuses on how such arrangements affect policy implementation. A centralized administrative system that delegates activities will have a different focus than a system that devolves responsibility to local levels and agencies. Such a crude dichotomy masks a range of possibilities but draws attention to alternative institutional approaches, as shown in table 4.1.

Questions of coordination and policy capacity lead to consideration of the need to manage what Allison termed the internal components and external constituencies of organizations (Allison 1992). Managing internal components either within agencies with differing responsibilities or in those with broad interests in coastal or marine management may be complex, but is a critical element in coordination and in enhancing capacity. Managing the relationships with external constituencies (nongovernment stakeholders, such as industry and business, as well as

Table 4.1   Delegated and Devolved Approaches to Implementation

	Delegated	*Devolved*
Focus	Central government decisions: new laws, etc.	Local implementation structure (network) involved in a policy area.
Policy process	From the center down and from government out to private sector and public.	From local (government and private sectors) out (and up?).
Evaluation criteria	Focus on attainment of formal objectives.	Effectiveness of response.
Key principles	Central coordination to achieve intended results.	Implementation as strategic interaction among multiple actors.

the more traditional NGOs) is often difficult given that government objectives are not always shared by other stakeholders.

All governments have responsibilities for development and implementation of policy. The structures and processes developed to undertake these activities form core institutional arrangements. In relation to issue areas such as coastal zone management, these arrangements can influence the efficacy of policy responses. There is a vast range of organizational options available to address problems associated with coastal management. These options include establishing a specific agency, including responsibility for coastal management within a specified agency, or coordinating a number of relevant agencies. This introduces the importance of horizontal governance as a factor affecting the implementation of integrated coastal management in countries within the Indian Ocean Region. An important additional factor is the way in which policy is implemented. This introduces the concept of vertical governance, the relationship between central and local agencies or governments.

What are the implications for managing the coastal zone? In short it means that we should pay close attention to the factors that will influence the choice of institutional design, and to the type of policy instruments used to implement policy, such as regulatory instruments (legislation and regulation), market or economic instruments (fees, charges, taxes), or community agreement or norms (Howlett and Ramesh 1995). While these different categories indicate the diversity of instruments available to governments, it is also important to note that none of these instruments are mutually exclusive. Most alternative (nonregulatory or nonmarket) instruments will be based on, or included in, legislation.

Addressing problems of coastal and marine management also necessarily focuses on horizontal coordination within government. The treatment of initiatives that cut across administrative responsibilities is not new, and different governments have developed a range of responses to such issues. One consequence of focusing on vertical dimensions of government may be to ignore the need for increased horizontal coordination between different government agencies.

A number of key factors contribute to improved coordination across government agencies. These factors include structural change, ensuring adequate linkages between central and local administration, and ensuring local administration has sufficient capacity (see Peters 1998). A focus on vertical and horizontal governance and of institutional arrangements to address problems such as those associated with coastal zone management also addresses the question of policy capacity. Policy capacity—the ability to provide an effective solution to a problem—is linked to broader questions of institutional design.

Policy capacity can be conceptualized in different ways. Two key elements are the ability to make decisions (a process or procedural dimension) and the quality of policy decisions (the substance of policy). Both of these elements of policy capacity are linked to effective integrated coastal zone management. Key agencies need to be able to maintain and extend their own capacity and to be able to display leadership in this area, but they also need to be able to work effectively with the range of other actors engaged in coastal management. Policy capacity is affected by a number of factors, including the relative size of agencies and resources, both human and financial, available to them. In many economies the last twenty years have seen a reappraisal of government activities and greater use of alternative delivery mechanisms and/or increasing partnerships with private and third sector organizations. These reforms may have increased the separation of responsibility for "policy" from "operations" (Bakvis 1997), and in some cases has contributed to a loss of policy capacity or effectiveness within agencies.

Lessons for Coastal and Marine Management

Coastal and marine management involves a range of actors and stakeholders. Given that the involvement and interests of governments at different levels is a fact of life in coastal management, attention should be drawn to ways in which a coordinated approach to coastal management can be implemented. The experience within the Indian Ocean Region highlights the importance of linking national initiatives to local action and providing means by which local capacity can be enhanced. This can be done in a variety of ways, and it important to reiterate that there in no single "one best fit" approach. What is clear from the range of government, academic, and NGO reviews on coastal and marine management within the region is that a more comprehensive and integrated approach should replace traditional sectoral orientations to coastal management activities, and that increased inter-agency consultation and cooperation is required. Additional attention to the inclusion of local governments and local communities as stakeholders will supplement these more inclusive governmental approaches (see Clemett 2003).

Linking the work of universities and research organizations such as the IORG, as well as that of individual scientists, with research undertaken by government agencies in coastal management will improve the baseline data and information for any future policy. The development of national standards for areas such as water quality and coastal development may involve national government leadership but should also include local government input and allow the range of coastal interests to be consulted during the decision-making process. Ongoing assistance should be given to local government bodies, particularly in terms of providing training for coastal planners and facilitating public consultation in local coastal decision making.

This chapter has explored the fundamental importance of the coastal and marine environment to all states bordering the Indian Ocean and has demonstrated that management of these areas is equally important. ICZM will increase in salience as development pressures increase and as coastal areas are subject to climate variability and change. We have seen that extreme environmental events, as shown in the case of the tsunami of December 26, 2004, can and do have significant impacts on the coastal zone that supports the vast majority of the region's population, industry, and infrastructure.

The last 20 years have seen increased attention on coastal management processes around the region, moving to the establishment of national coastal legislation and/or policy, shifting from sectoral to integrated management, as well as improving coordination and capacity, including within local governments and communities. These national initiatives, supported by ongoing regional cooperation, provide an opportunity to address pressing threats to the coastal and marine environment and also provide the opportunity to enhance environmental security of marine and coastal resources and coastal communities.

REFERENCES

Allison, G. 1992. "Public and Private Management: Are They Fundamentally Alike in All Unimportant Respects." Reprinted in R. J Stillman Jr., *Public Administration: Concepts and Cases,* 5th ed., Boston: Houghton Mifflin, 292–98.

Bakvis, H. 1997. "Pressure Groups and the New Public Management: From 'Pressure Pluralism' to 'Managing the Contract.'" In *Canadian Public Administration and New Public Management,* ed. M. Chariah and A. Daniels, 293–315. Toronto: Institute of Public Administration of Canada.

Bay of Bengal Programme. 2005. "About BOBP." www.bobpigo.org/aboutbobp.htm (accessed August 1, 2005).

Bergin, A., and M. Haward. 1999. "Australia's New Oceans Policy." *International Journal of Marine and Coastal Law* 14 (3): 387–98.

Brolsma, H. 2005. "Tsunami Detected at Antarctic Stations." *Australian Antarctic Magazine,* no. 8 (Autumn): 13.

Clemett, A. 2003. *Improving Policy-Livelihood Relationships in South Asia.* Briefing Note 7. Stockholm Environment Institute, University of York, UK.

Davis, B. W., and M. Haward 1994. "Oceans Policy and Overlapping Regimes." In *Coastal Zone Canada 94: "Cooperation in the Coastal Zone" Conference Proceedings,* vol. 1, ed. P. G. Wells and P. J. Ricketts, 155–64. Dartmouth, Nova Scotia: Coastal Zone Canada Association, Bedford Institute of Oceanography.

Francis, J., and E. Torell. 2004. "Human Dimensions of Coastal Management in the Western Indian Ocean Region." *Ocean and Coastal Management* 47:299–307.

Glazewski, J., and M. Haward. 2005. "Towards Integrated Coastal Area Management: A Case Study in Cooperative Governance in South Africa and Australia." *International Journal of Marine and Coastal Law* 20 (1): 65–84.

Haward, M. 1995. "Institutional Design and Policy Making 'Down Under': Developments in Australian and New Zealand Coastal Management." *Ocean and Coastal Management* 26 (2): 87–117.

———. 2001. "Developing Australia's Ocean Policy." *Oceans Yearbook* 15:523–39.

———. 2003. "The Ocean and Marine Realm." In *Managing Australia's Environment,* ed. S. Dovers and S. Wild River, 35–52. Sydney: Federation Press.

Haward, M., and L. P. Hildebrand. 1996. "Integrated Coastal Zone Management." In *Oceans Law and Policy in the Post-UNCED Era: Australian and Canadian Perspectives,* ed. L. Kriwoken, M. Haward, D. VanderZwaag and B. Davis, 141–72. London: Kluwer Law International.

Howlett, M., and M. Ramesh. 1995. *Studying Public Policy: Policy Cycles and Policy Subsystems.* Toronto, Oxford Univ. Press.

Kay, R. 2005. *icoast* newsletter (Internet Coastal Management Newsletter). July 13.

Kimball, L. A. 2001. *International Oceans Governance: Using International Law and Organisations to Manage Marine Resources Sustainably.* Gland Switzerland and Cambridge, UK: IUCN-The World Conservation Union.

Kwiatowska, B. 1994. "Institutional Cooperation in the Indian Ocean Region: Resource Development and Environmental Protection." Paper to Pacem in Maribus (PIM) XXII, December 4–8, Madras.

McClanahan, T. R., S. Mwaguni, and N. A. Muthiga. 2005. "Management of the Kenyan Coast." *Ocean and Coastal Management* 48 (11–12): 901–31.

NOAA (National Oceans and Atmospheric Administration). 1995. "Regional Perspectives: Indian Ocean." www.ncdc.noaa.gov/paleo/outreach/coral/sor/sor_indian.html (accessed July 13).

Norse, E., ed. 1993. *Marine Biological Diversity: A Strategy For Building Conservation Into Decision Making.* Washington, D.C.: Island Press.

Patlis, J. M. 2005. "The Role of Law and Legal Institutions in Determining the Sustainability of Integrated Coastal Management Projects in Indonesia." *Ocean and Coastal Management* 48:450–67.

Peters, B. G. 1998. "Managing Horizontal Government: The Politics of Coordination." *Public Administration* 76:295–311.

Potts, T., and M. Haward. 2007. "International Trade, Ecolabelling, and Sustainable Fisheries— Recent Concepts and Practices." *Environment, Development and Sustainability* 9 (1): 91–106.

Subramanian, B. R. N.d. "National Profile: India." www.globaloceans.org/icm/profiles/india/india.html (accessed July 20, 2005).

UNEP (United Nations Environment Programme). 2003. *Regional Seas Status Report.* Nairobi: United Nations Environment Programme.

WCED (World Commission on Environment and Development). 1987/1990. *Our Common Future,* Australian ed. Melbourne: Oxford Univ. Press.

WIOMSA. 2005. "About WIOMSA." *Western Indian Ocean Journal of Marine Science.* www.ajol.info/policies.php?jid=180 (accessed July 13, 2005).

World Bank. 2004. "Coastal and Marine Management: Coral Reef Degradation in the Indian Ocean." http://go.worldbank.org/VZD5H2IU80 (accessed July 13, 2005).

Yearbook of International Cooperation on Environment and Development. 2004. "Conventions within the UNEP Regional Seas Programme." Lysaker, Norway: The Fridtjof Nansen Institute.

PART II

EARTH

5 Earth Security in the Indian Ocean Region

FOOD, FISHERIES, AND BIODIVERSITY

MELISSA RISELY AND TIMOTHY DOYLE

Driving out from the center of Johannesburg through its suburbs, we were confronted—as every traveler there inevitably is—by the stark reality that the post-colonial world of Africa is clearly divided between the haves and have-nots. It is impossible to over articulate this split between worlds. It is as if travelers from the wealthier parts of the city enter through portals into separate states of existence. It is almost impossible to fathom that these two states of being exist alongside each other, that they are part of the same planet, let alone the same city. But no matter how prepared, each time one confronts this dichotomy it remains a shock, and on this occasion our transition from city center to city periphery was no different.

Centuries of imperialism, slave trading, and a plethora of first world get-rich-quick schemes have left vast parts of Africa in a dire condition, leaving most to live a level of unimaginable poverty. This poverty exists, increasingly, in cities. The shanty towns in and around Johannesburg are appropriately named and are indicative of all such towns across the IOR. Like most cities in the IOR, huge populations arrive every day on their doorsteps. These cities are ill-equipped to deal with this immense movement of people, the magnitude of which has never before been witnessed. As a consequence, entire cities are forming outside the established cities. Bandung in Indonesia, Mumbai in India, Bangkok in Thailand, and Johannesburg in South Africa all share this fate. These cities outside cities have little or no established infrastructure. There is often no access to energy sources. There is often no sewage system and running water, with no basic separation in the waste stream, with human waste draining to nowhere, flushed along with storm water as it tries unsuccessfully to seek the sea. Housing is marginal—the shelters in these shanty towns consist of discarded iron, propped up and weighed down with old tires and patched up with plastic shopping bags. These are places of disease, crime, suffering, malnutrition, and death.

But what drives rural populations to these "hells on earth"? There are many answers to this question. But one thing is sure. Many leave their rural existence not for the promises offered by global markets, but because of their lost ability to subsist on their ancestral lands. Increasingly, the still dominant peasant lifestyle of most people in the IOR is under threat. When people are forced to leave their rural

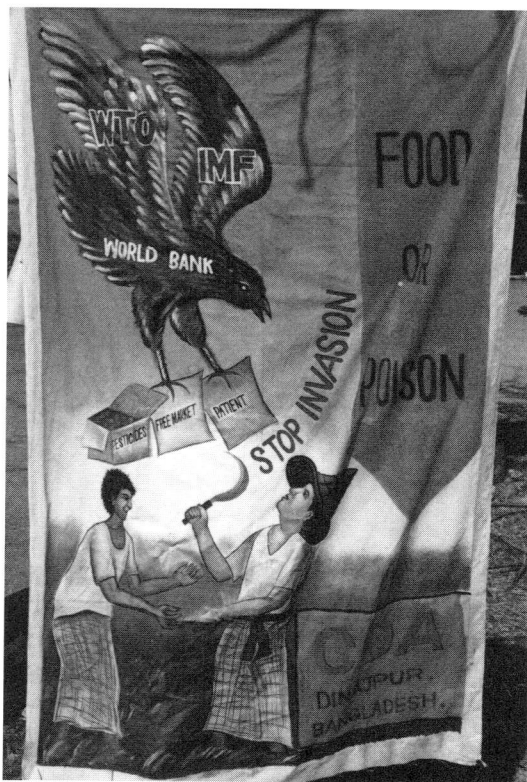

Figure 5.1.   Food sovereignty banner of Bangladeshi activists at the 2004 World Social Forum, Mumbai, India.
Source: Joel Catchlove.

lives and move to the big cities, they not only lose their ability to subsist, but they also lose their sacred links to the land of their families and ancestors; they lose their meaning systems and their song-lines; they become landless and rootless. It is usually the men who must leave their family abodes in search of work in the cities on the edge of cities. And those that are left behind—women, children, the eld-erly—largely fend for themselves. In this manner, people face the desperate periph-ery of existence, battling with ever increasing malnutrition and food shortages.

With the emergence of so-called free markets there has been increased pres-sure on communities and governments to involve themselves in agriculture on a far larger scale. This was illustrated vividly during a visit to a farm that had attracted considerable attention due to its ability to attain sponsorship from a large donor consortium that included the World Bank. This farmland, just five years prior to our visit, had not been "improved," with most of its land surface still cov-ered by native vegetation. In the last two years, the trees and other habitat had been removed and replaced with a large crop of jokobi. This crop is not for local consumption, as we were to discover, but had been planted as part of a bio-diesel project. This guaranteed the national government a large number of carbon credits, which it could sell off to first world polluters who had already achieved their omissions targets. The situation is outrageous, considering that it took place in a nation that has profound difficulty in feeding its people.

On our return to Australia, we were again confronted by the enormous contrast between South Africa and Australia. At the same time, however, the two countries share a number of food and biodiversity security issues. On Kangaroo Island in Australia, for example, food-bearing farmland has been bought by large agro-forestry companies, which have proceeded with enormous plantings of blue gums. The parallels between this and the jakobi plantings just outside of Johannesburg are striking. There is no intention to harvest the long-term crop, with no adequate port facilities available on the island. The crop is simply a means for the Japanese government to gather carbon credits associated with the Kyoto Protocol, and continue burning fossil fuels. What is far more alarming than continued carbon emissions, however, is the mass disappearance of food-producing lands across the region under monocultures that are useless to local inhabitants.

Similarly, while the focus on addressing food security issues tends to be on developing countries like those in Africa, even developed countries like Australia are confronted with the challenge of overcoming food insecurity. Malnourishment is not only a problem in poor countries, and is not always the result of too little food. Rather, it is often due to a lack of the rich and varied diet that is vital for human well-being. This is largely due to the high percentage of processed foods produced and consumed, offering lower nutritional value and variety than whole foods. In developed countries like Australia, up to 75 percent of food consumed is processed in some way.

As we entered our local supermarket to restock our kitchens following our trip away, we were struck by the amount of processed foods confronting us on the shelves. Much of the food products available bear little resemblance to their original state, and their sources are often questionable. We could truly relate to the arguments of Rosemary Stanton, a well-known nutritionist in Australia, that nutrition and food "literacy" are growing in importance as a whole generation of Australians is being brought up with limited knowledge or ties to their food sources. While communities in developing countries have strong ties to the land and food production, the majority of Australian communities tend to be divorced from their food sources. Local knowledge of food and food production has largely been lost. As the globalization and homogenization of agriculture and food production drives third world rural poor to cities and divorces them from their sense of "place," so too people in the developed world are divorced from the lands that feed and provide for them.

And so, while the poor in developing nations struggle to access staple foods, the bread, milk, and "butter" available in our local supermarket are highly processed, and many are even fortified with "engineering wonders" offering to, for example, lower our cholesterol levels. The food industry is therefore heavily pushing "functional foods" to cure the ill health of Western societies—ills that are largely a product of the incredible marketing success of "junk food" and sedentary lifestyles. Functional foods proposed in Australia and New Zealand include more fruits and vegetables genetically modified to have increased vitamin or mineral content or healthier fatty acid profiles (FSANZ 2005).

Both functional foods and junk foods have significant effects on the sustainability of the food supply and on the well-being of communities in Australia, and other countries of the developed world. They are closely tied to over consumption of food, which poses problems for both health and sustainability. It has been reported that obesity is responsible for at least 250,000 deaths per year in the United States (Bowden 2002), and Australia is not far behind. The high rate of meat consumption, including fast food burgers, is just one example. To produce one kilogram of lot-fed meat, 25–50 kilograms of grain and 100,000 liters of water is required. Cereals are therefore used to feed cattle rather than people in many instances. In developed nations, over 70 percent of cereals are used for this purpose.

While filling a shopping cart with packaged foods in the local supermarket, the gross inadequacy of the labeling also became apparent. Labeling on most foods in Australia is vague. For example: "made from Australian and imported ingredients." This highlighted to us that consumers have no way of knowing the environmental footprint that the production of such foods has caused, taking away both consumer choice and education about this important food security issue. The high "food miles" that many foods must travel, for example, involving an incredible amount of energy use, are hidden from view. It was clear to us, as Bowden also argues, that people living in rich countries need to ask questions about the food they eat, rather than blindly consuming it (2002).

Biodiversity—and in particular the fraction that constitutes "food"—is fundamental to human survival and sustainability. Quite simply, people (and animals) need to eat to live. The right to freedom from hunger is a fundamental human right, as food security is essential for people to live healthy lives. Biodiversity is the cornerstone of survival for poor people. Small-scale farming communities rely on diversity for food and income security through complex farming systems such as garden-scale farming and shifting cultivation.

The Australian environmental movements' reframing of "wilderness" issues as "biodiversity" issues in recent times reflects the recognition that environmental issues in poorer countries are about basic human survival—like access to food (Doyle 2005). In the third world, people live in "wild" habitats, and the poorest depend on the physical environment and common property for their livelihoods. Thus, the earlier preoccupation of the Australian environment movements on human exclusion from wild places in order to conserve them was not appropriate in these contexts. By necessity, the poor in developing countries of the Indian Ocean Region are acutely aware that human needs cannot be separated from the natural environment. Thus, the realization that "wilderness" conservation is a "luxury" pursuit in the majority world has brought the issues of human health, shelter, and food security onto the first world green agenda (Doyle 2005).

Thus, food security is inextricably linked to biodiversity and is defined by the United Nations as "the physical and economic access, for all people at all times, to enough food for an active, healthy life" (UN Food and Agriculture Organization 2005). Significant global conventions, such as the Convention on Biodiversity (CBD) and the World Food Summit in Rome in 1996, made commitments to enhancing biodiversity, and in the case of the latter, to try to halve world hunger by 2015. However, there is still too little being done and hunger has increased every year since the summit. For example, in 2004 there were 852 million gravely under-nourished people in the world—up 10 million from the previous year (FAO 2004). In addition to this, every day, more than 17,000 children under the age of five die from hunger- related diseases (WFP 2004). Most of these deaths occur in the IOR.

The number of starving people across the IOR is skyrocketing each year, despite the propaganda of neoliberal economists and international finance organizations. In eastern Africa, nowhere is the nexus between food security and traditional security more obvious. In Kenya, for example, deteriorating standards of living in Nairobi furnished the backdrop for the abortive coup attempt of August 1982. Somali troops clashed with civilians in the northern part of the country after a demonstration was held to protest the ill effects of economic crisis (Shaw 1996).

Despite this desperate situation, the efforts and resources spent on the international alliance to alleviate hunger and poverty remain meager, particularly when compared to the billions of dollars spent on the "War Against Terror." The amount of aid being provided for famine relief is decreasing as funds are redirected toward strengthening traditional national security through growing military resources (UN 2005). For example, in Ethiopia, it has been reported that the World Food Program reduced daily food rations for the 126,000 refugees from the Sudan, Eritrea, and Somalia—living in Ethiopian refugee camps—because the aid was redirected toward the War Against Terror (UN 2005).

It is therefore the case that, while biodiversity, and more particularly food security, is an essential element of human survival, increasingly it is taking second place to more traditional security agendas. In addition, it is becoming a commodity under the free market control of global entities such as the World Trade Organization (WTO) and transnational corporations (TNCs). It is rapidly becoming the foundation of major economic markets through, for example, biotechnologies and the patenting of genetic materials. This current world view has led to three major revolutions since the 1950s: the "Green Revolution," "Blue Revolution," and "Gene Revolution."

The Green Revolution of the 1950s and 1960s saw the transfer of Western industrialized agriculture from wealthy first world nations to poorer developing nations. Proponents saw it as a remarkable achievement due to the 100 percent increase in wheat production through the planting of more productive varieties and improving cultivation techniques (Aldridge 1996; Conway 1997). To proponents it heralded the introduction of "miracle seed" varieties to feed the world. However, there were only a few high-yield varieties, and the global use of fertilizers doubled in the 1970s following their introduction. Pesticide use increased by around five times. In 1998, industry sales of agrochemicals totaled US$31 billion a year (Bowden 2002).

The legacy of the Green Revolution is that 20 species now make up around 90 percent of our food supply out of thousands of potential food plants (Aldridge

1996). Hence, food security for all people in the Indian Ocean Region is being undermined. For example, in India in the 19th century around 30,000 native rice species were cultivated. By the start of the 21st century this had been drastically reduced to a meager 50 species (Bowden 2002).

In addition, chemical industrial agriculture requires intensive irrigation, which over long periods can raise the water table. The water table in the Indus Valley in Pakistan, for example, was 30 meters below ground before irrigation was introduced in the middle of last century, but in the space of several years, it rose to within centimeters of the surface in low-lying areas (Bowden, 2002). This, combined with the increase in fertilizer use, has led to increased salinity, resulting in significant land degradation and crop failure. The worst affected countries are India, Pakistan, Iraq, and Egypt, and Australia has also been significantly affected.

The same world view that led to the Green Revolution saw the world fish catch increase around 500 percent between 1950 and 1997, an increase now referred to as the "Blue Revolution" (Bowden 2002). Exports from the IOR to Japan and Europe increased dramatically. This trend has continued, and it is not surprising, therefore, that serious concerns have been raised about fish stocks being depleted too rapidly. Of particular note is the increase in commercial tuna fishing efforts by nations outside of the IOR. This has received significant media attention in Australia recently. The Australian Fisheries Management Authority reportedly accused Japanese fishers of illegally catching tuna worth $2 billion and systematically hiding their haul over the last 20 years (Darby 2006).

Chapter 7 of this book, by Clive Schofield, extends this discussion of fisheries insecurity, particularly in zones of rich living resources and weak maritime security such as Somalia. There is now more commercial fishing, and illegal fishing by foreign vessels, where there used to be small-scale artisanal fishing, leading to the over-exploitation of an important food source, which will threaten community livelihoods. In addition, maritime piracy is commonplace in these waters, and lack of governmental stability and international support has led to fisheries enforcement at the grassroots level.

Chapter 8, by May Tan-Mullins, Jonathan Rigg, and Carl Grundy-Warr, also explores the issue of fisheries security, but in the context of natural disasters. The December 26, 2004, Indian Ocean tsunami caused massive human and economic destruction, and fishing communities in coastal areas were among the most severely affected. A case study of three fishing villages in southern Thailand serves to illustrate that natural events cannot be separated from the social, political, and economic environments in which they occur. The authors examine how factors such as pre-tsunami structures, religious networks, and politics contributed to the different patterns of recovery and rehabilitation in these communities. It is argued that these factors are essential in enhancing our understanding of the resilience of these fishing communities. The chapter also considers how such "soft" information could be utilized to reinforce the livelihoods and environmental security of fishing communities in hazardous zones.

The livelihoods of poor people also hang in the balance due to the other great revolution of our time, the "Gene Revolution," often referred to as the "Doubly Green Revolution." The "Gene Revolution" is the topic of Richard Hindmarsh's chapter in this section. By the middle of the 21st century, there will be around 3 billion more people to feed, and the biotechnology industry is heralding itself as the solution to meeting growing food demand. Supporters of the technology claim that genetically modified crops will be an essential component of a global food security strategy (U.S. Department of State 2002; Green Nature 2002; www.uspolicy.be 2002, cited in Risely 2003). For example, scientists undertaking rice research sponsored by the United Nations Development Program claim that the modified varieties have enormous potential to improve food security in Africa, Asia, and South America (Agrifood Awareness Australia 2001).

However, critics are concerned about growing corporate control of plant breeding and the seed industry, and increased private ownership of genetic materials. Debates over who controls the new agricultural technologies, and who benefits from them, have been raging in recent years. Critics assert that genetic-industrial agriculture, following chemical-industrial agriculture, is enabling seed-chemical corporations to extend their control over farmers, and indeed the entire food chain (Scrinis 1999). Commercial rights under plant variety rights (or plant breeding rights) legislation allow breeders to control the use and availability of specific plant varieties, restricting seed varieties that are sold and grown, thereby concentrating control of the seed market to these trans-national corporations (Hobbelink 1991; Hindmarsh 1999). Intellectual property rights conflict with the rights of farmers to keep and reproduce seeds from year to year, instead creating a dependence upon agribusiness for both inputs and seeds. In particular, herbicide-tolerant varieties offer companies continued control with chemical herbicide and crop seeds sold as a pair. Seeds have also been modified to be sterile—the so-called terminator technology has been developed to ensure that farmers cannot re-use seed the following year.

Detractors argue that the reductionist logic of agricultural biotechnology continues to marginalize alternative approaches to agriculture, such as organics and permaculture. This is despite increasing reports from ecologists that greater biodiversity leads to a greater carrying capacity and ecosystem viability (Ho 2000). Biodiversity also helps crops to withstand climatic events and disease; and people benefit from a richer, varied diet.

But the industry argues: "If we are to banish hunger, famine and pestilence from this planet, we must become missionaries on behalf of scientifically based realism and tireless opponents of unfounded and divisive rhetoric" (Mycogen 1997, cited in Risely 2003). Therefore, any objections to the technology are claimed to be "unfounded," "divisive," and "anti-science." Proponents of the technology go even further to argue that opposition to agricultural biotechnology will mean continued starvation in poor countries: "Denial of the new technologies to the poor is synonymous to condemning them to continued suffering from malnutrition which eventually may deny the poorest of the poor their right to survival" (James 1999, 5, cited in Risely 2003). Thus, industry continues to maneuver to redefine biotechnology as "in the public interest" in both the developed and developing world.

These "revolutions" discussed above are the result of today's mainstream neoliberal economic theory that purports that liberalization of international trade and deregulation lead to growth and are, therefore, the best way forward for achieving economic and social justice. Some would argue, for example, that liberalization of the market has increased the opportunities of many to gain access to education, healthcare, and agricultural markets that was not possible in the past. The reports from the UN tell a completely different story, however.

The General Agreement on Tariffs and Trade makes it compulsory for developing countries to stop controlling importation of food and other agricultural products, as well as to reduce subsidies to peasants, exposing them to the competition of international markets. The Food and Agriculture Organization of the United Nations (FAO) insists that in the long term this will be profitable due to exportation opportunities. However, the unequal power relations make this impossible for many communities in the developing world. It is an illusion to view producers from throughout the world, and in this case the Indian Ocean Region, as being on "equal ground."

These power relations impact directly on food production and distribution and have a strong influence on trade. Global market competition will lead to the elimination of the weakest, which will ultimately mean the destruction of economies of majority world countries. What arrangements like the General Agreement on Tariffs and Trade (GATT) have done is to strengthen the monopoly control of transnational corporations (TNCs) on the food and agricultural sectors. These TNCs, for example can sell food products in developing countries at prices equivalent to half the local cost of production.

It can therefore be argued that international free trade has nothing to do with meeting basic human needs. This is made clear by the fact that hunger is not the result of an absolute shortage of food, but rather distributional inequities. As Foster and Leathers write: "The world has ample food. The growth of global food production has been faster than the unprecedented population growth for the past forty years. . . . Yet many poor countries and hundreds of millions of poor people do not share in this abundance. They suffer from a lack of food security, caused by mainly a lack of purchasing power" (Foster and Leathers 1999).

This is supported by Bowden (2002), who argues that although between 1960 and 2000 the amount of food available per person increased around 20 percent, the food available in poorer countries in 2000 was less than 2,100 calories per day, while in wealthier countries it was on average 3,200 calories per day. It can be argued that this inequity is largely due to the domination of free market ideals and that, as a result, access to food and health is now subject to the forces of the free market system (RAFI 1999, cited in Risely 2003). In other words, poor people simply cannot afford the new agricultural technologies being heralded as the solution to global hunger.

Further complicating matters for poor IOR communities is the direct threat to small-scale agriculture from globalization. In the Horn of Africa, around 80 percent of farmers are reliant on smallholdings. These are usually designed to supply food and sustenance for the extended kinship group, village, or community, with limited regional trade. Inevitably, larger farming practices are no longer designed to provide food security for local peoples. Rather, they are fashioned in a manner to service export markets. Alongside this shift in scale often comes a decline in the diversity of foodstuffs produced, with a move to monocultural pursuits.

Threats to sustainable agriculture are also shared by wealthier cities of the Western world. Good agricultural land is sold for housing development and agriculture itself is pushed out into areas with poorer soils that require greater irrigation and high use of chemical fertilizers. This in turn leads to increased environmental pollution, salinity, and soil and biodiversity erosion.

The centralization of agriculture into the hands of the state—often ill-equipped and untrained for wide-scale management—has had devastating impacts. One such impact has been the rapid migration of people to urban centers due to large-scale changes in food production and other elements of agriculture in rural areas.

It is for this reason that critics assert that the real push for high-technology solutions, such as biotechnology, is not the improvement of third world agriculture and food production, but rather to generate profits (Busch et al. 1990; Scrinis 1998). The new biotechnologies are seen to facilitate the further commodification and corporatization of agriculture (Scrinis 1998). This view is supported by the fact that plant biotechnology research and development is heavily skewed toward crops with high commercial potential. One of the first genetically modified (GM) products to be released was Monsanto's "Roundup Ready" soybeans, which a European Parliament Report concluded was "above all, developed for economic reasons, since development costs of a new herbicide are up to 20 times higher than those for a new (plant) variety" (European Parliament 1986). Currently, GM soybeans, canola, corn, potatoes, sugar beets, and cotton (for cottonseed oil) are approved for sale in Australia and New Zealand (Food Standards Australia New Zealand 2005).

It is likely then that gene technology will only intensify the problems related to the industrialization of agriculture, such as "increased hunger, malnutrition, landlessness, unemployment, cultural imperialism, dependency, corruption, corporate control, pesticide poisonings, ecosystem degradation, trade imbalances" (Hindmarsh 1993, 103). Modern biotechnology will have a profound effect on the production of necessity products, and those in control of these resources will exert considerable political influence. Inevitably, then, there will be both winners and losers (J. Doyle 1990, cited in Risely 2003).

Therefore, the liberalization of agricultural trade has, and will continue to have, a serious impact on food sovereignty and security in developing countries. People's basic right to food is being eroded. Prominent Indian environmentalist Vandana Shiva warns: "The diverse seeds now being pushed to extinction carry with them seeds of other ways of thinking about nature, and other ways of producing for our needs . . . uniformity and diversity are not just patterns of land use, they are ways of thinking and ways of living. . . . Monocultures spread not because they produce more, but because they control more. The expansion of monocultures has more to do with politics and power than with enriching and enhancing systems of biological production. This is true of the Green Revolution as it is of the gene revolution or the new biotechnologies" (Shiva 1993, 6–7).

Toward an IOR Agenda for Food Security and Sovereignty

Poor people do not have the income to buy food, whether it is in local markets or world markets. The only way to overcome this is to remove social and economic barriers that limit poor people's ability to achieve individual self-reliance in food supplies. Costly technologies, such as genetically modified crops, threaten to increase existing inequalities, poverty, and resultant food insecurity. Of greatest concern is that around five multinational corporations' control the world's food chain. The development, marketing, and patenting of seeds that require proprietary chemicals to grow is further concentrating power with these companies.

Many grassroots movements claim that too little time, opportunity, and assistance are provided to assist developing countries in testing and controlling GM crops themselves (UK Food Group 2003). Thus, there is significant risk that commercial interests will override democratic decision-making and local control of food security.

Some call for a new food economy with more food grown locally and growers paid a fair price, for example, products bearing the Fair Trade label, negotiated according to the social justice movement committed to ensuring employees and farmers are paid fairly and sustainable practices are used (Bowden 2002). According to Bowden, at present growers get very little of the money from their crops—coffee growers, for example, receive just 10 percent of the retail purchase price.

While neo-Malthusian arguments posit the cause of environmental degradation, such as deforestation, soil erosion, loss of biodiversity, and climate change, to population (Kirby and Moyo 2001), these models have been called into question in South Africa and South Asia. Fairhead and Leach (1996) have shown that in West Africa indigenous rural land users have been able to increase environmental productivity, not degrade it, through maintaining a balance between forest and grassland cover using traditional land management techniques.

In the Machakos District in Kenya there has been a resurrection of the landscape despite a six-fold rise in population. This has been linked to improvements in human welfare, indigenous initiatives, and ordinary people adapting to livelihood opportunities (Kirby and Moyo 2001). Contrary to the neo-Malthusian view, some argue that environmental improvement in some areas can be more easily achieved with higher populations, such as the case of Zimbabwe, where soil productivity has been created by labor-intensive garden-scale farming (Scoones 1997, cited in Kirby and Moyo 2001).

Despite the dominant industrial mindsets of the agrochemical industry, conservative agricultural institutions and some farming leaders, there is growing support for organic and biodynamic agriculture among some farmers and environmental NGOs. Australia currently has around 7.6 million hectares of certified organic agriculture (IFOAM 2004). Low-input technologies such as this, along with integrated pest management, for example, are making a significant contribution to food security (Pretty 1995).

Local people need to be at the center of any food security initiatives that are considered. Strategies will need to build on valuable local experiences and knowledge. The state-centric top-down approach to agriculture, ignoring grass-roots groups, is not conducive to achieving food security. As Zamora (1996) argues, local control of biodiversity is the best way to achieve food security and can be strengthened by regional cooperation. While state initiatives will remain important, it is at this local level that the principles of sustainability, the precautionary principle, and intra- and intergenerational equity can best be achieved.

REFERENCES

Agrifood Awareness Australia. 2001. "UN Report Highlights GM Food Hypocrisy." AFAA News. July 20. www.afaa.com.au (accessed July 2002).

Aldridge, S. 1996. *The Thread of Life: The Story of Genes and Genetic Engineering.* Cambridge: Cambridge Univ. Press.

Altieri, M. A. 1998. *The Environmental Risks of Transgenic Crops: An Agroecological Assessment.* http://www.pmac.net/miguel.htm (accessed October 2007).

Bowden, R. 2002. *Food Supply: Our Impact on the Planet.* London: White-Thomson Publishing.

Busch, L., W. B. Lacey, J. Burkhardt, and L. Lacey. 1990. *Plants, Power and Profit.* Oxford: Basil Blackwell.

Conway, G. 1997. *The Doubly Green Revolution: Food for All in the 21st Century.* London: Penguin.

Darby, A. 2006. "Tokyo's Stonewalling Comes at Great Cost," The Age. August 19. http://www.theage.com.au/articles/2006/08/18/1155408020868.html (accessed August 24, 2006).

Doyle, T. 2005. *Environmental Movements in Majority and Minority Worlds: A Global Perspective.* New Brunswick, N.J.: Rutgers Univ. Press.

European Parliament. 1986. *Commission on Agriculture, Fisheries and Food Draft Report on the Use of Biotechnology.* Brussels: European Parliament.

Fairhead, J., and M. Leach. 1996. *Misreading the African Landscape: Society and Ecology in a Forest-Savanna Mosaic.* Cambridge: Cambridge Univ. Press.

FAO (Food and Agriculture Organization). 2004. *The State of Food Insecurity in the World 2004.* Rome: FAO.

Foster, P., and H. Leathers. 1999. *The World Food Problem.* London: Lynne Rienner Publishers.

FSANZ (Food Standards Australia and New Zealand). 2005. *GM Foods: Safety Assessment of Genetically Modified Foods.* Canberra: Biotechnology Australia.

Green Nature. 2002. "United States Makes Push for GM Food Production." Agrifood News. February 22. http://www.afaa.com.au/news/news-718.asp (accessed December 2002).

Hindmarsh, R. 1993. "Overview of the 'Gene-Revolution'—A Need for a 'BAN.'" *Proceedings of the Ecopolitics VII Conference.* Griffith University, July 1993, 101–4.

———. 1999. "Consolidating Control: Plant Variety Rights, Genes and Seeds." *Journal of Australian Political Economy* 44:58–78.

Ho, M. W. 2000. "The End of Bad Science and Beginning Again with Life." Public lecture for the Conference on the Limit of Natural Selection, French Senate, Paris, March 8, 2000.

Hobbelink, H. 1991. *Biotechnology and the Future of World Agriculture.* London: Zed Books.

IFOAM (International Federation of Organic Agriculture Movements). 2004. *Uniting the Organic World.* Newsletter.

Kirby, J. and S. Moyo. 2001. "Environmental Security, Livelihoods and Entitlements." In *Negotiating Poverty: New Directions, Renewed Debate,* ed. N. Middleton, P. O'Keef, and R. Visser, 148–61. London: Pluto Press.

Pretty, J. 1995. *Regenerating Agriculture: Policies and Practices for Sustainability and Self-Reliance.* London: Earthscan.

Risely, M. 2003. *The Politics of Precaution: An Eco-Political Investigation of Agricultural Gene Technology Policy in Australia, 1992–2000*. Ph.D. thesis, University of Adelaide. February 2003.

Rogers, B. 2000. "The Nature of Value and the Value of Nature: A Philosophical Overview." *International Affairs* 76 (2): 315–23.

Scrinis, G. 1999. *Colonizing the Seed*. Melbourne, Australia: Friends of the Earth.

Shaw, T. M., and S. J. MacLean. 1996. "Civil Society and Political Economy in Contemporary Africa: What Prospects for Sustainable Democracy?" *Journal of Contemporary African Studies* 14 (2) (July): 247–64.

Shiva, V. 1993. *Monocultures of the Mind: Perspectives on Biodiversity and Biotechnology*. London: Zed Books.

UK Food Group. 2003. "GM Crops and Developing Countries." UK Food Group Briefing, July 2003. http://www.ukabc.org/gmcropsbriefing.htm (accessed June 2005).

UN. 2005. "Economic, Social and Cultural Rights: The Right to Food: Report of the Special Rapporteur on the Right to Food," Jean Ziegler, January 2005. New York: United Nations Economic and Social Council.

U.S. Department of State. 2002. "Senator Richard Lugar on Biotechnology: Chairman of Agriculture Committee Advocates New Techniques." U.S. Department of State Information Programs. http://usinfo.state.gov/topical/global/biotech/00012705.htm (accessed December 2002).

WFP (World Food Program). 2004. *World Food Program, 2004* World Hunger Map. Rome: WFP.

Zamora, O. B. 1996. "The Real Roots of Security." *Our Planet* 8 (4) (November 1996), http://www.ourplanet.com.

6

Food and Environmental Security in the Indian Ocean Region

INTERROGATING THE GM DOUBLY GREEN REVOLUTION

RICHARD HINDMARSH

Pressured by global population growth, which currently stands at 6.5 billion, the Indian Ocean Region, dominated by Africa, is a key site of global hunger. Of the estimated 850 million people worldwide classified as malnourished, some 200 million live in sub-Saharan Africa (Berthelot 2005). Many others of the global hungry also live in the Indian Ocean Region, especially in Asian countries, such as India, Bangladesh, Indonesia, Sri Lanka, and Thailand.

Despite many measures to purportedly address hunger and malnutrition, especially since the mid-1940s, with the creation of the high-yielding crop varieties of the so-called Green Revolution, and their transfer as industrial agriculture from the North to the South, hunger and malnutrition have persisted and worsened. Following the decreasing effectiveness of the Green Revolution, the message now, with the birth of modern agricultural genetics and genetically engineered crop varieties, is of a Doubly Green Revolution. Accompanying that message, increasingly, is the message of "food security," which, in the context of hunger, is a message of hope. This chapter critically interrogates these messages and finds that they are wanting, and that the populations most targeted by them will likely remain wanting of food security and, indeed, may be worse off. Instead, other agricultural systems and ways of public participation in technological change seem more appropriate as a message of hope.

"Food security" has many definitions. Most definitions refer to people not living in hunger or starvation,[1] or fear of starvation. This definition seems applicable to very poor or disadvantaged peoples. Other definitions go beyond this basic human need to a ready access at all times to sufficient, safe, and nutritious food that meets dietary needs and food preferences. This appears to represent more affluent peoples, perhaps middle-class ones. Finally, at the other extreme we find definitions such as the one by the U.S. Department of Agriculture that adds onto the second definition "an assured ability to acquire acceptable foods in socially acceptable ways (that is, without resorting to emergency food supplies, scavenging, stealing, or other coping strategies)."[2] The rich countries' definition thus implies the associated need for wealth security, for example, employment security, resource security, and perhaps military security.

But another type of security that food security is embedded in—that applies to all peoples and countries regardless of any wealth or hierarchical status—is "environmental security." But what does environmental security mean? we may ask. Most readers probably think of the health of natural environmental systems or the ability of agricultural ecosystems to provide a long-term and secure basis for farming and the provision of safe and nutritious food. But of course it also alludes to the human environment, the "ready access" part of the food definitions above, or the ability not to resort to coping strategies outside legitimate or socially acceptable strategies, such as access to employment, welfare, or land in order to be able to purchase or grow food.

The first type of food security that relates intimately to healthy biophysical environmental systems is well reflected in the long history of human beings. Initially, many ancient societies found food security through their agriculture, but over time, when some agriculture fell out of step with the (biological) carrying capacity of natural systems to support a given population, environmental disasters occurred. In Sumeria, Mesopotamia, Egypt, India, and China, population growth fueled demands on intensive agriculture to feed populations and/or to generate state income from exports. Salinization and erosion of farmlands resulted under the impact of irrigation systems, deforestation, and overgrazing by domesticated animals (Jacobsen and Adams 1958; Hughes 1998; Zettler 2003). Empires weakened or collapsed. What we might refer to as "food insecurity type 1" occurred: food insecurity due to collapsing ecosystems through the imposition of inappropriate agrifood production systems. The Persians, Greeks, Romans, Vikings in Greenland, Mayans in Central America, Native Americans in the Southwest, and Polynesians on Pacific islands also suffered this type of food insecurity, where hunger and starvation became commonplace.[3]

But of course food insecurity type 1 is now also commonplace in the modern world, with the adverse environmental impacts of intensive industrial agriculture. Industrial agricultural is entirely out of sync with natural systems; indeed, it is based on the purposeful transformation and industrialization of ecosystems in the direct interest of productivity gains for capital accumulation by agribusiness. In short, the integration of agriculture and industry increases economic incentives to push the land beyond its carrying capacity and to also displace the producer as the main site of the relations of production with agroindustry, which these days amounts to vast global conglomerates. These developments have thus introduced "food insecurity type 2," which relates to the social dimensions of the human environment to have ready access to food or the equitable capacity to grow food.

In sum, the history of modern agriculture is grim when it comes to the lot of the direct agricultural producer as well as to the environment. Under the impact of modern agriculture, much restructuring has occurred, especially vertical integration of the agrichemical and seeds sectors, where outcomes have include increased specialization, increased technological dependency on expensive inputs and corporate power, decreased reliance on farm labor due to mechanization and economies of scale, and acceleration of the trend toward fewer and larger farms. Many farming communities and lands in both the North and South have been decimated under the impacts of intensive monoculture agriculture to such a degree that monoculture agriculture is cast as one of three key human activities most impacting on the stability of Earth's natural ecosystems, alongside climate change and deforestation.[4] In the South, at the forefront of such developments was the Green Revolution.

The Green Revolution

The Green Revolution program to transfer industrial agriculture, informed by the design of high-yielding varieties (HYVs), began in 1943 with the Mexican Agricultural Program initiated by the Rockefeller Foundation. Earlier, in the 1920–1940s, the foundation had come to support new agricultural genetics hybridization developments with a U.S. "improved" corn crop (Berlan and Lewontin 1986, 45). Dramatic commercial returns had subsequently resulted from hybrid seed-corn having to be purchased each season by farmers (Kloppenburg 1988). This revitalized the commercial seed industry.

During the Second World War the idea of developing HYVs through genetics for poor countries of the South became negotiated between Rockefeller Foundation president Raymond Fosdick and U.S. Vice President Henry A. Wallace (formerly the secretary of agriculture, 1933–1940). While the public message of what became cast as the "Green Revolution" was to feed the hungry, it seemed that other motives steered these developments: one political and the other economic. Social stability was sought through increased food production and a strengthened middle-class peasantry (Cleaver 1972, 82), to counter the spread of communism in third world countries to make the world safe for profits—in this case, from hybrid seed (Wallace was the founder of the forerunner of Pioneer Hi-Bred) and sales of (Rockefeller) Standard Oil petrochemical products (see also Hindmarsh 2004, 332).

Subsequently, the Green Revolution has been described as a "volatile mix of business, philanthropy, science, and politics" (Kloppenburg 1988, 158), with its implicit goal being to diffuse hybrid HYVs with high response to agrochemicals, especially fertilizers to boost yields. This goal was confirmed when the Rockefeller's International Basic Economy Corporation invested heavily, in 1946, in the only Brazilian hybrid seed-producing firm. Other Western interests followed suit. For example, grain merchant Cargill initiated hybrid seed-corn production in Argentina in 1947 (Hindmarsh 2004, 332–33). Diffusing this program into Kenya in 1956, the U.S. Agency for International Development (USAID) and the Rockefeller Foundation funded a hybrid corn-breeding program under which purchasers of seed were required to buy fertilizers (see also Barkin and Suarez 1986, 29).

By the 1960s, Green Revolution programs had spread to Asia, with fertilizer sales rocketing. In India, they rose almost 30 percent (Shiva 1993). With approximately 90 percent of rice grown in Asia, in 1960 the Rockefeller and Ford foundations founded the International Rice Research Institute (IRRI) in the Philippines. To date, IRRI has produced more than 300 monoculture HYVs (Hindmarsh and Hindmarsh 2002, 3). Their adoption created further lucrative profits for agrochemicals because genetically uniform monocultures were vulnerable to insect and pest attacks, as well as to weed proliferation due to the intensive fertilizer use. In the Philippines, Standard Oil set up 400 agro-service centers for ESSO fertilizer, seeds, pesticides, implements, and extension advice (George 1976, 118–19). To further the enterprise, the Rockefeller and Ford foundations, with other western agencies, created the Consultative Group on International Agricultural Research (CGIAR) in 1971. Its research centers, now known as "Future Harvest Centers," employ more than 8,500 scientists in over 100 countries, and represent about 4 percent of total global expenditure on agricultural research. Sponsors include many countries in the North and key agricultural ones in the South (although in 1993, only 1 percent of funding derived from Southern governments) (Rangnekar 1996), the Ford, Rockefeller, and Kellogg foundations, and international aid and development organizations, including the World Bank (Hindmarsh 2004, 333).

But the promise of the Green Revolution to feed the hungry through increased productivity could only be realized on well-irrigated land by farmers with the financial capability to invest in the high-input package. As Kuyek outlined: "So, while Green Revolution varieties could achieve yields of 10 metric tonnes per hectare (t/ha) at research stations, in practice most farmers only got 3–6 t/ha. Production gains in a particular monoculture crop were also offset by production losses of other staples, vegetables and fodder crops. Even where gains were achieved, the Green revolution varieties were beset by disease and pest troubles that had previously not posed a problem" (2002, 1).

As Rangnekar (1996) has also highlighted: HYV IR8, which launched the Green Revolution because of its high yield potential, suffered from poor quality and a lack of resistance to common rice diseases and pests. However, the new varieties, through intensive promotion and state support, became so widely disseminated that genetic erosion also severely threatened traditional polyculture farming systems in some areas. For example, prior to the diffusion of HYVs, over 100,000 rice varieties thrived in farmer's fields in the Philippines, but by the mid-1980s, only two HYVs occupied 98 percent of that entire rice growing area.

Ecological degradation also resulted from increasing dosages of pesticides, along with salinity problems, soil erosion, and depletion of micronutrients, such as zinc, due to constant application of chemical fertilizers. This reduced yields and nutrition on many Green Revolution lands. Yields are now in wide decline or are stagnating. In addition, land consolidation led to marginal lands being cultivated with further environmental degradation, a situation also reflected in industrial countries (Hindmarsh 2004, 334).

Consequently, while adoption initially created new avenues of profit for large farmers—aided by land consolidation and a trend toward labor saving inputs such as tractors and agrochemicals—small and tenant farmers and landless laborers became severely disadvantaged. Despite a significant increase in agricultural productivity, George reported a widening income gap between rich and poor, which saw increasing tenure displacement, landlessness, unemployment, indebtedness, poverty, cultural breakdown, social conflict, and hunger and malnutrition (1976, 118–19). Such outcomes thus challenged the stated mission of the CGIAR to promote "policies to reduce poverty, improve food security and nutrition, and alleviate pressures on fragile natural resources" (CGIAR n.d.), and thus, notions also of environmental security.

Further challenging the Green Revolution was that eventually agricultural productivity began to decline. To meet that challenge, the CGIAR has embraced the notion of a "Doubly Green Revolution" through biotechnology (Conway 1998). The UN Food and Agriculture Organization (FAO) (2000, 2) offered a conservative version of its promise: "The 'green revolution' was responsible for accelerating food and agricultural, in particular, cereal production. However, the impact of the 'green revolution' is now on the wane. Biotechnology, if properly integrated with other technologies for food production, may offer a means of triggering the next 'green revolution.' It offers great opportunities for enhancing food and agricultural production, quality and nutritional improvement, prevention of pre- and post-harvest losses and bioremediation and environmental improvement."

The Doubly Green Revolution

The new promise is to again increase agrifood production and productivity, but this time through biotechnology, especially through genetically engineered or genetically modified (GM) crops and foods. GM crops will resist viruses, salinity, drought, and herbicides, incorporate naturally occurring bioinsecticides, or be boostered with new levels and concoctions of minerals and vitamins. The new bioindustrial approach to farming—molecular farming—is driven by life sciences conglomerates like Syngenta, Monsanto, and Bayer and by agricultural aid agencies from the North, which, they claim, have the hungry as their moral responsibility. That claim is furthered by the food demands of an estimated additional 85 million people a year, located mainly in the South. Cast as the new miracle crops, GM crops will do all this in a "cleaner and greener" manner than before.

But the policy foundations for the Doubly Green Revolution in the South began to be laid by Northern interests in the late 1980s. In 1989, a World Bank forum held in Canberra, Australia, called Agricultural Biotechnology: Opportunities for International Development shaped the agenda. Participants included western development and aid agencies, the Rockefeller Foundation, biotech and seed TNCs, and representatives of Southern countries housing centers of biodiversity (or genetic resources) alongside CGIAR centers and their gene banks.

The thrust of World Bank prescriptions was that developing countries should concentrate on "orphan" crop research, while the North, at the forefront of biotechnology development, should concentrate on commercially important ones. But, biotechnology transfer was conditional on Western patent systems and voluntary regulatory systems, and on the CGIAR collaborating more with the private sector even though the focus on intellectual property rights contradicted the traditional role of the CGIAR to process information, inventions, processes, biological material, and other research products as public goods (Hindmarsh 2004, 335).

Nearly a decade before this forum, the Rockefeller Foundation had helped lay the technological ground for this policy agenda. In the early 1980s, with GM developing earnestly in the North, the foundation investigated biotechnology prospects for the world's major food crops, and in 1984 began a 15-year "International Program on Rice Biotechnology" (IPRB) in the South. Similar to the earlier European and U.S. network it had incubated to develop molecular biology (Yoxen 1981), the foundation brokered an R&D network to develop and popularize the new molecular rice technological frame. The IPRB dispensed almost US$105 million for its technology generation and application phases (Hindmarsh and Hindmarsh 2002, 7). The first phase lasted seven years and funded research in 46 advanced research institutions, primarily in the United States, Europe, Japan, and Australia. It involved some 700 scientists from over 30 countries, including some 400 Asian scientists. Promising Asian scientists were sent to Northern laboratories that the foundation supported, and funding was provided to Asian facilities that supported them on their return. The network focused on incorporating specialized traits into rice varieties.

Scientific breakthroughs resulted: rice was the first cereal to be regenerated from a protoplast in 1986–1988; a DNA molecular marker map was achieved by 1988, and the first experimental transformation was accomplished in 1988–1990. Rapid progress occurred with host-plant resistance. In 1991, a detailed genetic map of rice—developed at Cornell University with Rockefeller funding—was disseminated to rice breeders worldwide to facilitate improved rice varieties (Rockefeller Foundation 1990). In 1993, the Asian Rice Biotechnology Network (ARBN)—coordinated by IRRI—was established to enhance the biotechnology capacity of national agricultural research systems (NARS) partners.

The second (application) phase focused on research for product development through technology transfer to research institutions and rice breeders. Again, research grantees and fellows were enrolled from North and South. By 1994, the program had supported 130 projects in 26 countries, with 69 located in developing countries (Hindmarsh and Hindmarsh 2002, 9; Hindmarsh 2004, 337). Promotional claims about feeding the hungry continued. The foundation, however, emphasized the technical approach and ignored important socio-political causes of poverty and hunger in the South, such as structural adjustment policies, debt, and inappropriate technology transfer. Also ignored were inclusive participatory approaches that the World Commission for Environment and Development's report *Our Common Future* called for in 1987. Even though the Rockefeller Foundation program admitted that farmers had a deep personal knowledge of farming conditions, a comprehensive assessment of their opinions was dismissed as too expensive (Evenson et al. 1996, 395–96). Contesting low-input alternatives that many small farmers (the majority of farmers in the South) supported were marginalized. In 1999, with the biotechnology rice program well under way, the foundation concluded that its infrastructure-building role was over in Asia and that it was time to turn to Africa.

Fruitful legacies for biodevelopment included India and Korea (as well as China) firmly integrating GM biotechnology into national rice research programs, with the Philippines, Thailand, and Vietnam also being enthusiastic and IRRI setting up the Asian Rice Biotechnology Network to engage in infrastructure building with NARS partners. Additionally, IRRI's 2002–2004 plan was strongly committed to bioproduct development, including herbicide-tolerant rice, in a "partnership" network with development NGOs, extension agencies, and private companies, including the Asia Pacific Seeds Association, of which members included national seed associations, government agencies, and public and private seed entrepreneurs, including biotechnology companies DuPont, RiceTec, Monsanto, and Syngenta (Hindmarsh 2004, 337).

IRRI also began developing "super rice" varieties targeted to produce 20 percent higher yields. By way of contrast, 20–25 percent increases in maize in Brazil were reported from the adoption of low input organic and agroecological practices, and yields in Ethiopia from composted plots rose between three to five times higher than those treated only with chemicals (Parrott and Marsden 2002). Even so, to the CGIAR's Technical Advisory Committee, low- or non- external input systems were inherently unsustainable and "incapable of feeding a growing population" (Rangnekar 1996), such as that in Africa.

Onward, to the Proposed Bio-Africa

Preceding its move to Africa, the Rockefeller Foundation requested the International Service for National Agricultural Research (ISNAR)—the policy and management center of the CGIAR—to analyze opportunities for greater investment in biotechnology research concerning African crops. ISNAR found that African agriresearch capacity depended upon donor agencies and lending institutions such as the World Bank, but was severely limited in funding, skills, and equipment. While international institutes and programs (especially U.S. and European ones) had developed good relations with African research institutes, and while 25 percent of African collaboration involved the CGIAR, biotech resources were scattered and focused on "low tech" applications like genetic markers to improve plant breeding (Komen et al. 2000). To boost biodevelopment, and similar to the Asian program, a focus on priority crops, strong institutes, earlier involvement of donor agencies, public-private sector initiatives, and intellectual property (IP) protection of proprietary technologies was recommended.

In 1999, the foundation began building on the work of its International Program on Rice Biotechnology that had started in Africa at the CGIAR's West Africa Rice Development Association (WARDA, now renamed The Africa Rice Center) to combine the best traits of Asian and African rices to create rice HYVs termed "New Rice for Africa" or "NERICAs" (WARDA 2001). Subsequently, the NERICA Consortium for Food Security in Sub-Saharan Africa was established as the implementing body of a proposed African Rice Initiative to step up dissemination of the new rice. In 2002, following its launch, a report followed called "Now Is the Time: A Plan to Cut Hunger and Poverty in Africa" (2002). Promoting that "judicious deployment of biotechnology and other improved technologies could lead to an agricultural revolution in Africa more dramatic than the Green revolution of the mid-twentieth century" (WARDA 2002, 3), it was endorsed by the Corporate Council on Africa, representing nearly 85 percent of U.S. private sector investment in Africa. Another promoter site of GM is BiotechAfrica.com. It relays rhetorical narratives that aim to orientate policy and normalize the new agricultural biology for development, called, for example, "Modified Crops and Hunger in Africa," "Africa Wrestles with Grim Choice," "How Science Can Save the World's Poor," "A Seed of Hope for Africa," or "Technology That Will Save Billions from Starvation."

These narratives and other ones of western development agencies, life sciences companies, proponent government agencies (for example, agriculture, science, technology, and trade), and free trade advocates embrace several themes. First, GM crops are promoted primarily as having environmental good and human health good, as well as having economic promise. For example, food security will be improved and poverty and hunger will be reduced. The increasing food demands of growing populations will be met through increased productivity, lower production costs and food prices, and improved nutrition. Better yields will be generated variously through varieties that may be drought-resistant, nutrient-rich, more resistant to viruses, insects, or herbicides, or a mix thereof. Here the projected beneficial consequences are targeted to a broad audience. In turn, for the individual farmer biotech varieties will have appeal in being affordable, responsive to local needs, and for subsistence farming. Some varieties may even reduce the need for, and high cost of, agrochemicals and water. In this set of themes, however, the primary reasons for GM crops, for example, profits or the resolution of environmental problems arising from an earlier round of innovations, are hidden. Instead, the conclusion is supposed to be inescapable that the welfare, security, and happiness of society depend on GM crops.

Another theme is based on "conversion" techniques of persuasion, which are designed to nullify negative opinion and reverse hostile attitudes. The main message is that fears concerning biotech are based on speculation rather than scientific facts. This also introduces the theme of scientific authority, which is often used to close controversy in scientific and technological debates (Etzioni-Halevy 1990). Key rhetorical messages employed here are that genetic modification is scientifically sound and environmentally safe, and that GM food is safe and nutritious. In this set of themes, alienating or negative references are avoided or omitted. For example, there is no mention of the intense debate in the North about narrow regulation of environmental release of GM organisms, or the economic and environmental risks of genetic pollution involving gene flow from GM crops to non-GM crops (Traavik 1999, Davies 2004), or adverse impacts on biodiversity and farming cultures from expansion of high-cost monoculture crops.

Yet another theme appeals to governments to look favorably on GM through messages of adverse consequence if GM is not adopted. For example, it is argued that food insecurity is caused by a lack of enabling policies and strategies for developing agricultural biotechnology. This runs onto convergent themes of fear and hope: for example, Africa cannot afford to be excluded or miss the promises of biotechnology; or that biotechnology is an essential part of the "broader solution." Finally, in following the problematizing approach, the solution is given that governments need to be involved in private-public partnerships, adaptation of (self-regulatory) biosafety models, incentive measures, and accessible proprietary models. In this set of themes, alienating or negative references are again avoided or omitted. For example, nothing is said about corporate control of agriculture and "biocolonialism," which builds upon neocolonialism and signals further foreign control of agrifood production as global life sciences conglomerates pursue market expansion through patented GM varieties. In 1996, Robert Fraley, Monsanto's CEO, elaborated, "What you're seeing is not just a consolidation of the seed companies, it's really a consolidation of the entire food chain" (cited in RAFI 1996, 2).

Already, the top ten life sciences companies control some 30 percent of the $23 billion global commercial seed market (ETC Group 2003). Products like Roundup Ready soy emphasize a focus on transgenic seed and in-built genetically engineered tolerance to a company's proprietary herbicides (Huang et al. 2002), where herbicide sales constitute 46.6 percent of world pesticide sales (Agrow 2003). Consumer groups and environmental groups like the Pesticide Action Network Asia Pacific are thus also concerned that GM crops will not only expand environmental degradation and undermine environmental sustainability, but also increase the health impacts on farm workers under the impact of industrial agriculture. The World Health Organization estimates that 25 million cases of acute occupational chemical pesticide poisonings already occur each year in developing countries (CABI Bioscience 2000, 1).

Yet another marginalized concern is the further appropriation of genetic resources from centers of biodiversity in the South to gene banks in the North under the expansion of industrial agriculture (Christie 2001). There is also concern about lack of GM food labeling—especially concerning GM foods with genes inserted from foods considered "unclean," or afforded religious attributes, or from non-food sources not readily identifiable, or of human-origin DNA. Moreover, safety concerns exist about new potential allergens and toxins being introduced into, or existing levels of toxins being increased in, foods by genes inserted from nontraditional food sources. Similar safety concerns involve the lack of surveillance mechanisms to detect whether GM foods may already be causing diseases, like cancer (Carman 2004). Clearly, all these impacts directly challenge notions of food security.

Critics also question a portrayed benefit of GM crop R&D to raise nutrient and mineral levels. They query: Just what is a healthy dose of vitamins and minerals delivered by the planned new GM functional foods? Can't too much of certain vitamins and minerals be just as damaging as too little? Wide criticism emanated about the transgenic beta-carotene enhanced rice, commonly called "Golden Rice," concerning its nutritional value, cultural acceptability, and social usefulness as pro-poor with the 70 patents and 16 material transfer agreements involved (Hindmarsh and Hindmarsh 2002, 19–20).

But, more specifically for Africa, questioning the portrayed African Doubly Green Revolution is that the first Green Revolution failed in Africa because agronomic conditions were mostly unsuitable for intensive monoculture agriculture (Kuyek 2002). HYVs were also unpopular for other reasons, as a letter to the editor of a South African financial newspaper summed up:

> more worrying is the claim by the big biotech companies that GM foods will help solve malnutrition in Africa. The causes of hunger in Africa, even SA [South Africa], are complex: war, poor land management, insecure tenure, land

hunger and planting inappropriate cash crops, such as tobacco, are only some. Genetically engineered seeds will not begin to deal with these. In fact, the higher cost of seeds and agricultural inputs GM crops require will chain African farmers to more debt. GM food is not Africa's savior. The solutions to malnutrition are political, not technological. African governments need to support small farmers to enable them to practice agriculture that is low-cost and high-yield and without the potential dangers to human health and the environment.

(Dieltiens 2000, 11)

For critics, such arguments further interrogate the suitability of unproven high-input technologies in the volatile and complex conditions of Africa, where so many people both farm and are poor. Drawing on agricultural researchers Ezumah and Ezumah (1996), Kuyek stated that barriers to productivity are not so much technical but socio-economic (2002, 3). In adopting the Lusaka Declaration 2002,[5] African consumer leaders agreed. Arguing that GM technology is not a solution for food security in Africa, they asserted that food security needs to be addressed through maximizing existing resources, through tackling distribution problems and promoting local foods that are low-tech and highly resistant, through protecting biodiversity from risks of GM technologies (Tsimese 2003, 4), and through opposing IP rights on genetic resources for food and agriculture. Their key recommendations are that national governments should set up a commission to independently audit the socio-economic impacts of biotechnology and that consumer organizations need to be included in the drafting and revisions of consumer protection legislations.

But with regard to inclusive processes, another problem raised is that through creating dependency on GM technologies, farmers face the likelihood of marginalization from R&D as highlighted in the Rockefellers' Asian rice biotechnology development program (Evenson et al. 1996, 395–96). The emphasis will remain on the expert top-down technical approach that offers only limited perceptions of local problems, and which in the case of many resource controversies, especially GM crops and foods in the North, has stimulated intense contestation. More broadly, the issue of local empowerment in decision-making has become so intense there that a participatory governance turn known as deliberative governance has begun to emerge in many countries internationally, especially in the European Union, in response to the failures of governments to manage industrial, technological, and environmental risks that are increasing despite a global growth in environmental regulatory apparatus. Such phenomena as the thinning ozone layer, chemical and oil pollution, nuclear fallout (for example, Chernobyl), the BSE crisis, GM food crops, and climate change, and their enduring scientific, social, and political uncertainties, have attracted strong pressure to open up expert policy advice and evaluation processes (Beck 1995, Carson 2002, Mayer 2003, Jasanoff 2004, Hindmarsh 2008). Public spaces for more inclusive social negotiation and collective representations and partnership approaches are being generated especially with regard to environmental and natural resource management, but also, increasingly, with regard to science and technology developments. But, what of the participatory turn in Africa?

Local Participation in Africa

Early developments with regard to the contemporary "participatory turn" in Africa were found at the 1998 Symposium of Food Security and Governance in Africa held in Durban (by the Toda Institute for Global Peace and Policy Research and the University of Durban). On one hand, Cyrus Ndiritu (director of the Kenyan Agricultural Research Institute, and later director-general of ISNAR in 2003) advocated molecular science, a stronger technical base, the private sector, investment capital flexibility, and adequate support mechanisms such as policy support and the development of marketing infrastructure in following what I refer to as a "bio-technocratic" policy style. In contradistinction, Elizabeth Gabona (of the Uganda Peace Research and Education Association) stressed an active role for citizens in food security governance for effective policy making in following what I refer to as a civic policy style, now being popularized worldwide among many new participatory policy responses in a number of fields (Abels 2005, Hindmarsh 2007).

Moving along to 2004, pro-biotechnology voice Florence Wambugu[6]—in arguing that the poor, especially women, needed empowering through democratic governance and human rights—opted for consultative processes that emphasized public acceptance of biotechnological innovations though farmer extension workers (2004, 239). But such consultation reflects the deficit model of science communication, the top-down public understanding of science model, that sets out to ameliorate a perceived deficit in public understandings without attending to the kinds of knowledge and understanding that the public can only bring to scientific issues (Wynne 2001).

Civic NGOs increasingly reject the deficit model and instead are adopting the line set earlier by Gabona and others at the 1998 Symposium of Food Security and Governance. They are becoming increasingly engaged in Africa over the issue of GM crops, and their pressure has already seen bodies supportive of biotechnology beginning to engage with the idea of more inclusive participatory forums. For example, the International Food Policy Research Institute (IFPRI) and the Food, Agriculture, and Natural Resource Policy Analysis Network (FANRPAN) conducted a multiple stakeholder initiative in Johannesburg in April 2003. Called the Regional Policy Dialogue on Biotechnology, Agriculture, and Food Security in Southern Africa, the corporate- and government-sponsored bodies stressed that in the complex debate about technological, political, economic, social, and scientific considerations, "civil society can provide much of the expertise and creative thinking that is required to identify needs, generate innovative policy options and implement agreements." It seems, however, that this initiative has progressed very slowly.

Another dialogue initiative, more inclusive of civil society organizations (CSOs), occurred in May 2005, also in Johannesburg. Called "Look, Listen and Learn: Promoting the Use of CSOs' Evidence in Policies for Food Security: An Action Research Project in Southern Africa," the initiative was the concept of the

Southern African Regional Poverty Network, the Overseas Development Institute, and FANRPAN. It aims to deepen the involvement of CSOs in food security policy processes with the increasing awareness of CSOs as an important component of policy through hands-on and grassroots experience.[7] In October 2005, yet another multi- stakeholder meeting, called "Food Security and Biotechnology," was held in Arrca, Ghana. It brought together both proponents and critics of biotechnology from 20 African countries. Highlighted by critics was the need for better information for the public on genetically modified organisms (GMOs), the need for labeling of GMOs in food products being imported into Africa, the need for GM-free zones to control for contamination, the need for effective biosafety legislation, and the need for "good governance" based on democratic principles and equitable distribution of resources and opportunities.

Conclusions

In reflecting upon the experience of the Green Revolution, upon monopoly corporate trends in the life sciences and the specter of biocolonialism for Africa, upon the associated environmental and social problems of GM agrifood production, and upon the overly technocratic activities and policy processes of GM infrastructure agents, it is increasingly apparent that the promotion of the GM "Doubly Green Revolution" as a moral imperative is more for economic reasons than for satisfying any sense of benevolence. Under these circumstances, it is more likely that the GM "Doubly Green Revolution" will increase the adverse impacts and failures of industrial agriculture than demonstrate broad benefits for the populous majority of poor farmers and rural society. Such impacts would offer severe consequences for developing countries of the Indian Ocean Region already suffering adverse impacts from inappropriate technology transfer and failed development. They diverge from both biotechnology and local narratives of food and environmental security. Indeed, they significantly contradict them.

To counteract such consequences and achieve better outcomes for food and environmental security in Africa, low input agriculture and deliberative governance avenues offer much: they empower local peoples and their valuable farming knowledge and offer creative, open, informed, accountable, and partnership-driven decision making. The threat remains though of their marginalization such that elite agrifood production systems continue to pursue what many consider to be inappropriate agricultural technologies that divert attention and valuable resources from the more fundamental problems affecting small farmers, and other more practical avenues to achieve food and environmental security.

NOTES

1. See: UN's Food and Agriculture Organization (2003), http://en.wikipedia.org/wiki/Food_security (accessed December 10, 2006).

2. Ibid.

3. See: http://www.crf-usa.org/bria/bria18_4a.htm (accessed September 18, 2006).

4. See: http://en.wikipedia.org/wiki/Food_security (accessed December 10, 2006).

5. See: http://www.greens.org/s-r/31/31-02.html (accessed September 20, 2006).

6. Florence Wambugu is affiliated with the Africa Harvest Biotech Foundation International, and is also a member of the Private Sector Committee of CGIAR, the DuPont Biotech Advisory Panel-USA, vice-chair of the African Biotechnology Stakeholders Forum (http://www.politicalfriendster.com/ShowConnectionphp?id1=5496&id2=3929 [accessed November 13, 2007]), and has worked for Monsanto (http://en.wikipedia.org/wiki/Florence_Wambugu [accessed November 13, 2007]).

7. See: http://www.sarpn.org.za/documents/d0001647/ODI_Nat-Consultative-Meetings_July2005.pdf (accessed January 10, 2006).

REFERENCES

Abels, G. 2005. "The Long and Winding Road from Asilomar to Brussels: Science, Politics and the Public in Biotechnology Regulation." *Science as Culture,* Special Issue, "Recombinant Regulation," ed. R. Hindmarsh and H. Gottweis 14 (4): 339–53.

Agrow. 2003. "Agrochemical Sales Flat in 2002." *World Crop Protection News,* February 26. http://ipm.osu.edu/trans/043_141.htm (accessed February 10, 2006).

Barkin, D., and B. Suarez. 1986. "The Transnational Role in Mexico's Seed Industry," *Ceres* 114:27–31.

Beck, V. 1995. *Ecological Enlightenment: Essays on the Politics of the Risk Society.* New Jersey: Humanities Press.

Berlan, J-P., and R. Lewontin. 1986. "The Political Economy of Corn." *Monthly Review* 38:35–47.

Berthelot, J. 2005. "The WTO: Food for Thought?" *Le Monde Diplomatique,* December. http://mondediplo.com/2005/12/10food (accessed April 14, 2006).

Business Times. 2001. "Asia's Biotechnology Sector Offers Investment Opportunities: Report." *Business Times,* November 20:3.

CABI Bioscience. 2000. "Pesticides: Is There An Alternative?" CABI press release, February 29.

Carman, J. 2004. "Is GM Food Safe to Eat?" In *Recoding Nature: Critical Perspectives on Genetic Engineering,* ed. R. Hindmarsh and G. Lawrence, 82–93. Sydney: UNSW Press.

Carson, L. 2002. "Community Consultation in Environmental Policy Making." *The Drawing Board: An Australian Review of Public Affairs* 3 (1): 1–13.

CGIAR. N.d. http://www.cgiar.org (accessed October 20, 2005).

Christie, J. 2001. "Enclosing the Biodiversity Commons: Bioprospecting or Biopiracy?" In *Altered Genes II: The Future?,* ed. R. Hindmarsh, G. Lawrence, 53–65. Melbourne: Scribe.

Cleaver, H. 1972. "The Contradiction of the Green Revolution." *Monthly Review* 24: 80–111.

Conway, G. 1998. *The Doubly Green Revolution: Food for All in the Twenty-First Century.* Ithaca, N.Y.: Comstock.

Davies, P. 2004. "Gene Flow and Genetically Engineered Crops." In *Recoding Nature: Critical Perspectives on Genetic Engineering,* ed. R. Hindmarsh, G. Lawrence, 71–81. Sydney: UNSW Press.

Dieltiens, V. 2000. "GM No Answer for Africa." *Financial Mail* (South Africa), August 11, p. 11.

Elster, J., ed. 1998. *Deliberative Democracy.* New York: Cambridge Univ. Press.

ETC Group. 2003. "Oligopoly, Inc.: Concentration in Corporate Power: 2003." *ETC Group Communique* 82:9.

Etzioni-Halevy, E. 1990. "The Relative Autonomy of Elites: The Absorption of Protest and Social Progress in Western Democracies." In *Rethinking Progress: Movements, Forces, and Ideas at the end of the 20th Century,* ed. J. Alexander and P. Sztompka, 202–26. Boston: Unwin Hyman.

Evenson, R., R. Herdt, and M. Hossain, eds. 1996. *Rice Research in Asia: Progress and Priorities.* Cambridge: CAB International in association with IRRI.

Ezumah. H., and N. Ezumah. 1996. "Agricultural Development in the Age of Sustainability: Crop Production." In *Sustaining the Future: Economic, Social and Environmental Change in*

Sub-Saharan Africa, ed. G. Benneh, W. Morgan, and J. Uitto, 215–44. Tokyo: United Nations University.

Gabriel, D. 2005. "Serious Concerns in Africa over GMOs Fuels Demands for Labelling and Safety Regulations." *Black Britain,* October 31. http//www.blackbritain.co.uk/Feature/details/22/Africa/ (accessed November 12, 2007).

George, S. 1976. *How the Other Half Dies.* London: Penguin.

Hindmarsh, R. 2004. "GM Policy Networks in Asia: The Discursive Politics of the 'Doubly Green Revolution.'" In *Biotechnology: Between Commerce and Civil Society,* ed. N. Stehr, 321–48. New Brunswick, N.J.: Transaction.

———. 2008. *Edging Towards BioUtopia: A New Politics of Reordering Life and the Democratic Challenge.* Perth, Australia: UWA Press.

———. 2008. "Environment, Water and Energy for the 21st Century: The Role of Deliberative Governance for the Knowledge Society." In *Knowledge Policy: Challenge for the 21st Century*, ed. G. Hern, D. Rooney, D. Wright, 189–203. Camberley, Surrey: Edward Elgar.

Hindmarsh, S. 2004. "Resistance in Asia: Voices of the People's Caravan." In *Recoding Nature: Critical Perspectives on Genetic Engineering,* ed. R. Hindmarsh and G. Lawrence, 202–20. Sydney: UNSW Press.

Hindmarsh, S., and R. Hindmarsh. 2002. "Laying the Molecular Foundations for GM Rice Across Asia." PAN Policy Research and Analysis Consultancy Report (May). Malaysia: Pesticide Action Network Asia Pacific.

Huang, J., C. Pray, and S. Rozell. 2002. "Enhancing Crops to Feed the Poor." *Nature* 418:675–84.

Hughes, D. 1998. "The Ancient Roots of Our Ecological Crisis." In *Environmental Ethics: Divergence and Convergence,* 2nd ed. ed. R. Botzler and S. Armstrong, 147–56. Boston: McGraw-Hill.

International Seed Federation. 1997. "Feeding the 8 Billion and Preserving the Planet." http://www.worldseed.org/ (accessed March 15, 2006).

Jacobsen, T., and R. Adams. 1958. "Salt and Silt in Ancient Mesopotamian Agriculture: Progressive Changes in Soil Salinity and Sedimentation Contributed to the Breakup of Past Civilizations." *Science* 128:1251–58.

Jasanoff, S. 2004. "Science and Citizenship: A New Synergy." *Science and Public Policy* 31(2): 90–94.

Kloppenburg, J. 1988. *First the Seed: The Political Economy of Plant Biotechnology, 1492–2000.* Cambridge: Cambridge Univ. Press.

Komen, J., J. Mignouna, and H. Webber (ISNAR). 2000. "Biotechnology in African Agricultural Research: Opportunities for Donor Organizations." Briefing Paper 43, February. The Hague: ISNAR.

Kuyek, D. 2002. "Genetically Modified Crops in African Agriculture: Implications for Small Farmers." Genetic Resources Action International. http://www.grain.org/publications/africa-gmo-2002-en.cfm (accessed December 8, 2005).

Mayer, S. 2003. "Science Out of Step with the Public: The Need for Public Accountability of Science in the UK." *Science and Public Policy* 30 (3): 177–81.

Parrott, N., and T. Marsden. 2002. "Real Green Revolution, Organic and Agroecological Farming in the South." Greenpeace Environmental Trust. http://dom01.dominohosting.com.au/magus/ofa.nsf/objects/OFAupdate0302/$file/OFAup date0302.htm (accessed October 17, 2006).

Partnership to Cut Hunger and Poverty in Africa. 2002. *Now Is the Time: A Plan to Cut Hunger and Poverty in Africa.* Washington D.C: Partnership to Cut Hunger and Poverty in Africa.

Rangnekar, D. 1996. "CGIAR: Agricultural Research for Whom?" *The Ecologist* 26 (6): 259–71.

Rockefeller Foundation. 1990. *A History.* http://www.rockfound.org/about_us/history/1990_1999.shtml (accessed November 20, 2006).

RAFI (Rural Advancement Foundation International). 1996. "The Life Industry." RAFI Communiqué, September.

Shiva, V. 1993. "Can Africa Afford a Green Revolution?" *Choices* 2 (2): 25/27.

Traavik, T. 1999. "Too Early May Be Too Late: Ecological Risks Associated with the Use of Naked DNA as a Biological Tool for Research, Production and Therapy." Research Report for DN 1999–1, Directorate for Nature Management, Tröndheim, Norway.

Tsimese, L. 2003. "Biotechnology Against Food Security: The Choice for Africa." *OpenDemocracy* (September 4): 1–4. www.openDemocracy.net (accessed January 19, 2007).

UN Food and Agriculture Organization. 2000. *Twenty-Fifth FAO Regional Conference for Asia and the Pacific: Implications and Development of Biotechnology.* FAO, APRC/oo/5.

Wambugu, F. 2004. "Africa's New Focus in Establishing Food Security, Agricultural Biotechnology: Finding Common International Goals." National Agricultural Biotechnology Council Report 16: 233–41.

WARDA (West Africa Rice Development Association). 2001. "Consortium Formed to Rapidly Disseminate New Rice for Africa." http://www.warda.cgiar.org/News/NERICAConsortium.htm (accessed November 20, 2006).

———. 2002. "Ivorian Prime Minister Launches New African Rice Initiative." March. http://www.warda.cgiar.org/News/ARI%20Launch.htm (accessed October 11, 2006).

Whitfield, K. 2001. "Digesting the GM Debate." *Supermarket to Asia* 5 (1): 36–37/39.

Wynne, B. 2001. "Creating Public Alienation." *Science as Culture* 10:445–81.

Yoxen, E. 1981. "Life as a Productive Force: Capitalising upon Research in Molecular Biology." In *Science, Technology and the Labour Process: Marxist Studies.* ed. L. Levidow and R. Young, 66–122. London: CSE Books.

Zettler, R. 2003. "Reconstructing the World of Ancient Mesopotamia: Divided Beginnings and Holistic History." *Journal of the Economic and Social History of the Orient* 46 (1): 3–45.

7 Plundered Waters

SOMALIA'S MARITIME RESOURCE
INSECURITY

CLIVE SCHOFIELD

Introduction

The demise of Somalia as a functioning state and the ongoing, seemingly endless conflict there is well documented. What is less well acknowledged and understood is the impact the failure of the Somali state has had offshore, particularly in environmental and marine resource terms.

Most discussion of Somalia's waters has tended to focus on the deterioration in the maritime security environment and particularly the threat to shipping posed by piracy. However, Somalia's enormous, resource-rich maritime domain is also threatened by rampant illegal, unreported, and unregulated (IUU) fishing on the part of foreign fishing vessels keen to exploit the absence of offshore surveillance and enforcement efforts. These activities have resulted in serious concerns that the marine environment and living resources in question are subject to overexploitation with a consequent danger of collapse.

This chapter will first provide a brief overview of the Somali geopolitical context, as this is critical to an understanding of the maritime security situation offshore. Somalia's maritime claims and resources will then be examined. Aspects of Somalia's maritime insecurity will then be explored as a prelude to an assessment of the environmental, economic, and security threat posed by IUU fishing in Somali waters. Finally, the Somali case will be set in its wider Indian Ocean context.

Fragmented and Failed

In many ways Somalia is the classic "failed state"—a recognized state in international legal and diplomatic theory but exhibiting none of the characteristics of a functioning state in practice. Following the fall of the Siad Barre dictatorship in 1991, Somalia collapsed as a functioning state and has subsequently been characterized by chronic political instability driven by deep-seated, and continuing, clan rivalries, leading to anarchic factional violence with appalling humanitarian and developmental consequences.

However, the common portrayal of Somalia as an ungoverned, and ungovernable, territory does not represent the whole truth. While Somalia has undergone profound political and territorial fragmentation and there are certainly large areas of the country that appear to be effectively ungoverned, this view is at least partially misleading. A closer examination reveals that distinct parts of Somalia have, in fact, enjoyed a degree of relative stability and security. This, in turn, has had a significant impact on management and security offshore.

Of particular significance in this context is the "Republic of Somaliland," located in northern Somalia, which declared its "independence" from Somalia on May 18, 1991. Ironically, this self-declared entity possesses most, if not all, of the key attributes of statehood that Somalia itself lacks (Hoyle 2000, 88). Nevertheless, Somaliland has failed to secure recognition for its de facto independence from any government. To the east of Somaliland is another autonomous territory, the self-styled "Puntland State of Somalia." The extent of the jurisdiction of the Puntland authorities in uncertain, however, as territorial disputes exist with Somaliland to the west and the extent of Puntland's control, as opposed to its claims, to the south is unclear.

The international community has proved deeply reluctant to countenance formal recognition of the fragmentation of Somalia and has instead backed efforts toward national reconciliation. Some progress toward this goal has been achieved, and a Transitional Federal Government (TFG) was formed in Djibouti under UN auspices in August 2000. The TFG has, however, proved to be deeply divided and,

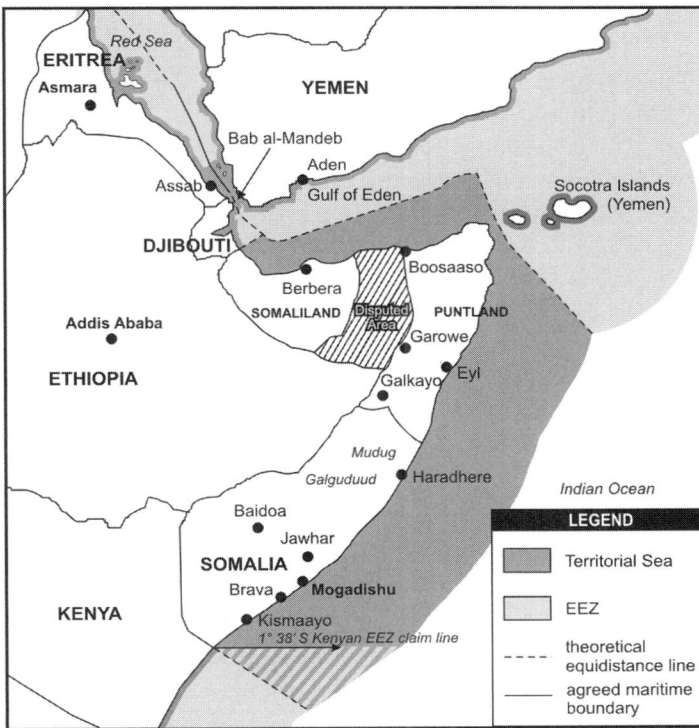

Map 7.1 Map of Somalia Coastline.
Source: Clive Schofield.

prior to December 2006, realistically controlled no more than a small area around the town of Baidoa, with the remainder of Somalia, including the Somali capital Mogadishu, remaining in the grip of a variety of clans, gangs, and warlords (with the exception of Somaliland and Puntland).

This scenario altered considerably from mid-2006 with the rise of a loose coalition of Islamic forces, gathered under the collective banner of the Union of Islamic Courts (UIC). The influence of the UIC spread rapidly through southern Somalia, and UIC forces seized control of Mogadishu from the militias in September 2006. This prompted a counterattack by TFG forces comprising a variety of militias, backed by intervening Ethiopian troops and supported by U.S. air strikes. By the end of 2006, TFG and Ethiopian forces had largely defeated their UIC opponents and entered Mogadishu.

However, the Islamic militias of the UIC have not been comprehensively vanquished. Furthermore, the deep divisions that characterized the TFG prior to the crisis provoked by the rise of the UIC have not been resolved and appear likely to reemerge. Indeed, there are strong indications that the warlords and their militias have reasserted themselves, and insurgent attacks have proliferated despite the deployment of the initial elements of an 8,000-strong regional peace support mission (Fletcher 2007). It therefore appears unlikely that the TFG can be transformed into a genuinely viable Somali-wide central government in the foreseeable future.

Maritime Somalia

At around 3,300 kilometers, Somalia's coastline is the longest on the African continent. As a result of this long coastal front, Somalia's potential maritime claims have been estimated at 1.2 million square kilometers (Jennings 2001, 404), though this figure is uncertain, primarily due to the lack of maritime boundaries agreed with neighboring states. Somalia signed the United Nations Convention on the Law of the Sea (LOSC) and ratified it on July 24, 1989. Somalia's claims to maritime jurisdiction are, however, problematic.

In particular, according to Article 1 (1) of Somalia's Law No. 57 on the Territorial Sea and Ports of September 10, 1972, Somalia claims a territorial sea "to the extent of 200 nautical miles," as compared with the international norm of 12 nautical miles (LOSC, Article 3). This excessive territorial sea claim has resulted in international protest on the part of the United States (Roach and Smith 1996, 158–61).

It is notable, however, that Somalia's 200-mile territorial sea claim predates LOSC and Somalia's signature and ratification of that convention. In fact Somalia is not alone in making such a claim, as a number of coastal states made analogous claims at a similar stage in the development of the law of the sea. These claims reflect the developing aspirations of coastal states at that time for extended jurisdiction over offshore resources (Prescott and Schofield 2005, 34). These objectives were largely met through the introduction of the 200 nautical mile breadth exclusive economic zone (EEZ) within LOSC. As a result, many 200 nautical mile territorial sea claims have been "rolled back" to the 12 nautical mile rule (Roach and Smith 1996, 151–53). A number of the states that retain 200 nautical mile territorial sea claims, such as Liberia and Sierra Leone, have, in common with Somalia, suffered from serious and long-standing economic and governance problems that have hampered any change to formal legal claims.

Similarly, the absence of a functioning central government means that Somalia has yet to delimit a maritime boundary with any of its maritime neighbors—Djibouti to the west, Yemen to the north and northeast, and Kenya to the south. When the time eventually comes for Somalia to negotiate these maritime boundaries, it seems likely that there is scope for dispute with Yemen and Kenya. The opposite coasts of Somalia and Yemen on the Gulf of Aden both have smooth configurations and are of comparable length. Consequently, there appears to be no reason to regard delimitation on the basis of an equidistance line to deliver an inequitable result (Prescott and Schofield 2005, 465). However, the proximity of Yemen's Socotra Islands to the northeast of the Horn of Africa would have a "significant blocking effect" on Somalia's claims were equidistance to be applied, and this may prove an obstacle to agreement (Bradley et al. 2000, 288). This is despite the fact that it is difficult to envisage these large and populated islands not legitimately claiming full continental shelf and EEZ rights.

With regard to the potential Kenya-Somalia maritime boundary to the south, a boundary based on a line of equidistance would trend in a broadly south-easterly direction because of the alignment of the coastline and the presence of small Somali islands in the vicinity of the terminus of the land boundary on the coast (Prescott and Schofield 2005, 465–66). Such a boundary alignment would be disadvantageous to Kenya. As a result, Kenya has defined a unilateral EEZ limit that runs due east along the 1°38′ south parallel and thus substantially to the north of a theoretical equidistance line (Bradley et al. 2000, 192, 288). Such a claim is unlikely to be acceptable to Somalia if and when the boundary comes to be negotiated.

Somalia's waters also lie in close proximity to key shipping lanes passing through the region. Of particular importance in this context is the Red Sea "choke point" of the Bab al-Mandeb Strait through which, it was estimated in 2004, around 3 million barrels of oil passes per day (EIA, n.d.).

Offshore Riches

Somalia has a relatively narrow continental shelf of around 50 kilometers breadth and consequently limited potential for seabed oil and gas resources. In contrast, Somalia's marine living resources are understood to be relatively abundant but traditionally under-utilized (FAO, n.d.). Although the Indian Ocean as a whole has generally not been regarded as highly productive in terms of fisheries, thanks to the existence of the Somalia Current marine ecosystem and its associated periodic but intense upwelling of nutrient-rich cold waters, Somali offshore areas can be viewed as especially productive and attractive (UNEP 2005, 45).

Any discussion of the state of Somalia's marine fisheries is hampered, however, by lack of up-to-date and accurate statistics. Perhaps, unsurprisingly, catch reports are generally unreliable, fragmentary, or nonexistent. Nonetheless, the FAO provides an assessment of Somalia's fisheries in a National Fishery Sector Overview, from which the following statistics can be drawn and a picture of the state of Somalia's fisheries built up (FAO n.d.).

On the basis of these admittedly "rough estimates," allied to a number of surveys conducted in the 1970s and 1980s, the FAO has suggested that Somalia's pelagic fish stocks may be capable of supporting a sustainable annual catch of around 200,000 tonnes. Other estimates as to overall annual sustainable potential marine production from Somali waters are rather less conservative, with figures of 380,000–500,000 tonnes (UNEP 2005, 45). Key large pelagic species include tunas, largely yellowfin, longtail, bonito, and skipjack, as well as big mackerels, such as Spanish mackerel. The seasonal abundance of these species varies considerably, reflecting their migratory patterns. A number of smaller pelagic stocks are also caught, such as the Indian oil sardinella, rainbow sardines, scads, and anchovies. Inshore, Somali waters also support a wide range of demersal species, with accessible stocks estimated at 40,000 tonnes per annum. Elasmobranchs (sharks and rays) are estimated at 30,000 tonnes per annum, and there are spiny and deep sea lobsters as well. With respect to spiny lobsters, which occur all along the Somali coastline, exploitation by the artisanal sector is understood to be light. Exploitation levels of deep sea lobsters by the industrial sector is unknown but thought to be heavy (FAO, n.d.) The FAO estimated that in 2003 Somalia's overall fish catch for direct human consumption stood at 18,000 tonnes (statistics from FAO, n.d.).

Somalia's artisanal fishery is concentrated in inshore areas. Further offshore, oceanic fisheries are dominated by distant water fishing nations (DWFNs). The presence of these distant water fleets fishing illegally in Somalia's largely unprotected waters has led to competition and conflict with Somali groups as well as concerns over overexploitation and the potential for collapse in the stocks of key species.

Danger Zone

Maritime Somalia is, however, an especially hazardous place to operate. In particular, Somali waters are renowned for maritime piracy and armed robbery at sea, with over 700 such incidents occurring in the period 1993–2005 (von Hoesslin 2006). Although there was a noticeable decline in piracy over recent years, 2005 witnessed a surge in the number of reported piracy attacks in the region. As a result, Somali waters "topped the piracy high risk areas," with 35 attacks taking place (16 actual attacks and 19 attempted), as compared with only two incidents in the previous year and three in 2003 (IMB 2007, 5, 24). It is worth bearing in mind in this context that reported attacks are estimated to represent only around one-third of the number of attacks that actually take place. The same period also saw a "dramatic increase in kidnap and ransom" activities off the Somali coast (von Hoesslin 2006). As a result of these seizures, as of November 2005 over 130 crew members were being held hostage as negotiations over their release continued (IMB 2007, 24).

Consequently, the International Maritime Bureau's Piracy Reporting Centre recommends that shipping not calling on Somali ports should keep "as far away as possible from the Somali coast," ideally more than 75 nautical miles or even as much as 200 nautical miles offshore and thus well out of VHF range of land (IMB

2007, 16). Strictly speaking, "piracy" within the meaning of Article 101 of LOSC only applies to acts taking place within the EEZ or on the high seas. The term is therefore inappropriate for most attacks taking place within Somalia's (overly broad) territorial sea. However, the IMB has adopted a more all-encompassing definition of piracy that applies wherever such an action takes place, and this broader definition is used for the purposes of the present discussion (IMB 2007, 2).

These incidents included attacks on a wide range of shipping, from relatively small vessels, such as traditional dhows and fishing trawlers, to larger merchant vessels. The latter category included cargo vessels charted by the UN to deliver humanitarian aid to Somalia, tankers, and, perhaps most strikingly, an audacious attack on a luxury cruise ship, the *Seabourn Spirit,* on November 5, 2005 (see Lehr and Lehmann 2007, 2–5).

The spatial distribution of maritime security incidents offshore Somalia is uneven, and there is a direct relationship between the internal political situation in Somalia and the maritime security situation offshore. In the north of the country, the self-proclaimed Republic of Somaliland has a firm grip on its claimed territory, including coastal areas, and its coast guard has proved to be effective in combating piracy off Somaliland's shores. This is evidenced by the fact that in the midst of the surge in piracy-related incidents in 2005, there were no reports of piracy attacks off the coast of Somaliland (Hansen and Mesoy 2006, 5).

To the northeast, the Puntland authorities have also established a force to undertake maritime patrols—the Puntland Coast Guard. Following training from a private maritime security company, the UK-based Hart Group, substantial progress was made in combating piracy off Puntland. However, the Puntland Coast Guard is a small force facing a large challenge. Additionally, the Hart Group was forced to withdraw following internal conflicts in Puntland in 2001–2002, leading to deterioration in the effectiveness of the coast guard (Hansen and Mesoy 2006, 5–6).

Further south, at least two major pirate groups or criminal syndicates exist, as well as numerous small groups. The two larger groups are the so-called Somali Marines, operating from bases (particularly the port of Harardhere) along the coasts of Mudug and Galguduud, located north of Mogadishu, and the self-styled "Somali National Volunteer Coastguard," based on Koyema Island in southern Somalia, south of Kismaayo (von Hoesslin 2006; Lehr and Lehmann 2007, 5).

The rise of the Islamic movement in 2006 transformed this situation. The spread of the UIC's influence throughout much of southern Somalia from mid-2006 achieved the seemingly near impossible task of establishing substantial stability in these areas, and this development also had a significant impact on law and order offshore. The UIC publicly "declared war" on piracy on the basis that such acts are contrary to Islamic law (IMB 2007, 24). Although increased international patrolling coupled with precautionary measures on the part of passing ships also helped to reduce the number of piracy attacks in Somali waters, the UIC's crackdown clearly had a dramatic impact and was credited with virtually eradicating piracy off southern Somalia in the second half of 2006 (IMB 2007, 17, 24–25).

It appears though that, now that the UIC has been largely defeated (at least for the present), there has been a resurgence of piracy off southern Somalia. This is unsurprising, given the TFG's track record of exerting control over the militias that have reemerged along the coast (IMB 2007, 24).

Maritime Somalia is also characterized by drug and gun running, as well as by its being a conduit for people-smuggling operations, especially via Somaliland and Puntland to Yemen, which frequently result in significant loss of life when the over-loaded and/or dilapidated boats sink (Adow 2004). Furthermore, significant maritime terrorism attacks have taken place in the vicinity of Somali waters, notably the ramming of the USS *Cole* in Aden in October 2000, and the suicide attack on the French tanker *Limburg* off Yemen in October 2002. These incidents have under-scored international unease over the security of shipping passing through the region (Schofield 2004, 47).

Plundered Waters

The comprehensive failure of the Somali state, coupled with enduring internal conflict, has had a profound impact on the exploitation of Somalia's offshore living resources. Somalia's long coastline and extensive zones of maritime jurisdiction are largely unmanaged and effectively unprotected. Although Somalia's Law No. 57 states, at Article 5 (1), that "fishing in the territorial sea and regular transportation of persons and goods between Somali ports are reserved for vessels flying the Somali flag, and other authorized vessels," with no functioning state there have been no recognized maritime security forces to monitor or enforce this requirement.

This scenario, allied to the presence of abundant, high-value stocks, has proved an irresistible attraction to foreign distant water fishing fleets. Despite the evident dangers of operating there, large numbers of opportunistic foreign fishing vessels have sought to exploit Somalia's resource-rich and unpoliced maritime spaces through IUU fishing operations. Indeed, it has been estimated that "700 foreign-owned vessels are fully engaged in unlicensed fishing in Somali waters" (FAO n.d.). These vessels have been able to exploit Somalia's offshore living resources with "near impunity" (Jennings 2001, 403).

Foreign fishing vessels reportedly hail from within the immediate region, including Egypt, Kenya, Pakistan, Saudi Arabia, Sri Lanka, and Yemen, and from further afield, including Belize, France, Honduras, Japan, South Korea, Spain, and Taiwan (Coffen-Smout n.d.; Jennings 2001, 411). In this context Belize has been employed as a flag of convenience for French and Spanish fishing concerns in order to circumvent European Union rules prohibiting fishing by member states in Somalia's maritime areas (Jennings 2001, 418).

The activities of the foreign fishermen in Somali waters are clearly conducted in defiance of international law. The waters within which they operate are claimed by a sovereign coastal state and, as that state has no recognized government, there is no authority with the right to license foreign fishing. Consequently, all fishing in Somali-claimed waters by foreign vessels is illegal (Jennings 2001, 415).

Estimates as to the value of IUU catches from Somalia's maritime jurisdiction vary from in excess of US$90 million to US$300 million per year (von Hoesslin

2006; Lehr and Lehmann 2007, 13, quoting UN figures). These activities are taking place against a backdrop of poverty, famine, and humanitarian crisis in Somalia. The irony of this situation is not lost on the Somalis, with one Somali academic commenting: "Foreigners are supplying less fresh protein to Somalia [in aid] than they are taking from Somali waters" (quoted in Jennings 2001, 407).

Pirates or Protectors?

The presence of foreign poachers has led to confrontation between foreign fishers and local fishermen, especially where the former have been tempted inshore and are competing for the same resources. Coastal communities have witnessed large, technologically advanced, and often well-armed foreign fishing vessels operating in a destructive manner, without regard for the marine environment or sustainability of stocks, and out-competing their own generally smaller and under-equipped boats. In response they have sought to protect "their" rights, and Somalia has experienced what has been described as the effective "decentralization of fisheries enforcement to the grass-roots level" (Coffen-Smout n.d.).

Numerous foreign fishing vessels have been "arrested" or simply attacked. Some illegal fishing vessels have reportedly tried to counter attempted boardings by employing high-pressure or boiling water hoses. These devices allegedly also have been used to chase local fishermen away from productive fishing grounds, and there have been reports of foreign fishers destroying gear on Somali boats and attempting to ram and sink or disable local fishing vessels. These violent clashes give every indication of escalating, with both sides reportedly arming themselves with automatic weapons (Jennings 2001, 409–10; Lehr and Lehmann 2007, 13–14; Mwangura 2005). The motivation behind many attacks is the desire on the part of Somali fishermen and local interests to stop—or at least to gain some benefit from—the illegal and unchecked exploitation of Somalia's offshore resources by foreign poachers. Other attacks, however, represent piracy in a more traditional sense.

However, just as IUU fishing is contrary to international law, the actions of local Somali groups are similarly problematic. This is the case because such enforcement action is clearly not being taken by or under the auspices of the competent authorities of the Somali state, as these don't exist. Even more established sub-national entities, such as Somaliland and Puntland, "do not have legal standing to take actions against foreign fleets" (Jennings 2001, 415). Consequently, illegal foreign fishers habitually label their Somali opponents as "pirates" (Coffen-Smout n.d.). There is a Somali proverb about a "she-camel who bites other camels but at the same time screams as if she were the one being bitten" (hashu iyadaa geella cunayasa cabaadaysana), and some say it is apt to describe the complaints of these foreign poachers (Kulmiye 2001).

IUU fishing therefore at once serves as both justification for local enforcement action, where coastal communities seek to protect their livelihoods and perceived legitimate property rights, and as a pretext for piracy. Resolution of the IUU fishing problem has thus been directly linked to addressing the piracy threat around the Horn of Africa (Hansen and Mesoy 2006, 13).

A further irony is that the waters around the Horn of Africa are among the most intensively patrolled in the world. In the post 9/11 security environment, the existence of a failed state such as Somalia translates, in Washington's view, into large areas of effectively ungoverned territory that terrorist organizations could exploit, especially where arms are readily available and border controls are lax or nonexistent. The bombing of the U.S. embassies in Kenya and Tanzania in August 1998 and the Paradise Hotel in Mombasa in November 2002 highlighted the scope for terrorism in the region. The known presence of al-Qaeda-linked Islamic terrorist organizations, such as al-Itthad al-Islamiya, combined with the fact that the missiles used in the Mombasa attack are widely believed to have reached Kenya from Yemen by way of Somalia, underscored U.S. concerns (Schofield 2004, 46). With this in mind, the United States established the Combined Task Force—Horn of Africa (CTF-HOA) in December 2002, with a base established in Djibouti in May 2003.

In the maritime context, maritime terrorism attacks in the region, especially the aforementioned suicide attacks on the USS *Cole* and *Limburg,* have led to the deployment of an international naval flotilla, Combined Task Force 150 (CTF 150), as part of Operation Enduring Freedom. CTF 150 is essentially a maritime counterterrorism force tasked with patrolling the Red Sea, Gulf of Aden, and Arabian Sea in the vicinity of the Horn of Africa with the aim of "deterring terrorists from using the maritime environment and disrupting terrorist attack planning" (Combined Task Force 150 n.d.; Schofield 2004, 47–49). To this end, CTF 150 has conducted tens of thousands of shipping queries and performed hundreds of vessel boardings. Unfortunately, this significant maritime surveillance and interdiction effort in the region is simply not focused on, or tasked to address, the complex and, for coastal Somali communities, vital issue of illegal fishing.

On the Brink of Collapse?

There are justifiable fears that certain important fish stocks in Somali that are subject to intensive and unregulated exploitation are in danger of catastrophic collapse. However, the picture varies from species to species and spatially between inshore and offshore areas.

Despite the depredations of IUU fishing vessels, stocks close to the Somali coast are understood to be in a reasonably good state of health. This is because these areas are dominated by the artisanal sector, which is understood to only lightly exploit commercial demersal species there. The exception to this rule relates to high-value shark species, sought by both the artisanal and industrial fishing sectors, and the lobster fishery, which are thought to be overexploited (FAO n.d.; UNEP 2005, 46–47).

This generally positive scenario is at least partially due to the destruction of the fisheries infrastructure in the course of Somalia's internal conflicts. The uncertain political and economic situation on shore has also resulted in severe problems of supply—for example, of new fishing gear and engine parts. These difficulties have tended to restrict the development of traditional artisanal fishing along the Somali coast. Coastal communities and the inshore fishery have also had to contend with another alarming threat to their livelihood and environment, as there exists "strong suspicion of illegal dumping of industrial and nuclear wastes along the Somali coast" (FAO n.d.). This practice reportedly has been going on in Somalia since the early 1990s (UNEP 2005, 33). Furthermore, approximately 650 kilometers of the Somali coast was impacted by the December 2004 tsunami (UNEP 2005, 48).

In contrast, key pelagic species, such as tunas and mackerel, are believed to be under significant threat. Although only lightly exploited by the artisanal sector, these stocks are clearly "heavily exploited" by the foreign-flag distant water fishing fleets that dominate the industrial marine fishery further offshore of the Somali coast (FAO n.d.). It is, however, impossible to say with confidence whether these resources are being overexploited or if stocks are on the brink of collapse, due to the paucity of reliable data. In light of the estimated scale of IUU fishing in Somali waters, both in terms of the number of vessels and the size of the illegal catch, however, suspicions of over-fishing must be regarded as highly credible. Biodiversity and marine environmental concerns also exist as a result of substantial bycatch of turtles, dolphins, and dugong by IUU fishing vessels as well as their use of fishing gear and practices proscribed elsewhere and intensive fishing, including destructive bottom trawling, in sensitive, inshore nursery and breeding grounds (Coffen-Smout n.d.; Kulmiye 2001; Lehr and Lehmann 2007, 13).

Conclusions

Maritime Somalia boasts seemingly abundant stocks of high unit value species such as tunas, sharks, and lobsters. These resources, especially the large pelagic stocks, have the potential to be "of vast importance to the economy" of Somalia (FAO n.d.). This is particularly the case given the peripheral role fisheries have traditionally played in Somalia (currently accounting for around 2 percent of GDP) and the significant increase in domestic demand for fish in recent years, with per capita consumption rising at least tenfold in the last two to three decades, from 0.16 to 1.6 kilograms per year. Ironically, demand currently outstrips local supply, with the shortfall being met with imports from some of the very same DWFNs that illegally exploit Somalia's waters (FAO n.d.).

The exploitation of these offshore resources could, therefore, play a crucial role in local food security as well as helping Somalia to overcome serious developmental challenges in the future. However, foreign fishing fleets are taking advantage of the complete absence of regulatory mechanisms, systematically plundering Somali's marine resources. It also seems highly likely that such unchecked IUU fishing in Somali waters poses a serious threat to the long- term health of the fishery and thus profoundly undermines Somalia's marine environmental security. IUU fishing is, furthermore, intimately linked to piracy and, in effect, guarantees a continuation in the maritime insecurity that plagues Somali waters.

What, Then, Is to Be Done to Address This Challenge?

The obvious and ideal scenario would be the emergence from the peace process of a functioning and credible Somali government. Unfortunately, the TFG, faction-ridden, sustained by foreign intervention, and with uncertain control over its constituent militias, remains deeply flawed and does not appear to represent the answer. Indeed, the TFG is realistically unable to exert serious control far beyond its present base at Jowhar. Instead, the warlords and militias appear to be reasserting themselves in the wake of the setbacks suffered by the UIC. A revitalized Somali government therefore remains a distant prospect.

Alternatively, although the TFG is unlikely to establish its own coast guard or navy in the foreseeable future, it could conceivably provide a source of authority to combat illegal activities in Somali waters. The TFG could therefore authorize an interested state or states to undertake surveillance and enforcement activities on behalf of Somalia, thereby filling the legal and institutional void. Similarly, it has been suggested in the past that the international community should take responsibility for Somalia's offshore areas in the form of some sort of "marine protectorate" (Jennings 2001, 418) or "interim marine management governance framework" (Coffen-Smout n.d.; see also Mwangura 2005). Both the president of the TFG and the UN's representative in Somalia advocated solutions along these lines in 2005 (Hansen and Mesoy 2006, 12; Lehr and Lehmann 2007, 13). The obvious candidate for this type of undertaking would seem to be CTF 150.

However, there appears to have been little enthusiasm for this type of proposal internationally. It has been alleged that a key part of the reason for this is the existence of strong vested interests on the part of distant water fishing nations whose vessels are involved in IUU fishing in Somali waters and who therefore desire a continuation of this practice. The "marine protectorate" concept can also be viewed as compromising Somalia's sovereignty as well as having more than a hint of neocolonialism about it—something that is unlikely to endear it to states around the region (Jennings 2001, 420).

Furthermore, with regard to CTF 150, while this international maritime force certainly has substantial maritime resources in the region at its disposal, its primary mission is counterterrorism. Extending CTF 150's operations to counter illegal activities at sea, such as piracy, let alone the unbridled IUU fishing currently taking place in Somali waters, would inevitably seriously stretch CTF 150's operational resources and therefore potentially compromise this core objective (Lehr and Lehmann 2007, 18–19). Although India has shown some interest in taking on the role of maritime surveillance and enforcement in Somali waters and would also have the advantage of carrying no colonial baggage, further progress on this issue has not been forthcoming. In any case, it is feared that external intervention could prove divisive and lead to renewed conflict within Somalia (Hansen and Mesoy 2006, 12).

A further option that is perhaps more realistic, though not without its pitfalls, is for the international community, individual interested governments, or even private security companies to engage with local partners in Somalia. Such a strategy would build on the success of the efforts of the authorities of Somaliland and Puntland. The potential for this type of response to be effective is illustrated by the Puntland Coast Guard's arrest of a Spanish fishing vessel, the *Alabacora Quatro*.

Significantly, Puntland and the Hart Group subsequently instituted proceedings against the vessel in a UK court and gained a conviction on a charge of illegal fishing (Hansen and Mesoy 2006, 5–6). This type of response can, however, prove problematic where there are no such relatively stable government structures involved, as is the case for much of southern Somalia (Lehr and Lehmann 2007, 20–21). As such, this type of initiative can be viewed as a half-measure at best.

Casting the Net Wider: Implications of the Somali Case for the Indian Ocean Region

Somalia can justifiably be thought of as an exceptional case within the region and indeed the world. Certainly no other Indian Ocean state matches Somalia for comprehensive territorial fragmentation and collapse of state institutions. Nonetheless, aspects of the Somali case are instructive for the region as a whole.

The absence of maritime surveillance and enforcement that is the root of the Somali IUU fishing problem is, in fact, symptomatic of the challenges currently being faced by developing states around the region, albeit in a unique and extreme way in the Somali case. Indian Ocean coastal states, in common with coastal states worldwide, have proved to be keen claimants of extended zones of jurisdiction, particularly 200 nautical mile EEZs (as opposed to the Somali 200 nautical mile territorial sea).

Within claimed EEZs, coastal states have considerable sovereign rights, especially over marine resources. Indeed, the advent of the EEZ regime has been described as the "most significant reallocation of fisheries property rights of the 20th Century," resulting in the transfer of property rights to "90 per cent of the world's then active fisheries" (Hanich and Tsamenyi 2006). Developing an appropriate legal and management framework and acquiring the operational capability to undertake effective maritime surveillance and enforcement operations in these enormous zones of jurisdiction represents a significant, and daunting, challenge. Conducted thoroughly, such an undertaking inevitably demands sophisticated infrastructure and management, placing serious demands on the coastal state's human and financial resources. For many coastal states, including Indian Ocean developing states, this appears to be well beyond their means.

As a result, many Indian Ocean EEZs are vulnerable to IUU fishing. In this context, the Somali case also serves to highlight, in the starkest possible terms, the rapacious and opportunistic nature of distant water fishing fleets and the IUU fishing phenomenon. Somalia's dire maritime situation also illustrates the limitations of international law and politics in terms of safeguarding vulnerable marine living resources and environments and restraining illegal fishing. In theory, maritime Somalia is protected under the terms of international conventions such as the Convention on Biological Diversity and the precautionary approach enshrined in the FAO's Code of Conduct for Responsible Fisheries and the UN's Agreement on the Conservation and Management of Straddling Fish Stocks and Highly Migratory Fish Stocks (UNFSA) (Jennings 2001, 416–18). These international legal instruments have, however, provided little protection to maritime Somalia. Similar problems are also clearly evident in the broader Indian Ocean. This is especially the case concerning the management and exploitation of highly migratory stocks, such as tunas, which migrate through the waters of multiple coastal states as well as the high seas. As the high seas are not under the jurisdiction of any state and, under international law, the freedom to fish is retained, these stocks are especially vulnerable to illegal fishing—despite the conventions and agreements outlined above.

It is vital to the future well-being and sustainability of Somalia's marine resources and environment that Somalia regain its place in the international community and rebuild capacity to protect its own resources. Unfortunately this seems to be a distant dream. With regard to the wider Indian Ocean, however, the outlook is substantially more positive, though considerable challenges remain. Enhanced efforts in terms of maritime surveillance and enforcement are vital to deterring IUU fishing. While this raises serious issues in terms of national capacity, the success of sub-national entities such as Somaliland and Puntland illustrates what can be achieved, even with severely limited resources and legal standing.

With regard to international legal mechanisms, Somalia's lack of representation on the international stage has been termed "a devastating handicap," as "Somali interests are neither voiced nor heard" in the international arena (Jennings 2001, 414–15). In contrast, other Indian Ocean littoral states are represented internationally and thus have an opportunity to influence outcomes. In this context there is an urgent need to bolster relevant regional fisheries management organizations (RFMOs), notably the Indian Ocean Tuna Commission (IOTC). The IOTC currently suffers from incomplete membership, poor participation rates, lack of adequate statistical information (which undermines stock assessment and the setting of catch quotas), and the absence of effective inspection schemes to combat IUU fishing. Nonetheless, steps are being taken to address these shortcomings and significant progress has already been made to establish conservation and management measures (Mbendo and Tsamenyi 2007, 11–15). This progress gives rise to the justifiable hope that Somalia's unfolding maritime resource and environmental disaster need not be replicated around the Indian Ocean as a whole.

REFERENCES

Adow, M. 2004, "Somalia's Trafficking Boom Town." BBC News Online, April 28. http://news.bbc.co.uk/2/hi/africa/3664633.stm (accessed May 3, 2004).

Bradley, R. E., M. A. Pratt, and C. H. Schofield. 2000. *Jane's Exclusive Economic Zones* 2000–2001. Coulsdon, U.K.: Jane's Information Group.

Coffen-Smout, S. N.d., "Pirates, Warlords and Rogue Fishing Vessels in Somalia's Unruly Seas." http://www.chebucto.ns.ca/~ar120/somalia.html (accessed April 30, 2007).

Combined Task Force 150. N.d. http://www.cusnc.navy.mil/command/ctf150.html (accessed April 30, 2007).

EIA (Energy Information Administration). N.d. World Oil Transit Chokepoints, Bab el-Mandeb. http://www.eia.doe.gov/cabs/World_Oil_Transit_Chokepoints/Bab_el-Mandab.html (accessed April 20, 2007).

Fletcher, M. 2007, "The Warlords of Death Return to Steal City's Brief Taste of Peace," *The Times* Online, April 26. http://www.timesonline.co.uk/tol/news/world/africa/article1706367.ece (accessed May 1, 2007).

FAO (Food and Agriculture Organization). N.d. "Somalia Fishery Sector Overview." http://www.fao.org/fi/website/FIRetrieveAction.do?dom=countrysector&xml=FI-CP_SO.xml&lang=en (accessed November 9, 2007).

Hanich, Q., and B. M. Tsamenyi. 2006. "Exclusive Economic Zones, Distant Water Fishing Nations and Pacific Small Island Developing States: Who Really Gets All the Fish?" Paper presented to the conference Sharing the Fish—Allocation Issues in Fisheries Management, Perth, February (publication of conference proceedings pending).

Hansen, S. J., and A. Mesoy. 2006. "The Pirates of the Horn—State Collapse and the Maritime Threat." *Protocol Strategic Insights,* no. 3 (March): 4–13.

Hoyle, P. 2000. "Somaliland: Passing the Statehood Test?" *Boundary and Security Bulletin* 8 (3) (Autumn): 80–91.

IMB (International Maritime Bureau). 2007. "Piracy and Armed Robbery Against Ships." *Annual Report, 1* January–31 December 2006. London: ICC International Maritime Bureau.

Jennings, T. 2001. "Controlling Access in the Absence of a Central Government: The Somali Dilemma." *Ocean Yearbook 15.* Chicago: Chicago Univ. Press, 403–27.

Kulmiye, A. J. 2001. "Militia vs Trawlers: Who Is the Villain?" *The East African Magazine,* July 9. http://www.ecop.info/english/ind-oce-pir-somalia.htm (accessed April 30, 2007).

Lehr, P. and H. Lehmann. 2007. "Somalia—Pirates' New Paradise" In *Violence at Sea,* ed. P. Lehr, 1–22. London: Routledge.

Mbendo, J., and B. M. Tsamenyi. 2007. "Regional Cooperation: A Case Study of the Western Indian Ocean Tuna Fishery." Unpublished paper, Marine Biodiversity and Fisheries in the Indian Ocean Region: Opportunities and Threats, Indian Ocean Research Group (IORG), 4th Conference, Muscat, Oman, February 18–20.

Mwangura, A. 2005. "Indian Ocean Piracy: Somalia." http://www.ecop.info/english/ind-oce-pir-somalia.htm (accessed April 30, 2007).

Prescott, J. R. V., and C. H. Schofield. 2005. *The Maritime Political Boundaries of the World.* Leiden/Boston: Martinus Nijhoff Publishers.

Roach, J. A., and R.W. Smith. 1996. *United States Responses to Excessive Maritime Claims.* The Hague: Martinus Nijhoff.

Schofield, C.H. 2004. "Horn of Africa Conflicts Threaten US Anti-Terrorism Efforts." *Jane's Intelligence Review* 16 (6) (June): 46–51.

UNEP (UN Environment Programme). 2005. "The State of the Environment in Somalia: A Desk Study." UNEP, Geneva/Nairobi. http://www.unep.org/DEPI/programmes/Somalia_Final.pdf (accessed May 2, 2007).

von Hoesslin, K. 2006. "Making Sense of Somalia's Anarchic Waters." *Philippine Star* Online, March 25.

Legislation/Legal Documents

Republic of Somalia. Law No. 57 on the Territorial Sea and Ports, September 10, 1972. http://www.un.org/Depts/los/LEGISLATIONANDTREATIES/PDFFILES/SOM_1972_Law.pdf (accessed April 26, 2007).

United Nations. 1983. "United Nations Convention on the Law of the Sea (LOSC), Montego Bay, Jamaica, 10 December 1982 (in force as from 16 November 1994)." New York: United Nations.

8

Responses and Resilience of Fisherfolks on the Tsunami Event in Southern Thailand

MAY TAN-MULLINS, JONATHAN RIGG, AND CARL GRUNDY-WARR

Introduction

In this era of environmental insecurity, with increasing natural disasters—possibly caused by global warming—we have been made to realize that we are no longer "in the times of procrastination, of half measures, of soothings and bafflings, expedients of delays" (Sir Winston Churchill, 1936). In fact, we are entering a period of consequences.[1] The inconvenient truth of increasing environmental insecurity has shifted the discourses of sustainable development. In the Indian Ocean, the December 26, 2004, Boxing Day Tsunami questioned the readiness of communities to cope with such disasters, their abilities to recover, and their resilience in an event of massive destruction. In this chapter, we examine the eastern rim of the ocean, in particular the communities in Phangnga and Krabi provinces, southern Thailand, and investigate factors attributed to the ability to recover and rehabilitate in such changing conditions.

In a review paper of the study of natural disasters published in 1997, David Alexander wrote that it is "now widely recognized that 'natural disaster' is a convenience term that amounts to a misnomer" (1997, 289). Disasters are, in short, never only "natural"; they are fundamentally social: "The crucial point about understanding why disasters happen is that it is not only natural events that cause them. They are also the product of social, political and economic environments (as distinct from the natural environment), because of the way these structure the lives of different groups of people" (Wisner et al. 2003, 4). Some scholars (e.g., Bankoff 2001 and 2004) have stretched this point further still to propose that the "disaster" discourse is fundamentally Western. This is not to challenge the fact that "natural" disasters kill and injure people and destroy livelihoods, but to note that the debate over disaster has arisen in a particular intellectual milieu where it is often implicitly assumed that they are, first, afflictions of the poor(er) world and, second, that they attain precedence in local people's minds and experiences over other threats to life and livelihood.

The reality of people's lived experiences in the Global South is that, often, vulnerability to natural hazards is embedded—in terms of perception—in a much wider set of vulnerabilities. While it may be easy for scholars, governments, multilateral organizations, and development practitioners to separate an event such as the December 2004 Indian Ocean tsunami from the day-to-day threats that people face, it is nonetheless telling that those millions of people who die before they should in the countries of the poorer world are likely to do so for other, run-of-the-mill reasons, such as under-nutrition and an absence of medical care. It is for this reason that scholars have sought to view and understand natural disasters, and particular recovery from such disasters, in terms of the inequalities and exclusions that structure society and everyday life. This is not to argue, however, that we can conflate vulnerability and poverty. While there is a significant overlap between populations who are vulnerable and those who are poor, this is far from perfect. As we explore below, the 2004 tsunami, for example, led to the death of almost as many wealthy (comparatively) international tourists in Thailand as it did poor Thais or migrant workers from other countries. Furthermore, recovery transitions do not mirror, to the degree that we can impute one from the other, patterns of wealth and destitution or of power and powerlessness. The tsunami provided the possibility for a historical break in established ways of functioning, a small widow of opportunity for the poor, marginalized, and excluded, whether they be communities, households, or individuals, to challenge and up-turn the status quo.

The tsunami also offered a development challenge. The disaster led to an outpouring of generosity reflected in the unprecedented scale of donations from governments, international agencies, private groups, and individuals totaling more than US$7 billion, the most raised in connection with a single event in the course of history (see Telford and Cosgrave 2007). More important than the sheer scale of the response, however, is its composition and the implications this has for our understanding of the aid "industry."

This new politics of aid allocation not only offers new spaces of opportunity (refer to Rigg et al. 2005), but also presents new vulnerabilities that arise from such patterns and mechanisms for aid disbursement.[2] Indeed it could be argued that what we see in some areas is the worst of both worlds. Continuity is reflected in the politics of aid distribution through centralized agencies with their, inter alia, over-bureaucratized and unwieldy decision-making structures, lack of attention to local context, inability to foster substantive and substantial local participation, and prioritization of geopolitical goals over humanitarian concerns. At the same time, the new politics of aid, while it may overcome some of the objections directed at the old politics of aid, has its own difficulties and objections to contend with. Some of these focus on managerial issues, including the duplication of effort, a lack of skills and capacity, poor accounting, and the difficulty of harnessing scale economies. Others, though—and these are the more profound and intractable—take the form of cultural and political impediments. The important role played by social capital, manifested through various ethnic, kinship, and religious networks, creates new possibilities for participatory exclusions to be built into aid disbursements. These, moreover, are often disguised and partially legitimated by the claims that can be made in the direction of local and traditional norms and structures.

What we see in those areas affected by the tsunami is pre-existing strengths and vulnerabilities being reproduced in the patterning of official aid. On-going discrimination linked to ethnicity, religion, class, or gender is the most obvious patterning factor (EWC 2005, 5). Particularly in countries where corruption and bureaucratic manipulation are rife, certain individuals and groups may use their political connections at the local level to receive aid, sometimes at the expense of others (EWC 2005, 1). This may be interpreted as the reproduction of pre-existing architectures of power and influence in the distribution and allocation of aid. When states fulfill the primary role of rehabilitating survivors and restoring livelihoods and, in effect, become the arbitrators of the geography of aid, then we can use power structures in place prior to a disaster as an easy reference back to "normal" lines of command. This, then, explains the continuing marginalization of certain groups, with a disaster merely reinforcing the pre-existing context (see also Wisner et al. 2003).

However, some groups are able to utilize the same established "discriminations" to their advantage, using them to lever assistance from official bodies. For example, in our research we found that a group of historically marginalized sea gypsies (or Moken) on the southern Thai island of Koh Lanta were able to "utilize" the political sensitivities connected with their marginality to "pledge alliance" to the central Thai government and, in this way, to obtain aid and assistance at a much quicker pace than many other mainstream Thai residents in the area. What this demonstrates is that it is not always possible to read off patterns of distribution of assistance on the basis of prevailing structures of power and authority. Before the tsunami, the Moken identity was a barrier to development and inclusion in the Thai state; following the tsunami the Moken used identity politics to pressure that Thai state into privileging their claims for assistance over those of other groups. To be sure, such structures remain important, but from crisis comes opportunity, and we found in post-tsunami communities in southern Thailand an injection of new contingencies, and these being reflected in geographies of assistance. It is not just local individuals and groups who can take advantage of these new contingencies; so too can business and the agencies of the state. How communities affected by disasters are able to recover depends on a number of factors, such as the kind and extent of damage, the timeliness and effectiveness of assistance from various institutional actors, village cohesiveness, and community access to economic, social, and political resources.

In this chapter we examine and assess the explanatory purchase that can be achieved through viewing the 2004 tsunami through the lens of the wider social, political, and economic structures that govern everyday lives. We do this through looking at three culturally, socially, and geographically different fishing villages, and examine how their differences contributed to their different abilities to recover and rehabilitate. We suggest that the continuity of social capital—here understood as the ability to mobilize access to resources through pre- or post-tsunami social networks—plays a crucial role in response and recovery activities through the differential access it provides to aid and assistance. Other factors, such as identity politics and media attention, also contributed to the different abilities of communities and individuals to recover from the tsunami.

The Research Context

The tsunami hit the west coast of Thailand, including outlying islands and tourist resorts. Most of the country's 400-kilometer-long western coastline was pounded by waves of 3–5 meters. Resorts in Krabi and Phangnga provinces sustained extensive damage. Officially, there were 5,395 confirmed deaths in Thailand, with another 2,932 people listed as missing.

The field research was mainly based in three sites: Koh Lanta, Koh Phi Phi (both in Krabi province), and Khao Lak (in Phangnga province), with the field period extending over a two-month period between June and July 2005, and December 2006. Working from north to south, sites and settlements surveyed were: Ban Nam Khem, Ban Laem Pom, Laem Pakarang, Ban Bang La-Hone (Ban Bang La-On), Ban Tung Wa, Ban Bang Niang, Ban Tap Tawan, Khao Lak, Ban Nam Sai, Phra Nang Bay, Phi Phi Islands (Koh Phi Phi), and Lanta Island (Koh Lanta). These locations were chosen to represent both the tourism and fishery sectors, and both local and non-local populations. In this way we hoped to gain an insight into the varied impacts of the disaster and the different ways in which communities and households / individuals responded.

Quantitative and qualitative in-depth interviews were conducted with over 150 residents (mainly from fishing villages and the tourism industry) in the affected

Figure 8.1 An impermanent shrine constructed on a beach at Khao Lak, near Ban Nam Khem in Thailand commemorates some of those who died during the 2004 tsunami. *Source*: May Mullins.

areas. Our interviewees included local people, community leaders, those engaged in the tourist industry, non-governmental organization (NGO) workers, and volunteers. We identified interviewees partly through an NGO based in Krabi and the Tsunami Volunteer Centre in Khao Lak. This was carried forward and complemented by a snowballing approach to identifying further people to interview. The main research objectives were to investigate the social patterning of effects and recovery—in terms of damage, deaths, livelihood impacts, and response rates and effectiveness—and the importance of "leadership," community cohesion, and social capital in explaining resilience and recovery. More importantly, given the subject of this chapter, issues connected with the ease of access to aid and equality of aid distribution were also illuminated through these questions.

Out of these 150-plus residents, 35 informants from Ban Neung responded to the semi-structured questionnaire, which included questions investigating the immediate effects of and responses to the tsunami, the medium-term impacts on livelihoods and health (including issues of resilience and support), and questions that might tentatively identify longer-term changes and effects. The questionnaires helped to illustrate the importance of aid agencies in the process of aid recovery, both in the short and medium term. Taken together, this two-pronged approach yielded a rich data set through which we have been able to cross-check and verify our conclusions, and which has helped to elucidate the varying roles of aid agencies in the local context. That said, we are also all too well aware that in a post-event context where many have died it is even harder than usual for researchers and their subjects to remain "objective." Sheer emotion colored the fieldwork, shaped the way we interacted with people in the study sites, and, no doubt, had an influence on the material and data that we collected.

The three fishing villages in this chapter's discussion are Ban Nam Khem (in Khao Lak) and Ban Hua Laem and Ban Sanga-U (on Koh Lanta). Ban Nam Khem is—or was—a Buddhist fishing village about 25 kilometers north of Khao Lak. There were around 1,000 households in the village. The village was severely affected by the tsunami and large parts were destroyed. Most of the survivors spent the first few nights in tents; later the government built more solid temporary quarters. By March 2005 work had begun rebuilding the village: new houses, new roads, new electricity pylons—effectively a new village was created from the destruction of that morning in late December. Villagers who had lost family members and whose lives and livelihoods were focused on or close to the sea did not find it easy to return to the site of such devastation and personal anguish. After the tsunami, Ban Nam Khem was divided into two villages, Nam Khem 1 and 2.

In Ban Nam Khem 1, various local and international donors built 52 houses (mainly AIT [Asia Institute of Technology] and CIDA [Canada], the MOSES Foundation, and Worldvision), supported an occupational loan scheme, and provided loans of 150,000B (US$4,700) per family, without interest, for five years (the MOSES Foundation). According to the community leader, Mr. Sakda, the villagers were in debt to various mutual funds as they could not earn adequate income for daily expenses immediately after the tsunami. This loan scheme was valuable in helping the villagers to rehabilitate and recover. In 2006, most villagers were working in seafood factories, in the fish ball and squid industries, or were doing manual labor. The daily wage for all this work was approximately 100–150B (US$3.15–US$4.70).

The inhabitants in this village were also on constant alert for the next tsunami, and deeply troubled by any news of earthquakes in other places. The villagers believed that another tsunami could hit at anytime, and they did not trust the warning system put in place by the authorities. To this end, they had erected their own, alternative system of public loudspeakers to relay warnings while checking with disaster call center 1860. By December 2006, however, lack of funds for maintenance and repair meant that the speakers were not working.

Ban Hua Laem is a Muslim village located on the southeastern tip of Koh Lanta Yai. Although geographically divided across three bays—and therefore consisting of three discrete settlements (Ban Hua Laem 1, 2, and 3)—the village(s) is/are grouped under one administrative unit. This meant that aid and assistance were disseminated to the three villages through an administrative system that treated them as singular; further distributions were then made by local leaders. A total of 193 families were affected by the tsunami, and 23 houses destroyed.

The main local leaders in Ban Hua Laem were—and are—the village headman and the Muslim religious leader, or Tok Imam. Following the tsunami, however, these conventional leaders were joined by a large number of NGOs, including Worldvision, the International Red Cross, the Lions Club, Porobchor, Puk Phrak Issara (a Buddhist organization), Yadfon (a small- scale fisheries NGO), and Santhichoon (a Muslim organization). Commercial firms also made donations to the village, including Michelin and CP Foods (Charoen Pokphand). Finally, the Chaipattana Foundation (founded by the Thai Royal Family), Princess Chulaborn, and several other wealthy individuals made donations for the rehabilitation of this village.

Located on the southeastern coast of Koh Lanta Yai, Ban Sanga-U is a "sea gypsy" or Moken community. The Moken had settled in the area about 25 years ago. By the time of our visit at the end of 2006, 139 new houses had been built by various NGOs and individual donors, including a Taiwanese monk who had personally donated 25 boats to the villagers. There was also a newly built resort, owned by the ex-governor of Krabi, located next to the village. The main local leaders in Ban Sanga-U were the village headman and two members of the Tambon Administrative Organization. Contrary to the romanticized version of the event, which suggests that the sea gypsies saved themselves from the tsunami through some innate knowledge of the sea, these villagers did not anticipate the tsunami and only escaped disaster because their houses were built on stilts.[3]

These three villages—Ban Nam Khem, Ban Hua Laem, and Ban Sanga-U—present different cultural and developmental contexts in terms of their abilities to obtain aid, recover, and rehabilitate. Research was set out to investigate what factors contributed to these differing abilities to recover. Particular attention was directed at religion and kinship networks, social structure and social capital, positioning of minority identity, access to mass media, and linkages to political largesse and NGO networks.

Different Abilities to Access Aid: Old Structures, New Opportunities

Patterns of aid and assistance, and therefore of recovery and rehabilitation, reflected the prior status of each of the three study villages. Ban Hua Laem, for example, as one of the few fishing villages on Koh Lanta, was firmly on the administrative map and, as a result, received formal aid disbursements from organizations such as UNICEF, the UNDP, and the Thai Red Cross. Other NGOs provided donations of rice, water, medicine, clothing, blankets, kitchen utensils, and basic infrastructure materials to help people rebuild their homes and boats in the first weeks after the tsunami. The Muslim community at Ban Hua Laem also spoke of collective efforts to clean-up affected sites and distribute aid donations in the early days. As the months progressed, the community was able to replace fishing boats through official channels to the Fisheries Department, and acquired more than a dozen new boats through two royal projects led by the Crown Prince and Princess Royal.

At the same time, the community activated their religious network and linkages to the world, prepared a visual record of the destruction to the village, and approached organizations in Kuwait for financial support. Through the greater "ulama" religious network, Ban Hua Laem managed not only to obtain aid for themselves, but also put the plight of the tsunami victims to the 56 country members of the Organization of the Islamic Conference. As a result, not only Ban Hua Laem but affected non-Muslim villages (such as Ban Nam Khem) received aid, such as fans and rice cookers donated by the Kuwaiti government. Ban Hua Laem thus activated local, national, and transnational social networks in their efforts to rebuild the community. Similarly, the Buddhist residents of Ban Nam Khem utilized their religious networks in the immediate aftermath of the tsunami, and stayed in local monasteries until temporary housing was constructed.

Ban Sanga-U villagers' identity as minority Chao Lay (sea gypsies) brought even more attention to their plight in the media, resulting in an abundance of aid in the post-tsunami period. Indeed, residents complained that there was too much food in the days following the wave, and even though only one house was destroyed, NGOs rebuilt all the existing houses, and even added more houses for families who wished to move out from their extended families. This positioning reinforced Li's (2000) emphasis on agency, and concepts of articulation and positioning regarding how indigenous people identify themselves. Li argues that self-identification of indigenous people draws upon historically sedimented practices, landscapes, and repertoires of meaning, which emerge through particular patterns of engagement and struggle, and then potentially realign the ways they connect to the nation and to government. The response in Ban Sanga-U was indicative of just such a process, using media designations of their (socially excluded) minority status to fast-track aid. Underprivileged became, in the context of the tsunami, privileged relative to other affected communities.

The Role of Social Capital

Other than activation of networks in times of crisis, and positioning of identity, social capital played a similar, if not more important, role in determining access to and the allocation of aid, especially at the local scale. Pierre Bourdieu (1985, 248) defines social capital as the "aggregate of the actual or potential resources which are linked to possession of a durable network of more or less institutionalized relationships of mutual acquaintance or recognition." These networks, which are manifested through local structures, often stretch across a number of scales, from networks within the community, to those that span district or regional boundaries, or even beyond international borders. At the same time, historical legitimacy, cultural coherence, and economic reciprocity between the members of the community are also important determinants of a person's ability to accumulate social capital.

According to Portes (1998), social capital stands for the ability of actors to secure benefits by virtue of membership in social networks. To possess social capital, a person must be related to others, and it is those others, not the individual, who are the actual source of his or her advantage. It is primarily the accumulation of obligations from others according to the norm of reciprocity. As has been noted elsewhere (e.g., Putzel 1997), there is a dark as well as a bright side to social capital. This was evident in our research in southern Thailand, where social capital was a source of strength and benefit to some through various extra-familial networks, and at the same time played a negative role through networked practices of exclusion and cronyism.

Positively, connections beyond the immediate family are instrumental in oiling the wheels of individual mobility. Such connections and networks are frequently invoked as an explanation for access to employment, mobility through occupational ladders, and entrepreneurial success (Portes 1998). In relation to the tsunami, social capital was also used to obtain aid, secure employment, and reinforce livelihoods. For example, Ban Hua Laem on Koh Lanta is a cohesive village rich, seemingly, in social capital and with effectively functioning and broadly representative community groups. This permitted organizations to quickly and adequately provide and distribute donations and basic infrastructure materials to help people rebuild their homes and their lives.

While we would not wish to reify the "community," the village economy, unlike the tourism industry, operated more like a community collective, with mutual support and trust. In the Muslim fishing village of Ban Hua Laem, reciprocity and trust were clearly evident and the common history, collective experience, and cultural coherence of the village clearly helped to create place-based social networks that provided a fertile setting for social capital to operate (see Tan-Mullins 2005). In other words, it was the strength and coherence of "communities" that created the space not only for community-initiated and -focused recovery and rehabilitation efforts, but also for the mobilization of local, national, and international assistance.

While such social capital may reside in highly localized and apparently traditional structures with historical roots, they provide a context, and a legitimacy, that non-local actors are attracted to and can work with. Such localized networks, therefore, can have an effect beyond the immediate scope of the network itself. The important point here is that when it comes to understanding patterns of aid disbursement we often need to look beyond the network.

But this local strength also has negative implications, most obviously with regard to the way in which pre-existing and entrenched structures can exclude certain members of the community. An informant in one village was accidentally "missed out" and excluded from the compensation scheme by the government and the Royal family. Constant reminders to the headman yielded the reply "thiao lang" (later). This fear of exclusion was intense during the immediate post-tsunami period, especially for those who were either forced to leave their villages because their houses were so badly damaged or who fled their homes because of fear. An example would be a family from Ban Hua Laem who were so afraid that the aid agencies would leave them out that they planted messages along the village lanes referring to their location in the jungle.

Another example is in Ban Nam Khem outside Khao Lak, which was completely devastated; the whole village was rebuilt by the Thai Royal Army. Every house conforms to the same single-story design, irrespective of the size of each family's original house. The glaring exception to this was the headman's house, which was a more substantial three-story affair. This was because the headman was able to utilize the local pre-existing architectures of power and the political and social connections to access a larger share of assistance. When an informant was questioned as to the reason, she replied:

> Prok wai pen phuu yai baan, thung mii baan yai!
> When you are the village headman (phuu yai = big man), you need a big house (baan yai)!

According to our quantitative survey, 19 of the respondents had received some form of compensation, a little over half the sample. Most of this was quite rapidly paid out to the victims of the tsunami, with 16 of the 19 receiving compensation by the end of February 2005 (two months after the event), and the remaining three in March. However, while the response, in this sense, was fairly rapid—so that the usual lament of "too little, too late" cannot be applied—the large majority, some 28 of the respondents, felt that the support did not go far enough. Significant complaints—beyond "not enough"—to emerge from the survey were:

> "The government only helps big business"
> "The village head does not help everyone"
> "The village head does not let us know what help is available"
> "Aid and money are not distributed everywhere"
> "Aid and money are not for everyone"

These comments, allied with the information from interviews, highlight the difficulty of penetrating beyond the existing structures of power and authority that exist at the district, village, and national levels. As we found, aid and assistance flow unequally to and within communities, often reflecting links and associations between more influential villagers and the official hierarchy.

More importantly, this form of unequal flow of aid did not just exist within the local social network, but also extended to NGO networks and businesses. There were numerous examples of incompetence, oversight, pilfering, and corrupt practices. One of the biggest industries in the post-tsunami era was construction. However, some of the rebuilt tsunami houses were extremely poorly constructed; we found one house in Koh Lanta that was reported to have cost 120,000B but which could not have cost more than 50,000B, judging from its build quality and structure. In Koh Lanta, an NGO required recipients to sign for 20 planks of wood, but would only actually distribute 15 planks to the villagers. Equipment intended for villagers went missing—800 nets intended for the local fishermen mysteriously disappeared, for example. Numbers were also inflated to lever more money from donors. In Ban Hua Laem, according to one informant, a local NGO coordinator listed 80 people working on reconstruction while no more than 45–47 villagers were actually involved.

There were also unintended consequences that arose from the sheer generosity of the response. At its simplest, initial donations were so high that some victims became dependent on further donations (*The Nation,* December 16, 2005). Less obviously, the abundant supply of new fishing boats had the effect of depleting fish stocks. One report quotes Manit Komsan, a fisherman from Ranong's Suksamran subdistrict, complaining that "too many boats are competing for too few fish." "Prior to the tsunami, villagers fished on a self-sufficiency basis," said Adul, deputy secretary of the Federation of Southern Small-scale Fishermen (FSSF), a network of fishing communities in 13 provinces on the Andaman Sea. "But now they have new boats and gear, and many want to catch more fish. Some are going further out to sea to areas where big commercial fishing boats operate" (*The Nation,* December 18, 2005).

Resilience and Recovery of Fisherfolk?

Despite large, albeit uneven, amounts of aid and assistance being directed to these fishing villages, we observed a total transformation of livelihood in most communities. Material possessions may have been replaced, but livelihoods and living patterns proved to be less recoverable. In Ban Nam Khem, the surviving inhabitants were reluctant to return to their village, partly because their newly built houses were poorly designed and partly because of a newly forged fear of the sea. Fishermen preferred to work as poorly paid land-based laborers, instead of fishing with the newly donated boats. Yet the ability of fishermen to transform their livelihoods through access to alternative opportunities relied on each individual's and household's social and family networks. As many formal institutions and networks were crippled or undermined following the tsunami, this provided a space for revitalized and renewed informal and traditional social networks to play an important role. In a similar vein to Scott's notion of a "moral" village economy (Scott 1976), where collective security in times of trouble was guaranteed through patron-client relations, the victims of the tsunami sought patrons to support themselves in the rehabilitation and recovery phases and, more particularly, to ease their access to alternative livelihoods. Although this "favor" puts the victims in a subordinate position, there is a strong normalizing moral imperative at work where such collaboration is seen to be for the collective and common good.

Of course, those who had no alternative opportunities had no choice but to continue fishing. Sompong Talaayluat of Ao Hua Laem on Koh Lanta continued to work as a fisherman despite his fear of the sea and of another tsunami. He would like to move away from the shore because his daughters dare not sleep in their house anymore. But moving would make fishing more difficult and he would worry about his boat. Although no one died in Ao Hua Laem, Sompong Talaayluat was well aware of the death and destruction wrought by the tsunami. Replacing Sompong's boat was an easy exercise, requiring little more than money. Recovering from the psychological trauma was much harder. The invisible effects of the tsunami proved to be much more intractable.

Conclusion

This chapter has focused on the different abilities of villages and individuals in southern Thailand to recover from the tsunami. Religious networks, political identities, and social capital were all important contributors to the patterns of recovery we observed. This, then, brings consideration of issues such as social networks, historical legitimacy, cultural coherence, and economic reciprocity to fore in any interpretation. It is these which often led to differential treatment between and within communities and, in consequence, the unequal response rate following the tsunami. Communities and individuals were able to "activate" different types of networks during the recovery process. On the one hand, in-place and locally contingent social structures and networks permitted the immediate activation of pre-existing social capital. This in turn contributed to a quicker response rate in terms of the sourcing, securing, and acquiring assistance, thus hastening recovery and rehabilitation.

The need to activate trans-provincial and trans-national networks was prompted by the failure of the state to meet the needs of the local population in the aftermath of the tsunami. Partly this was due to incompetence, corruption, and cronyism. However, it was also clear that tourist-related businesses were considered less deserving than other affected parties. Local officials regarded the tourist industry as alien to the local context and, in a sense, out of place. The tourist-related businesses could not, therefore, call on the state's largesse by appealing to a localist agenda.

There is one more point to make in conclusion, and that concerns the issue of scale. We recognize and accept that many of these processes, structures, and networks operate across scales. Nonetheless, scale remains centrally important and we do not believe that it is possible—or even desirable—to ignore the role of scale in unpicking an understanding of the politics of aid. The tsunami had place-specific impacts. The meanings attached to networks, alliances, and allegiances are often scale dependent. And if we are to ask the question "What does aid accomplish?" rather than just "What does aid aim to do?" then the answer involves a studied concern for the local (see Li 1999, 2005).

Box 8.1   Lessons from Disaster

Settlement and Livelihood Issues

Resolve issues of land rights and land allocation.
Site housing at a convenient distance from storage, production, and processing sites.
Livelihood options of the survivors should be diversified through education and skills development.
Particular attention should be paid to historically marginalized communities and victims of conflict.

Coastal and Marine Development

Adopt a broad approach to coastal development to widen local opportunities.
Protection and restoration of coastal habitats and biodiversity should be undertaken.
Activities that pollute, degrade, or otherwise harm the coastal environment should be regulated.
Restoration programs should be participatory.
Small-scale fishing vessels should be distributed only if there is evidence that there has been a shortfall in replacing vessels (to prevent over-fishing).
Appropriate and selective fishing gear compatible with the status of the fishery resource should be distributed only if there is evidence that there has been a shortfall in replacing gear (to prevent over-fishing).
Systems for effective registration of craft, gear, engines, and fishers should be established.
Participatory programs to improve and strengthen management regimes toward conservation of fishery resources and protection of fish habitats should be undertaken.

Aid Coordination and Future Threats

Mechanisms for coordination of tsunami rehabilitation at different levels, and between various actors, should be put in place.
Government-NGO partnerships for coordination should be fostered.
Transparent, single-window mechanisms for registering complaints should be introduced.
Regional and other imbalances in provision of assistance should be addressed.
Mechanisms to promote accountability of different actors (governments, NGOs, and others) should be established.
Local and traditional institutions should be strengthened and the government and NGOs should work with these institutions.
Programs to enhance community-based disaster preparedness and training should be initiated/continued.

NOTES

The research team gratefully acknowledge the financial support of the U.S. National Science Foundation (NSF project number 0522133) and the National University of Singapore. We would also like to thank the team leader of the NSF project, Dr. Ben Horton. In addition we would like to record our thanks to Sophia Buranakul and Wendy Firlotte in Krabi, the Prince of Songkhla University, Amasari Batchara, and to all our respondents and the governmental and non-governmental agencies and organizations who gave up their time to talk to us and who so willingly spoke about an event that was traumatic for all and tragic for many.

1. Gore 2005.

2. A fuller discussion of the geographies of aid distribution can be found in Tan-Mullins et al. 2007.

3. Typing "Moken" and "tsunami" into a search engine reveals scores of articles recounting this version of events: "But there's one group who live precisely where the tsunami hit hardest who suffered no casualties at all. They are the sea gypsies [or] Moken. . . . . And, as Correspondent Bob Simon reports, they miraculously survived the tsunami because they knew it was coming. It's their intimacy with the sea that saved the Moken. They're born on the sea, live on the sea, die on the sea. They know its moods and motions better than any marine biologist" (CBS News, March 20, 2005, http://www.cbsnews.com/stories/2005/03/18/60minutes/main681558.shtml [accessed August 17, 2007]).

REFERENCES

Bankoff, Greg. 2001. "Rendering the World Unsafe: 'Vulnerability' as Western Discourse." *Disasters* 25 (1): 19–35.

———. 2004. "Time Is of the Essence: Disasters, Vulnerability and History." *International Journal of Mass Emergencies and Disasters* 22 (3): 23–42.

Bourdieu, P. 1985. The Forms of Capital. In *Handbook of Theory and Research for the Sociology of Education,* ed. J. G. Richardson, 241–58. New York: Greenwood.

EWC (East-West Center). 2005. "After the Tsunami, Human Rights of Vulnerable Populations." Human Rights Centre, University of Berkeley, California. http://www.reliefweb.int/rw/RWB.NSF/db900SID/VBOL-6JEE3A?OpenDocument (accessed February 17, 2006).

Gore, Al. 2005. *An Inconvenient Truth.* Dimension Pictures.

Li, T. M., 1999. "Compromising Power: Development, Culture and Rule in Indonesia." *Cultural Anthropology* 14 (3): 295–322.

———. 2000. "Constituting Tribal Space: Indigenous Identity and Resource Politics in Indonesia." *Comparative Studies in Society and History* 42 (1) (January): 149–79.

———. 2005. "Beyond Failed: 'The State' and Failed Schemes." *American Anthropologist* 107 (3): 383–94.

The Nation, December 16, 18, 2005.

Portes, A. 1998. "Social Capital: Its Origins and Applications in Modern Sociology." *Annu. Rev. Sociol.* (24): 1–24.

Putzel, J. 1997. "Accounting for the Dark Side of Social Capital: Reading Robert Putnam on Democracy." *Journal of International Development* 9 (7): 939–49.

Rigg, J., L. Law, M. Tan-Mullins, and C. Grundy-Warr. 2005. "The Indian Ocean Tsunami: Socio-Economic Impacts in Thailand." *Geographical Journal* 171 (4): 6–11.

Scott, J. C. 1976. *The Moral Economy of the Peasants: Rebellion and Subsistence in Southeast Asia.* New Haven, Conn.: Yale Univ. Press.

Tan-Mullins, M. 2005. "Politics and Ecology of Southeast Asia, Through the Lens of Coastal Communities of Indonesia and Thailand." In *The Naga Challenged: Southeast Asia in the Winds of Change,* ed. V. Savage and M. Tan-Mullins, 417–48. Singapore: Marshall Cavendish.

Tan-Mullins, May, Jonathan Rigg, Lisa Law, and Carl Grundy-Warr. 2007. "Re-Mapping the Politics of Aid: The Changing Networks and Structures of Humanitarian Assistance in Post-tsunami Thailand." *Progress in Development Studies* 7 (4) (December): 327–44.

Telford, J., and J. Cosgrave. 2007. "The International Humanitarian System and the 2004 Indian Ocean Earthquake and Tsuanmis." *Disasters* 31 (1): 1–28.

Wisner, B., P. Blaikie, T. Cannon, and I. Davis. 2003. "At Risk: Natural Hazards, People's Vulnerability and Disasters," 2nd ed. London: Routledge.

PART III

RAIN

9

The Essence of Life

WATER SECURITY IN THE INDIAN
OCEAN REGION

MELISSA RISELY AND TIMOTHY DOYLE

We are sitting at the mouth of the Murray River, the largest river in Australia. We are waiting patiently for the arrival of a famous Australian long distance swimmer—Susie Moroney—who, in an act of symbolic protest at the ill-health of the river system, has vowed to swim its length, from source to mouth. This enormous river system begins in Queensland, thousands of miles away to the North, and winds itself through New South Wales, Victoria, and then finally flows through to the sea in South Australia, where the warmer waters of the Indian Ocean meet the Antarctic. Or, that is what used to happen. On this particular day in 2003, and on many other days leading up to this, the largest river in Australia has stopped flowing to the sea. While waiting for the swimmer's appearance, we decide to walk from the Goolwa side of the mouth (an historic town once bustling with activity as the port that linked the continental trade from the river to the trade of the Indian Ocean) to the other side, where the mighty and magical Coorong begins, the land of the Ngarrindjeri, the indigenous people of this region. Once upon a time, walking on water would have been the exclusive domain of gods, the holy, the deified. But today, we mere mortals began walking across the sandbar that separated the river from the sea. The feeling we incurred was simply bizarre. We were doing "the unnatural," and we both agreed that if ever there was a single case of environmental disaster that most abruptly described the impact of European invasion to this Great South Land, then this was it: the cessation of the life source itself, the wringing out of an entire river system.

The Murray River is dying. Now, in 2007, Australia is experiencing its worst drought ever, with record low inflows to the Murray-Darling basin. It is having an effect on all members of the community, from farmers to residents of cities and towns. And what makes this issue even more serious is that this environmental catastrophe is happening on the driest inhabited continent on earth. In 2000, a World Health Organization report argued that unless fundamental changes to water usage, agricultural practices, and industrial practices were addressed along the river system, then Adelaide, the capital of South Australia with a population of over a million people, would be unfit for habitation by as early as 2050. One of the key problems contributing to this extreme degradation and environmental insecurity is that state governments have only shown interest in the river system where it exists within their own borders. The problems of upriver and downriver states have generated little interest. Australia is a federation of states, and the problems of other states have historically been ignored by domestic state governments. Although there has been a long-standing federal authority in existence to tackle these cross-border issues—the Murray-Darling Basin Commission (Doyle and Kellow 1995)—attempts to increase flows have been largely unsuccessful, due to a lack of political will founded on the politics of narrow, state-based self-interest. As we shall see later in this part dedicated to water issues, these problems are even more exacerbated in regions where rivers flow through national boundaries, not just state ones.

The initial sparks that have led to the Murray disaster began with a post-war, nation-building exercise: the building of the Snowy Mountain scheme, in the upstream reaches of the system. Mega dams, along with other mass engineering solutions, are not solutions at all, but actually are contributors to human and environmental insecurity. Unfortunately, just as wealthy nations on the planet have accepted their pitfalls, the technology is being sold to the third world, with the result being, for example, in India and China, attempts to engineer linkages to make all river systems into one large system. Apart from the obvious mass displacement of peoples, the negative environmental outcomes of these colossal engineering and nation-building efforts will be long-term and unimaginable in the scale of their ecological devastation.

It is not just the Murray, but in fact all Australian rivers and estuaries that are in crisis because of human regulation of environmental flows, the effects of intensive irrigation and pollution, vegetation clearance, and inappropriate development and land management. Diversion of water from Australian rivers has led to altered flooding regimes in wetlands and floodplains, and, as a result, has reduced the diversity of vegetation in many of these areas (CSIRO 2005).

Australia is the driest and flattest continent, with the highest variability in rainfall. These conditions predispose the continent to salinity problems. One-third of Australia's fruit and vegetable crops are irrigated, with an estimated farming revenue of $3.1 billion (CSIRO 2005). This amounts to a total irrigated area of around 2.5 million hectares using over 16,000 gigaliters of water (ABS 2004). Of this amount, an average of 11,580 gigaliters is from the Murray-Darling basin. Thus, over-extracting both surface and ground waters in the Murray-Darling basin leads to poor water quality through rising salinity. An audit undertaken by the Murray-Darling Basin Commission in 1999 showed that under current management systems around 3 to 5 million hectares of land will become salinized during the next 100 years due to rising groundwater tables. This would result in significant costs to agricultural productivity and have a serious impact on major wetlands in the basin. Therefore, as the demand for water grows, there is an urgent need to be more strategic in the foods that we produce with limited water.

Recently, another report documenting the rapid decline of river red gums in the Lower Murray River was released, documenting that tree decline has increased substantially between 2002 and 2004, from 51 percent of all trees counted in 2002 to 75 percent of trees in 2004. This rate of decline will likely see the deaths of all red gums along the river in the foreseeable future. The ecosystem services of these giant trees, including the mitigation of salt and erosion, and the provision of habitat, cannot be replaced (Owen 2005).

During this particular afternoon, quite a crowd joined us at the mouth to welcome Susie Moroney as she emerged from the fetid green pool that, as children, we had once called the Mighty Murray. For the final one hundred or so meters, Moroney, towel draped over her shoulder, walked the river, sand and mud oozing through her toes, before diving into the clear waters of the ocean.

Water is the essence of all life. From a human perspective, it is the availability of potable water that dictates the conditions of all our lives on earth. It is indeed the crux of human survival. As such, access to safe drinking water is recognized as a basic human right, enshrined in the UN Declaration of Human Rights.

Also, as superbly argued by Eva Saroch in her study on the geopolitics of the Mekong (featured in this section), for nation-states, water flowing through their territories is a centrally defining facet of their identities. In the modern state-centric imaginations, the idea of water is often linked closely to national development, national security, ideological priorities, and foreign policy objectives. "Since river basins are often being perceived by the governments concerned as heartlands of critical importance for the overall success of national developmental programs, they occupy a central place in the national discourse of 'security,' 'power,' and 'development'" (Saroch, this section).

Of all the freshwater on earth, only 0.3 percent is found in rivers and lakes, and yet this is where most of the water that people use in their daily lives comes from (Gleick 1996). This is despite the fact that around 70 to 75 percent of the earth's surface is covered in water—hence its often being described as the "blue planet"—as over 96 percent of the total water supply is found in oceans. Of the remaining fresh water, over 68 percent is locked up in icecaps and glaciers, mainly in Greenland and Antarctica.

Thus, water is not always readily available and humans have had to adapt. In India, water has defined the lives of the population for thousands of years. Over time, communities in India have learned to cope with the erratic rainfall of the monsoon climate. In recent times, however, the increasing population and development demands are changing this balance. These same stressors are particularly significant in Asia, a continent that supports more than half of the world's population with only 36 percent of the world's water resources (UNESCO 2003). Significant injustices currently exist in relation to water security: one-sixth of the world's population does not have access to safe water, and more than a third don't have adequate sanitation facilities.

Water management is therefore a critical issue all over the world, including the IOR. The slow move toward conscious water management began at the UN

Conference on Environment and Development held in Rio in 1992 with the development of Agenda 21—the global partnership for working toward sustainability. The Millennium Development Goals for 2015 (set at the UN Summit of 2000) also recognize the importance of water for achieving sustainability.

Out of this recognition, the United Nations has declared the period from 2005 to 2015 the "International Decade for Action" in relation to "Water for Life" (UNESCO 2005). According to the UN, every individual needs a minimum of 15 liters per day, with half of that for outright survival. The rest is needed for cooking, basic hygiene, and sanitation to help avoid disease. Despite the dependence that all communities have on water, and the struggle that many poor communities have just to get enough water to survive, in wealthier countries such as Australia it has become an almost invisible aspect of our way of life. Nevertheless, our standard of living requires immense water resources: it takes around 18 liters of water to produce one liter of petrol and around 1,300 liters of water to produce a microchip (Bouguerra 2006).

From basic survival to maintaining living standards, water also has vital cultural value. Water is at the source of almost all religious faiths and is associated with birth, life, death (through drought and floods), reproduction, and even power. To those who believe in evolution, the fluid element is the origin of all life on earth. In the origin myths of many countries, such as Africa for example, water is a central theme (Bouguerra 2006).

Thus in many countries, such as India and Africa, water is sacred. For this reason, rivers that flow through their communities are revered and even worshiped. In some parts of Africa people still present offerings to lakes and rivers to show them gratitude for giving life to crops and to ensure bountiful harvests in the coming growing seasons. In Africa, many ancient customs in traditional communities serve to protect water and the water cycle by recognizing the need to respect natural cycles and avoid over-exploitation. In Kenya, for example, the Masai worship Engai, the god of rain, leading them to respect all life and ecological principles. This has enabled them to live in an environment where the temperature often reaches 50° Celsius and rainfall is less than 60 centimeters per year (Bouguerra 2006).

In Southeast Asia, the Mekong River is particularly revered. It begins in the mountains of Tibet and flows through China, Myanmar, Thailand, Laos, and Cambodia to Vietnam. This mighty river determines the lives of over 60 million who live on or near its banks and who depend on it for food, water, and transport. Because of this dependence, water plays a significant part in the shaping of these river cultures.

This is reflected in the many cultural festivals that celebrate rivers in the Indian Ocean Region. Burma, with its own significant river, the Irrawady, celebrates a water festival, Thingyan, in April, marking the beginning of the Burmese year. In Jaipur in India, a similar festival is held at the end of March called the feast of Holi. The purpose of both of these festivals is to celebrate, show respect for, and gain the favor of the gods (Bouguerra 2006).

Water, then, is far more than just a resource, which is often the focus in more developed countries of the IOR. Rather, it is also linked to spirituality and culture, and it captures the human imagination. First and foremost though, water is a basic element of survival—and many communities have great difficulty accessing enough water to live a healthy life. This is due to both water quality and water scarcity issues.

While it is widely recognized that rivers and lakes around the world are in crisis, in Australia, we tend to take safe drinking water for granted. In poorer nations such as India, however, most of the country's water supplies are contaminated by sewerage and chemical runoff from agriculture. The rapid increase in agrochemical use in the past 50 years in particular has contributed to the pollution of both surface and ground waters.

Water quality has also been affected by poor land management practices that have led to erosion and therefore increased suspended solids in water bodies that receive runoff. Deforestation is a major cause of this increased sediment load. More than 6,000 million tons of topsoil is washed into India's rivers each year (World Bank 1999). Runoff from rubbish dumps exacerbates this problem. Growing population pressures and increased development have led to increased environmental degradation and pollution. It is estimated that by 2025 the overall water demand in India will equal the available water resources in the country (World Bank 1999).

In India's industrial sector, wastewater generation has been estimated at around 55,000 million cubic meters per day, of which around 68.5 million cubic meters are dumped directly into local rivers and streams without prior treatment (Development Alternatives 2001).

Almost 70 percent of India's surface water resources and a growing number of its underground reserves are contaminated by toxins (Development Alternatives 2001). Leaching from landfills and garbage pits also transports toxins, including heavy metals, into the water table. Contamination of the water table is almost irreversible and so will continue to pose dire problems for a clean and safe water supply.

Contamination from arsenic is a large problem in water wells of Bangladesh and West Bengal, leading to significant health problems among the population. Closing of many of these wells, however, has led to increased risk of acute bacterial contamination and therefore water-related diseases. It is therefore clear that water quality and water accessibility are inextricably linked. Degraded water contributes to water scarcity by rendering the resource unusable. For example, polluted water and poor sanitation leads to the proliferation of water-related diseases such as gastro-intestinal illness, malaria, and schistosomiasis, as well as scabies and trachoma. In 2000, over 2 million people died from water sanitation-associated diseases (UNESCO 2003). The majority of those affected tend to be children under five years old.

In India, access to drinking water has improved in recent years; however, gross disparity remains across the country. A significant percentage of communicable diseases in India and Bangladesh are related to unsafe water. It is estimated that around 100,000 children die each year in Bangladesh due to diarrheal diseases (Water Partners International n.d.).

Therefore, water pollution is significantly decreasing the usable water supply due to growing population and development pressures. UNESCO estimates suggest that by the middle of this century, at best 2 billion people in 48 countries will be water-scarce, at worst the figure could be as high as 7 billion in 60 countries. These water accessibility issues are shared by poor and wealthy nations alike; however, it is poor communities that are most affected. They live in marginal areas affected by floods, pollution, scarce water resources, and loss of natural sources of food (UNESCO 2003).

The importance of long-standing traditional land and water management to help curb water scarcity cannot be underestimated. The effects of moving away from these approaches are crystallized in the case of India. Women and girls walk up to five kilometers each day to collect water. Women continue to bear many of the costs associated with increasing water scarcity as the principal users and collectors of daily water supplies. The time that it takes to undertake this essential activity also continues to perpetuate the poverty cycle in many regions where people struggle to meet their daily water needs.

In India, six of the 20 major river basins fall below the water scarcity threshold of 1,000 cubic meters per year, and five more are expected to be added to the list within the next 30 years (World Bank 1999). This is despite India's being one of the wettest countries in the world. Currently, water is not being harvested efficiently. Arguably, this is because there has been a shift in harvesting methods, from those that have been in place since antiquity toward modern irrigation practices.

Whereas the traditional approach emphasized ecological principles, was low in cost, and contributed to social cohesion and self-reliance, modern systems are exploitative of both the environment and communities (Ghosh 2004). Benefits are seen far more by the rich than by poor peasant communities. Two of the biggest factors involved have been the commercialization of agriculture and the introduction of large-scale cultivation of cash crops. Growth in population, increased development, and therefore increased water demand have also meant that traditional means alone could not meet this demand. This situation is not unique to India either—in several African nations, such as Kenya and Zimbabwe, water scarcity is also becoming critical.

The influence of climate change on the future availability of water is the subject of intense debate. The majority view is that global warming is occurring and this is likely to change future climate patterns. For communities such as those in the coastal region of the Mekong delta, higher sea levels due to global warming would increase salt water intrusion, which would be made even worse by dam blocking in the upper catchment. This means that certain water-dependant areas, such as farming areas, are likely to experience water scarcity while other areas may get higher rainfall. Thus, while water scarcity is a significant problem in many countries and during different seasons, floods also pose a threat to many communities in the IOR. In Bangladesh, for example, during the summer monsoon each year, about one-third of the country is flooded. These floods force people from their homes and hinder the country's economic development.

Figure 9.1 Some parts of southern and eastern Africa are blessed with water; in other parts drought remains the norm.
Source: Timothy Doyle.

With a rapidly growing global population, obtaining sufficient water will be an increasing environmental and financial challenge. It should be reiterated here that scarcity is heavily influenced by human behavior and government policies—it's not just about absolute supply. Growth in food demand will probably be the most important cause of pressure on water resources. In regions such as east and south Asia, most of the increased food production is expected to come from irrigated agriculture, putting even greater pressure on water supplies (Dyson 1996). Australian agriculture also uses a significant amount of water and is one of the country's largest exporters. Improving water use efficiency is going to be a major challenge for Australia in the coming years and will be essential for sustainable development. In addition, Australia's management of water and the impact on agriculture and the environment are likely to become significant trade issues in the near future (Harris 2001).

Water security is therefore closely linked to food security (as raised in section 2 of this volume)—sufficient water for food production is obviously an important part of ensuring an adequate food supply. Poor water quality can also lead to food insecurity through, for example, a decline in fish stocks. For many people, such as those in Cambodia, fishing is a way of life and not just a source of income. However, as fish become scarce and their value increases, it enters the global market and becomes unaffordable to many local people. This in turn leads to the displacement of many people as private wealthy fishing companies take over (Doan n.d.). Thus, ensuring food security for all communities is another important reason to get the management of water right.

Further exacerbating problems is the increasing move from water as a basic element of survival to water as a resource, and now increasingly to water as a priva-
tized commodity. Political decisions around water are predominantly made on the
basis of economics and profits rather than biophysical or cultural premises (Harris
2001). Increasingly, then, the social, religious, cultural, and environmental values of
water are trivialized, as economic tools cannot adequately deal with them.

In many poor countries of the IOR, this economic bias has the potential to
impact on communities and affect political stability. This approach, through
increasing globalization, has the potential to widen the economic gap within and
between countries in the region and also to adversely affect traditional social
structures. In Australia, there is a growing divide between rural and regional areas
and cities, which Harris (2001) refers to as the "Balkanization" of society. This poses
a fundamental threat to water justice.

This shift in view to water as a commodity has led Australia to move toward
economic instruments to manage water. While this approach has some merit, the
market focus fails to take into account the essential moral and ethical dimensions,
such as the rights of other species and other generations (Harris 2001). The same
mindset that has led to this market approach has also lead to the focus on technological approaches to solve the growing water crisis. The most significant of these
has been the enormous number of mega dams constructed in the past several
decades.

Since the 1950s, 40,000 dams over 15 meters high have been constructed around
the world to try and augment existing water resources. In India, there have been
over 1,554 large dams constructed in the past three decades. This approach has been
based on a view of water largely as another raw material for commodity production in agriculture and industry—with its management therefore treated as a stock
rather than a part of the hydrological cycle (Shiva 1991). As Shiva points out, this
engineering bias that dominates water management fails to take into account an
understanding of the relationship between water and other elements of the
ecosystem, as well as the limits on water use enforced by the hydrological cycle.

Shiva highlights the Kabini project in India as a demonstration of the detrimental environmental and social consequences of the disruption in the hydrological cycle due to the damming of water supplies. This project led to the clearing of
30,000 acres of forests to re-establish villages located in the 6,000-acre submersion
area. As a result, local annual rainfall fell from 60 to 45 inches and there is high
water siltation rates and soil salinity. As stated by Shiva, this is a classic example of
how such engineering projects—aimed at increasing water availability or stabiliz-
ing flows—actually contribute to the water crisis rather than help to solve it.

In Australia, the Snowy Mountains Hydro-Electric Scheme is the largest engineering project the country has undertaken. It was developed to supply water to
the farming industries of inland New South Wales and Victoria. This sizeable
scheme that started in 1949 and finished in 1974 consists of sixteen major dams and
seven power stations. It diverts surface water from the Snowy Mountains, which
originally flowed into the Snowy River, into the dams, where the water is then used

to make electricity. The water then flows into the Murray and Murrumbidgee Rivers. This process has changed the nature of all three of these major rivers. When the dams were first built, many ecosystems were also flooded. In some sections of the Snowy River, only 1 percent of the original flow remains (Australian Government n.d.).

In 1998, the state governments of New South Wales and Victoria set up the Snowy Water Inquiry, with one of its aims being to reinstate environmental flows. As a result, they agreed to restore 21 percent of the original flow to the Snowy River by 2010 (Australian Government n.d.).

The Mekong River in Southeast Asia is also under threat from the large number of major dam constructions within the river basin. The annual flood-drought cycles, as well as enriched sediment washed down from the upper catchments, are essential for its ecosystem functions as well as for agricultural production, particularly rice, on the floodplains and riverbanks. For people living in the Mekong delta, any changes in water flow during the dry season could have severe detrimental impacts on their livelihoods. However, increased electricity demand due to growing population and development pressures is leading the push toward hydropower.

The 1960s saw a series of dams constructed along the Mekong River through support from international organizations such as the World Bank, as part of efforts to provide economic and technological assistance to developing countries. Initially these dams contributed to increased food supply and standard of living; however, environmental impacts, such as soil erosion, salinity, decreased water quality, and declining biodiversity, soon began to be felt.

This in turn led to increased tensions between upstream and downstream regions as well as between local people and dam developers. Doyle's chapter in this section documents just two of these people's campaigns against the construction of large dams: one in Australia, and one in India. In each case, it was a collective fight against a mega dam that has been the most significant environmental campaign in both countries' experience. The battle to "Save the Franklin River" in the Australian island-state of Tasmania was, without doubt, the most important single environmental campaign in Australia. Similarly, the fight for the Narmada in India has dominated the ecopolitics of India for a decade and a half. Both campaigns emerged at approximately the same time: in the early to mid-1980s. The Franklin campaign was fought intensely, and ended quickly and "successfully"; the Narmada campaign has continued since its time of emergence until the present day. The differences and similarities between these two anti-dam campaigns are many. The first brutally obvious difference between the two campaigns relates to the alternative positioning of the human being in relation to nature/environment: there can be no more profound difference than this. The second relates to what, at first glance, appears to be the shared philosophical and tactical position of nonviolence. A closer look, however, reveals deep rifts in the interpretation of the concept as practiced by both movements. In many ways, it is through the study of the actual opposition to dam-building that Doyle has uncovered the essential elements of the environmental position found in first world versus third world countries within the IOR. Through the analysis of the actual strategies and tactics of the environmentalists themselves, the differences between the post-materialist position of the minority world activists and the post-colonialist position of the majority world activists becomes more clear.

Thus, large water projects also have significant political effects (which are analyzed and contextualized in Eva Saroch's contribution to this section on water). Globally, there are 215 international rivers and 300 groundwater aquifers shared by two or more countries, and so it is not surprising that conflicts occur over these shared resources (Bayarsaihan 2003). Incompatible water uses and the downstream impacts of upstream activities are prime causes. To date, planning for water use has largely failed to deal with this interconnectedness adequately, leading to interstate conflicts.

In many regions, increasing violence over shared water resources threatens the welfare of communities and the security of the region as a whole. India has been involved in disputes with neighbors such as Pakistan, Nepal and Bangladesh over water allocations in shared river basins, the historical and political context of which is detailed by Radha D'Souza. Major dam projects centralize water control and distribution, removing the capacity for local decisions and risk management. This has obvious implications for justice, in that river communities are denied their basic right to control their own lives. This imperial logic and its basis are discussed in more depth by D'Souza.

On a more local scale, there are also inter-sectoral conflicts, such as the diversion of drinking water for irrigation, or for industry from agricultural and domestic use (Shiva 1991). State-planned and -managed water projects are generally aimed at the expansion of commercial agriculture, thereby undermining traditional, common management of water resources. As Shiva remarks, this type of state intervention has led to the concentration of water access in the hands of the rich and powerful.

Thus, water security is inextricably linked with politics. In the 1990s, the Mekong River Commission promoted the Agreement on the Cooperation for the Sustainable Development for the Mekong River Basin, signed by Thailand, Laos, Cambodia, and Vietnam. The purpose of the agreement was designed to ensure cooperation and coordination between nation-states in the use and conservation of river water. However, as discussed by Saroch in this section, the agreement is weak due to the lack of participation of the upper countries of China and Myanmar and its inability to resolve conflicts in water use among countries.

While large dam construction remains on the agenda of developing countries in the IOR, in affluent communities there has been some move away from major dam construction, and in arid and semi-arid regions, toward desalination to treat saltwater for household and industrial use. Desalination is used in Middle Eastern oil-producing countries and, on a smaller scale, in Australia. There is an increasing push toward desalination to meet the water needs of a growing population, however the significant amount of energy needed to drive the desalination process is the main barrier to its wider application. The most common and proven desalination technology is reverse osmosis, which requires 4.7–5.7 kWh/m^3 for pre-treatment, brine disposal, and water transport (Hoffman 2004).

Thus, water security is also inextricably linked to energy security and vice versa. In the case of desalination, significant amounts of energy are needed to conduct the process and run the desalination plant. Further interconnectedness can be seen in the formation of hydropower, discussed earlier, which is dependent on the availability of water. Similarly, geothermal power plants require water also. In the future, if there is a move toward hydrogen for energy, large quantities of water will be required to provide hydrogen via electrolysis. Thus, in order to address water security, adequate energy is required to draw water from underground aquifers, to transport water for domestic and industrial use, and to treat water for re-use.

There has been a significant political push from governments, such as the Australian government, to pursue the above techno-fixes to water supply problems. In this push, advances in biotechnology have also been heralded as holding the potential to save water by increasing the drought-tolerance and salt-tolerance of plants. One of the major problems with a focus on such technological advances is that they mostly take place in industrialized countries. Poorer developing nations cannot afford to buy into these technologies and they also often do not have adequate regulatory frameworks. It is therefore urgent to look into alternative water technologies, such as water reclamation and re-use, if sustainability and water security are to be achieved long-term.

More positive stories can be found from the work of some NGOs, who are not so intent on turning environmental security into nation-state power, but rather see it as essential to the everyday lives of people across the IOR. Not-for-profit organizations such as Water Partners International are working with communities to help them better meet their water and sanitation needs. They have helped communities to build latrines and establish public water points. In addition, Water Boards, headed by women of the community, have been established to manage the water points. Health education and training also forms part of these assistance programs. It is within these anecdotes, however small-scale and few in number, that creative solutions can be imagined and implemented.

REFERENCES

Australian Bureau of Statistics. 2004. "Water Account for Australia 2000–2001, 4610.0. Implications of Water Reforms for the National Economy." Prepared for the National Program for Sustainable Irrigation by the Centre for International Economics, Canberra

Australian Government. N.d. "The Snowy Mountains Scheme." Australian Government Culture and Recreation Portal, http://www.cultureandcreation.gov.au/articles/snowyscheme/index.htm (accessed August 2006).

Bayarsaihan, T. 2003. "Shared Water Resources: Whose Water?" Asian Development Bank, http://www.adb.org/documents/periodicals/adb_review/2003/vol35_1/shared_water.asp (accessed July 2006).

Bouguerra, M. L. 2006. "Water: Symbolism and Culture." Institut Veolia Environment, Report No. 5. http://www.institut.veolia.org/en/cahiers/water-symbolism/ (accessed August 2006).

CSIRO. 2005. "Irrigation in Perspective: Irrigation in the Murray and Murrumbidgee Basins, a Bird's Eye View." CRC for Irrigation Futures, Commonwealth of Australia.

Development Alternatives. 2001. "Troubled Waters: Water Issues in India." www.devalt.org/water/WaterinIndia/issues.htm (accessed August 2006).

Doan, P. N.d. "The Mekong River Basin: Anti-Dam Movements and the River's Survival." Unpublished paper.

Doyle, T., and A. Kellow. 1995. *Environmental Politics and Policy Making in Australia.* Melbourne, Australia: Macmillan Education Australia.

Dyson, T. 1996. *Population and Food: Global Trends and Future Prospects.* London: Routledge.

Gleick, P. H. 1996. "Water Resources." In *Encyclopedia of Climate and Weather,* vol. 2, ed. S. H. Schneider, 817–23. New York: Oxford Univ. Press.

Ghosh, S. 2004. "Revival of India's Traditional Water Conservation and Harvesting System: A Necessity to Combat Water Scarcity." *Agricultural Research Extension Network Newsletter,* no. 49 (January): 10.

Harris, G. 2001. "Water, Science and Society." Speech given at the Melbourne Town Hall, Saturday, May 19, 2001.

Hoffman, A. R. 2004. "The Connection: Water and Energy Security." Institute for the Analysis of Global Security (IAGS), http://www.iags.org/no813043.htm (accessed August 2006).

Owen, P. 2005. "Briefs." Conservation Council of South Australia Newsletter (December), 12.

Shiva, V. 1991. *Ecology and the Politics of Survival: Conflicts over Natural Resources in India.* New Delhi: Sage Publications.

UNESCO (United Nations Educational, Scientific, and Cultural Organization). 2003. *Water for People, Water for Life: The United Nations World Water Development Report.* Paris France: UNESCO Publishing.

———. 2005. "2005–2015: International Decade for Action–Water for Life." www.unesco.org (accessed August 2006).

Water Partners International. 2004. "Water Partners International 2004 Annual Report: October 1, 2003 to September 30, 2004." www.water.org.

10 *Mapping the Mekong Basin*

GEOPOLITICAL IMAGINATIONS
AND CONTESTATIONS

EVA SAROCH

Introduction

Rivers are the arteries of the earth, sustaining life in all forms. In the past, many great civilizations flourished along the banks of the Mekong River. The glorious Angkor civilization is a vivid example indicating the crucial role of this great river in its birth and progress. The Mekong River has been the epitome of socio-cultural synergies, representing a mosaic of harmonious confluence between sustainability, culture, nature, and humankind and thus unifying and binding the Mekong region into an open and "adaptive" place despite socio-cultural heterogeneity and diversity. But the birth of the territorially defined sovereign nation-state—an important facet of the modernity project—and the unflagging conviction that nature can be mastered and controlled fundamentally transformed the human-ecology relationship. The nation-state-based "cartography" of modernity transformed "nature" into "commodity."

For nation-states, water flowing through their territory is a national property. Thus rivers that do not acknowledge geopolitically imposed borders or boundaries from above on the terra firma are territorialized, nationalized, and securitized. Furthermore, in the modern state-centric elitist geopolitical imaginations, the idea of water is often linked closely to national development, national security, ideological priorities, and foreign policy objectives. Since river basins are often being perceived by the governments concerned as heartlands of critical importance for the overall success of national developmental programs, they occupy a central place in the national discourse of "security," "power," and "development." It is also important to note that the discourses of development, as pointed out by Geáróid Ó Tuathail (1994, 228), "are never simply shorn of politics. Rather, 'politics' of development . . . is a politics circumscribed and disciplined by an unquestioned adherence to Western notions of modernity, progress as well as development."

Deeply embedded in the Foucauldian power/knowledge nexus, the compact called development (between the nation-states and modern Western science), often blurs and reduces all forms of ethnic, cultural diversities and traditional knowledge to create a flatland called "modernity" (Visvanathan 1998). The "vision" of development is "conquest." As such, the other side of development is disaster. In this sense, both development and disaster are the two sides of the same coin. We will return to this point later on.

In the Southeast Asian countries, the "peace dividend" of the early 1990s triggered economic boom, and simultaneously set off the pace for numerous hydro development plans in the Mekong basin. These hydro development plans, though earlier initiated in the1960s, were now revived under the entirely different climate of development and environmental thinking. Once imagined through the lens of "development," the Mekong River, a life-sustaining resource, was transformed and categorized as a "corridor of commerce," a "virgin object" to be developed as a potential source of hydroelectricity that will fuel the region's predicted rising energy needs (Bakker 1999). The major analytical concern of this chapter is to show how various (hydro development) projects of "mapping" the Mekong River basin have been an integral part of the geopolitics of the "making" and "unmaking" of places and peoples. Located within various geopolitical imaginations of "centers of power" (states as well as donor agencies), these dynamic geopolitical imaginations produce different maps of meaning that in turn give rise to equally diverse "written" geographies of the river. For the purpose of this chapter, mapping is, as aptly pointed out by Matthew Edney (1997, 21), "an intellectual process of creating, communicating and accepting geographical conceptions, whether at an individual or socio-cultural level." The chapter also maps out the "landscape of disaster" that these development projects have endowed on nature as well as to the "marginalized" stakeholders, the coastal as well as the riverine communities.

A Brief Profile of River Mekong

The Mekong River is 4,500 kilometers (2,800 miles) long, with a catchment area of approximately 795,000 square kilometers, and is the tenth largest river in the world. Its biological diversity can be compared to that of the Amazon River (Ojendal 1996). The source of the Mekong River is in the Tibet mountains and is called Dza Chu River (River of Rock). The Mekong flows out of the Tibetan ice fields and through the mountains of Yunnan in southern China, before tumbling into the flood plains of Thailand, Laos, and Cambodia and entering the sea through its delta in Vietnam. It is the world's eighth largest river in terms of water volume (total runoff annually is about 475,000 million cubic meters). More than 250 million people inhabit the region, of which over 50 million live in the basin itself (Guttal 2003). The lower Mekong basin is defined as the watershed area downstream of China and Burma, which includes parts of Thailand and Vietnam. Over the past 30 years, the population of the Lower Mekong basin has doubled. An estimated population increase of another 30 to 50 percent by the year 2025 will bring the basin population to over 100 million. Pressure on natural resources will increase dramatically, as will the demand for additional food, water, and energy (Mekong Region Cooperation "Basin Development Plan" 2005).

As mentioned earlier, the Mekong basin is shared by six countries, however, the river is not evenly distributed in time and space. For instance, approximately,

85 percent of the Mekong basin lies in the national territories of Laos and Cambodia. As far as China and Myanmar are concerned, the Mekong River carves not so much part of each country: China, has only 1.7 percent of Mekong basin in its territory and Myanmar 3.5 percent.

About 80 percent of the population in the region is dependent on agriculture (farming and fisheries) as the main source of livelihood. The Mekong freshwater system is the third most diverse in the world, with more than 1,200 fish species, many of which are endemic to specific tributaries of the Mekong. More than half of the protein intake of the region's people comes from fish (Guttal 2003).

The Mekong River and its tributaries possess the largest potential water resource, with the total hydropower potential of the Mekong river system estimated at 17,000 megawatts for the tributaries and 13,000 megawatts for the main stream (Cogels 2005). These water resources have the ability to support on-going economic development in terms of irrigation, hydropower, navigation, water supply, and tourism (Sokhem 2004).

Burgeoning population and accelerating demands from agriculture, domestic, and industrial sectors have led to increasing competition among water-using sectors and between countries. The countries of the Mekong region share asymmetrical power relations in both economic and political terms. For the poorer riparian nations, hydro development is depicted as the only resource capable of generating large amounts of foreign exchange, critical for development and economic stability. On the other hand, for wealthier economies such as Thailand, Malaysia, and China, hydro development is a "common spring board" for more economic development. Guided by such a vision, all the countries in the Mekong basin have developed a fascination for the "mega projects" that have not only become symbols of "national pride" but are also sites of ecological and social disasters.

Mapping and Marketing the Mekong River

Throughout the nineteenth and twentieth centuries, a key idiom in the nation-state's "grammar" of development was the damming and taming of rivers (see Anderson 1991). The saga of nation-state development and modernization was increasingly symbolized by great water works or grandiose dam projects, such as the TVA in the United States, Egypt's Aswan High Dam, China's Three Gorges, India's Bhakra dam, or Pakistan's Tarabela dam. These dams were seen by and large as the testimony to the power and unity of the state. Driven by various competing geopolitical imaginations, the six riparian states—China, Laos PDR, Myanmar, Cambodia, Thailand, and Vietnam—along with bilateral or multilateral donor agencies, have mapped, profiled the "natural" resource as an "economic" resource, and have transformed it into a category of control and power. For the investors, the Mekong basin became a sub-region "ripe for economic growth." As for the Asia Development Bank, the biggest donor, the Mekong represented a "natural economic area" (ADB 1996, 1).

The Greater Mekong Subregion (GMS)—a term given by the Asia Development Bank—is one of the world's fastest-growing sub-regions. In 2002, its average per capita gross domestic product (GDP) was $3,288 ("The Mekong Region: An Economic Overview" 2004). It is worth noting that Malaysia and Thailand of the GMS qualify to be in the category of "high performing East Asian economies," along with China, Hong Kong, Indonesia, South Korea, Singapore, and Taiwan. Whereas the other four countries of the GMS (Cambodia, Myanmar, Lao PDR, and Vietnam) are not part of this category as they are in transition from centrally planned to market economies. All these states are facing demands for water to generate electricity, to supply irrigation systems, and to service new urban and industrial areas (Chenoweth et al. 2001). Large-scale hydropower projects have become integral to national development for either meeting electricity demands or for generating profit by exporting power. Economic growth and demand for electricity are projected to continue growing strongly in most markets (see Ford 2005; Macan-Markar 2005). Dictated and driven by their respective hydrographic imperatives, each riparian state has dammed the Mekong River, which only 20 years ago was one of the world's most untouched rivers. To meet energy demands, massive hydropower dams were constructed, for example, the 136-megawatt Pak Mun dam by the Electricity Generating Authority of Thailand (EGAT), which was completed in 1994 with $24 million in financing coming from the World Bank. If this trend continues, the river could become one of the most dammed in the world, with more than 100 other major dams, diversions, and irrigation projects planned and thousands of smaller schemes already impacting on people downstream (Vidal 2004).

In Thailand, as well as in most of the other major economies in Southeast Asia, as mentioned earlier, economic growth and industrial output have resulted in a rapid rise in demand for electricity. Though Thailand itself still has a considerable amount of surplus generating capacity (approximately 25 percent of its total capacity), with increasing demands this too will disappear within the next five years (Ford 2005). Currently, Thailand consumes 1,448 kilowatt-hours (kwh) of electricity per capita, a number far higher than some of its neighbors, such as China, where power consumption is 827 kwh per capita, or for that matter Vietnam, where it is 286 kwh per capita, or Burma, at 68 kwh per capita (Macan-Markar 2005). This, along with the deregulation of the power sector, could indeed affect the hydro-generating capacity of the country. The state-owned Electricity Generating Authority of Thailand continues to dominate the power sector but is facing tough competition from private companies who are entering the power market.

It is also important to note that any large-scale modernization project such as a dam has indirect relations to trade. Thailand's future as a hub of foreign direct investment (FDI) depends on having a stable electricity supply, and therefore it must cooperate with China and Japan to construct hydropower plants in Myanmar, a riparian state where the investment will be the cheapest. In this context, as aptly pointed out by Suphot Dhirakaosal, Thailand's ambassador to Rangoon at the BIMSET Meeting in July 2004, "We now have an abundant supply of energy, but we must have a stable energy supply for further FDI expansion. Hydropower development in neighboring Burma is the cheapest investment that Thailand can share with countries like China, Japan and South Korea" (Ashayagachat 2004). According to Thailand, in order to bring modernization and economic prosperity to Myanmar, Thailand, as a strategic partner of Burma, should cooperate closely with Rangoon (Ashayagachat 2004). The State Peace and Development Council (SPDC) of Myanmar planned to build several dozen additional hydropower projects, adding more than 25,000 megawatts of capacity. Hydropower currently accounts for about one-third of Burma's electricity production (1,500 megawatts) (Ashayagachat 2004). For Myanmar, in a period of mounting international debts, it is a tempting opportunity to export power to Thailand, but such development initiatives are not without huge ecological and social costs.

For Malaysia, the development of its water resources has been the basis for the socio-economic development of the country. Population growth and urbanization, industrialization, and the expansion of irrigated agriculture are imposing rapidly increasing demands and pressure on water resources, besides contributing to rising water pollution. In order to have a clean and renewable resource, hydropower development has been given precedence over the other three sources of energy (oil, gas, coal). With this in mind, the Bakun Hydro Electricity Power project was first proposed in the 1980s as part of a series of dams to exploit the hydroelectric potential of Sarawak's rivers. The original proposal was met with massive agitation by the local indigenous communities and the proposal was scrapped in 1990. But in September 1993, seen as a panacea for the problems of electricity supply in Peninsular Malaysia, it was revived (see Hertlein 2000). For the government, the project was not only a cheap source of energy but also a catalyst for the country's industrialization program. Apart from this, the RM9 billion (US$2.6 billion project, with an expected completion date of 2010, could also provide power for the Philippines and the whole of Kalimantan and West Malaysia (see Yahya 2002).

Beyond Malaysia, the biggest hydropower exporter in the region is likely to be the Laos PDR. With its abundance of hydropower potential and modest domestic demand for power, Laos is soon to become the "battery" of Southeast Asia, or "the [hydropower] Kuwait of Asia" (Ashayagachat 2004). However, according to many critics, "the Laos government is living in a dream world, believing that it can push development through without hurting the country's cultural (ethnic) and natural resources" (Development Comes at a Cost: Conserving the Xe Kong River basin in Lao PDR in the Face of Rapid Modernization 2005). To fulfil such a "development vision," the country planned the largest hydro development project—the Nam Theun 2 scheme—to be built across a tributary of the Mekong in Laos. Thailand has been a major force behind this venture, since it is being built with the aim of selling power to EGAT to supply Thai demand for electricity (see The Nam Theun 2 Hydro Electric Project; "The Contested Landscape of Nam Theun, Lao PDR: The Role of Thailand"). In addition, Bangkok's interest in identifying external sources of electricity stems from the fact that it wants to develop a regional power grid for the ASEAN countries. Furthermore, through this power grid, these ten countries will be able to buy power from each other (Ford 2005). Nam Theun 2 is not only pivotal for the ASEAN power grid but also for the international donor agencies that have stakes in the project: the consortium that set up the Nam Theun 2 Power Company (NTPC) is comprised of Electricité de France (EDF), with a 35 percent stake, plus the government of Laos (25 percent), the Electricity Generating Public Company of Thailand (25 percent), and the Italian Thai Development Public Company (15 percent) (Ford 2005). It is important to note that these donors, too, are guided by their set of economic and political motives that are deeply entrenched in the overall politics of development. This also brings into sharp focus the politics of donors and the geopolitics of who gets what, where, when, and how from such mega structures.

As far as Vietnam is concerned, while the Central Highlands has great potential for hydropower development in tributaries of Mekong River, the Mekong delta in Vietnam's territory is rich in natural resources that are favorable for agricultural development. At the economic front, unlike most other states in the region, Vietnam is experiencing a more rapid rise in demand for electricity than economic growth. The economy is growing at a very healthy 7–8 percent a year, but the government predicts that demand for electricity will increase by a massive 15 percent per year between 2005 and 2010 (Ford 2005). As per the Asia Development Bank's "Technical Assistance Report on Socialist Republic of Viet Nam" (2005), electricity demand in Vietnam grew at an annual rate of 15 percent during 2000–2004 and is projected to continue to grow at this rate until 2010, and then at 12 percent per year until 2015. To meet its growing electricity demands, in 2004 Vietnam Electricity (EVN) was forced to sign a deal to import electricity from China. Furthermore, to exploit its hydro potential the country planned a number of mega hydro projects on the Mekong and its tributaries with the help of foreign donors. Some of the biggest power projects are the Son La scheme, which will generate approximately 2,400 megawatts of power when completed in 2012, and the Dong Nai 3 and 4 plants, which are scheduled for completion in 2008 and will provide a generating capacity of 520 megawatts. And in December, EVN began the construction of the 330 megawatt Se San 4 scheme (ADB 2005). As already mentioned, the donors have played a major role in providing financial assistance to these mega projects, with the lead taken by Japan. Mitsubishi of Japan leads a consortium that is currently working to modernize the Da Nhim hydro plant. The Sumitomo Corporation of Japan has also been awarded a contract to complete the development of the Buon Kuop plant on the Srepok River in Dac Lac province (ADB 2005).

China, the upper riparian nation-state that is, conventionally speaking, more powerful than the downstream countries, will require a lot of energy to meet the needs of one-fifth of the world's population and support industrial development. Some of this energy is going to come from hydro development in the upper reaches of the rivers that flow through the other Mekong countries (Dore and Yu 2004). China, over the years, plans to build seven cascade hydropower dams in the Upper Mekong basin. The 126-meter-high Manwan dam was officially completed in 1996, but its reservoir was filled earlier in the 1992–1993 dry season. This was followed by the 110-meter-high Dachaoshan dam that was completed in December 2002. Construction on the third dam, Xiaowan dam, began in 2001 and is expected to be complete by 2013. Hydropower development in Yunnan province in the PRC is likely to have a great impact on hydrology of the Mekong basin—with a potential installed capacity of 15,600 megawatts and active storage of 23,200 million mega-liters by 2025 (as cited in Landovsky 2006). As part of their long-term and large-scale plans for economic development, Chinese officials recently announced that China will increase its dependence on renewable energy sources from around 5 percent to 15 percent (Walsh 2004). Hydropower is a from of renewable energy, and it is clear from already existing plans and the commercial activities of Chinese energy companies that a substantial part of this increase will be accounted for by building dams in and around Yunnan province. Here it is important to note that in Yunnan, the hydropower projects are critical for Yunnan's economy and a major feature of China's "Go West" policy. The purpose of the "Go West" policy, or the "Great Western Region Development," is to reduce the gap between eastern and western China (Antaseeda 2002).

Looking at the future, it is likely that large-scale dams and river infrastructure will continue to be the most contentious developments in the Mekong River basin. They are emblematic of the contested visions and development paths being set for the region through processes that have had little accountability or relevance to those whose lives are most affected by such development agendas. The enormity of the "landscape of disaster" is increasing day by day. Apart from the ecological havoc created by these mega structures, the life of the riparian communities and the economic, political, social, and cultural activities that are interwoven are threatened. Let us take brief look at the other, darker side of these development agendas.

The "Landscape of Disaster": Socio-Ecological Concerns and Anxieties

The socio-ecological impacts of large dams are in most cases very serious, and its gross neglect, despite growing evidence and protest, is rather surprising. Sandra Postel has argued that "for all its impressive engineering, modern water development has adhered to a fairly simple formula: estimate demand for water and then build new supply projects to meet it" (1996, 7). As a result, the freshwater ecosystems have been hit hard by reduced and altered flow patterns, deteriorating water quality, infrastructure construction, and land conversions. It must also be remembered that massive dams are much more than simple machines to generate electricity and store water. They are a concrete, rock, and earth expression of the dominant ideology of the technological age—icons of economic development and scientific progress to match nuclear bombs. Mega dams are not only sites and symbols of national development, with the "nation" and "development" as its beneficiary, but they are also sites of erasure—of various economic, cultural, ecological, and political spaces (Routledge 2003, 53).

Mega hydro projects like the Pak Mun and Bakun dams in Thailand, while providing cities with electricity and water, have led to massive human and ecological disaster (Phongpaichit and Baker 1998). In the case of Pak Mun dam, the villagers claim that their livelihoods have been destroyed by the failed development policies of the government. The villagers could no longer survive on their land, as the Pak Mun dam had blocked fish migrations from the Mekong River, thereby causing a significant decline in fish catches, which had serious consequences for the people of this area (Swain and Chee 2001).

These severe negative impacts have lead local people to hold protests against the dams. A euphemism frequently used by those protesting against the Pak Mun dam is, "Fighting to let the river run free" ("Demystifying the Pak Mool Imbroglio" 2000). In December 1996, a group of indigenous people arrived at the dam site's airport with banners saying, "Do not invest in this project: this project will destroy our culture" ("Demystifying the Pak Mool Imbroglio" 2000). Similar protests have been staged against the Bakun dam. This dam not only threatens the region's forests, rivers, and soils but the traditional economy too. More than 10,000 indigenous people have been displaced by the construction of the dam (see Swain and Chee 2001). Their resettlement has not ended their woes. It is important to remember that displacement reflects a breakdown in the basic mechanism of society and a crisis of national identity. In that sense, displacement is not only of the "place" but also of the "socio-cultural space." Even if the displaced are resettled, it is only in terms of place, as the socio-spatial consciousness, deeply embedded in their mentalscapes, haunts them in their new "homes."

In China, too, in its southwestern Yunnan province, dam projects have forced riverbank communities to migrate, often at dire economic and social cost (Macan-Markar 2002). Similarly, in the case of the proposed US$1.1 billion World Bank-financed Nam Theun dam in Laos, the human-ecological impact is simply obfuscated from the developmental discourse. It is estimated that the dam will impoverish up to 120,000 people, displace 5,700 people, and saddle the country with enormous debts (Vidal 2004). It is interesting to note that those who stand to benefit and those who stand to bear the burden of such a policy are not located in the same place or even the same country. For example, in the case of Nam Theun dam, the beneficiaries are located in Thailand, whereas the massive population in Laos will suffer the negative consequences of such an ecologically and socially blind project.

China's dam engineering works are threatening the livelihoods of up to 100 million people in Southeast Asia (see Bayron 2004; Vidal 2004). According to one analyst, "if all these dams go ahead, the river's hydrology will be significantly altered and no one can begin to understand the social or ecological consequences. China can do what it wants with impunity. It is a dangerous situation." Moreover, China being an upper riparian, does not think it is accountable to the downstream countries. In this sense "China holds all the trump cards" Vidal 2004). The Manwan hydro-electric dam across the upper Mekong, finished in 1996, has been frequently blamed by Thailand and other countries for reduced fishing and also for causing flash floods when water is released without warning. The floods in the Mekong delta in Vietnam and Cambodia in 2002 were blamed partly on the Chinese dam (Antaseeda 2002).

Similarly, China's Dachoashan dam is likely to reduce the river flow and affect the livelihoods of 60 million people downstream in Southeast Asia. In early 2004, the dam was blamed by downstream countries for the low and unusual fluctuations in the flow of the Mekong River (Pearce 2004a). This led to an emergency meeting of the Mekong River Commission and an "official request" for information on the dam operations from China (Pearce 2004b). According to Witoon Permpongsachareon, director of Terra, a Bangkok-based environmental group, "China acts like it doesn't need to care about countries downstream. It has to recognize that the Mekong isn't just theirs" ("China Eyes River for Development" 2001). Since China is not a member of the Mekong River Commission, however, it is not obliged to cooperate in this regard.

The massive damming in the upper Mekong has raised concerns and anxieties among the downstream riparian communities. As the turbines are switched on and off to meet hourly changes in demand, their reservoirs empty and fill and the river downstream experiences fluctuations in water levels of up to a meter a day. After the construction of the Manwan dam, the mean minimum discharge of the Mekong River on the Thai-Laos border decreased by 25 percent ("Downstream Impacts of Hydropower and Development of an International River: A Case Study of Lancang-Mekong" 2004). This affects the river's hydrology and the marine environment also. For those downstream, the deterioration of the ecosystem means a decrease in food security and disrupted economic and social structures, all of which are tightly interlinked to a healthy ecosystem.

In particular, the impact of the upstream damming is clearly visible in the dwindling number of fish catch in the lower Mekong basin, which has profound effects on the lives of fishing communities. Voicing concern generated by Chinese damming plans, the Cambodian prime minister emphatically stated, "Cambodia's Tonle Sap lake, a vital source of fish of the country, could dry up if development projects are not handled carefully on the Mekong River upstream from the lake" ("Downstream Impacts").

Conclusion

Ecological issues challenge not only state sovereignty (boundaries of territorial spaces and ecological spaces seldom coincide), but also the political organization of "development." Development practices that are divorced from the ethics of sustainability can never benefit more than a minority because, by and large, such practices result in the destruction of the ecology and the displacement of peoples. The intellectuals of statecraft and eco-managers of the economies of the Mekong region, in their quest for hydro energy, continue to (ab)use the natural resource to sustain certain power structures. The critical question remains as to what extent the hydro energy-driven economies of the Mekong will continue to exploit and plunder their natural resources for the short-term gain of energy production. The magnitude of ecological as well as social destruction that these economies have delivered brings to the forefront, first, the bitter truth that the "sustaining power" of the Mekong River is getting fragile. The hydro-ecological system upon which the life of the region depends is being threatened. Second, it not only questions the energy-driven policies undertaken by the riparian nations of the Mekong basin but also calls for a paradigm shift from the state-centric geopolitics of mastering nature to a sustainability paradigm where a vital link exists between economy and ecology. In the resource "conserving" economies, natural resources are produced and reproduced through a complex network of ecological processes, where production becomes an integral part of this economy of natural processes (Shiva 2002). Such a paradigm is not restricted to water per se, since the notion of sustainability is captured in the larger context of the sustainability of ecology, the economy, as well as the maintenance of the ecological services provided by water in the environment. Furthermore, the ecological sustainability paradigm is based upon the premise that water is a gift from nature, a finite, life sustaining "commons" that can neither be bounded nor owned and sold as a property or a commodity (Shiva 2002). Since two-thirds of humanity depends on land, water, and biodiversity for livelihoods, their destruction or privatization creates poverty for the people, who are left without food, water, and means of livelihood. Deeply embedded in the sustainability paradigm is the ethos: water should not be traded, overused, wasted, or polluted, so that even those at the margins of marginality have a reasonable access to this life-sustaining resource. But sadly, in the Mekong River basin, like other basins of the world, there exists the predominant undercurrent of old geopolitical thinking of mastering nature and entrenched interests in favour of large dams. As Dipak Gyawali (2001, 45) puts it, "much as the environmentalists and social activists all over the world may want, it is too early to write an obituary for large dams. Though there are signs of new and alternative thinking."

REFERENCES

Anderson, B. 1991. *Imagined Communities: Reflections on the Origins and Spread of Nationalism,* 2nd ed. New York: Verso.

Antaseeda, Poona. 2002. "Upstream Power Play." http://www.searin.org/Th/Mekong/Mek_dam_nE3.htm (accessed July 22, 2006).

ADB (Asian Development Bank). 2005. "Technical Assistance Report on Socialist Republic of Viet Nam: Implementation of the Environmental Management Plan for the Son La Hydropower Project." http://www.asiandevbank.org/Documents/TARs/VIE/39537-VIE-TAR.pdf (accessed August 22, 2006).

———. 1996. *Economic Cooperation in the Greater Mekong Subregion.* Manila: Asian Development Bank.

Ashayagachat, A. 2004. "Push to Build Hydro Projects in Burma." http://www.searin.org/Th/SWD/swd_n_e18.htm (accessed August 22, 2006).

Bakker, K. 1999. "The Politics of Hydropower: Developing the Mekong." *Political Geography* 18:209–32.

Bayron, H. 2004. "China's Dams Threaten Mekong, Conservationists." http://www.cambodianonline.net/articles200475.htm (accessed August 22, 2006).

Chenoweth, J. I., H. M. Hector, and J. F. Bird. 2001. "Integrated River Basin Management in the Multi-Jurisdictional River Basins: The Case of the Mekong River Basin." *Water Resources Development* 17 (3): 365–77.

"China Eyes River for Development." 2001. U.S Water Newsline. http://www.uswaternews.com/archives/arcglobal/1chieye10.html (accessed August 22, 2006).

Cogels, O. 2005. "Regional Cooperation Programme for Sustainable Development of Water and Related Resources in the Mekong Basin." http://www.mrcmekong.org/mekong_program_ceo.htm (accessed August 22, 2006).

"Damming the Mekong: A River in Trouble." 2004. http://www.panda.org/about_wwf/ what_we_do/freshwater/our_solutions/policies_practices/removing_barriers/dams_initiative/ examples/mekong/index.cfm (accessed August 22, 2006).

"Demystifying the Pak Mool Imbroglio." 2000. http://www.searin.org/Th/PMD/PMDa/ PMDaE9.htm (accessed August 22, 2006).

"Development Comes at a Cost: Conserving the Xe Kong River Basin in Lao PDR in the Face of Rapid Modernisation." http://assets.panda.org/downloads/tmflaosjune05.pdf (accessed August 22, 2006).

Dore, J., and X. Yu. 2004. "Yunnan Hydropower Expansion: Update on China's Energy Industry Reforms and the Nu, Lancang and Jinsha Hydropower Dams." USER Working Paper 2004-4. Unit for Social and Environmental Research, Chiang Mai University, Chiang Mai, Thailand.

"Downstream Impacts of Hydropower and Development of an International River: A Case Study of Lancang-Mekong." http://www.searin.org/Th/Mekong/mek_down_impact_ en.pdf (accessed August 19, 2006).

Edney, M. 1997. *Mapping an Empire: The Geographical Construction of British India: 1765–1843.* Chicago: Univ. of Chicago Press.

Ford, N. 2005. "Southeast Asia Turns Back to Hydro." *International Water Power and Dam Construction Magazine,* November 10. http://www.waterpowermagazine.com/story.asp?storyCode=2032402 (accessed August 19, 2006).

Guttal, S. 2003. "Marketing the Mekong: The Asian Development Bank and the Greater Mekong Sub-Region Economic Cooperation Program." http://www.jubileesouth.org/news/ EpZyVyEAZFESZsvoiN.shtml (accessed August 19, 2006).

Gyawali, D. 2001. *Water in Nepal.* Kathmandu: Himal Books.

Hertlein, L. 2000. "The Resettlement of Indigenous People Affected by the Bakun Hydro-Electric Project, Sarawak, Malaysia: The Coaltion of Concerned NGOs on Bakun (Gabungan) Malaysia." http://www.dams.org/docs/kbase/contrib/soc198.pdf (accessed August 15, 2006).

Landovsky, J. 2006. "Institutional Assessment of Transboundary Water Resources Management." Human Development Report Office Occasional Paper 39. http://hdr.undp.org/en/ reports/global/hdr2006/papers/landovsky%20jakub.pdf (accessed November 22, 2007).

Macan-Markar, M. 2002. "Mekong's Dams Wreak Havoc on Rural Poor." *Asia Times* Online, April 10. http://www.atimes.com/se-asia/DD10Ae04.html (accessed August 15, 2006).

———. 2005. "Thai-Burma Dam Planned over Troubled Waters." http://www.newsmekong. org/thai-burma_dam_planned_over_troubled_waters (accessed August 14, 2006).

Mekong Region Cooperation (MRC). 2005. "Basin Development Plan." http://www. mrcmekong.org/programmes/bdp.htm (accessed August 19, 2006).

Öjendal, J. 1996. Mainland Southeast Asia: Co-Operation or Conflict over Waters? In Hydropolitics: Conflicts over Water as a Development Constraint, ed. L. Ohlsson, 149–77. Dhaka: Univ. Press Limited.

Ó Tuathail, G. 1994. "Critical Geopolitics and Development Theory: Intensifying the Dialogue." *Transactions of the Institute of British Geographers* 19:228–38.

"Outline of the Mekong River: From Tibetan Mountains to the Mekong Delta." http://cantho.cool.ne.jp/mekong/outline/mekong_river_e.html (accessed November 22, 2007).

Pearce, F. 2004a. "China Drains Life from Mekong River." *New Scientist* 2441. http://www.newscientist.com/article.ns?id=mg18224411.700 (accessed August 19, 2006).

———. 2004b. "Chinese Dams Blamed for Mekong's Bizarre Flow." *New Scientist.* http://www.newscientist.com/article.ns?id=dn4819 (accessed July 24, 2006).

Phongpaichit, P., and C. Baker. 1998. *Thailand's Boom and Bust.* Chiang Mai: Silkworm Books.

Postel, S. 1996. "Dividing the Waters : Food Security, Ecosystem, Health and the New Politics of Scarcity." World Watch Paper No. 132. September. Washington, D.C.: World Watch Institute.

Routledge, P. 2003. "Voices of the Dammed: Discursive Resistance amidst Erasure in the Narmada Valley, India." *Political Geography* 22 (3) (March): 243–70.

Shiva, V. 2002. *Water Wars: Privitization, Pollution and Profit.* London: Pluto Press.

Sokhem, P. 2004. "Cooperation in the Mekong Basin in Implementing Integrated River Basin Management (IRBM): From Negotiation Stage to a More Concrete Joint Planning and Implementation." http://www.adb.org/Documents/Events/2004/NARBO/1_5_Pech_paper.pdf (accessed July 22, 2006).

Swain, A., and A. M. Chee. 2001. "Political Structure and 'Dam' Conflicts: Comparing Cases in Southeast Asia." http://www.worldwatercouncil.org/fileadmin/wwc/Library/Publications_and_reports/Proceedings_Water_Politics/proceedings_waterpol_pp.95-114.pdf (accessed July 18, 2006).

"The Contested Landscapes of the Nam Theun, Lao PDR: The Role of Thailand." http://www.mekong.es.usyd.edu.au/case_studies/nam_theun/thailand/thailand.htm (accessed July 20, 2006).

"The Nam Theun 2 Hydro Electric Project (NT2)." http://web.worldbank.org/WBSITE/EXTERNAL/COUNTRIES/EASTASIAPACIFICEXT/LAOPRDEXTN/0,,contentMDK:20172670~pagePK:141137~piPK:217854~theSitePK:293684,00.html (accessed July 20, 2006).

"The Mekong Region: An Economic Overview." 2004. http://www.adb.org/Documents/Reports/MREO/2004/summary.pdf (accessed July 15, 2006).

Vidal, J. 2004. "Dammed and Dying: The Mekong and its Communities Face a Bleak Future." *The Guardian,* March 25. http://www.guardian.co.uk/china/story/0,7369,1177292,00.html#article_continue (accessed July 12, 2006).

Visvanathan, S. 1998. "Mrs Brundtlannd's Disenchanted Cosmos." In *The Geopolitics Reader,* ed. G. Ó Tuathail, S. Dalby, and P. Routledge, 237–44. London: Routledge.

Walsh, J. 2004. "The Mekong." http://www.suite101.com/article.cfm/east_asian_history/110144 (accessed August 16, 2006).

Yahya, A. H. 2002. "Sarawak Has Potential to Become Power House for South East Asia." http://www.earthisland.org/borneo/news/articles/020527article.html (accessed July 21, 2006).

11

Water Resources Development and Water Conflicts in Two Indian Ocean States

RADHA D'SOUZA

Introduction

The political relations between India and Pakistan remain consistently adversarial in the Indian Ocean Region. Yet the Indus Treaty signed in 1960 between India and Pakistan has endured despite the unabashedly hostile nature of the political relationship between the two states. There are other paradoxes. The World Bank and the United States played a strong mediatory role in the treaty negotiations and mobilized bilateral and multilateral organizations, and a consortium of Western governments to back its mediation with large infusions of aid to "stabilize" the conflicts over the waters of the Indus.

If the Indus Treaty mediation is a success story, it is significant that the World Bank has not extended that experience to other states and conflicts elsewhere. Finally, for well over a century science and development policy circles have unequivocally advocated that the river basin is the natural unit for water resources development and planning. The Indus Treaty went against the grain of the unity of the river basin thesis, at a time when the prestige of the view was unchallenged. The rivers of the Indus were divided between India and Pakistan, with India getting exclusive rights over the three eastern tributaries on her territory: the Ravi, Beas, and the Sutlej, and Pakistan getting the three western rivers on her territory: the Indus, Jhelum, and Chenab.

Partition of the Indian subcontinent into India and Pakistan in August 1947 and the signing of the Indus Treaty in 1960 represent key moments in the contemporary politics and economics of the subcontinent. In the unfolding of the two events, national/internal factors played out in response to dramatic changes in the global world order at the end of World War II. It is important to contextualize the conflict and cooperation over Indus waters to understand what drives both processes between two influential states in the region. Analysis of both conflict and cooperation needs to be anchored to wider geo-historical and structural processes of colonialism, neocolonialism, and imperialism in the region.

The Imperial Logic of Water Resources
Development: Early Colonization

The political boundaries of the British Empire in Asia were the result of the outcomes of colonial wars in the region between Britain and other European powers
on the one hand, and between Britain and native rulers and populations on the
other. The conclusion of the Anglo-Russian war (from 1807–1812) in favor of
Britain during the Napoleonic Wars played a decisive role in securing the northern
borders of the British Empire in South Asia. Thereafter, Britain could concentrate
on reigning in and subjugating native rulers and peoples to secure the territorial
limits and develop new forms of imperial governance in the region. Important
events that secured the northern boundaries of the British Empire were the outcomes in the Anglo-Afghan Wars,[1] the Anglo-Sikh Wars,[2] and the Anglo-Persian
War.[3] The Afghan Wars and the Persian War carved out the territorial limits within
which the writ of the British Empire could run; and the Sikh Wars consolidated
colonial rule within the Indian sub-continent. These territorial and geopolitical
regimes endured until the World Wars, which brought new instability, new wars,
and a new post–World Wars regime. The politics of water complemented militarism and colonial wars in important ways to secure imperial governance.

Although British penetration of the Indus basin began in 1809, its consolidation
occurred after the annexation of Sind and Punjab in the 1840s. The Sikh army in
the Punjab was defeated in 1846. In 1848 there was the second Anglo-Sikh war,
where the Sikh army was once again defeated. In 1849 the English East India Company disbanded the Sikh army. The disbanded soldiers let loose on the countryside
posed a serious threat to the security of the East India Company. The success of
the military campaigns forced attention to administration and governance to consolidate the annexations.

The East India Company deployed its military engineers to construct the
Upper Bari Doab Canal works in the Indus basin, primarily to give employment to
the Sikh army veterans and to settle them in agriculture in the canal colonies established after the construction. Fear of famines too played an important role in the
decision to undertake the Upper Bari Doab Canal projects (Michel 1967, 60–66). In
South Asia, famines are invariably followed by periods of political instability. Since
then, water resources development in the Indus basin has had a political logic.

In 1861, the Maharaja of Patiala, the ruler of one of the Native States[4] in the
Punjab region, proposed a second canal, the Sirihind Canal, which was accepted by
the English East India Company. The Maharaja had supported the British troops at
a critical juncture in the First War of Independence (the Indian Sepoy Mutiny in
British history texts). The defeat of the Sultanate in Delhi in 1857 conclusively
established British supremacy as the leading imperial power in the world and established direct Crown rule over the dominions of the East India Company. The
Sirihind Canal was, thus, a reward from the empire.

Soon thereafter the Maharaja of Jammu and Kashmir proposed developmental
works on the upper reaches of the Jhelum in the Indus basin, and it was refused.
The state of Patialia was surrounded by British territories, whereas the state of

Jammu and Kashmir was a frontier state buffering the politically and militarily difficult Afghanistan. In their dealings with the Native States, the guiding principle in water resources development in the Indus basin and elsewhere was to ensure that Britain controlled the headworks (Michel 1967, 64–71). Arguing in support of the Sirihind Canal, Captain J. H. Dyas, the executive engineer for the East India Company, wrote: "Governments are always liable to change, but a properly made canal will endure for centuries, if not for all time, and every Government is equally interested in its maintenance" (quoted in Michel 1967, 70).

The logic was clear. Once built, water resource technologies and land colonization would dictate a policy logic that subsequent governments would find difficult to renege from. Subsequent developments in the Indus basin during the Cold War reaffirmed the logic of imperial engineers.

Interest in further expansion of developmental projects on the Indus basin waned thereafter as the economic rationale of profitability and revenue did not follow the political logic of stabilization of the region. In 1892, severe famines and political unrest prompted resumption of developmental works in the basin. By the early 20th century, the World Wars brought demands for electricity to produce war supplies. By 1947 the Indus basin, covering an area of 364,700 square miles and developed through the logic of conquests and military campaigns, had become a fully integrated economic system involving population settlements supplying raw materials to Britain's industries. Michel points out:

> So it is not too much to say that modern irrigation provided the framework around which both West Pakistan and those portions of the Indian Punjab [. . .], grew to their present economic importance. Each new canal was followed by a migration, by the foundations of new towns, including the mandi, or market-towns, deliberately spaced along the roads and railways to serve an irrigated hinterland, and by the development of modern infrastructure of transportation and trade (Michel 1967, 13).

The unity and interrelatedness of the Indus basin was achieved, not through any natural acts of the river per se, or ancient regimes, but by colonial conquests and canal building mediated through science and technology, military and civilian.

Economic Integration, Identity Politics, and Water Resources

The economic integration brought about by canal construction in the Indus basin was premised on a unified administration. This administration entails governance, politics, and above all the role of the state. In the colonies, the state as an institution carries within it an internal schism in that the economic laws and institutions are oriented toward imperial interests of capitalism located outside the colonial society and political institutions oriented toward keeping a culturally diverse population within bounds of colonial rule (D'Souza 2005, 2006). In the Indian subcontinent, the legal and institutional insulation of economics was carried out through the politics of economic integration and articulated through the rhetoric of "progress." The legal and institutional mechanisms of governance were premised on identity politics and articulated through the rhetoric of "representative govern-ment" (D'Souza 2004a, 2006; Washbrook 1997).

The partition of Bengal in 1905 is seen as a watershed in colonial governance. Its significance lies in the fact that it marks the transition of colonial rule from an administrative state to a constitutional state (D'Souza 2006, chapter 4). Lord Curzon, the then Governor- General of India proposed the division of the province of Bengal ostensibly for administrative convenience. The growing nationalist movement led by the educated elite of Calcutta and the Bengali aristocracy protested against the partition. The influence of the elite in the subcontinent had increased sig-nificantly after Queen Victoria's Proclamation of 1858 allowing Indians to enter the civil services and recognizing feudatory interests in land. The partition of 1905 was revoked in 1912 due to the nation-wide protests. The revocation was not to status quo ante however. Rather, Bengal was partitioned instead into the provinces of Bengal, Bihar, Assam, and Orissa based on the language groups of the populations.

People in the Indian subcontinent have historically lived under multiple identi-ties, and continue to do so. Religion, caste, village, language, regions, race, and history, among other identities, intersect within normative orders and codes of conduct. The colonial administration privileged one identity above all others and institutionalized the privilege through the legal and constitutional regime.

The Morely-Minto reforms in 1908 based on the recommendations of the sec-retary of state in London, Lord Morley, and the Governor-General in India, Lord Minto, introduced the principle of identity politics as a legal criterion. The Indian Councils Act 1909 institutionalized the principle. The statute continued to be the basis of governance and subsequent constitutional reforms. Under the Act, repre-sentation of South Asians in the central and provincial governments was increased and Muslims were given separate electorates. Thus religion was added to language as the basis for political representation. Subsequently, the principle was extended to Dalits (marginalized castes) in the 1930s, a principle that was later incorporated into the Indian Constitution. Other hallmarks in the constitutional developments were the Government of India Act of 1919 and the Government of India Act of 1935, which defined the character of constitutional federalism that developed in the subcontinent. Together the legal developments gave a constitutional form to colo-nial governance.

Simultaneously with identity politics, legal and institutional developments relating to water in the subcontinent advanced economic integration and central-ized administration. The reforms of 1905 and 1909 did not extend the principle of "devolution" and representative government to economic matters. The Act of 1919 transferred limited powers over water to the provinces but retained significant overall control with the central government. In the wake of the economic depres-sion of the 1930s and challenges to British supremacy by other Euro-American powers in the international arena, the Act of 1935 transferred authority over water in the Indian subcontinent to provincial governments, largely with the aim of attracting international investment in water projects, and improving supplies to war efforts in the wake of World War II.

Thus the principle of an integrated economy in the subcontinent, of which water was an integral part, was at tandem with the identity politics that is necessarily fractious along noneconomic criteria, as if the economy was bereft of cultural identity and as if identities were not underpinned by economics. Capitalist states in the West fostered class politics based on economic interests. The colonial state in India, in contrast, fostered communal politics wherein communities were tied to imperial economic interests in the centers of capital in specific ways.[5] In this hiatus lies the nub of post-war imperialism in the subcontinent.

The bloody and traumatic partition of the subcontinent (effectuated through the Indian Independence Act 1947) and the cooperation over Indus waters (effectuated through the Indus Water Treaty of 1960 after partition), need to be seen as the logical culmination of identity politics on the one hand and the dictates of economic integration on the other. In the colonial era the conflicting trajectories of identity politics and economic integration were underpinned by the colonial state and its laws and institutions. What underpins the conflict-cooperation tension in the Indus basin post-independence? In the post-independence era the cooperation-conflict dialectic was played out in the context of the geopolitics of the post-war world order dominated by the Cold War. Once again water resources development had a political logic under the new forms that imperialism took in the new world order.

Disintegration of the Empire in South Asia

In the narratives of the partition, the communal conflagrations between Hindus and Muslims emphasize political actions of different groups in the subcontinent, a "who-did-what" approach, and British policy responses to their actions. Such an approach draws attention away from the wider global context within which the partition occurred, which is significant for the conflict-cooperation dialectic of developments that followed partition in the Indus basin.

The demand for an independent state for Muslims of the subcontinent was made formally for the first time in 1940 via the Lahore Resolution (Michel 1967, 2–3). From being a strategy for political bargaining it became a reality when in 1946 Jawaharlal Nehru, later India's first prime minister, rejected a broad-based federation with considerable autonomy for provinces as proposed in the plan for independence known as the Cabinet Mission Plan. Nehru's reasons were that a strong center was necessary for economic development. After that, the partition was an exercise in haste. Within five weeks a large subcontinent came to be carved up into two nations (Michel 1967, 134–94).

Partition occurred at a unique moment in the history of the subcontinent, a moment of collapse of the edifice of the colonial state. In this collapse, the struggle for independence and a separate state for Muslims are just two factors. The others include the international context, economic and political, that brought about the collapse. In the words of Michel:

Though victorious in World War II, the British in 1946 and 1947 were plagued with political and military problems in Germany, Greece, Turkey, Palestine,

Iran, Malaya as well as in the subcontinent, where the repatriated members of the Indian National Army, which had fought for the Japanese, were being greeted as heroes. In England the Labour Party, though conscious of its repeated pledges to India, was anxious to get along with reconstruction and with the building of a socialist society. Thus, within the space of a few months, the phrase "Quit India" was transformed from an Indian National Congress slogan to a policy of British Government. [. . .] Britain was not only willing but eager to "Quit India." (1967,1–2, 147)

During the crucial years of 1941–1942, during World War II, the United States and Britain were already engaged in dialogues over the nature of the post-war world order through the Atlantic Charters and negotiations over Britain's war debts to the United States. In that context the United States pressured Britain to "resolve" the question of Indian independence, for fear India might oppose the Allies in the World War. The United States was, however, too preoccupied with the developments in Southeast Asia pursuant to Japanese advances to intervene directly (Venkatramani and Shrivastava 1963).

Modernist segments of the leadership of the nationalist movement came to believe in the possibility of developing into a major capitalist power based on the economic boost that the World Wars had given to Indian industries. They envisioned independence as a transfer of power from Britain to the modernist segments, keeping the legal and institutional framework of the state in tact. The Government of India Act of 1935 was adopted in all its essential features as the constitution of Independent India. Independence was not therefore a fundamental socio-economic transformation of society from within, as was the case with the Chinese revolution. Their insistence on a strong centralized "developmental" state meant, with regard to unification of the Indian subcontinent after independence, the modernist segments of the nationalist leadership took an authoritarian, often unilateralist approach.[6] The demand for secession by a section of the Muslims in response to the near unitary state proposed for Independent India was the first of such demands.

The demand for Pakistan occurred during a fluid international situation when Britain could not hold on to the colonies, the United States was unable to consolidate its growing influence in the region, and the nationalist leadership had not consolidated their hold over the state apparatus. The fluidity of the international context of partition became significant for water resources development after independence in the Indus basin.

The identity politics that began in 1905 ended in 1947 with the partition plan that was based on the religious identities of the populations. Muslim majority districts that wished to secede from India formed Pakistan. As India claimed to be a secular state, the remaining areas continued to be part of India. The partition involved dividing up the assets of the two states, including the engineering works and water resources developed on the assumption of a unified administration. However, the principle of religious identity conflicted with economic unity of the basin.

The Indus basin includes the states of Jammu, Kashmir (in India and Pakistan), East Punjab (in India) West Punjab (in Pakistan), Haryana (in India), and Sind (in Pakistan). The headworks of the projects on the upper reaches of the river system from where the water was supplied to the vast agricultural regions set up around the canal colonies downstream were premised on military logic, not religious identity. Dividing the basin along religious affiliations of the populations involved drawing a line across the middle of the basin, leaving the headworks in India.

The civil war that was the culmination of identity politics since 1905 escalated after independence into war over Kashmir. Pakistan first committed its military formally to the dispute over Kashmir around April 1948, the same month that the first standoff on water took place. A Standstill Agreement was signed between the two countries at the time of independence, valid until March 1948, to allow the status quo on water supplies to the canal systems to remain. On April 1, 1948, the agreement lapsed. India, taking a strictly legalistic interpretation of the agreement, stopped supplies to the canal waters for a month. They were resumed again in May 1948 (Gulhati 1973; Michel 1967). By then the political and military conflicts over Kashmir and the conflicts over Indus waters in predominantly agrarian societies became inextricably tied. In the new UN system that emerged after the end of World War II, however, the principle of separation of economics from politics could be advanced to a level that would have been hard to conceive of under the colonial state in the empire system.

In the UN charter, self-determination was envisioned as a formal right in the traditions of Western liberal law, where all states, capitalist and colonial alike, had formal equality in international relations analogous to the right to equality in citizen-state relations within a state. The new colonial states became subjects of international law and subjected to the twin rhetoric of decolonization and development as the guiding policy. India and Pakistan were recognized under the UN system as two independent sovereign nations. The culmination of identity politics into civil war assumed the form of an international inter-state conflict after that. In the new world order, Britain could pull out of her responsibilities for the consequences of the policies of economic integration and identity politics fostered under colonial rule. In law, India and Pakistan, as independent sovereign states, had to settle the fallout from the collapse of colonial administration. In that context, any reassertion of imperial domination in the region required picking up the threads of imperial governance, but within the changed context of monopoly-finance capital, the new legal and institutional regimes, and the ideological leadership of the United States.

The World Wars ended the phase of industrial capitalism spanning from the mid-18th century to the early 20th century, and with it the regime of law and institutions developed under it, especially after the Vienna Convention of 1815. By the early 20th century, capitalism had entered a new stage of monopoly-finance capitalism. The upheavals from 1905–1945 may be seen as a period of transition. The new world order that emerged at the end of World War II created a new legal and institutional order, a new regime, conducive to the monopoly-finance capital stage of capitalism. The new world order replaced the post-Napoleonic world order and the legal and institutional framework for the empire system that had developed after the Vienna Treaty under the leadership of Britain (D'Souza 2006, chapter 2).

This new world order centered upon reconstruction. Reconstruction meant economic reconstruction of the physical and institutional infrastructure for capitalism and market transactions destroyed by the World Wars; containment of the socialist block that came to include one-third of the world's population in 25 nations; and restructuring colonial relationships ruptured during the World Wars. Monopoly-finance capitalism made it possible to further institutionalize the separation of economic institutions from political ones, introduced under colonialism. Large-scale investments from distant places ensured economic control, provided international legal and institutional regimes, and insulated economic interests from political turmoil in newly independent states that emerged at the end of World War II. Restructuring colonial relationships took two forms: "development" as a global project of accumulation, and the UN system as the legal and institutional framework for the new form of imperialism in the finance-capital stage of capitalism (D'Souza 2006, chapter 2).

The regime change in the Indus basin was more in the international order than the domestic. Domestically, both India and Pakistan retained the essential features of the colonial state and the constitutional framework developed under it (D'Souza 2002; Mustafa 2001). Once again, like during early colonization, the regions surrounding the Indus basin underwent cataclysmic changes.

The successful revolution in China on the India-Pakistan border; the Soviet occupation and withdrawal from Iran across Pakistan's border between 1946–1949; the United States' political interferences in Iran to reinstall the Shah and the economic blockade by Britain from 1951–1954; the rise of Soviet influence in Afghanistan following the Third Afghan War; and the post-partition tensions on the new Indo-Pakistan border posed new challenges for the United States as the new imperial power at the end of World War II, in a similar way to Britain at the end of the Napoleonic wars. In that context, further escalation of the Indo-Pakistan conflict would inevitably draw the Soviet Union into conflict, with China close at hand. Once again, military logic prompted "technology-fix" as a solution for problems of consolidation of imperialism in the region. Once again water resources development in the Indus basin had a political and military logic.

The Imperial Logic of Water Resources Development: The Cold War Era

In February 1951, David Lilienthal, formerly of the Tennessee Valley Authority and the U.S. Atomic Energy Commission visited India and Pakistan. The visit was ostensibly as a freelance writer for *Collier's* magazine in the United States. Lilienthal was no ordinary freelance writer, however. Prior to the assignment, he consulted with the secretary of state and President Truman, who briefed Lilienthal on the visit and asked him to be his "eye" (Gulhati 1973, 92).

On his return, Lilienthal's influential articles became the basis for international policy and action on the Indus basin. His suggestions were part of an overall assessment of the United States' strategic interests in Asia, South Asia in particular. In his article titled "Another Korea in the Making?" Lilienthal wrote:

> The direct issue is whether the historic region of Kashmir and Jammu . . . shall be part of India or of Pakistan. . . . *On one of this disputed region's frontiers lies Red China, and on the another, Red Tibet. Along another frontier is Soviet Russia. . . . A plebiscite*[7] *at this time might contribute to rather than discourage war.* . . . The practical procedure in my judgement should be not the adjudicating of a dispute between two enemies, whether before the World Court or a board of arbitrators, *but the setting up of proper living conditions.* . . . Why the flow of the Punjab's lifeblood was so carelessly handled in the partition no one seems to know (article appended in Gulhati 1973, 440–47, emphasis added).

Lilienthal went on to propose: "The whole Indus system must be developed as a unit—designed, built and operated as a unit, as in the seven-state TVA system back in the U.S. Jointly financed (perhaps with World Bank help) an Indus Engineering Corporation, with representation by technical men of India, Pakistan and the World Bank, can readily work out an operating scheme for storing water wherever dams can best store it, and for diverting and distributing water" (Gulhati 1973, 445).

Lilienthal's conception of water resources development and military logic was: "Working together on a common project that is not political but functional, a part of life, and based on technical skill and human need, is the way to inject a creative decent note into the rapidly degenerating quarrel between Pakistan and India over Kashmir. . . . With a mutual project under way, with these brothers again working together on big things, then the political issues of Kashmir may be solvable, *the UN's heavy commitment discharged without force, and 'another Korea' prevented*" (Gulhati 1973, 445, emphasis added).

The article became the basis for the president of the World Bank, Eugene R Black, a good friend of David Lilienthal, to take initiatives (Michel 1967, 224).[8] Lilienthal's proposals implied the return of a unified administration, one that was more complex than the unified administration on which the Indus basin developments were premised under the empire. It proposed to do this through the international development organizations such as the World Bank, corporate entities, bilateral and multilateral assistance, and development of international law and policy that came to characterize water resources development in the post-war era (D'Souza 2004b).

The basis of Eugene Black's intervention was, as Lilienthal had suggested, that the development of Indus water resources should be dealt with on an engineering basis. The logic of identity politics had gone too far, however, to make a return to any unified administration as envisioned by Lilienthal possible. Far from maintaining the integrity of the Indus basin, the World Bank was eventually forced to agree to the division of the basin between the two states, with three rivers each following the Harmon Doctrine of absolute sovereignty (Mehta 1988). The treaty went against the grain of the principles that development organizations were promoting everywhere and eventually came to be incorporated into international law through the Helsinki Rules of 1966 and the UN Convention on Transboundary Waters of 1996. The principles were the cornerstone of dam building in the "Third World" on which much of the "developmentalism" of the post-war world order was based.[9]

The territoriality envisaged in the idea of a "natural unity of the river basin" in water resources law and policy undercuts political sovereignty. It presumes a legal and institutional infrastructure, to which at least some economic rights must be ceded. In turn the infrastructure furthers economic integration, regionalization based on global capital investments, leaving the identity of nations with a weakened economic base, and thereby continuing the very structural patterns set in motion by early colonization. Not surprisingly, the World Bank was not enthusiastic about repeating its "success" story elsewhere.

The Indus Treaty was backed up with the Indus Basin Development Fund, between Pakistan and a consortium of "friendly Governments" (the United States, Canada, the United Kingdom, West Germany, Australia, and New Zealand), to underwrite the Indus Treaty on water sharing as it would "advance the cause of peace in the Indus Basin at a total cost of one billion dollars" (Michel 1967, 248). The Indus Treaty of 1960 is in fact an annexure to the Indus Development Fund Agreement, and Michel takes this as an indication that "that the Bank and the 'friendly Governments,' chiefly the United States, had actually purchased an agreement" (Michel 1967, 254). The purchase came at a political and social cost for both countries.

For Pakistan, the negotiations for the continued infusion of funds to sustain the technological gigantism of the Indus projects paralleled the geopolitical importance of Pakistan for the United States. Thus, after an initial period of political instability following the partition, in 1954 Pakistan joined two military alliances—namely the South East Asian Treaty Organization (SEATO) and the Central Treaty Organization (CENTO), led by the United States. SEATO, formed under the Manila Pact, was an important initiative under the Truman Doctrine of containment during the Cold War. Another important but less successful Cold War alliance was the CENTO, formed under the Baghdad Pact signed in 1955, including Iraq, Turkey, Pakistan, Iran, and Britain, underwritten by military aid and supplies from the United States.

During this period, Pakistan's bargaining position on the Indus was significantly stronger. By the 1960s that position changed in the wake of the Indo-China war in 1962. During this time, Pakistan protested Western aid to India against China. It impaired infusion of military and nonmilitary aid to Pakistan. By 1965, funding for Pakistan's Third Plan had started to thin down, affecting the water resources projects planned pursuant to the Indus Treaty in 1960 (Michel 1967, 240–314). Thus, foreign policy and economic policy were again closely tied after the Indus Treaty, as much as before. The Soviet intervention in Afghanistan in the 1980s changed all that. Military and nonmilitary aid to Pakistan resumed, with positive consequences for water projects in the Indus basin developments. Thus economic assistance has gone hand in hand with political loyalties.

The Partition of India put on leash her ambition to emerge as a modern industrial nation. Partition created another independent state on her borders over whose foreign policies she had no control, yet, whose foreign polices dictated her own. If India started out to find an independent space for its foreign policy through the nonaligned movement in the late 1950s, the India-China war made any pretensions of nonalignment difficult to maintain. With SEATO and CENTO partners at her borders, made possible due to the emergence of Pakistan as an independent state, India was pushed into the Soviet "sphere of influence" when it signed the Indo-Soviet Friendship Treaty in 1971.

The war in Afghanistan, with the United States and the Soviet Union backing different sides in the civil war, heated up the Cold War on India's northern borders. The geopolitical developments had a significant influence on the way India conceptualized the development of the Rajasthan Canal project built to utilize waters from the Indus basin. Rehabilitation of Sikhs dislocated from the canal colonies in West Punjab took priority over design or ecological questions, especially as a section of the Sikh population had staked their claims to an independent state. Although the Bhakra dam project on the Indian side of the Indus basin had been planned before independence, it was altered significantly after independence to divert water from the Indus rivers to Rajasthan, along the Pakistan border.

The separation of economic questions from political ones in the Indus basin—one through discourses of water resource development, the other through regional security dialogues—led directly to the onset and consolidation of the Cold War in the region. Michel observed: "The waters dispute left room for maneuver. It represented an area where the expertise of engineers and the ingenuity of lawyers and statesmen could be coupled with the incentives of international financing to produce a settlement" (1967, 9).

The Kashmir question was "frozen" as a result, throughout the Cold War. When it returned, it was in a changed world context, after the end of the Cold War, the rise of neoliberalism, and the "war on terror." The plebiscite promised under UN resolution 91 in 1951 never happened. Instead, with huge infusions of investments in water resource developments in the Indus basin, the strategic interests of the United States in the region, both public and private, were consolidated during the Cold War. Water resources projects on the Indus boosted private sector investments, especially from the United States (Michel 1967, 281–88).

Thus, the Cold War, played out through the post-partition hostilities between India and Pakistan, had a significant impact on the trajectory of water resources development in the Indus basin. These impacts were economic (in terms of funds available for development), political (in terms of choices in foreign policy), and technological (in that both countries were forced to take recourse to large-scale engineering structures with social, ecological, and economic ramifications). The technological and military orientation of water resources development commenced during colonial rule and continued after independence, putting water out of the hands of agriculturists and into the hands of national bureaucracies dependent on international funds to support the economy.

The transborder conflict-cooperation tensions in the Indus basin have a long-term impact on the people of the basin on both sides. The populations of both states, beleaguered by the border wars, are held back from pursuing democratic social transformations of the colonial state that has become a structural feature of society, the formal independence notwithstanding. The structural features are characterized by the legal and institutional dimensions of the state that internalize the schism between the economic and the political dimensions of social life. The reality makes any real self-determination or independence elusive and makes the people on both sides of the border vulnerable to the logics of imperial economics and politics in the region. On both sides people are left to deal with the ecological effects, environmental effects, social inequity, the empowerment of the elite, and their national priorities being "hijacked" by the priorities of the capitalist/imperialist nations. These problems are well traversed in the growing critical literature on dams and development.

Concluding Remarks

The end of the Cold War has once again renewed political, military, economic, and ideological crises everywhere. The regions surrounding the Indus basin are once again in turmoil: Afghanistan, Iran, India, Pakistan, China, and Russia. Equally, the rise of neoliberalism in international organizations and the emphasis on "governance," "economic efficiency," and "open economy" have changed the most important condition that made water resources development in the Indus basin a "success" story in the eyes of many: i.e., large infusions of funds at low costs to support state-led water resource planning premised on technological "giganticism." Once again the dramatic changes in the geopolitical alliances in the region are at tandem with renewed tensions over the Indus waters (Lautenbach 2005; Luce and Bokhari 2005). The "expertise of engineers and ingenuity of lawyers coupled with incentives of international financing" (Michel 1967, 9) that sustained the conflict-cooperation dynamic in the Indus basin was driven by the logic of the Cold War. Whether that dynamic can continue after the end of the Cold War must remain a question for another study.

It is the imminent "coming apart" of the post-war world order that poses new questions for water resource developments and security in the region. In the wake of the end of the Cold War and the rise of neoliberalism, a number of so-called new social movements have emerged (see Doyle, this volume). Among them, the movement against dams and development has built strong alliances and a concerted critique across national boundaries.[10] These movements are based primarily on the citizen-state axis, where citizens protest the consequences of the development paradigm adopted in the post-war era. In the Indus basin, too, popular movements against dams, such as South Asian Solidarity for Rivers and Peoples, form cross-border coalitions. The military and security dimensions of water resources developments in the two states remain to be teased out. To do so, the critique of dams and development, and environmental security as a framework for analysis, need to be anchored to wider theoretical questions about wars in the development of capitalism and imperialism. The task is a challenge for those who wish for real peace and prosperity in the Indian Ocean Region.

NOTES

1. First Anglo-Afghan War: 1839–1842; Second Anglo-Afghan War: 1848–1849; Third Anglo-Afghan War: 1919–1921.

2. First Anglo-Sikh War: 1845–1846; Second Anglo-Sikh War: 1848–1849.

3. Anglo Persian War: 1856–1857.

4. The British Empire in the Indian subcontinent included two types of states: the Provinces and the Indian States, also know as Native States or Princely States. The Provinces, formerly under the East India Company's rule and known as Presidencies, were under direct Crown rule. The Princely States were legally independent states with defense treaties with the British that reduced them to the status of protectorates.

5. Chua (1995) discusses the ways in which economic policies impinge upon communitarian identities in Asia.

6. See Menon (1956) for details.

7. UN Security Council Resolution 91, which passed in March 1951, called for a cease- fire along a de facto line of control and a plebiscite to be held under UN supervision to decide which of the two nations the people of Kashmir wished to accede to.

8. The diaries of Lilienthal, as well as the memoirs of Gulhati, reveal how personnel in the state departments, the World Bank bureaucracy, public and private enterprises, law firms, and the press were personally and socially close and how personal friendships brought about political results.

9. See Sklar (1994); Usher (1997); D'Souza (2006).

10. See, in this connection, the work of the International Rivers Network.

REFERENCES

Chua, Amy L. 1995. "The Privatization-Nationalization Cycle: The Link Between Markets and Ethinicity in Developing Countries." *Columbia Law Review* 95 (March): 223–303.

D'Souza, Radha. 2002. "At The Confluence of Law and Geography: Inter-State Water Disputes in India." *Geoforum* 33 (2): 255–69.

———. 2004a. "The Democracy-Development Tension in Dam Projects: The Long Hand of The Law." *Political Geography* 23 (6): 701–30.

———. 2004b. "Re-Envisioning Transboundary Water Disputes as Development Conflicts." In *Geopolitical Orientations, Regionalism and Security in the Indian Ocean*, ed. D. Rumley and S. Chaturvedi, 172–193. New Delhi: South Asian Publishers.

———. 2005. "The 'Third World' and Socio-Legal Studies: Neo-Liberalism and Lessons from India's Legal Innovations." *Social and Legal Studies* 4 (4): 487–513.

———. 2006. *Interstate Conflicts Over Krishna Waters: Law, Science and Imperialism*. Hyderabad: Orient Longman.

Gulhati, Niranjan D. 1973. *Indus Waters Treaty: An Exercise in International Mediation*. Bombay: Allied Publishers.

Lautenbach, Dale. 2005. World Bank Names Neutral Expert on Baglihar. Press release, May 10. Washington, D.C.: World Bank.

Luce, Edward, and Farhan Bokhari. 2005. "Pakistan to Seek World Bank Mediation." *Financial Times,* January 12.

Mehta, Jagat S. 1988. "The Indus Water Treaty: A Case Study in the Resolution of an International River Basin Conflict." *Natural Resources Forum* 12 (1): 69–77.

Menon, V. P. 1956. *The Story of the Integration of the Indian States*, 1961 ed. Bombay: Orient Longmans.

Michel, Aloys Arthur. 1967. *The Indus Rivers: A Study of the Effects of Partition*. New Haven and London: Yale Univ. Press.

Mustafa, D. 2001. "Colonial Law, Contemporary Water Issues in Pakistan." *Political Geography* 20: 817–37.

Sklar, Leonard, and Patrick McCully. 1994. *Daming the Rivers: The World Bank's Lending for Large Dams.* Berkeley Way, Calif.: International Rivers Network.

Usher, Ann Danaiya, ed. 1997. *Dams as Aid: A Poliitcal Anatomy of Nordic Development Thinking.* New York: Routledge.

Venkatramani, M. S., and B. K Shrivastava. 1963. "The United States and the Cripps Mission." *India Quarterly: A Journal of International Affairs* 19 (3): 214–65.

Washbrook, David. 1997. "The Rhetoric of Democracy and Development in Late Colonial India." In *Nationalism, Democracy and Development: State and Politics in India*, ed. by S. Bose and A. Jalal, 36–49. Delhi: Oxford Univ. Press.

12 *Struggles for River Security*

MOVEMENTS AGAINST DAMS

TIMOTHY DOYLE

Introduction

Many political networks involved in environmental movements in India and Australia pursue concepts of sustainable development, environmental justice, and environmental security.[1] It is important to understand that while some of these struggles for environmental emancipation (see last chapter of book) appear similar at first glance, they are culturally very distinct, both in their overall goals and in the strategies used for achieving them. This chapter investigates two environmental campaigns that, in part, champion more sustainable forms of environmental security. Both these struggles formed around the impetus to stop the building of mega dams: the Narmada and Franklin dam campaigns. One of the campaigns for environmental emancipation—the Franklin—takes place in a predominantly affluent country—Australia—while the Narmada campaign continues to be fought in a majority world country—India.

The following quotations are taken from two separate articles: the first, by P. P. Karan, refers to a common trait of three Indian environmental movements, Chipko, Silent Valley, and the Save the Narmada movements (the latter being a specific case study in this chapter). The second quotation was written by Cassandra Pybus, with direct reference to the Save the Franklin campaign in Australia.

> They cut across social and cultural cleavages that might have been expected to be divisive. They unite people who differ by sex, age, religion, ethnicity, caste, class, and region by stressing shared interests in saving the environment. . . . The integrative nature of the movement cuts across ancient and powerful ethnic barriers. (Karan 1994, 8)

> The Franklin dispute was a trauma for Tasmania. It was a time of extreme volatility where allegiances to political positions became emotionally-charged articles of faith. Families were ruptured by conflict; no-one was able to stay aloof. The scars of that time have cut deep into the political psyche and have been a long time healing. Perhaps nowhere is that more evident than in the Labor Party, which was torn apart by conflict and indecision. (Pybus 1990, 18)

Both quotations are interchangeable; because, regardless of global or cultural context, one of the key defining characteristics of these struggles is their new social movement (NSM) form. This structural form defies and, for the period of specific struggle, overrides barriers and borders, such as those generated by classes, religions, established political parties, and even families, which were previously regarded as inviolate and impermeable. Environmental movements rally and protest on a contextual basis. Strange bedfellows appear from the center as well as from the extremes of the traditional left-right political continuum in multifarious situations. Not only this, these NSMs strike new identities, some for a fleeting moment; others more lasting. Obviously this NSM characteristic to drift through barriers, or to violently disperse them, has positive and negative ramifications. In both India and Australia, the ability of environmental movements to do so has on the one hand created a tremendously broad coalition of support that has been utilized, on occasions, to empower the powerless. Alternatively, this ability of NSMs to spread tentacles of influence with scant regard for tradition has created confusion, tensions, and sometimes violence and death in the communities that have been penetrated and recategorized.

In the case of movements for sustainable development studied in this paper, this shared identity, if and whenever it happens, is a long way off from emerging. Regardless of very recent trends that suggest an increasing interplay between different cultures'/countries' environmental movements, the empirical reality is very different. In fact, it is still their profound differences in ideology and focus rather than their similarities that define the green movement experience in India and Australia, rather than cross-boundary, shared political activities/identities. Many of these differences can be characterized by the geopolitical categories generated by the differences between majority versus minority worlds.

Apart from Australia and India's sharing an ocean (the Indian Ocean), there are several historical and political similarities that make a comparative political analysis of this type appropriate. Both countries are democracies; both countries were invaded by the British; and, as a consequence, both countries operate as a federation of states with an extremely powerful bureaucratic and electoral center. Both types of government also refer to themselves as being "secular"; but the colloquial meaning of these terms is quite different. In the Indian context, "secular" usually refers to a tolerance and respect accorded to each citizen to practice his/her own religious observances. In Australia, "secular" more often refers to the fact that Australia is actually a "nonreligious" society, even at the individual level.

Both countries are also part of Greater Asia, though, again, this political category is subject to disputation. European settler elites, who dominate the current regime in Australia, have consistently tried to view Australia as a European outpost or, more recently, a junior partner of the United States operating in the region. More important, perhaps, is the fact that few Indians would regard Australia as part of Asia.

Finally, both countries share questionable records in relation to their treatment of their indigenous peoples, though in the case of Australia the genocide has been far more all-embracing.

There are also many differences. India is usually seen as a "third world" nation, with vast numbers of citizens experiencing a poverty that only a small percentage of Australians experience (usually among certain sectors of its indigenous peoples and what is increasingly being referred to as its "underclass"). Australia inhabits a rather confused place in geopolitics, though it is usually referred to as part of the more affluent "first" world. For the purposes of this chapter, I will refer to India as a majority world nation, and Australia as a minority world nation. This categorization makes further sense when one considers that over 1 billion people live in India, while Australia is a minnow in the population stakes, with only 19 million citizens.

Movements against mega dams have grown in stature since the early 1980s. In their groundbreaking work in 1984, Edward Goldsmith and Nicholas Hildyard wrote of the vast societal impetus behind the building of large dams, and the enormous obstacles that environmental movements and others faced in their opposition to such enterprises. They state: "To add to their difficulties, they [environmentalists] must also confront the entrenched belief that large-scale water development schemes [with their resulting hydroelectricity] are an essential part of the process of economic development—a process that we have been taught to see as the only means of combating poverty and malnutrition, and assuring health, longevity and prosperity for all. To challenge dams is thus to challenge a fundamental *credo* of our civilization" (Goldsmith and Hildyard 1984, 231). Both countries share a rather significant past in the specific terms of their environmental agendas. It is a collective fight against a mega dam that has been the most significant environment campaign in both countries' experience. The battle to "Save the Franklin River" in the Australian island-state of Tasmania was, without doubt, the most important single environmental campaign in Australia. Similarly, the fight for the Narmada in India has dominated the ecopolitics of India for a decade and a half. Both campaigns emerged at approximately the same time: in the early to mid-1980s. The Franklin campaign was fought intensely, and ended quickly and "successfully"; the Narmada campaign has continued since its time of emergence until the present day.

The Franklin Campaign

The campaign to save the Franklin River and its surrounding forests from being dammed by Tasmania's Hydro-Electric Commission (HEC) began in the late 1970s but reached a crescendo in 1983, at the very time the Save the Narmada Movement was beginning to catch the attention of the Indian population. So powerful was the Franklin campaign that environmental politics in Australia was never the same again. It moved the "environment" symbol from being a relatively peripheral one, to part of the central business of governments, both state and federal. The Franklin campaign was attributed with single-handedly bringing down the conservative federal government, and replacing it with a Labor government that upheld the cause of the river against the dam. The battle for the Franklin was a wilderness campaign. Patrick McCully, in his excellent study on the politics of big dams, explains that the Gordon-Below-Franklin dam "would have flooded part of one of the last great temperate wildernesses of the Southern Hemisphere. It would have inundated rare temperate rainforest, one of Australia's most spectacular gorges and archaeologically important caves with evidence of occupation 20,000 years before" (McCully 1998, 322).

Australians were bombarded with images of absolute beauty, untouched forests cascading down to the water's edge in remote Tasmania. Its supporters included the environmental non-governmental organization (ENGO) the Tasmanian Wilderness Society (TWS), whose major objective was to protect the unique natural habitat of the river and its surrounding forests from development. Wilderness campaigns such as the Franklin have dominated the Australian (as well as North American) environmental agenda. The key political message of wilderness movements is that the environment (nature)—and its nonhuman component parts—have rights to exist independently of human values and perceptions. This position has been referred to by Inglehart and others as post-materialist (Inglehart 1977), in that pursuit of this political goal is usually reserved for societies that have already fulfilled their basic hierarchy of needs necessary for survival.

In December 1982, environmentalists staged several blockades at the construction site of the Franklin dam. At its peak, 1,200 demonstrators were arrested during this "non-violent action," and in the interim the Franklin area was classified as a "World Heritage" site (Doyle 2000). Eventually, the "anti-dam," newly elected Labor Party had to take the issue to the High Court, which ruled that the Commonwealth government's external affairs powers "allowed Federal legislation giving domestic effect to international treaties, such as the World Heritage Convention, to prevail" (Tighe 1992, 126). The Franklin and its surrounding wilderness had been saved.[2]

The Narmada Campaign

The environmental protest with the biggest profile in India over the past decade and a half is, without doubt, the campaign fought over the damming of the Narmada River in western India (Swain 1997, 7). The Save the Narmada Movement (SNM) commenced in the 1980s as a battle for the resettlement and rehabilitation of people being displaced by the proposed mega dam—the Sardar Sarovar Project (SSP)—in the Indian state of Gujarat. The SSP is just one of a number of major dams being built on the Narmada River: the fifth largest river in India. Sheth writes: "The reservoir will submerge about 37,000 hectares of lands, of which about 11,000 hectares are classified as forests. It will displace about one lakh persons of 248 villages (19 of Gujarat, 36 of Maharashtra, and 193 of Madha Pradesh). The anti-project activists give more than double this figure as the project-affected persons (PAPs)" (Sheth 1997, 253).

The exact number of displaced persons is obviously debated vociferously by different parties, but they must be understood within the larger context of displacement that mega dams have brought to India. In a popular book that shook India on publication in 1999, Arundhati Roy estimates that at least 33 million people have been displaced by mega dams in India over the past fifty years. Roy writes of the ecological carnage of big dams, the dam concept having originated in the North but now deemed too dangerous for minority worlds, only fit for the consumption of the third world: "Big dams started well, but have ended badly. . . They're undemocratic. They're the Government's way of accumulating authority (deciding who will get how much water and who will grow what where). They're a guaranteed way of taking a farmer's wisdom away from him. They're a brazen means of taking water, land and irrigation away from the poor and gifting it to the rich. Their reservoirs displace huge populations of people leaving them homeless and destitute. Ecologically too, they're in the doghouse. They lay the earth to waste. They cause floods, water-logging, salinity, they spread disease" (Roy 1999, 7–8).

There is no space here for an in depth critical analysis of the phenomenon of mega dams.[3] Nor is their an opportunity for a full chronological account of the campaign as it has been championed by its key ENGO[4] proponent, the Narmada Bachao Andolan (NBA) of the Save the Narmada Movement. The campaign has already transpired for over a decade and a half. Just a few events within this vast campaign can be touched upon here. First, as aforementioned, the Narmada issue, more than any other environmental campaign in India, managed to unite a wide variety of social movement actors that were previously fighting disparate and more localized campaigns. At its Harsud Convention in 1989, for example, 45,000 people attended, including project-affected persons and activists belonging to approximately 200 NGOs (Sheth 1997, 255–56).

Next, in 1992, the NBA managed to ensure the withdrawal of the World Bank's funding of the project. This was a huge win, with the World Bank's reputation almost permanently tarnished in future "development" projects across the globe. The NBA and the broader movement, with its charismatic leaders Babe Amte and Medha Patkar, have pursued numerous successful, nonviolent actions of satyagraha (literally, firmness in truth). In 1994, for example, at a "dharma" every protester's hands were tied to symbolize their commitment to nonviolence. This did not stop the protesters from being badly beaten by police, but won for the movement a deep respect from many parts of the Indian populace.

In 1995, the NBA took its fight to the Indian Supreme Court, and won a four-year stay on the continued construction of the huge Sardar Sarovar dam. In October 2000, however, the Supreme Court decided to allow the construction of the dam to a height of 138 meters as originally planned. The Gujarat state government, and the National BJP government hailed this decision as a victory for the people and a defeat for the NBA. The NBA begs to differ, for the battle for the Narmada has always been more than just whether a dam was going to be built or not. In an interview with "Shripad," an NBA leader, it was made quite clear that the goal of the struggle was always much broader: "The goal has always been to empower people to fight for their own rights; to create a just society; to create a space in that society for justice and environmental responsibility" ("Shripad" 2000).

One trend in this vast environmental campaign is without question. From its early beginnings, with its focus purely on human displacement, gradually the focus of the Save the Narmada Movement shifted to the protection of the ecological integrity and pursuit of environmental justice for the entire valley (Karan 1994, 6).

Comparative Analysis

The differences and similarities between these two anti-dam campaigns are many. Only two sets of factors can be discussed here at any length. These two characteristics, however, are powerful and salient indicators that make it extremely clear how different these two environmental movements actually are. The first brutally obvious difference between the two campaigns relates to the alternative positioning of the human being in relation to nature/environment: there can be no more profound difference than this. The second relates to what, at first glance, appears to be the shared philosophical and tactical position of nonviolence. A closer look, however, reveals deep rifts in the interpretation of the concept as practiced by both movements.

The Human/Environment Relationship: Wilderness versus Human Survival

The most obvious difference between these two environmental, anti-dam movements is that the Franklin was a campaign largely fought for "other nature," while the Narmada campaign fought primarily for "human nature" (no doubt these boundaries are more blurred than this). First of all, there are vital demographic differences that influence these contexts. Millions of people work and live in the Narmada Valley (including the indigenous "adivasis"), while the indigenous peoples who lived in southwestern Tasmania were rounded up over a century ago in one of the most brutally "successful" genocidal "experiments" ever witnessed on the planet. It was only since the arrival of the Europeans that the Franklin and its watershed became a wilderness "free of people." Perhaps a precursor to qualifying as a post-modern, "first world" society is that indigenous peoples have to be wiped out and/or marginalized first: only then can the original boundaries, barriers, and other features that are the songs of the land itself be truly discarded and replaced with those more popular tunes profitable to the projects of global free markets. If this is so, then Australia almost fully qualifies,[5] while India has yet to reach this point.

However, there are much broader and more salient reasons that explain, more fruitfully, the differences in this focus in the Franklin/Narmada comparison. In the minority world, "environment" usually denotes an instrumental nature, "out there somewhere," away from humans, a nature which can be molded, used, and perfected by humans. In this manner, environment, in the more affluent North, has been dominated by issues such as "wilderness" (mainly forests). The term "wilderness" relies on a concept of "true nature," without the imprimatur of humans stamped upon it: the Christian garden before the great sin. In Judeo-Christian societies, the human/"other nature" split is a defining feature of its cosmology. Consequently, movements in the North bearing the green cloak may be dominated by questions such as which particular parts of nature must be hermetically sealed from human access; or, more profitably, how can this external environment be "managed" more efficiently.

According to Tagore, Indian society has emerged from a "forest society" and has always seen humans as part of nature, rather than separate. He writes: "The culture of the forest has fuelled the culture of Indian society, The culture that has arisen from the forest has been influenced by the diverse processes from species to species, from season to season, in sight and sound and smell. The unifying principle of life in diversity, of democratic pluralism, thus became the principle of Indian civilization" (quoted in Shiva 1992, 196).

Obviously, many other religions, such as Hinduism, Islam, Jainism, etc., as well as nonreligious ideologies, have been layered, palimpsest-like, over this "original" cosmological script. So, the origins of this human inclusiveness in nature in modern India are confused by the over-layering of other types of boundaries of identity. In actual practice, therefore, certain sectors of Indian society are just as dismissively dualistic as Western societies when it comes to their separation and treatment of "other" nature. For example, Indian political elites often describe the activities of environmentalists by referring to them as "boys and girls interested in saving tigers and trees" (Baviskar 1995, 235). Baviskar continues: "Such an understanding of what is 'environmental' echoes the thoughts of those who see development as an essentially benign process, marred only by a few regrettable externalities such as environmental pollution. 'Tigers and trees' are perceived as trivial concerns, luxuries that elites can afford to indulge in, since they have already gained the benefits of development. This interpretation of the conflict as 'environment' versus 'development' has tended to prevail in government discourse."

Of course, this is another example of the power of the environment symbol. Different sectors in different societies define it differently for both substantive and strategic reasons. Some seek to expand its umbrella; others seek to reduce it. In Baviskar's quotation, it is evident that certain sections of the Indian elite seek to limit the boundaries of identity of the environmental movement by publicizing their denigratory interpretation of the narrow focus of green activists. Often, this "tigers and trees" focus is then discursively connected to the fact that Indian ENGOs are simply pawns of the North, promoting post-materialist agendas.

But even side-stepping these religious/cultural divisions/explanations, it must be said that in many cultures in the South, regardless of religion, the human/nonhuman nature split is not as evident within environmental discourse. Most environmental issues in the South, as perceived by the bulk of the environmentalists themselves, are human survival issues, such as sustainable shelter, food, and water supply, employment, and disease control (Doyle and McEachern 1998, 2). Consequently, the "luxury" of pursuing nonhuman welfare issues is not available to most people. In this manner, through obvious necessity, humans are not regarded as separate from the rest of nature: the ecological degradation/human devastation nexus simply presents itself. Shiva comments: "The ecology movements that have emerged as major social movements in many parts of India are making visible many invisible externalities and pressing for their internalization in the economic evaluation of the elite-oriented development process. In the context of a limited resource base and unlimited development aspirations, ecology movements have initiated a new political struggle for safeguarding the interests and survival of the poor, the marginalized, including women, tribals and poor peasants" (Shiva 1991, 19).

Environmental issues, in this regard, are more central to questions that challenge status quo, "grown-up" politics. Although wilderness networks such as those dominant during the protests against the Franklin dam still exist within Southern environmental movements, they are in a minority. Environmental movements in the majority world perceive issues of social justice and equity as central goals. In short, it is not just a question of which parts of nonhuman nature are "protected," as in the case of minority worlds, but rather issues of the maldistribution and overconsumption of resources dominate majority world green agendas. There is very little that is post-materialist about the majority world. The post-materialist thesis sometimes (but far from always) provides a suitable description of green movements in the minority worlds of the North, but it has very little applicability in the South.

Nonviolence

Regardless of the fact that there is little direct contact between the two countries' activists, there can be no doubt that there are some important similarities. Shared personnel, or lack there-of, does not exclude the movement of ideas across boundaries. The most significant shared ideological component is, of course, nonviolent action (NVA). In many parts of the world strict nonviolence is no longer a defining characteristic of environmental action. In the United States, for example, the eco-saboteurs of deep ecological "nonorganizations" such as Earth First! believe they have a right "to defend mother earth" with militant actions. In Britain, animal rights organizations and the anti-roads movement have consistently used violence against property to pursue their goals (Wall 1999). In the Philippines, this level of violence includes the tactic of pursuing guerilla warfare in order to protect people's access to a livelihood when threatened by the activities of giant multinational mining corporations. In Australia and India, however, the most important shared ideological component of both movements is nonviolence.

No doubt, this shared experience is almost wholly due to the dramatic influence of Mahatma Gandhi. Gandhi's teachings emerged as a powerful influence in the Australian context, due largely to the merger of the peace movement with the environment movement in the late 1960s and early 1970s (Summy and Saunders 1986). One of the key campaigns of the peace movement had been against nuclear war, and this focus was extended in the 1970s to include opposition to uranium mining, which was seen as part of the "nuclear cycle" contributing to nuclear militarization. In addition, nonviolent techniques also infiltrated the early Australian movement from the United States Movement for a Free Society, again, in the early 1970s. Finally, the Tasmanian Wilderness Society, which was the key ENGO during the "battle for the Franklin," possessed a very influential network of Quakers (or Friends) that helped shape this nonviolence focus.

In the case of the Narmada, the ever dominant philosophy of nonviolence is at times overwhelming. Indeed, the existence of an ideology of nonviolence is one of the centrally defining characteristics of what can, and cannot, be classified as an "environmental" campaign in India. In a work on environmental politics in India, Sumi Krishna (1996) attempts to explain why the more violent/militant "tree wars" of the Gonds of Adilabad, the Naxalites, and the Jkarkland Movement in Southern Bihar are not regarded either by most environmentalists in India, or by the Indian ruling elite, as part of the "green terrain." Krishna argues that the dominance of the ideology of nonviolence, and its concomitant distaste for militancy within the Indian green movement, among other factors, explains this border between two movements with many similar goals, such as the empowerment of poor people against the encroachment of the state and multi- national interests (Krishna 1996, 152).

It is critically important, however, to understand the deep differences between Australian and Indian understandings of nonviolence. The Franklin protest was nonviolent in that people passively gave themselves up to police for arrest, and did not inflict violence upon their opposition. This western definition, however admirable, is an extremely narrow understanding of nonviolence when compared to NVA as practiced by the NBA and its supporters.

The Narmada NVA experience was different in its level of risk, as well as its depth of philosophy and broadness of purpose. For example, how many Franklin protesters were willing to die for their cause? In the Indian magazine *Frontline,* which has covered all aspects of the Narmada dispute since its emergence, the level of risk was made quite clear: "By the monsoon of 1993, villages nearest to the dam site, at Kervadia in Gujarat, faced submergence, and Patkar was forced to use the card of 'jal samarpan': threatening to drown herself in the floodwaters if the Government did not halt construction and constitute an independent review of all aspects of the SSP" (Swami 1994, 116).

On numerous occasions, Medha Patkar and supporters faced death, either through extended hunger strikes, through beatings ministered by "officials," or through refusal to leave villages threatened with submergence: a willingness "to meet the waters."

"Satyagraha" (literally translated as "firmness in truth"), however, is more than just a case of heightened risk: it is a term that embraces an entire "way of living," rather than just being a "passive resistance" tactic at a time of conflict. At the personal level it may relate to vegetarianism and acts of self-discipline. At the societal level, nonviolence is a dramatically radical political philosophy that strikes at the very heart of the modern nation-state. Baviskar contends: "The slogan of 'Our rule in our villages' calls for non-cooperation with the state, the Gandhian method of passive resistance against exploitative authority. Jan andolan (people's movement), or decentralized and non-violent collective action, is posited as a political alternative to the dominant political system . . . village self-government is theoretically consistent as a form of decentralized political action that tries to create a political alternative to mainstream politics" (Baviskar 1995, 224–25).

Although there were many occasions when traditional political and legal avenues were pursued by the NBA and its supporters, it was always, first and foremost, a mass mobilization campaign, designed to empower the adivasis (indigenous peoples) and small Patidar farmers (landholders with five to ten acres) directly threatened by the dam. The philosophy and practice of nonviolence in organizations like the NBA has led to the education, empowerment, and mobilization of Indian villagers in the valley. Prior to this empowerment, for the fifty years since India has gained nationhood, most of these people had no formal education, no subsidized food, no health care. And on the few occasions when there has been government contact—in the words of Himanshu Thakkar of Delhi's Centre for Water Policy— "it has created points of access into forest society with a view of exploitation on behalf of the state" (Thakkar 2000).

Both environmental campaigns, the Franklin and the Narmada, share the fact that they included a diversity of responses. Both played legal games; both dabbled in party politics; both protested directly and nonviolently; both challenged the state's intentions by dragging the issues onto the international stage.

Regarding the latter, in the case of the Franklin, environmentalists appealed to the international scientific community in a bid to have the southwest of Tasmania listed as a "World Heritage" site. The Save the Narmada Movement, linking with U.S. NGOs such as the Environmental Defense Fund and the Friends of the Earth (Sheth 1995, 72), briefly moved the campaign to Washington in efforts to place international pressure on the World Bank to withdraw its funding for the project. In both cases, these international strategies proved successful. This diversity of approaches in both campaigns is a true signal of new social movement political strategies.

Despite this multitude of strategic pathways, there are clear overall trends. TWS was dominated by appeals-to-elites strategies; Narmada was a mass-mobilization campaign. The Franklin campaign, despite the presence of more radical networks within it, was largely played within the established institutions of politics: an appeal-to-elites. Martin writes of the Franklin experience as follows:

> Civil disobedience can be used for several purposes. It can be: a method for involving people in meaningful experience in challenging unjust laws or actions, a way of demonstrating to others the depth of commitment felt by a group about an issue, a means to obtain publicity and apply pressure on politicians. The Tasmanian blockade was all of those things. . . . Yet for the TWS organizers, the blockade was mainly used to obtain publicity and thus to apply pressure on national politicians, it was not seen as part of a long-term strategy involving grass- roots involvement in non-violent action. The main emphasis throughout the campaign was on saving the Franklin within the context of present political structures, by a change in policy at the top, rather than a restructuring of political institutions. (Martin 1984, 116)

Of course, the overriding goals of the two movements, with such different interpretations of the environment symbol, also ultimately led to very different types of political tactics and strategies, though both still operate within the new social movement form. To be fair, elements of the "wilderness" ideals of the Save the Franklin movement can be considered far-reaching and quite radical in terms of providing serious questions about the future valuing of "other nature." Despite this, however, many of these goals can be achieved in the short-term, within politics-as-usual: environmentalists advocating these goals have rarely challenged systemic inadequacies dealing with fair and equitable resource distribution; they have rarely contributed directly to the lives and deaths of human beings, as was the case in the Narmada Valley.

Conclusions

There is an emerging body of evidence that globalization will enlarge the level of interaction between environmental movements of different ilks. Many campaign structures are changing to make full use of the Internet. For example, at the recent climate change conference in The Hague, an international green campaign was run almost exclusively in cyberspace. There can be no doubt that this interactivity has multiplied since the first emergence of the Franklin and Narmada campaigns. The Narmada movement, typifying many other environmental struggles in the majority world, began as a fight for the rights of people's livelihoods against the mega development of the state and transnational capital. Later it began to adopt the "environment" label, and discussion of a "green agenda" emerged. There can be no doubt that the latter type of arguments came from Northern environmental movements, and that these movements, in a sense, sought to coopt Southern struggles into a global frame that would strengthen the Northern resistance against a Northern "enemy." In this sense, there are substantial elements of ecological imperialism here, with the more "dangerous" arguments of the South being omitted or sidelined. Krishna comments on this changing agenda in the Indian context as follows: "Liberal opinion, and both national and international NGOs, empathized with the motif of trees. They also related much more easily to the broad issue of conservation than to the specific politico-economic questions of employment, labor conditions, and local industry. . . . [It] has transformed outraged response into a meditation on ecology" (Krishna 1996, 157).

But, as happens with social movements, it is not so simple. There is also dramatic evidence that in more recent times, Southern movements are increasingly driving the global green movement agenda, including those incorporating concepts of sustainable development, with many Northern NGO and CBO players taking a subservient role—for now. For the flow of history is a mirror opposite in the green movements of the minority world. Like the Franklin, many began as postmaterialist movements, interested in trees, parks, and threatened species, but many minority world environmentalists are gradually coming to terms with the fact that people are also part of the environmental equation: they are not separate from nature. As a consequence, we have seen the beginnings of environmental justice and democracy movements evolving in the North for the first time. This has occurred due largely to the amplified power of Southern movements in recent times.

Princen and Finger, in their study of environmental NGOs across the globe, support this argument when they write: "Just as Northern NGOs are becoming more institutionalized, Southern NGOs are building organizational skills and financial independence and, as a result, increasingly demand greater autonomy and less dependence on Northern supporters. . . . As Southern NGOs are becoming more independent and setting the international agenda, Northern NGOs are looking to the South for ideas, as well as to establish their own international credibility" (Princen and Finger 1994, 8).

It would be vacuous, however, to suggest that power moves equally both ways, like the tide, and that in the end some form of global balance will be struck by this increased interplay between social movements of the majority and minority worlds. As there is no such thing as a free market, or a free lunch, there is also no such thing as a free political space. The amorphousness and structurelessness of new social movements (alongside their cyberspace equivalent in the supposedly equally structureless Internet) will ultimately deliver results to the more powerful players.

At this chapter's outset, I mentioned the fact that within the "new world order" there has been a move toward promoting both global and local meaning systems over those of the nation-state. This is certainly a good description of the current period. Local identity systems, based on sacred senses of place and community, are currently very visible in their opposition to global capitalism, and this explains, in many ways, the multitude of very different movements, both gathering under the umbrella of "environment" and other social causes. But this "glocalisation" (Newman 2000) may be just a transition phase. Paradoxically, the championing of the "local" by an increasingly global movement of resistance that includes environmental movements may ultimately decimate this well-documented local diversity of experience in favor of more homogenous, simplistic dichotomies and dualisms utilizing Western capitalism as the base point upon which everything else is measured. In this manner, environmentalism, as "the other," with its ambiguous but increasingly shared strands of support and meaning, may also be acting as a globalizing catalyst, leading to the creation of a diaspora of vast proportions—a globe crawling with environmental refugees—condemning the majority world to a place that is at once beyond boundaries and, at the same time, within a prison cell of global poverty and ecological degradation.

But the future, of course, is not a time or place within fixed, defined boundaries. This chapter, in seeking to record the empirical reality of two national environmental movements—both fighting against the construction of mega dams—is more of a celebration of differences than similarities: more evidence of the fact that there are many environmental movements across the earth, rather than one. Movements pursuing more sustainable forms of environmental security across the globe must persist in this salutation of diversity and resist the all-powerful but understandable urges to overly homogenize opposition, using the justification of global resistance and, in doing so, creating *one* environmental movement. A more creative and longer lasting relationship between the minority world nations like Australia and majority world nations such as India will emerge from a continued respect and reverence for diverse localized experiences found within a multitude of ecological communities, both human and nonhuman.

NOTES

1. Not all environmental movements endorse the concept of sustainable development. In fact, many green networks are violently opposed to it, seeing it as a concept championed by business interests to co-opt the more oppositional limits-to-growth arguments of more radical environmentalists. See Doyle 1998.

2. For full accounts of the Franklin dam campaign and its movements, see: Green 1981, The Wilderness Society 1983; Connolly 1981; Thompson 1984.

3. For a thorough and thoughtful analysis of the politics of mega dams read: McCully 1998. In addition, as aforementioned, one of the earliest and most ground-breaking popular critiques of mega dams emerged out of the journal *The Ecologist,* edited by Edward Goldsmith in London, in the mid-1980s. See, for example, Goldsmith and Hildyard 1984. Many arguments against the Aswan and other dams made within this special edition of *The Ecologist* are still used today by anti-dam movements around the world.

4. There are many different terms in different cultures for the equivalent of nongovernmental organizations. In the United States, for example these groups are often referred to as civil society. In India, and other parts of the majority world, these NGOs are sometimes also referred to as Citizen-Based Organizations (CBOs). In this light, NGOs are seen as much larger, more institutionalized, and often international organizations.

5. To acknowledge this attempt at genocide in the case of Australian indigenous peoples is something that has only recently been aired in public forums. It must be voiced, however, with the knowledge that not all aboriginal peoples, or even all Tasmanian aboriginal peoples, were annihilated. It is important to understand that Australian aboriginal peoples have survived the attempted decimation.

REFERENCES

Baviskar, Amita. 1995. *In the Belly of the River: Tribal Conflicts over the Development in the Narmada Valley.* Delhi: Oxford Univ. Press.

Connolly, B. 1981. *The Fight for the Franklin.* Sydney: Cassell.

Doyle, T. 1998. "Sustainable Development and Agenda 21: The Secular Bible of Global Free Markets and Pluralist Democracy." *Third World Quarterly* 19 (4): 771–86.

———. 2000. *Green Power: The Environment Movement in Australia.* Sydney: Univ. of New South Wales Press.

Doyle, T., and McEachern, D. 1998. *Environment and Politics.* London: Routledge.

Goldsmith, Edward, and Hildyard, Nicholas. 1984. "The Politics of Damming." *Ecologist* 14 (5–6): 221–31.

Green R. 1981. *The Battle for the Franklin.* Sydney: Fontana.

Inglehart, R. 1977. *The Silent Revolution.* Princeton, N.J.: Princeton Univ. Press.

Karan, P. P. 1994. "Environmental Movements in India," *Geographical Review* 84 (1) (January): 32–42.

Krishna, Sumi. 1996. *Environmental Politics: People's Lives and Development Choices.* New Delhi: Sage.

Martin, B. 1984. "Environmentalism and Electoralism." *Ecologist* 14(3):. 110–18.

McCully, Patrick. 1998. *Silenced Rivers: The Ecology and Politics of Large Dams.* New Delhi: Orient Longman Limited.

Newman, P. 2000. "Theoretical and Methodological Issues Relating to Boundaries." Paper presented at "Rethinking Boundaries: Geopolitics, Identities and Sustainability" conference, University of Punjab, India, February. 20–24.

Princen, T., and M. Finger. 1994. *Environmental NGOs in World Politics: Linking the Local to the Global.* London: Routledge.

Pybus, C. 1990. *The Rest of the World Is Watching*. Sydney: Pan Macmillan.

Roy, A. 1999. *The Greater Common Good*. Bombay: India Book Distributors.

Sheth, Pravin. 1997. *Environmentalism: Politics, Ecology, and Development*. Jaipur: Rawat Publications.

Shiva, Vandana. 1991. *Ecology and the Politics of Survival: Conflicts Over Natural Resources in India*. Tokyo: United Nations Univ. Press.

———. 1992. "The Green Movement in Asia." In *Research in Social Movements, Conflicts and Change: The Green Movement Worldwide, Supplement 2*, ed. Louis Kriesberg, 195–215. Greenwich, Conn.: JAI Press.

"Shripad." 2000. Interview at NBA headquarters, Vadadora, Gujarat, March 24.

Summy, R., and M. Saunders. 1986. *A History of the Peace Movement in Australia*. Armidale, N.S.W.: University of New England.

Swain, A. 1997. "Democratic Consolidation? Environmental Movements in India." *Asian Survey* 37 (September): 818–832.

Swami, P. 1994. "Narmada Diary." *Frontline, India* (December 30): 116.

Thakkar, Himanshu. 2000. Interview, at Centre for Water Policy, New Delhi, March 17.

The Wilderness Society. 1983. *The Franklin Blockade*. Hobart: The Wilderness Society.

Thompson, P. 1984. *Bob Brown of the Franklin River*. Sydney: Allen and Unwin.

Tighe, P. 1992. "Hydroindustrialisation and Conservation Policy in Tasmania." In *Australian Environmental Policy*, ed. K. Walker, 124–55. Sydney: Univ. of New South Wales Press.

Wall. 1999. *Earth First! and the Anti-Roads Movement*. London: Routledge.

PART IV

FIRE

13 *Fire and Firepower*

ENERGY SECURITY IN THE INDIAN
OCEAN REGION

TIMOTHY DOYLE

As "Westerners" traveling in Iran in what George W. Bush has called part of the "Axis of Evil," what quickly became apparent to us was that Iranians, like all who dwell in the IOR, wrestle with the daily grind of securing access to the vital ingredients for survival. Most environmental issues in Iran are reminiscent of those experienced in many parts of the majority world. They are issues of human survival: shelter, energy, water, and food security, all of which are threatened by rapid and uncontrolled industrialization. This industrialization is centered on the petrochemical industry, with few of the environmental safeguards and end-of-pipe technologies available to more affluent societies.

Energy issues are increasingly apparent on national environmental agendas, and Iran possesses approximately 40 percent of all known natural gas deposits on the planet. Mechanisms to transport this gas to neighboring countries via pipelines for market returns are now being explored.[1] In addition, Iran is currently developing a nuclear capacity, which brings with it an additional range of environmental problems and traditional security issues to confront.

Air and water pollution in the Iranian capital, Tehran, as in numerous other regions in the IOR, have now reached a critical stage. The city itself lies in a valley beneath a massive mountain range. As a consequence, the capital sits in a convergence layer that traps the fetid and polluted air of the overcrowded city. Iran also wrestles with major water shortages. Moving south, through the center of Iran, we travel across a vast flood plain of biblical proportions, framed to the west, north, and east by distant, majestic mountain ranges capped with ice (not tundra but pebbles). But in arriving at the famous cities of Shiraz and Esfahan, people scratch at forms of agriculture that are sustained by only 150 milliliters of water per year.

Traveling further south, and then east, we arrived at the ancient city of Bam, devastated only months earlier by an earthquake that claimed the lives of 40,000 people. The earthen houses of Bam had been constructed using the old methods, with no vertical struts. The sad reality was that during the earthquake, the roofs of the shelters had fallen to the floors, killing all within. Again, it seems the poorest exist and live their lives in the most vulnerable environments.

A few post-materialist green issues do exist, such as the preservation of icon species such as the Persian Cheetah, and the limited conservation of the Caspian Sea. More importantly, however, is to understand that what exacerbates the poverty of both urban and rural Iran is the international trade embargo placed on it by the international community. Poor people, bearing the brunt of successive wars, and conquests by various imperial powers, do not understand or care about the political intricacies of the trade embargo: they are simply hungry. So, in the context of air, water, and earth, Iran shares the plight of most who dwell in the IOR.

There is one significant difference between Iran and much of the Middle East however, when compared to their oceanic neighbors: the country, or more specifically the government that rules it, is rich in energy, specifically nonrenewable resources: oil and gas. Traveling to the north of the country, one confronts the magnificent Caspian Sea (discussed at length by Aparajita Biswas in this volume), a rich oil and gas field. The Middle East is synonymous with the politics of fossil fuels. It has been central to the globe's oil-based economy for nearly a hundred years, since the first discovery of "black gold" in Persia in 1908. In part, these resources allow Iranians to survive. But, this discovery has become a double-edged sword, effecting enormous exploitation and pain. Billon and Khatib argue: "after 'black gold' was discovered in Persia in 1908, this resource drastically exacerbated the stakes in the struggle over the spoils of the Ottoman Empire and the Western security imperatives to prevent the (re)emergence of a powerful regional rival" (Le Billon and El Khatib 2004, 109).

This cornucopia of fossil fuel energy resources has been Iran's salvation as well as its main source of suffering. It was entirely appropriate, then, that the second IORG conference—held in February 2004—focused on energy security. This event occurred at an interesting time. First, it happened to coincide with the Iranian national election. Second, it occurred not long after the U.S. invasions of Iraq and Afghanistan. Third, it happened at a time that many commentators are now referring to as the third major oil shock since the Second World War (Rumley and Chaturvedi 2005, 1). Finally, it was early on in the U.S. opposition to Iran's plan to develop a nuclear industry. In all these events, the politics of energy control is never far from the surface.

The Iranian national election of 2004 was intriguing to watch. Walking through the streets and markets of Tehran, we were confronted by a fascinating demographic phenomenon: three quarters of the Iranian population is under 25, with two-thirds of the people being women. Many of the men have been killed in a series of wars, including the murderous Iraq–Iran war, which spanned the decade between 1980 and 1990, in which over 1million were killed on the Iranian side alone. Iran's theocratic ruling elite defies this demographic, however, being both a patriarchy and a gerontocracy (Doyle and Simpson 2006).

Middle-class, urban Iranians live an existence clearly split between private and public lives. In the public realm, the world of the Mullahs dominates. Women are constantly reminded by passers-by to alter their head-dress to cover some offending hair that has emerged from beneath. Religious police scout parks and other public spaces, making sure young men and women are not demonstrating outward signs of affection. However, in the private realm, the world behind closed doors, women wear Western dress and men consume alcohol. It is also in this domestic realm that dissenting opinions to the state are sometimes heard.

It was in such circumstances that we found ourselves in the lead-up to the national election. In very recent times, the regime had ruled out many of the candidates from standing for election. So, although there were electoral mechanisms in place reminiscent of democracy, candidates had to be endorsed by the ruling regime beforehand and, as a consequence, many more progressive candidates had been ruled out in the weeks leading up to the election. As we sat in one particular living room, a United States CNN news service was being broadcast on the television, critically evaluating the likely outcome of the "undemocratic" poll in Iran, predicting that massive numbers would refrain from voting due to the majority of Iranian citizens protesting against the current regime and the "fixed" elections. The very next story on the bulletin depicted a recently completed Russian-built nuclear reactor. One of the agreements the Iranians had made with Russia before the construction of the reactor was that it would return nuclear waste to Russia, the very substance needed to create weapons-grade fissile material. However, at the completion of the construction phase, Iran had decided to treat the majority of its own waste. The reporter raised questions regarding the ultimate intentions of Iran in relation to a suspected uranium enrichment program. This led to conclusions being drawn, and consequently the CNN broadcast linked the undemocratic nature of the elections with the proximity of nuclear weapons of mass destruction.

It was interesting to observe how some of our hosts (mainly young students) responded. Some agreed with the notion of refraining from voting in order to lodge their silent protest. But the majority in the room, even though supporting the progressive movement, felt that it was the wrong time to question national unity—however flawed—due to what they understood to be the threat of an imminent invasion by the United States and their "Coalition of the Willing." One of the students, who we will identify by the pseudonym of "Ahmed," articulated this position as follows: "You see . . . Iran is now surrounded by U.S. and British armed forces. In many ways, in terms of your conference, the United States is now a defacto Indian Ocean state due to its heavy military presence in the gulf region. . . . We are in a sandwich between Afghanistan and Iraq. . . . The Americans want our oil . . . and our gas. They will use any argument in an attempt to galvanize international opposition against us. The nuclear issue is their entry point. . . . It is the wrong time for internal divisions."

By the end of the week, when the national election votes were counted, approximately 65 percent of Iranians had cast their votes. This is quite a high figure in electoral systems that do not demand compulsory voting. It is hard to provide an accurate breakdown of figures that would explain voting trends under authoritarian regimes like Iran's. No doubt, some who voted supported the regime. But despite a progressive campaign strongly supported by the international press for nonparticipation in the election, it is clear that many progressives followed Ahmed's line of reasoning. Of course, it must be reiterated, that in a war-ravaged culture like Iran's, fear of future wars is heightened. The United States surrounds Iran on two sides, both at the Afghan and Iraqi borders. Many Iranians understandably fear invasion by the United States. This galvanizes the society, limiting internal opposition to the regime, as a greater, external enemy is imagined approaching.

Energy security is not only the power that provides heat and light, but energy also metamorphoses into firepower. Fire, then, is also a form of defense, and, therefore, is a key part of environmental security that relates to the ability to defend oneself from annihilation by those who seek the source of one's "fire." Energy, then, is central to larger issues of military security in Iran in three ways: first, fossil fuels in the Persian Gulf and Caspian Sea regions are, in large part, the reason for the U.S. and British presence (and has been the source of conquest for over a hundred years); second, nuclear energy has become the international flashpoint in relation to Iran that may justify further military engagement; and third, in relation to nuclear energy, it is a possible source of mass weaponry. "The International Energy Agency (IEA) estimates that world energy consumption growth in the Asian region is likely to be between 4 to 6 percent. It is also estimated that Asia is set to overtake North America as the leading energy consumer in the next 10 to 15 years" (Luthra 2005, 19).

In parts of the Indian Ocean Region, rapid industrialization is taking place. Energy needs for the future are immense. Importantly, the region is also seen as a key source of energy supply. Also, the ocean and its ports are part of essential transport routes for the globe's energy industries. It must not be overlooked, however, that the current state of play in relation to energy, as it affects people's everyday lives, is that the energy uses of the majority of people within the IOR are rarely included in such official statistics. The reason is simple and disturbing. Although exact figures are extremely difficult to come by, it is estimated that across the globe, at least 2 billion people live outside the oil/gas/electricity nexus that fuels the first world. Most of these people live in the Indian Ocean Region. Theunis Aldrich—from the Institute for Global Dialogue, based in Johannesburg—estimates that in rural Africa 54 percent of people are without access to electricity. Most people across the region are reliant on micro-scale collection and utilization of energy. By far the most common reality relates to the everyday lives of women who, at the grassroots level, gather biomatter, usually in the form of animal dung, agricultural wastes, and sparse wood stocks for all energy needs. Household energy accounts for most rural energy use: in India, the figure sits at 75 percent of all energy usage. The burning of such fuels has obvious health risks. Most energy consumed in rural households (where most people live) is for cooking, 90–100 percent in Africa (Karekezi et al. 2002); and 90 percent in India (Neudoerrfer et al. 2001). The rest is used for heating and lighting.

In the IOR, renewable energy is not seen as an expensive luxury item, only to be used in a manner that builds upon heavy reliance on centralized fossil fuels energy systems. Due to the fact that most people in the region will not, in the foreseeable

Figure 13.1 Indigenous people across the region are often forced to live next to radioactive waste dumps.
Source: Joel Catchlove.

future, gain access to the national grid, even at the nation-state level, there is heavy emphasis on pursuing alterative energy strategies. In 1982, for example, India became the first country to create a Department of Non-Conventional Energy Sources (Whitta 2004). Conventional energy sources in India are highly inefficient, with 23 percent of power lost during transport and distribution (Joshi et al. 1997, 191). As a consequence, the Indian government has been extremely active in pursuing renewable energy technology, such as solar, wind, and biofuels, attempting to garner 20 percent of all energy needs from renewable projects. As Joshi suggests: "This . . . would create a substantial reduction of both environmental damage and also the problems of security and sovereignty" (1997, 190).

The connection of energy to security and sovereignty are crucial to understand. When people do move up the "energy ladder," they are confronted with a loss of control of their energy sources and face increasing centralization of the resources in the hands of nation-states and transnational corporations. Energy no longer becomes the domain of the micro-economies of the village or other kinship groups. Instead, it becomes fundamental to the development and security status of the nation-state itself. With this transition from local to national also comes a move to the transnational arena. In his excellent article that conceptualizes energy security for the IOR, Girish Luthra argues that in this manner "energy has also been a key attribute of changing international power equations during the last fifty years, and continues to be a dominant theme in the emerging geopolitical environment" (Luthra 2005, 18). So energy, more so than any of the others three elements of environmental security investigated in this volume, is also seen by many as comprising a traditional security issue. Luthra continues: "Unlike some other forms of security, it is more 'vulnerability based' rather than 'threat based.' It also implies making strategic choices in political, economic, social, military and environmental realms, and comprises elements of both collective as well as national security" (Luthra 2005, 20).

Once the transition is made to play the centralized energy game at the nation-state level in poorer economies, as is usual with larger industrial and commercial enterprises, the majority of countries in the IOR find themselves in an additional bind. For not only do their own people lose control of their energy resources, but the state also becomes heavily reliant on the energy that is determined by its first world partners. More than half of Asia and Africa import over 50 percent of all their commercial energy (Sayigh 1999). These countries export crops and other primary resources with little or no value added. They command low prices, but import energy at high prices. Through this economic construct, the IOR countries become extremely reliant on the trading whims of transnational capital, and energy control becomes the primary function of national and military security. It is in this manner that poorer nations are disciplined into accepting the dominant global game of fossil fuel politics, and more recently to invest heavily in nuclear power. Both sources of energy are ultimately controlled by states existing, at least in a geographical sense, outside the region. Chaturvedi and Rumley write:

> It needs to be acknowledged at the very outset that energy security, unlike other aspects of non-traditional security, has always been intimately related to military security. More often than not, it is the hegemonic consumer-states that have sought to maintain an uninterrupted supply of energy at an affordable price, through the threat and/or actual use of military power. . . . With the energy- military security nexus peaking and asserting itself nearly globally, the prospects of a serious conflict in the Indian Ocean region between the impera-tives of energy-social security broadly defined, and the quick-fix strategy of "securitizing" energy flows practiced by the hegemonic power(s) cannot be dismissed that easily. Those who choose to address the individual and societal dimensions of energy security have been widely criticized on several grounds, especially after the painful events of 9/11 and its aftermath (Chaturvedi and Rumley 2005, 286).

The ability of energy issues to cross the conceptual and often arbitrary bound-aries separating traditional and environmental security explains, to a large extent, the diverse content of this section. It is for this reason that we started this chapter with a first-person piece written in the Middle East. The article by Aparajita Biswas concentrates its analysis in a more traditional *statecraft* fashion, examining the impact of the post–Cold War period on the energy security of the Indian Ocean Region. In her analysis she is eclectic in drawing from three different schools of thought to decipher recent events: the strategic, the liberal, and the nontraditional security approaches. Adam Simpson, looks at the transnational dimension relating to electricity generation. He does not focus on the energy requirements of the nation-state involved; instead, he questions the centralized development paradigm of the large corporations and nation-states involved, and questions the costs of these profit-based exercises on the communities that live in the vicinity of these projects.

The last paper, by Dennis Rumley and Timothy Doyle, takes the traditional/ alternative security nexus one step further, investigating the burgeoning nuclear industry in the IOR. The study of nuclear energy politics sees energy issues surpass what Luthra has previously called the "vulnerability based" dimensions of energy security, to visit its "threat based" security characteristics that align it to military security. It is for these critical purposes that, in the remaining pages of this chapter, I wish to further introduce this issue: for, in the early days of the millennium, the poorest region on the planet is fast becoming "the nuclear ocean."

The Indian Ocean as the Nuclear Ocean

While many parts of the more affluent world are moving away from nuclear power as an industrial and domestic energy source, the Indian Ocean Region (IOR) is rapidly increasing its nuclear energy profile. Most often, this increase in nuclear profile is evidenced in discourses linked to the nuclear proliferation of weaponry. Because of the IOR's informal status as "Ocean of the South," the environmental security focus on nuclear power has not been sufficiently explored, as the possibilities of nuclear accidents—whether in mining, power generation, reprocessing, transport, or storage—are seen as risks that those "less affluent" are expected to take. With the IOR's increased nuclear profile, it is critical that environmental security concerns are included alongside the more traditional security concerns.

Like climate change and population growth, nuclear issues cross nation-state boundaries. Just as many parts of the industrialized world have come to the realization that the nuclear option cannot be sustained in an environmentally secure fashion, parts of the majority world have now embraced the technology. The Indian Ocean Region is currently undergoing rapid nuclearization, with many countries now embracing the technology for the first time. For most Indian Ocean countries, the issues of nuclear waste—its safe transport and its final disposal— have not been high on their environmental or nuclear agendas.

Issues pertaining to nuclear power have until recently been omitted from debates about environmental security. One of the key reasons behind this is that nuclear issues are already considered as part of the mainstream, traditional, hard security or defense debates. This focus on nuclear energy is almost always from the angle of weaponry and arms proliferation, and is almost always centered on the identities of nation-states. It is not, therefore, so much a case of introducing nuclear issues into the security rhetoric out of the policy cold, but rather, dragging some of its related issues out of "traditional" security debates and then including them in the more alternative human and environmental security discourses. In this vein, for the purpose of this research, I have deliberately not entered into the debate over nuclear weapons build-up in the region (which of course is already high on the international security policy agenda); instead, I have sought to recast the nuclear question in the IOR as an environmental security issue: principally dealing with the ever-increasing problem of nuclear waste—its transport and its storage. This alternative focus has allowed me to engage with nation-states in the region, such as Iran, Pakistan, and India, creating a dialogue of cooperation on the issues of nuclear and energy security, whereas a more traditional focus would have been prohibitive (Doyle 2005).

Nuclear power as an energy source brings with it a complex range of problems, including the storage and transport of nuclear waste. However, it is important to note that, with the exception of Australia, opposition to nuclear power within the IOR has been minimal. Most of the anti-nuclear campaigns in the Australian context are either aimed at halting the nuclear fuel cycle at its base (that is, to challenge the validity of mining uranium ore itself) and/or objecting to the construction of a storage facility for the waste products of these processes. The reasons for this are many. First of all, the majority of the Indian Ocean is usually classified as *third world*, and nuclearization has normally been a characteristic of industrialization. But most importantly, the dangers of nuclear accidents—whether they occur during plutonium production or during the handling and storage of waste products— are often regarded by majority world governments as constituting acceptable levels of environmental risk. In the current case of Iran, with fears of a U.S.-led invasion dominant in domestic policy circles, the possibilities of a nuclear accident are not rated highly on either security or environmental agendas. Worries over such environmental risks are often regarded as *luxury* concerns.

Nuclear reactors and nuclear waste dumps are either being constructed or are under consideration for the first time in many parts of the IOR. Australia is currently in the early stages of building a new nuclear reactor to replace its old research reactor at Lucas Heights in Sydney. Other IOR nations, including India, Pakistan, Iran, and South Africa, have all either recently developed a nuclear program or are in the initial stages of development. Linked to these reactors is the need to consider more permanent repositories for nuclear waste, as well as issues that relate to the transport of such waste. Traditionally, the key problem for the globe in relation to waste has been waste disposal *after* atomic reaction occurred. But because most countries in the IOR region have infant nuclear programs, this problem has not yet reached its future magnitude. But what is already pressing in these less affluent countries are issues of primary waste management which relate directly to the mining process itself. In wealthier countries such as Australia, the management of these wastes through the utilization of tailings dams is usually based on adequate levels of technology, although there are still dangerous leakages reported at disturbingly regular intervals. In the poorer parts of the region, these basic storage problems, and hence environmental risks, are exacerbated by limited access to the same level of appropriate technologies available to first world countries. It appears that these risks are considered by both state and corporate players to be acceptable.

Let us consider the case of India. India has embarked on the three-stage nuclear energy program that its government believes will reach its full fruition by 2020, with 20,0000 megawatts of electricity produced. One of the key problems for India relates to its very low-grade uranium stocks, necessitating mining on an extremely large scale with few economic margins available to pursue adequate environmental and safety measures. As a consequence, "normal" safety standards pursued in the minority world are almost nonexistent in South Asia. In India's main uranium mine—Jaduguda—200 trucks of ore pass through the village everyday. Uranium tailings lie unprotected in front of the local school. The liquid waste from the mine is dumped into the tailings dams and then diverted into a channel that ends up in the Subernarekha River. In one of the villages, Chatikocha, 500 people live below the embankment   of   the   tailings   dam   (Mahapatra   2004).   Saluka Himbram, the head of the village, talks of living next to the mine and the tailings dam: "Abnormal births have become common. Half of the women have problems in delivery and miscarriages. . . . We feel like vomiting when the wind, carrying fine dust from the pond, reaches us. . . . The tailing pond must be causing the problem" (quoted in Mahapatra 2004).

The critical message here is that environmental security issues relating to uranium mining and nuclear energy will be magnified in the less affluent world. The case of Australia may allow us to imagine a nuclear future for the Indian Ocean—to wrestle with potential waste issues—but the cold reality is that the Indian Ocean, as a nuclear ocean, will exhibit levels of environmental degradation that can be scarcely understood in Western thinking. In simple, political terms, the lives of people are more expendable in the majority world of the IOR, and this in turn has a devastating impact on their environments.

At the regional level, it is not just waste generated within the region; but also the ever- increasing waste which passes *through* the region that must be considered. This vital issue is taken up in the final chapter in this section by Dennis Rumley and Timothy Doyle. Apart from dismissively being regarded as simply en route states for the international trade in waste reprocessing, countries of the IOR are also increasingly being looked at as possible repositories, or "dumping grounds," for international nuclear waste. If the only waste product of nuclear energy was high-levels of radioactivity, with an initial half life of 24,000 years (as is widely reported for high-level waste), then the Indian Ocean would already have been targeted for nuclear waste storage. For, as is already well-documented by the environmental justice movement, it is the poorer nations who accept the waste of wealthier societies, in exchange for money. And within those countries, it is the poorest communities who are forced to dwell alongside these repositories (Bullard 1993).

At this juncture, the environmental security concerns of waste storage and transport become intermeshed, once more, with more traditional security concerns of nation-states and their defense. Because spent nuclear fuel can be reprocessed to produce weapons of mass destruction—as well as energy—the placement of such waste dumps is highly politicized. Of the Indian Ocean countries, as mentioned, Australia has been specifically targeted as a possible nuclear dump by the transnational corporation Pangea. In the late 1990s, Pangea placed the policy spotlight on Australia due to its apparent political and geomorphological stability. Though there is some merit to the geomorphological arguments, imagining that political stability could survive thousands of years is, at best, rather comical and nonsensical and, at worst, downright dangerous. Currently, Pangea has backed off its Australian target, while the Australian Federal Government has taken over the running—this time advocating a low to medium density national waste repository in either South Australia, Western Australia, or the Northern Territory.

At the broader level of anti-nuclear movements across the globe, it is extremely interesting to see these movements emerging for the first time in the majority world. As aforesaid, these movements also share an active disdain for the build-up and utilization of nuclear weapons within traditional security discourses. Environmental security issues such as nuclear energy include human security issues that cross the political boundaries of nation-states, gathering momentum in ecological and geopolitical regions such as the IOR. It is the immensity of these problems, paradoxically, that demand regional cooperation if they are to be successfully addressed. This cooperation, with great hope and conviction, may one day provide environmental security—human security—for all who dwell in the region.

Conclusion

Of course, in the IOR most people will have no access to nuclear energy, or any other form of centralized, state-controlled energy. The only time that most will confront the reality of nuclear energy will be when they are faced with wastes and toxins from the nuclear cycle, or have to live with the coercive threat posed by potential nuclear conflict. Decentralization of energy projects, with an emphasis on alternative and sustainable energy sources, must continue to be pursued within the IOR. Energy programs that support the development of micro-hydro projects, improved biomass use, community-scale solar, and wind energy projects are all means of maximizing the capacities of communities in the region to stabilize rural life through employment and an improved lifestyle. Jefferson argues that allowing communities to continue to control their own energy sources—but improving them through the use of appropriately scaled, alternative technologies— "may slow down or avoid some of this population drift [to urban areas]" (Jefferson 1997, 20).

At this micro scale, there have been positive attempts in recent times to increase the efficiency of wood stoves. In Africa and India, there has been some limited success with these schemes, although many users are dissatisfied with the decrease in heat that the new stoves produce, and their inability to keep insects at bay due to their reduction in smoke production (Karekezi et al. 2002). In Indonesia, however, the stoves have received a more positive endorsement, with local peoples approving of the improved taste that the newer cooking process produces.

Many renewable energy advocates believe there is energy security in diversity, that a well "developed" society is one that does not overly rely on one power source, such as electricity. Despite the apparent merits of diversity, the fact remains that international economies and the hegemonic powers that are built upon them are further disciplining poorer nation-states and communities into taking part in the global cash economy. One way in which this is done is to insist on much larger-scale energy projects. These infrastructural developments controlled by the state, corporations, and international financial regimes often demand monocultures of energy that are centrally controlled. With the move from rural communities to urban centers over the coming decades, it is imagined that the centralization of energy will continue. More and more peoples in the majority world will be further regimented into accepting fossil fuel and nuclear-generated energy through grid extension and singular reliance of electricity. In this manner, the people of the IOR will find their way into the statistical calculations of such organizations as the International Energy Association, as they will rate as "real people." In a positive light, there are some benefits of being in the mainstream of the global market. But for the large numbers who will remain outside of these energy monocultures, there will be little or no alternative energy infrastructure provided, and they will continue their lives as "nonentities."

NOTE

1. One of the major projects that looks increasingly likely to go ahead is a gas pipeline from Iran to India via Pakistan (Simpson 2006b).

REFERENCES

Bullard, R. 1993. *Dumping on Dixie.* Philadelphia: Westview Press.

Chaturvedi, S., and D. Rumley. 2005. "Towards and Indian Ocean Energy Community? Challenge Ahead." In *Energy Security and the Indian Ocean Region,* ed. D. Rumley and S. Chaturvedi. New Delhi: South Asian Publications.

Doyle, T. 2005. *Environmental Movements in Majority and Minority Worlds: A Global Perspective,* New Brunswick, N.J.: Rutgers Univ. Press.

Doyle, T., and A. Simpson. 2006. "Traversing More Than Speed Bumps: Green Politics under Authoritarian Regimes in Burma and Iran." *Environmental Politics* 15 (5): 750–67.

Jefferson, M. .1997. "Sustainable Energy Options." In *Sustainable Energy Supply in Asia,* vol. 1, ed. P. Chaturvedi, 19–20. New Delhi: Concept Publishing Company.

Joshi, M. D., and D. Vaja. .1997. "Meeting Energy Needs through Renewables: Can It Meet the Socio-Economic Needs of 930 Million Indians." In *Sustainable Energy Supply in Asia,* vol. 1, ed. P. Chaturvedi, 190–200. New Delhi: Concept Publishing Company.

Karekezi, S. 2002. "Renewables in Africa: Meeting the Energy Needs of the Poor." *Energy Policy* 30 (11–12) (September). http://80-infotrac.galegroup.com.proxy.library.adelaide.ed.auu: 2048/itweb/adelaide (accessed March 21, 2004).

Karekezi, S., and W. Kithyoma. 2002. "Renewable Energy Strategies for Rural Africa: Is PV Led Renewable Energy Strategy the Right Approach for Providing Modern Energy to the Rural Poor of Sub-Saharan Africa?" *Energy Policy* 30 (11–12) (September). http://80-infotrac. galegroup.com.proxy.library.adelaide.ed.auu: 2048/itweb/adelaide (accessed March 21, 2004).

Le Billon, P., and F. El Khatib. 2004. "From Free Oil to 'Freedom Oil': Terrorism, War and US Geopolitics in the Persian Gulf." In *Geopolitics of Resource Wars: Resource Dependence, Governance and Violence,* ed. P. Le Billon, 109–137. London: Frank Cass.

Luthra, G. 2005. "Conceptualising Energy Security for the Indian Ocean Region." In *Energy Security and the Indian Ocean Region,* ed. D. Rumley and S. Chaturvedi, 18–33. New Delhi: South Asian Publishers.

Mahapatra, R. 2004. "Eyewitness: Radioactivity Doesn't Stop at the Mines in Jaduguda." *Down to Earth* 12 (23): 23–25.

Neudoerffer, R. C., P. Malhotra, and P. V. Ramana. 2001. "Paticipatory Rural Planning in India—A Policy Context." *Energy Policy* 29 (5) (April): 371–81.

Rumley, D., and S. Chaturvedi. 2005. "Introduction: Energy Security and the Indian Ocean Region." In *Energy Security and the Indian Ocean Region,* ed. D. Rumley and S. Chaturvedi, 1–17. New Delhi: South Asian Publishers.

Sayigh, S. 1999. "Renewable Energy: The Way Forward." *Applied Energy* 64 (1–4): 15–30.

Whitta, K. 2004. "Renewable Energy Use in the IOR: The Potential to Meet Energy Security Needs." Unpublished paper submitted as part of Environmental Studies Honours Program, University of Adelaide, Adelaide, South Australia.

14 Issues of Energy Security and the Indian Ocean Region

Energy is likely to be at the heart of a major transformation of the global political scenario in the next few years. The post–Cold War world order that saw the fundamental changes in the mid-1980s is again on the threshold of a major change. Whereas the disintegration of the Soviet Union in 1991 and the intertwined association of globalization and capitalism shaped the contours of international relations in the mid-1990s, the outset of the 21st century will see oil as the most likely catalyst of change.

The energy security issue assumes paramount importance in the oceanic regions of the world, which, besides being richly endowed with natural resources, are also the source of a large portion of the world's production of hard minerals, like manganese and hydrocarbons. A simple definition of energy security, one that was more or less consensual before the 1990s, was "enjoying sufficient supplies at an acceptable cost." However, the concept has lately been at the center of a highly controversial debate, some stressing the "supply" element, others the "cost." The first concept of energy security might be thought to be "realist" or "strategic," since it is viewed mainly as a struggle to control the sources of a strategic energy resource, i.e., oil. According to this approach, since oil is a scarce, highly priced, and geographically concentrated commodity, it can be used as a "weapon" of blackmail in the international scene. Thus, proponents of this approach recommend energy self-sufficiency or, at least, the diversification of supply sources and of energy mix, and the establishment of reserves to help face a sudden tightening of supplies.

However, this strategic approach has been challenged by the "liberal" school of thought on energy security, which made its presence felt during the 1980s. According to their view, given the regular discovery of new oil fields, the growing role of the non-OPEC producers, and the development of hedging instruments such as the futures market, oil is becoming less strategic and should be considered as a normal commodity. Thus, government intervention would be desirable only in a situation of market disruption. As such, state intervention would be legitimate only in the basic regulation of the market, information gathering and diffusion, research and development, and international cooperation.

The two approaches presented above share some important characteristics. Both are supply-oriented, focused on oil, and state-centric. However, the rise in environmental awareness, the development of transnational terrorism in the 1990s, and new schools of thought in the field of international relations have recently produced a new, nontraditional perspective on energy security. For example, Stoett and Pretti argue that energy security should be assessed at all the different steps of the energy cycle: production, transportation, and waste. Advocates of such an approach thus encourage the development of a new energy paradigm that will be both more secure and cleaner than the actual model of energy development (Stoett and Pretti 2003).

Keeping the above approaches in mind, this chapter addresses the salient security concerns associated with the issue of energy, which has assumed colossal importance in recent years. An attempt has been made to examine and assess this issue by means of a regional geographical analysis, with the Indian Ocean Region being the focal point.

Change in the Pattern of Energy Consumption

Since the 1990s, the world has witnessed a significant shift in energy consumption patterns. The share of developing countries in global energy consumption has increased noticeably since the 1970s. In 1971, Asia—including the Organization for Economic Cooperation and Development (OECD) and the Pacific region—accounted for only 14 percent of the total world demand for energy. Today its share has doubled to 28 percent. In fact, Asia has emerged as the largest oil-consuming region in the world, one percentage point ahead of North America. In 2000, South Asia accounted for approximately 3.9 percent of the world's commercial energy consumption—up from 2.8 percent in 1991. By 2010, the energy use in developing Asia (including China and India, but excluding Japan, Australia, and New Zealand) is projected to surpass consumption of all of North America (Horsnell 1997).

According to the *World Economic Outlook,* Asia's share of oil in the global total will continue to increase and reach 35 percent by 2020. The increase will be evident mainly in China, India, and Southeast Asian countries. In volumetric terms, this means that demand for energy in Asia, which was 19 million barrels per day in 1997, will grow to over 28 million barrels per day in 2010 and more than 37 million barrels per day in 2020 (World Bank 2003). However, given the limited and declining production of oil in the region, the incremental demand for oil needs to be met with imports. For example, Southeast Asia is already a net importer of oil, in spite of the presence of oil-exporting countries in the region, like Malaysia, Indonesia, and Vietnam. Going to South Asia, the region consumed around 2.5 million barrels per day of oil, but produced only 0.80 million barrels per day in 2000, making it a net importer of around 1.7 million barrels per day. India and Pakistan account for most of the South Asian oil production (South Asia Regional Country Analysis Brief 2004). The Middle-East is expected to remain the major source of oil to both South and Southeast Asian countries.

Besides oil, there has also been a significant increase in the demand for natural gas in Asia. The Asian gas market splits into that for LNG (Liquefied Natural Gas) and pipeline gas. The International Energy Agency (IEA) projects that the demand for LNG in Asia will be more than doubled in 2020—of all forms of energy, demand for natural gas in Asia is expected to grow the fastest. Natural gas provides 9 percent of Asia's total energy needs; when China and India are excluded, Asia consumes 15 percent of natural gas as a share of its primary energy resources. In South Asia, natural gas reserves are around 58.6 trillion cubic feet, or about 1 percent of the world's total. The region consumed and produced around 1.99 trillion cubic feet of natural gas in 2000. Around 48 percent of this production is consumed by Pakistan, another 40 percent by India, and 17 percent by Bangladesh (IEA 1996).

Southeast Asia has also seen a considerable growth in the use of pipeline gas, primarily among the member countries of the ASEAN, with Indonesia, Malaysia, Brunei, Vietnam, and Thailand having significant gas reserves.

Gas Pipelines: Some Issues of Cooperation and Conflicts

In recent years, energy pipeline projects have attracted global capital in the Indian Ocean Region. Multinational oil companies like Unocal, Spie Capag, and Total Fina Elf of France, for example, have made significant investments in the region. However, while the emerging markets have created opportunities for cooperation in the hydrocarbon sector, they have also created conditions for conflict. There is intense competition among oil firms and nation-states to gain control over precious energy resources like oil and gas, especially in today's era of globalization. Due to this competition, political processes—both local and global—are continuously shaping the dynamics and complex interrelationship between the oil firms and nation-states on one hand, and NGOs like environmental and human rights organizations on the other. At the core of politics related to exploration of oil resources are vital issues such as exploration of new oil fields in virgin areas, smooth management of crude oil flows toward refineries through well-guarded pipelines, enhanced profit revenues through oil extraction, and the likely impact of such activities on the environment, development, and governance.

The Yadana pipeline project is a case in point. It became the focal point of domestic and international debate and is discussed by Adam Simpson in this volume. There are important security issues involved in the gas trade. It may be recalled that during the peak of the Cold War, the United States had strong reservations about Europe's opting to import gas from the former Soviet Union. Europe could secure their agreements only after agreeing to limit imports from the Soviet Union to 70 percent of the total requirement and to develop the giant Troll field in Norway as a fallback measure. Moreover, the security of supplies becomes all the more critical, as gas is used mostly in power generation.

Meanwhile, the "great game" is once again being played in the Caspian Sea basin and Central Asia, over access to energy and transit facilities ("Yadana Pipeline Project" 2000). In this rerun of the first great game—the 19th-century imperial rivalry between the British Empire and Tsarist Russia—players once again position themselves to control the heart of the Eurasian landmass.

Today, the United States has taken over the leading role from the British. Along with the Russians, new regional powers such as China, Iran, Turkey, and Pakistan have entered the arena, and transnational oil corporations are also pursuing their own interests. Like the "Great Game" of the early 19th century, in which the geopolitical interests of the British Empire and Russia clashed over the Caucasus region and Central Asia, today's struggle between Russia and the West may hinge on the issue of who controls the oil reserves in Eurasia. Control over these energy resources and export routes out of the Eurasian hinterland is becoming one of the key issue in post–Cold War politics.

For example, in the case of the great oil and natural gas fields of Turkmenistan, immediately north of Afghanistan, the U.S. government has for decades strongly supported U.S.-led business group Cent Gas, a consortium led by Unocal, for the construction of a US$3.5 billion oil pipeline from Turkmenistan to the Arabian Sea via Afghanistan, and a gas pipeline from Turkmenistan across Afghanistan to Pakistan. It would lead from Krasnovodsk on the Caspian Sea to Karachi in the Indian Ocean. The project is perceived as the quickest way to bring Turkmenistan gas to the fast-growing energy markets of South Asia.

It is interesting to note here that both the United States and Russia are concerned about the gas pipeline from Turkmenistan, but for different reasons. The vital interests of the United States and other Western allies are served by making Afghanistan a prime transshipment route for the export of vast oil, gas, and other natural resources of Central Asia. The U.S. government fully backed the route as a useful option to free the Central Asian states from Russian clutches, and to prevent them from getting close to Iran. To help it canvass for the project, Unocal hired the prominent former diplomat and secretary of state Henry Kissinger and a former U.S. ambassador to Pakistan, Robert Oakley, as well as an expert on the Caucasus, John Maresca (Yadana Pipeline Project 2000).

As for Russian interests in the two pipelines, geopolitically Russia aims to gain control over the oil and gas resources in the Caspian basin, and to keep U.S. companies out, unless they operate on Russia's terms. Russia's interest is that without the gas pipeline, Turkmenistan remains hostage to the Russian gas transportation system as a means to access the Western markets. This is leverage Russia is not likely to give up. Likewise, Moscow helped facilitate the abortive coup in Turkmenistan in late 2000 to sideline the gas pipeline project from Turkmenistan via Afghanistan to the Indian Ocean and Pakistan, and possibly India. In fact, Moscow sought to prevent Central Asian states from building corridors to the Indian Ocean and the formation of a transportation axis connecting Turkmenistan and Uzbekistan to the Indian Ocean, via Afghanistan and Pakistan. Russia has also figured that both in the short-term and mid- term, it would be cheaper for it to obtain gas from Central Asia than for it to make huge investments to develop its own gas fields in Siberia. The extent of Russian interest can be judged from its continued support for the Northern Alliance, despite the U.S. and NATO presence in Afghanistan and despite U.S. objections.

However, the situation in Iran is most unenviable. Iran faces serious obstacles in mobilizing foreign investments and modern technology for development of its oilfields because of prolonged American sanctions. The unilateral American economic sanctions were imposed on Iran during the hostage crisis, following the Islamic Revolution in 1979. Thereafter, in 1995, President Clinton issued Executive Orders 12957 and 12959 pursuant to the International Emergency Economic Powers Act. This was a declaration of a national emergency with respect to Iran, and banned commercial energy development contracts between Iranian and American corporations; it also imposed restrictions on Iranian imports, primarily oil and natural gas. The U.S. Congress unanimously passed the Iran-Libya Sanctions Act (ILSA) in August 1996, which imposed mandatory and discretionary penalties on non-U.S. companies, in case they invested more than $20 million annually in the Iranian energy sector. Moreover, the dominant position of the United States in the international financial system enabled the U.S. Congress to integrate support for International Monetary Fund and World Bank assistance loans within American economic sanctions. In March 2003, President Bush extended the economic sanctions imposed on Iran, because of the latter's support for international terrorism and attempts to acquire weapons of mass destruction (Kleneman 2004).

In this evolving scenario, Iran is actively pursuing energy diplomacy to sustain its economic growth. With its estimated 26,600 billion cubic meters of oil reserves, the second largest in the world, Iran is frantically looking at the emerging energy markets.

In Asia, Iran perceives China to be its important strategic ally. The budding relationship that is developing between these two countries has received a great amount of international attention recently, particularly in the wake of their signing two mega oil and LNG energy deals in October 2004. A contract was signed by Sinopec (China's second largest oil company) and Iran for an estimated $70 billion to $100 billion, for the shipment of LNG to China. As part of the deal, Sinopec also agreed to purchase 250 million tons of LNG over thirty years and to develop the Yadavaran oil field in southwest Iran (Stobdan 1999).

The other LNG project that has attracted a lot of attention is another deal between China and Iran. Through this deal, the Zhuhai Zhenrong Corporation is set to buy 2.5 million tons of super-cooled, compressed natural gas per year from Iran, starting in 2008. It is expected to rise to 5 million tons a year from 2013. The Zhenrong Corporation, which is also one of China's four major state oil traders, had signed a memorandum of understanding with the Iranian ministry of petroleum to undertake development and production of three Iranian oil fields as part of the LNG purchasing plan. It should be pointed out here that there is huge pressure on Chinese state oil firms to secure foreign oil and gas assets, in order to fuel its fast-growing economy, especially as domestic oil and gas outputs are declining (Hufbauer et al. 1998).

Besides China, Iran has also signed a major oil deal with India. In its US$40 billion deal with the National Iranian Oil Company (NIOC), India made a commitment to import natural gas from Iran over a 25-year period, and to develop two Iranian oil fields and a gas field. As a part of the deal, India's ONGC Videsh Ltd. (OVL) gets a 20 percent share in the development of Iran's biggest onshore oilfield, Yadavaran. The Indian Company (OVL) will also get 100 percent rights in the

300,000 barrel per day Jufeir oilfield. The stakes in Yadavaran translates to 60,000 barrels per day of oil for India. Significantly, China also operates in this oilfield and has a 50 percent share (Rashid 2002).

However, U.S. sanctions in Iran have created major impediments in a decade-old Iran-Pakistan-India gas pipeline project. It may be recalled that a memorandum of understanding was signed between Iran and India in 1993 for a 1,700-kilometer pipeline. It would pass through 700 kilometers of Pakistan territory. In 2000, the government of Pakistan affirmed that it would permit a gas pipeline linking Iran's massive gas reserves to India, across its territory. Pakistan will get gas and transit fees to the tune of US$400 million to US$500 million per year for the Iranian gas supply to India.

Pakistan has also offered security guarantees for the pipeline. India is interested in this project because of its incremental demand for gas, which is expected to reach 400 million standard cubic meters per day. According to Iranian sources, the pipeline could save India up to US$300 million every year in energy costs. Significantly, Pakistan has signed a memorandum of understanding with Russian energy firm Gazprom to pursue the construction of the trans-Pakistan gas pipeline from Iran to India and to enhance oil and gas cooperation. However, it has been reported that U.S. pressure is building up on Islamabad not to enter into an energy deal with Iran at this juncture. Thus, an Iran-Pakistan-India gas line project flies in the face of American efforts to isolate Iran regionally (Bhadrakumar 2005).

However, while both India and Iran have expressed their determination to go ahead with the project even in the face of U.S. threats, questions remain about Islamabad commitment, which is vital to the project since the pipeline will have to pass through Pakistan. In fact, for India, the Iranian pipeline is only a part of the grander scheme of pan-Asian energy corridors—pipelines crisscrossing Myanmar and Bangladesh in the east, and Turkmenistan and Central Asia in the northwest, in addition to the Iran pipeline. However, all these proposals are continuously held back because of the cold relations between India and Bangladesh. The disagreements between these two countries have slammed the progress for discussions on a natural gas pipeline from Myanmar to India, which would have to pass through Bangladesh territory, forcing India to look into the expensive option of creating a deep sea pipeline through the Bay of Bengal that would bypass Bangladesh.

Again, regional politics also plays a major role in defining the game. As the international gas pipelines have to transit through many countries, it depends on multi-country agreements for the smooth and continuous supply of gas.

Nevertheless, the trends of cooperation and collaboration between states and global companies have opened up many opportunities in the hydrocarbon sector. The Dolphin project—the world's biggest gas project—was conceived as a joint venture between the United Arab Emirates Offset Groups (UOG), Total Fina of France, and Enron. It was an ambitious scheme to transport natural gas from Qatar's huge offshore North Field via an undersea pipeline to UAE, an example of the emerging dynamics of market integration among the neighboring countries. Through the Dolphin project, Qatar—the leading producer of natural gas in the

Persian gas region—was able to provide gas to neighboring states like Abu Dhabi and Dubai, which were looking for gas to diversify their economies. At present, the Dolphin project is also supplying gas to countries like Oman, Pakistan, and India (Gerald 2001).

Interestingly, one notices a significant change in the debate on energy security in the 1990s. The energy security calculus today is very different from that of the 1970s and 1980s, when oil shocks and fear of global supply shortages determined government resource policies. The notion that conflict may arise over energy competition, fuelled by a perception of supply shortage, is not the main concern of states today. Rather, the changing patterns in trade, a greater reliance on the Middle-East for oil, and, therefore, a greater reliance on open access to sea-lanes and shifting strategic relationships are sources of conflict that may have an impact on the region's energy security. In fact, some scholars argue that the common challenge of increasing external reliance on energy supplies among Asian states would create an incentive to cooperate, not compete.

Traditional and Newly Emerging Regional Security Concerns

Given the dominance of oil as the energy source of choice and Asia's dependence on the Middle-East for oil, issues like open access to sea-lanes and domestic instability raise concerns regarding the security of the sea-lanes in the Indian Ocean Region. For instance, domestic stability in Indonesia and Malaysia—on both the sides of the Strait of Malacca—is critical to the security of these lanes.

In the Indian Ocean Region, access to energy sources is a critical security issue, given the structure of its energy needs and expected future consumption patterns. The region attained enormous importance mainly because of its geographical location and strategic waterways. The first route is around the Cape of Good Hope, onward to Western Europe and the United States, and the other route is eastward, through the Malacca Strait to Japan. The area is important because the two vital choke points lie here, namely the Strait of Hormuz and the Strait of Malacca. These two routes account for more than 60 percent of oil transits (Cordesman 1999). The Strait of Hormuz is the world's most critical oil choke point, it being the only shipping channel in and out of the Persian Gulf. Over 14 million barrels of oil flow through this strait each day to Asia, Western Europe, and the United States. At its narrowest, the strait consists of 2-mile-wide channels for inbound and outbound tanker traffic within the Oman side of the strait, as well as a 2-mile-wide buffer zone. It represents the most important strategic passage in the world, solely because of its access to the oil fields of the Middle East. It forms a strategic link between the oil fields of the Persian Gulf, the Gulf of Oman, and the Indian Ocean.

However, the most serious concerns in the region are focused on Iran and Iraq, the greatest long-term threats to U.S. interests in the region. This is because of the strategic location of the strait, which provides a vital connection between the Persian Gulf and the rest of the world. In early 1995, Iran deployed some 6,000 troops to Musa and other islands at the entrance to the strait. This trade route is so important that any closure of the strait would trap about 7 to 10 percent of the global very large crude carriers (VLCC) fleet in the Persian Gulf.

The other important strategic passage of the world is the Strait of Malacca, because it supports the bulk of the maritime trade between Europe and Pacific Asia, accounting for 50,000 ships per year (600 per day). This straight is the primary sea route from the Middle-East and Africa to Japan, Korea, China, Chinese Taipei, and other Pacific Rim countries. The strait, which is only 3 kilometers wide at its narrowest point, connects to the South China Sea, another extremely important shipping lane and a conflict region. Any closure of the Strait of Malacca would mean freight disruption and an increase in sailing time and freight rates (Cordesman 1999).

However, apart from the territorial disputes and insecurities about sea-lanes of communication, there are also potential concerns relating to Asia's new relationship with the Middle-East—largely based on Asia's growing energy requirements and the Middle-East's ability to supply them. There are apprehensions regarding the safe export supply of oil because of the history of political instability in the Middle-East. In addition, Asia's increasing dependence on the Middle-East heightens the strategic importance of sea-lanes from the Persian Gulf across the Arabian Sea and the Indian Ocean, through the Strait of Malacca and nearby waterways, and finally across the Southeast China Seas to China, Japan, and Korea. Moreover, the Iraq war, in particular, revived concerns over the impact of a disturbance in the Middle-Eastern supplies or a U.S. naval blockade in this strategic area.

Finally, from a geopolitical perspective, strengthening Asian–Middle-Eastern ties over energy implies new strategic interests for Asia in the Middle-East, which may complicate Asia–U.S. relations. It has been reported that China is building up bases along sea-lanes in the Middle-East to protect its oil shipments. According to the report "Energy Security in Asia," China is looking at the possibilities of pipelines traversing Pakistan and Bangladesh territory, as part of its "string of pearls" strategy to bypass the narrow Strait of Malacca, which experiences 40 percent of the world's piracy and through which 80 percent of China's oil import flow. China has also constructed a port in Gwador in the Pakistani province of Baluchistan. The location of Gwador is significant because of its proximity to the Strait of Hormuz. Consequently, the port would compete with a port facility at Chabbar in Iran, which is being jointly developed by Iran and India to access the landlocked states of Central Asia and Afghanistan. China's "string of pearls" strategy also forms part of a wider Chinese policy to encircle India (Gertz 2005).

Further, China is looking not only to build a blue water navy to control the sea-lanes, but also to develop missile and undersea mines capabilities, to deter the potential disruption of its energy supplies by potential threats, including the U.S. navy, especially in the case of a conflict with Taiwan. The report noted that the vast amount of oil shipments through the sea-lanes, along with growing piracy and maritime terrorism, prompted China, as well as India, to build up naval power at "choke points" along the sea routes from the Persian Gulf to the South China Sea. Iran is also building its bases near the Strait of Hormuz.

Another important development in international relations is a major shift of Russian foreign policy. President Putin of Russia outlined in 2000 a comprehensive plan to connect Europe and Asia through a project transformation of Russia's infrastructure. He stressed Russia's "natural" role as a bridge and hub linking Asia, Eurasia, and Europe through joint development of major projects that transcend energy, electricity, and power engineering, to include rail, sea, air, and space satellites and communications. He feared that failure to build "Russian Asia" would invite the hegemony of China, Korea, or Japan in this region. Putin also announced that problems in the development of Siberia on the state agenda were "key, pressing, [and] strategic ones" (Blank 2003).

Ultimately, the projects mentioned above also connect with Russia's ambitions for North- South corridors linking Russia, Iran, India, and Central Asia. The main components of this these North-South corridors are (1) navigation between ports of India across the Arabian Sea to the southern port of Bandar Abbas; (2) a new container terminal in the port of Bandar Abbas; (3) a railway connection between Bandar Abbas and Iranian ports on the Caspian Sea side; (4) Caspian Sea navigation; (5) a container terminal at the seaport of Olya; and (6) a railway connection between the Russian region and with northwestern ports for transit cargo (Regine 2002).

This grand design can materialize only with massive foreign investment and support. It would make Russia the hub of a vast network of Eurasian inland trade and transportation, and would materially stimulate the growth of inner and Russian Asia, thereby greatly strengthening Moscow's international political standing. Russian officials say that shipping oil via Russia's railroad network, with its East-West routes, would require 20 days of transit, as opposed to sending shipments through the Suez Canal that take 45 days. As a result, the cost per container would fall by US$400 to 500 while simultaneously netting Moscow hundreds of millions of dollars in transit charges, taxes, and customs revenues, all while also effectively competing with the Suez Canal and the EU's TRACEA and Silk Road projects that bypass Russia. One assessment of this projected corridor claimed in 2000 that it would tie together Finland, the Baltic, Russia, several Gulf states, and India.

In pursuance of its proactive "Look East" policy, Russia's foreign minister toured India, Pakistan, and Bangladesh in 2003. This policy reportedly attempted to revive the five-year-old proposal for an axis between Russia, India, and China against U.S. ascendancy, to ensure a multi-polar world that, in cooperation with Iran, would turn the oil-rich Central Asian region into their domain. It may be recalled that this proposal, which would put in place extensive military agreements and pipeline networks, was originally put forward by Russian prime minister Yevgeny Primakov. It appears to be gaining ground with the four nations.

Consequently, a Russian naval task force—the largest after the disintegration of the Soviet Union—has been deployed for an indefinite period in the Indian Ocean and surrounding areas. Although Russia has denied any active involvement of its navy in the Indian Ocean area, analysts claim that Russia wants to register itself there, as the maritime focus after the Cold War and especially after 9/11 has shifted to the Indian Ocean Region. Moreover, according to analysts, Russian presence in the Indian Ocean underlines the importance of "exercising control" over the Indian Ocean, through which pass vital oil routes from West Asia. It would also give Russia the leverage to access the vast Asian market for oil and gas.

On the other hand, Russia and China have also established the Shanghai Cooperation Organization (SCO), a regional Central Asian grouping that includes Tajikistan, Uzbekistan, Kazakhstan, and Kyrgyzstan. The SCO is looking to form a larger coalition, including India, Pakistan, and possibly Iran. Moreover, the relationship between India and China has gained unprecedented momentum in recent years. Both countries have decided to focus on the mutual benefits of economic interdependence. Politically, too, China has agreed to back India on the issue of claiming a coveted seat on the UN Security Council. Both of them have signed 25-year gas and oil deals with Iran, collectively valued at between US$150 and 200 billion. Again, both are also deepening their defense cooperation with Iran (Bedi 2003).

It is important to note here that these new developments would have serious ramifications in the Asia–U.S. relationship. The alliance of countries like Russia, China, Iran, and India has the potential of shaping the economic, environmental, and geopolitical future of these countries and the world. On the one hand, the stronger energy ties between China and Iran will weaken America's leverage to negotiate economic, military, and nuclear nonproliferation issues. At its core, the new alliance is a mutually beneficial arrangement based on the satisfaction of each country's needs. But perhaps more importantly, the alliance presents a united front in the face of what is perceived as a common threat posed by the United States. Taken separately, China and Iran are formidable regional powers. However, when taken together, they become an foreseeable and influential force on many levels.

Western thinkers are anxious about the role of Asian powers like China, India, and Iran and the possible impact in the international arena. During her recent visit to India, U.S. Secretary of State Condoleeza Rice voiced Washington's "serious concern" at the prospect of a US$4 billion gas pipeline bridging these economies, but stopped short of saying the United States would impose sanctions arising from provisions of the Iran-Libya Sanctions Act.

Concluding Remarks

It may therefore be concluded that the conflict over increasing energy needs is not inevitable. The need to access energy resources on the world stage can be as much a catalyst for cooperation as it can be for conflict. There is a need for continuous contact and dialogue between nations and global actors. For example, India's quest for energy security is being impeded by its sometimes tense relations with energy suppliers, energy transit countries, and energy competitors. While China has either resolved or shelved its border disputes, India has active conflicts with all its neighbors. Apart from poor relations with Pakistan on its western borders, the ongoing violence in India's northeast (with sporadic attacks on pipelines) and India's poor relations with Bangladesh and Myanmar have prevented it from fully exploiting its proximity to a region rich in energy resources on its eastern borders. Thus, it is imperative to continue the process of dialogue between consumers, governments, oil companies, and human rights activists, to arrive at a common approach to the security question as well as regional sensitivities associated with oil exploration. Here, regional organizations in the Indian Ocean Region can play a major role in diffusing tensions between nations, and help to bring about understanding and cooperation between them on the key energy security issue.

REFERENCES

Anderson, John R. 1996. "Multinational Naval Co-Operation into the 21st Century," Halifax, Halifax Maritime Symposium, May 22–23.

Bedi, R. 2003 "Now It Is Russia's Turn to Look East." *Asia Times,* June 18. www.atimes.com/atimes/Central_Asia/EF19Ag01.html.

Bhadrakumar, M. K. 2005. "India Finds a US$40 Billion Friend in Iran." *Asia Times,* January 11. www.atimes.com (accessed January 11, 2005).

Blank, S. 2003 "Russia's Grand Delusion." *Asia Times,* March 5, 2003. http://www.bu.edu/iscip/vol14/blank.html (accessed October–November 2003).

Cordesman, A. H. 1999. *Geopolitics and Energy in the Middle-East.* Washington, D.C.: Center for Strategic Studies.

Doha, G. B. 2001."The Dolphin Project Will Set a New Standard for the Gulf Gas Sector." http://www.ameinfo.com/16654.html (accessed July 17, 2001).

Gertz, B. 2005. "China Builds Up Strategic Sea Lanes." *Washington Times,* January 18.

Gundzik, J. P. 2005. "The Ties That Bind China, Russia and Iran." *Asia Times,* June 4, http://www.atimes.com/atimes/China/GF04Ad07.html (accessed June 4, 2005).

Horsnell, P. 1997. *Oil in Asia; Markets, Trading, Refining and Deregulation.* London: Oxford Univ. Press.

Hufbauer, G. C., J. J. Schott, K. A. Elliott. 1998. *Economic Sanctions Reconsidered: History and Current Policy, 1998.* Washington., D.C.: Institute for International Economics.

IEA (International Energy Agency). 1996. *Asia Gas Study.* Paris: IEA.

Kleneman, L. 2004. *The New Great Game: Blood and Oil in Central Asia.* New York: Grove Press.

Rashid, A. 2000. "China Forced to Expand Role in Central Asia." July 19, 2000. http://www.iicas.org/english/enlibrary/libr_26_7_00_1.htm (accessed July 19, 2000).

South Asia Regional Country Analysis Brief. "South Asia Regional Overview." October 2004. http://www.eia.doe.gov/emeu/cabs/bhutan.html.

Stobdan, P. 1999. "The Afghan Conflict and Regional Security." *IDSA, Strategic Analysis* 23 (5): 719. http://www.ciaonet.org/olj/sa/sa_99stp02.html.

Stoett, P., and D. Pretti. 2003. Energy Security: A Risk Vulnerability Analysis. Centre d'Études des Politiques Éstrangères et de Sécurité (CEPES). http://www.er.uqam.ca/nobel/ieim/article-cepes.php3?id_article=493.

World Bank. 2003. *The World Economic Outlook, Energy Sector, 2003.* Paris: The World Bank.

Velasquez, Manuel. 2005. "Unocal in Burma." Santa Clara, Calif: Markkula Center for Applied Ethics. http://www.scu.edu/ethics/practicing/focusareas/business/Unocal-in-Burma.html.

"Yadana Pipeline Project." 2000. www.Earthrights.org/Burma.

Gas Pipelines and Security in South and Southeast Asia

A CRITICAL PERSPECTIVE

ADAM SIMPSON

I regret very strongly that a company . . . owned by the government, was part of a deal which bought gas from Burma and hence opened up the conditions for the suppression of the Karen [communities] in the area where the gas pipelines have to pass. So I think that—for better or worse—we have blood on our hands.

Sukumbhand Paribatra, 1997
Former Thai Deputy Foreign Minister (cited in Giannini
et al. 2003, 167)

Introduction

This chapter examines security issues relating to electricity-generating cross-border natural gas pipeline projects, but it does not, unlike much of the energy security literature, focus specifically on the energy requirements of the nation-states involved. Rather, a critical security approach is undertaken, which questions the development paradigm used to justify the projects and analyzes the human and environmental security of communities in the vicinity of the pipelines.[1]

Gas pipeline projects undertaken in majority world countries of the global South, such as those discussed here, are rarely vetted through a process of environmental or social impact assessment. If these processes do occur, they rarely have input from local or indigenous peoples and have little impact on the project itself. This situation is exacerbated when the political regime promoting or administering the project is particularly repressive or authoritarian in nature (see Doyle and Simpson 2006). Yet, it is often the case that the communities surrounding these projects are indigenous, dispossessed, or marginalized and have little chance of mitigating the adverse effects that flow from the development. Most of the benefits of the projects are reaped further afield, in elite circles of the urban centers where the development decisions are usually made. The interests of these elites are largely antagonistic to the general populations, despite populist overtures, and this is reflected in development decision-making processes (Goldsmith 1996, 257). Attempts by developers and governments to either enrich elites or, at best, provide electricity for the urban middle classes invariably result in ethnic minorities or indigenous peoples baring the brunt of the environmental and social costs associated with the projects while having little input into the development process itself.

While the discourse of energy security is often employed by the pro-development lobby, the environmental security of local communities can be severely undermined but is rarely considered. Environmental security can be either defined narrowly or understood more broadly, as demonstrated by the multifarious definitions offered throughout this volume. A broad definition includes the energy security deficit felt by many communities in majority countries who often see no relief from the deficit when an energy project is completed. While the discourse of energy security justifies the project, communities living in the vicinity of the project may remain without electricity even after the project is completed and have other elements of their security, such as food or water, undermined.[2] In this situation it becomes poignant to ask whose security is actually being addressed and whose interests are being served by the project (Eddy 2004; Simpson 2007).

The projects to be discussed in this chapter include three transnational gas pipelines in the Indian Ocean Region (IOR), at various stages of their development, that link together a proposed South Asian regional energy grid with the proposed Trans-ASEAN gas pipeline grid (Chaturvedi 2005, 125). Of particular interest is the Yadana gas pipeline, the first cross-border pipeline in Southeast Asia, which runs from southern Burma into Thailand and which, in many ways, is prototypical for this kind of project. It has been a contentious project in both Burma and Thailand and was the subject of two long-running human rights court cases in the United States. The role of the authoritarian Burmese military regime, the State Peace and Development Council (SPDC), was central to social and environmental dislocation throughout the project, although transnational corporations and the Thai governments of the 1990s were also complicit.

There are now other regional gas pipelines being developed where similar problems are, or are likely to, arise. The Thai-Malaysian gas pipeline project is virtually complete, but there have been numerous occasions when an increased martial presence in Thailand's predominantly Muslim south has resulted in the arrest or beating of local residents who are protesting against the project due to social and environmental concerns. The southern region of Thailand, where the pipeline and gas separation plants are being constructed, has been in the grips of an insurgency against the Buddhist-dominated central government since 2004.

The Shwe gas pipeline, expected to run from Burma to India—potentially through Bangladesh, with possibly another running to China—is still at the planning stage, but already the Burmese military has increased its presence in Arakan State in western Burma, and reports of forced labor are already appearing. There are concerns that the same environmental destruction and contempt for human rights that occurred in the Thai-border region during construction of the Yadana pipeline will be meted out to the local and indigenous peoples during this project.

While often reprehensible, these situations juxtaposing energy projects with environmental destruction and human rights violations have, nevertheless, stimulated discussions examining linkages between these issues, which has led to the concept of *earth rights,* the nexus between human rights and environmental protection that can also be understood as an element of human and environmental security (Greer and Giannini 1999, 9–11; Simpson 2005, 256–57; Simpson 2007). This chapter examines these three pipeline projects through the conceptual prism of earth rights and the contested discourses of energy and environmental security. While discussing these issues in India and Bangladesh, this chapter will focus primarily on issues in Thailand and Burma, as they each play host to two of the three projects examined.

Conceptualizing Energy Security

Energy security is a nebulous and contested concept, but most analyses, even if espousing a broad definition, employ a predominantly state-centric approach (Dupont 2001; Luthra 2005). There are numerous reasons for this fixation, many of which relate to academic or government research funding opportunities, but it also fits neatly with the predominant large-scale and hierarchical, top-down development paradigm of "high politics" prescribed by financial institutions such as the International Monetary Fund (IMF) and World Bank and adopted by governmental elites across the world.

This discourse of energy security is employed by government and business elites to justify top-down investments in large-scale energy projects, which require significant initial capital injections and subsequent industrial-scale capital returns. Central to the commonly employed concept of energy security, therefore, is industrialization as a core national development goal. This top-down approach to development has caused ecological destruction on a vast scale, causing greater environmental insecurity (Barnett 2001), and tends to perpetuate, rather than ameliorate, inequalities (UNDESA 2005). After decades of the global pursuit of capitalist industrialization, even the World Bank now recognizes that inequality both within and between countries is increasing and that this can be a major inhibitor to development. Despite this belated recognition, the World Bank still unashamedly applauds "inequality of outcomes" as playing an important role "in providing incentives to invest in education and physical capital, to work, and to take risks" (World Bank 2005, 3). In addition to economic inequalities, the existence of rich hydrocarbon deposits, such as gas in the Indonesian province of Aceh, can result in a "resource curse" that tends to increase social and military conflict rather than reduce it (Ross 2003, 33–35).

In applying this industrial development philosophy over the last few decades Thailand has used significant energy resources for its industrialization while its neighbor, Burma, has used relatively little. According to Hewison, since the late 1950s many of Thailand's leaders have established a developmental social contract whereby top-down paternalistic governance is offset by industrialization and an expansion of the middle class (2005, 323–26). Burma's military leaders, since 1962, have been less successful at industrializing but have maintained more repressive authoritarian regimes (Doyle and Simpson 2006, 751–52).

Both Burma and Thailand, however, still retain significant fossil fuel energy reserves, with Burma announcing between 2004 and 2006 the discovery of huge natural gas reserves in the Bay of Bengal, possibly twice the size of the recoverable gas of the Yadana field. The relatively small allocation to Burmese industry has usually resulted in the export of its energy, and there are plans for pipelines from this reserve to India and China, or possibly Thailand via the Yadana field (Yuthana 2005).

The main focus in Thailand has been on extraction, delivery, and conversion into sufficient electricity to ensure unrestricted industrial development, with associated increasing inequality demonstrating the "principal beneficiaries [have been] political and economic elites" (Bello et al. 1998, 246). Thailand has been particularly successful at creating an excessive electricity supply with an unnecessarily large reserve margin of over 25 percent. Consequently, the aim of successive Thai governments has been for Thailand to be a regional energy-exporting hub facilitating the energy security of Asia as a whole.

The Burmese SPDC, while generally less successful at providing domestic electricity, has had similar aspirations, signing long-term agreements in 2006 with both India and China. Former prime minister and dominant powerbroker of the Burmese military regime General Than Shwe suggests Burma could become a "reliable source for the region's . . . energy security without failing in its responsibility to contribute toward regional peace, security and prosperity"—a responsibility, some would argue, it has yet to fulfil (Simpson 2005, 255).

Malaysia, which has jointly developed the Thai-Malaysian gas pipeline project, has industrialized heavily but has gas reserves for approximately 50 years and is therefore keen to rely on gas for the foreseeable future (Enerdata 2004). In contrast to these relatively energy rich countries, India, previously gas self-sufficient but expected to be among the top four consumers of energy by the middle of this century, will be importing approximately 80 percent of its gas requirements by 2020 (Chaturvedi 2005, 124; Raju 2005, 195).

Of all energy sources, the demand for natural gas, as a cleaner energy source than either oil or coal, is likely to grow the fastest in both Asia and the Indian Ocean Region. With India joining Australia as the Indian Ocean representatives in the Asia-Pacific Partnership on Clean Development and Climate in 2005, natural gas is now considered a key element of "clean development," admittedly alongside "civilian nuclear power" and "clean coal" (U.S. Department of State 2005). In addition to the case studies in this chapter, numerous gas pipeline projects, including one from Iran to India via Pakistan, are being touted as the answer to the region's increasing energy requirements (Chaturvedi 2005, 127; Devraj 2004). The oppressive political situation in Iran is unlikely to allow significant public debate on this project (Doyle and Simpson 2006, 752). Most countries in the region are, therefore, likely to be engaged in such projects in the name of energy security in the near future, and it is important to recognize particularly salient issues that can arise. While the concept of energy security has significant philosophical connotations attached to it, the technologies used in these projects are, themselves, not void of political baggage, and a brief exposition of these concepts follows.

The Politics of Electricity Generation

The social and environmental issues in these IOR countries relating to the physical construction of these pipelines are significant, but there are also issues that transcend the geographic locality of the pipelines that should be examined. While electricity generation using natural gas produces less pollutants than oil or coal, it still generates greenhouse gas emissions, atmospheric pollution, and the potential for toxic oceanic mercury pollution due to drilling, leading to contamination of fish stocks (Fahn 2003, 222). Thailand currently relies on gas for 70 percent of its electricity generation, but the global dependence on hydrocarbon energy sources in the long-term is in terminal decline. Electricity generation, which is the pipelines' *raison d'être,* is one of the two main sectors targeted globally for replacement with renewable energy sources (Wawryk 2004). Some analysts, such as Dupont, argue that environmental issues will compel governments to adopt alternative cleaner energy systems "long before fossil fuels near exhaustion" (2001, 69).

While rapidly industrializing countries such as Thailand have generally displayed little compunction about making gas or petroleum products the central platform of energy policy, their governments have also sponsored initiatives to increase renewable energy production. These initiatives are, however, generally insignificant in comparison with the resources allocated to hydrocarbon technologies. This result is hardly surprising when affluent countries such as Australia and the United States lag so badly in renewable energy production (Wawryk and Bradbrook 2002, 124–25).

In relation to electricity generation, the focus of Thailand, Burma, India, and Bangladesh has generally been both gas-fuelled power stations and mega dam hydropower, despite the recommended obsolescence of mega dams (Simpson 2007). These technologies favor large construction and oil or gas companies. Moreover they both have environmental and human costs that are rarely considered when calculating the cost of the energy produced. This results in favorable comparisons with more ethical and benign forms of electricity generation, such as solar power. In addition, the kleptocratic politics of money and patronage in these countries have often resulted in poor investment decisions being made on the basis of political favors and personal gain rather than national benefit. Gas pipeline projects in the Indian Ocean Region, as with big dams, "are a way of centralising resources and siphoning them off" (Arundhati Roy, in Denton 2004).

The politics, or intrinsic bias, attached to electricity-generating technologies, as with all technologies, should also not be overlooked (Mander 1996, 347–48). Technologies such as industrial-scale fossil fuel electricity generation require centralized control and extremely large financial investments, providing governments and businesses with mouth-watering opportunities for corruption and enhanced centralization of control. Solar and wind power generation generally reduces dependence on governments and large corporations through the decentralization of electrical power generation and distribution. This can result in a similarly subversive decentralization of political power, which is unattractive both to governments and big business.

In addition, the criteria that are used to measure the success of a particular technology are socially constructed and are set by a social subgroup, usually the engineers and technocrats that benefit from adherence to the technology (Kline and Pinch 1999, 114). In the following three case studies, the projects result in an increased centralization of political and economic control, a development favored by the governments and corporations who employ the technocrats who both design *and* assess the projects.

Case Study 1. Yadana Pipeline: Burma-Thailand

The Yadana ("Jewel") gas pipeline project was formally initiated in July 1992 when the French petroleum corporation, Total, signed a contract with the state-owned Burmese company, Myanmar Oil and Gas Enterprise (MOGE). Unocal, the American oil and gas company, joined the partnership soon after and the Petroleum Authority of Thailand (PTTEP) signed on in 1995.

The pipeline was completed in 1999 and runs east from the well site in the north-eastern Indian Ocean, across Tenasserim Division in the southeast of Burma and travels 260 kilometers into Thai territory across Kanchanaburi province. The pipeline terminates at Ratchaburi where the Electricity Generation Authority of Thailand (Egat) has built a power plant that converts the gas to electricity. While there are concerns regarding environmental destruction and a lack of public consultation in the project in Thailand, these pale in comparison with the earth rights infractions that occurred on the Burmese side of the border. On both sides of the border it has been communities living in the vicinity of the project who have paid the heavy price of the projects while business elites in Thailand and the West and the military elites in Burma have reaped its benefits.

Even prior to the signing of the contract the Burmese military junta, the State Law and Order Council (SLORC), since renamed the State Peace and Development Council (SPDC), used the pipeline project as an excuse to conduct military offensives against indigenous ethnic minorities in the region. The Karen National Union (KNU), one of the ethnic minority insurgent groups fighting the Burmese military regime in Rangoon, had a small outpost at the pipeline border crossing point that was particularly targeted by the SPDC. In determining the pipeline route the SPDC generally avoided areas with more entrenched opposition but by heavily militarizing the areas that surrounded the pipeline the project undermined the communities' earth rights, destroying both the environment and the civil rights of the community (Giannini et al. 2003, 18).

On the other side of the border, the Thai Government has, since the late 1980s, made token efforts to minimize the environmental impacts of large projects by passing environmental legislation to control development. One aspect was an

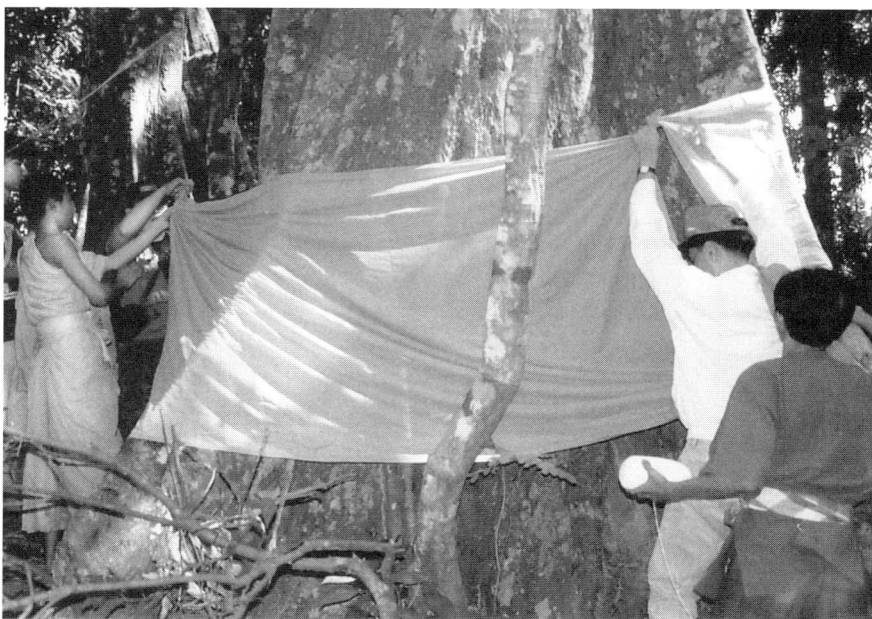

Figure 15.1 Buddhist protests against the Yandana Pipeline.
Source: Adam Simpson.

attempt, in 1992, to make Environmental Impact Assessments (EIAs) mandatory prior to governmental approval for projects such as Yadana. Unfortunately, in this case, government assent was given in 1995 while the EIA was only completed two years later. In addition to this inherent illegality, the Environmental Impact State-ment (EIS) was produced only in English, which resulted in the large majority of the residents in Kanchanaburi province, through which the pipeline passes, unable to access it. The language used in EIAs is often complex for native speakers; in a second language it would be incomprehensible. There were also numerous inconsistencies between the EIS and the reality of the project, which resulted in significant environ-mental degradation on the Thai side of the border (Simpson 2005, 261–62).

In both Burma and Thailand there has been significant destruction of dense closed-canopy rainforest leading to severe erosion and degradation of the ecosys-tems. At least 23 kilometers of dense rainforest in Burma, and 9 kilometers of rain-forest in Thailand, were bisected by the building of the pipeline, damaging the ecological integrity of those areas (Giannini et al. 2003, 146). The Thai route passed through Huai Khayeng Forest Reserve, which later became Thong Pha Phum National Park. The area was classified as a 1A Watershed Forest, the highest con-servation rating in Thailand. This environmental destruction caused certain com-munity members, some who had successfully opposed the Nam Choan Dam project of the 1980s, to form the Kanchanaburi Conservation Group and oppose the Yadana pipeline (Fahn 2003, 199; Simpson 2005, 262).

In Burma, without environmental impact assessment, forest areas have been decimated with unchecked logging by the military not uncommon (Giannini et al.

2003, 153). Along the Yadana pipeline route this effect has been exacerbated by another gas pipeline, the Yetagun, undertaken by a consortium originally led by Premier Oil of the UK and constructed parallel to the Yadana in Burmese territory. The entry of the Burmese military into the previously inaccessible mountainous Thai-Burma border regions with the building of new roads to construct and protect the pipeline has also intensified the conflict with ethnic insurgents in the region and placed additional pressures on the environments of local communities. Villagers are often forced to cut down entire stands of bamboo and rubber and betel nut plantations to provide building materials for the construction of military camps (Giannini and Friedman 2005, 40). This wholesale clearing of vegetation, with little or no regard for traditional or sustainable practices undermines the integrity of the environments and can result in severe monsoonal erosion and flooding.

Even more disturbing than the destruction of the local environment has been the repression of the indigenous Mon and Karen ethnic communities near the pipeline through the routine use of forced labor and systematic sexual and physical abuse. Forced, or slave, labor is common in Burma with the military forcing millions from ethnic or rural populations to work on infrastructure development. In 2004 the International Labor Organization expressed "grave concern" over the continuing scale and scope of forced labor in Burma and in November 2006 its governing body moved toward taking rare legal action involving the International Court of Justice (ILO 2004; 2006).

One of the Burmese military's strategies for undermining insurgents both within the pipeline area and other parts of Burma is the "Four Cuts" program which restricts insurgent access to food, funds, intelligence and recruits. This strategy generally results in extreme hardship for local villagers as the *tatmadaw*, or Burmese military, ensure villagers retain little or no surplus from their harvests (Giannini and Friedman 2005, 27–28). Systematic or ad hoc expropriations of food, crops, goods and land have been commonly used both to starve insurgents and supply Burmese military camps but the effect on local villagers is the same; a severe and deleterious degrading of villagers' earth rights and environmental security.

Another aspect of the Four Cuts program is the relocation of villages and communities which often puts the displaced communities in "life-threatening conditions" (see "Forced Labor and Forced Relocation" in ILAB 2000). By dislocating communities from their environments where they have often lived for generations, the military gains psychological and physical power over the insurgents and their ethnic brethren. When the predominantly animist Karen communities are forcibly removed from their villages and forests they lose an essential part of their identity. This situation can lead to illnesses the communities directly attribute to no longer having the animist spirits of their environment watching over them (Simpson 2004, 34).

In addition to forced labor and portering for the soldiers, villagers are also required to work as human shields or human mine sweepers. The military owns automated mine sweepers but villagers are often used instead to discourage ethnic insurgents from laying land mines (Mahn et al. 2003, 21–23). As under other authoritarian regimes, rape and sexual assault have been used as an instrument of repression by the military to undermine the tight community of these ethnic villages. Over the last decade several human rights groups have documented hundreds of cases of rape and sexual assault committed by Burmese soldiers, with the implicit imprimatur of their officers (Doyle and Simpson 2006, 756). These reports are supported by recent fieldwork suggesting that forced sexual servitude for several days at a time, including repetitive gang raping by soldiers, is still commonplace in conflict areas controlled by the military (Giannini and Friedman 2005, 24–27). Many of these case studies emanate from Mon and Karen communities in the Thai-Burma border region where the Yadana pipeline crosses from Burma into Thailand.

The opposition to the Yadana pipeline took a variety of forms and stretched from the razed villages of eastern Burma to the courtrooms of the United States with a major settlement being achieved with Unocal in 2005 (ERI 2005; Simpson 2005, 266–68). Despite minor victories the environmental security of these ethnic minorities on the Burmese side of the border has been severely undermined by the Thai government's pursuit of energy security and the Burmese military's need for hard currency to maintain its grip on power. The Yadana pipeline now provides approximately 30 percent of Burma's foreign exchange, most of which is spent on the military (BCUK 2005; Mukherjee 2004; Simpson 2007). Meanwhile, Burma's Tenasserim Division, through which the pipelines travel, has one of the lowest levels of per capita electricity consumption in the country (SGM 2006, 19).

On the Thai side of the border there was little genuine public consultation and a severe degradation of the local environments. Legal action was taken against several activists who engaged in legitimate and non-violent forest protests and the Thai state has itself suffered huge financial losses over a delay in the project because of a 30-year take-or-pay contract (Simpson 2005, 260). While most of the serious repression on the Yadana project was carried out on the Burmese side of the border there is another pipeline project in the south of Thailand where the Thai government's goal of energy security has undermined the Muslim ethnic minority's earth rights and environmental security.

Case Study 2. Thai-Malaysian Pipeline

In 1994, the Petroleum Authority of Thailand (PTTEP) and Petronas of Malaysia signed production sharing agreements to exploit natural gas from the Malaysia-Thailand Joint Development Area (JDA) in the Gulf of Thailand, and to transport the gas via a pipeline across the southern Thai province of Songkhla to connect with the already existing Malaysian pipeline grid. As a result, most of the concerns emanating from the new project have centered on the Thai side of the border, which is also the focus here. There are serious ongoing concerns that deleterious impacts upon local communities and their environments are currently occurring and will continue throughout the operation of the project.

The Trans Thai-Malaysian pipeline (TTM) project called for offshore drilling, the construction of two gas separation plants (GSPs) in Chana district in Songkhla, and the laying of a gas pipeline from the GSPs on the coast to the border with

Malaysia in Sadao district. The concerns held by environmentalists, academics, and local communities included an increase in air pollution, changes to the rural lifestyle of the local inhabitants, and increased coastal pollution, including mercury from the drilling, in an area predominantly populated by small-scale Muslim fishing families. In addition, the local villagers argue that a GSP is being built on public land, donated in an Islamic religious ceremony to the community over half a century ago.

While the Yadana pipeline was built throughout the 1990s under the auspices of various government coalitions, the TTM was largely undertaken during the Thai Rak Thai (TRT) government of Thaksin Chinawatra between 2001 and 2006. Thaksin was one of the wealthiest men in Thailand, and the TRT enterprise was an explicit attempt by Thaksin and other major domestic capitalists to capture state power to protect and promote domestic capital (Hewison 2005). Following Thaksin's election landslide in January 2001 and enhanced majority in February 2005, NGOs faced significant pressures in relation to their activities, and this impacted on local communities' ability to engage with the development process (Simpson 2006).

There is ample evidence that the pipeline will not benefit the local people, but peaceful attempts to influence decision makers have met with, at best, indifference, and at worst, violent repression. Despite the legitimate community concerns over the lack of transparency and public consultation, the Thai government has repeatedly cracked down on protesters in a repressive and militaristic manner. Muslim residents of Taling Chan (where the GSPs were to be built), attempting to attend a public meeting in October 2000, while the Democrats were still in power under Prime Minister Chuan Leekpai, were confronted with barbed wire barricades and police roadblocks (Supara 2004, 51–55). In December 2002, a peaceful demonstration against the pipeline by community activists in Hat Yai, a town near the pipeline route which then-Prime Minister Thaksin was visiting, resulted in a repressive police response that left both demonstrators and policemen injured. To rub salt into the wound, the police then prosecuted twenty protestors for encouraging the use of force and causing a public disturbance.

The movement against the pipeline grew into the largest civic group in the country during this time, but Thaksin repeatedly attacked the protesters as promoting violence and as dishonest recipients of foreign funding. Video evidence in the Hat Yai court case, however, showed the demonstration was nonviolent. In contrast, several hundred police had baton-charged the seated protestors, beating several people brutally—reminiscent of the scenes beamed around the world of the repression during the two massacres in the deep south during 2004—and overturning a truck and other vehicles (Simpson 2006, 24–25).

Repeated human rights violations due to heavy-handed police and military tactics at these and other protests drew heavy criticism from both international and domestic critics. The increasingly repressive tactics led the UN Special Envoy for Human Rights, Hina Jilani, to describe the situation facing Thai civil society as encouraging a "climate of fear." In July 2005, the UN Human Rights Committee expressed concern over the lack of public participation in the TTM Project where "violent suppression of peaceful demonstrations" by law enforcement officers was undertaken (HRC 2005, 24).[3]

In December 2004 a decision was brought down in the court case against the Hat Yai protestors, with all 20 acquitted. Nevertheless, the government's authoritarian approach in the south to both peaceful protesters and Muslim communities more generally saw the separatist insurgency, which until early 2005 had been contained within the three provinces south of Songkhla, spread north with three almost simultaneous bomb blasts in Hat Yai. The problems in the south prompted Thaksin's government to announce an emergency decree in July 2005 that granted law enforcement officers immunity from criminal and civil prosecution and suspended jurisdiction of the administrative courts to prosecute human rights violations, leaving citizens with no redress for abuses (Simpson 2006, 26). There were ongoing concerns that social and environmental activists would be targeted under these powers, as they had been in the past (HRC 2005, 3–4).

The rationale of energy security has often been used to undermine dissenting views against this and other energy projects in Thailand. The question of whether these projects are necessary remains. For instance, one of Thaksin's military advisers suggested that the Thai-Malaysian pipeline project would position Thailand as a regional hub for natural gas, and the Department of Energy suggested that the entire initial gas volume would be *exported* to Malaysia due to limited domestic demand (Supara 2004, 54, 71). This stance makes little sense, as arguments of energy security were used to promote the Yadana pipeline, which *imports* gas from Burma. It seems straightforward to argue that in a situation where Thailand imports gas from one end of the country and exports gas from another, at least one of the projects is superfluous and the suffering and environmental degradation that it caused could have been avoided.

The environmental security and earth rights of the Muslim fisherfolk in Chana district in particular have been undermined by this project. With their traditional way of life under threat and their inability to participate in development decisions, their understandable response has been to attempt to express their concerns through protest. Government attempts to de-legitimize these concerns have left these communities marginalized further from the development process, and decisions to grant private companies exclusive access to communal lands was the final straw for many. While attempting to suppress the southern insurgency through military means on the one hand, Thaksin's authoritarian development model sowed the seeds of further discontent on the other. Despite the authoritarian approach taken in Thailand during this and other development projects, it pales in comparison with that meted out across its western frontier in Burma.

Case Study 3. Shwe Pipeline: Burma-India

While the Yadana project undermined earth rights in the east of Burma, in the west the proposed Shwe ("Gold") gas pipeline to India promises to wreak havoc on a scale possibly greater than that of the Yadana (Doyle and Simpson 2006, 757). The offshore A-1 and A-3 Shwe gas fields have potentially more than twice the gas reserve of Yadana, increasing the stakes for the Burmese military junta further. The South Korean company Daewoo has a 60 percent stake in the fields and is the main international player in the projects, although Indian and Chinese corporations also have interests. The possible pipeline routes for the India pipeline run from the Bay of Bengal to the Indian city of Kolkata (Calcutta), via Arakan (Rakhine) and Chin States in Burma and either northeast India or Bangladesh. Intransigence by Bangladesh on related trade issues meant that by 2006 India was considering bypassing it altogether. An additional potential pipeline from the Shwe gas fields to Kunming (Yunnan province) in China was announced following the signing of a memorandum of understanding between the two countries in 2006, but few details were known at the time of writing so the focus here remains on the Indian pipeline.[4]

As with all the pipeline projects, the local communities' environmental concerns about the Shwe pipeline are intimately intertwined with human rights issues. In the northeast of India there is a high level of ongoing political violence from ethnic factions, and the pipeline is unlikely to be welcomed by tribal insurgents, except as a new target for extortion and sabotage. Despite a peace agreement between insurgents and the Mizoram government in mid-2005, which ended almost a decade of conflict, there are still major issues, such as repatriation of thousands of internally displaced peoples, that could cause renewed unrest. Construction of the pipeline across Bangladesh itself may also invoke security concerns after a wave of 400 explosive devices were set off virtually simultaneously in 63 (out of 64) districts across the country in August 2005.

On the Burmese side of the border there are concerns that local communities will be displaced and their environments significantly degraded, with little regard for the health and livelihood of those communities. If the pipeline traverses Arakan State it will result in significantly greater militarization in the area, leading inevitably to increased forced labor, forced relocation, torture, and sexual violence against women. Already there are militarization pressures. Since 1988 the number of infantry battalions based in the Western Command, an area that includes Arakan State and part of Chin State, has increased from 3 to 43 (SGM 2006, 22). Any increased militarization will put increased pressure on local communities and environments even before the pipeline is constructed. The areas likely to be traversed, bisected, and degraded by the pipeline also include several ecologically sensitive sub-regions that include globally endangered coastal rainforests and pine and subtropical forests (ERI 2004).

Energy security for local communities, in the form of electricity, is limited throughout Burma, as there are significant and widespread electricity shortages, but the exploitation of this gas field is unlikely to alleviate this problem. Even Sittwe, Arakan's capital city, receives only four hours of electricity per day from diesel generators, but there have been no proposals from the SPDC to use the gas for domestic electricity production (SGM 2006, 19). The gas will be used exclusively for export, providing foreign exchange for the SPDC, which spends 40 percent of its budget on the military while spending less than 0.5 percent on health (Simpson 2007).

Despite a joint statement by the three governments of a "win-win opportunity" for the "benefit of people of the region" the pipeline is likely, as with the Yadana before it, to primarily serve the interests of domestic military, government, and business elites and their transnational partners while causing misery and suffering for communities surrounding the pipeline. Despite some international pressure and the SPDC's Order No. 1/99 in March 1999, which officially outlawed forced labor in Burma, there is ongoing evidence that forced labor continues unabated in rural areas (Naing et al. 2002). Slave labor, initially erroneously described as "volunteer work," has been camouflaged further and is now implemented under the euphemism of "unity work" (Giannini and Friedman 2005, 34). While in early 2007 the Shwe pipeline was yet to be finally approved and the route was still being debated, there were already reports trickling in of forced labor being used in Arakan State to clear a pipeline route. In August 2005, the Bangladesh-based Narinjara News reported that 500 Arakanese villagers were forced to clear the forests in the path of the pipeline, level the path by cutting the hills and filling the earth with hand tools, and to build temporary bridges to cross creeks. There are also reports that this is resulting in significant refugee flows of ethnic minorities across the border from Arakan into Bangladesh. Once the final route is approved and agreed upon by the three countries, it is highly likely that this slave labor and displacement will only increase.

Throughout 2004–2006, the Bangladesh government repeatedly linked cooperation on the project to three issues that it wanted to see resolved with India: the removal of trade barriers between the two countries, the establishment of a land-based trade corridor with Nepal, and permission to purchase hydropower from Nepal and Bhutan. A major concern for the people of Bangladesh, however, is that the construction of a gas pipeline through the country will encourage governments to export their own limited reserves, undermining the people's future energy security (gas currently supplies two-thirds of Bangladesh's energy needs) (Luthra 2005, 27). Despite pressure from the World Bank and U.S. corporate interests, Bangladeshi governments have consistently refused to export their own gas, as the future energy needs of their sizable population may be dependent on it (Vallette and Kretzmann 2004). Joseph E. Stiglitz, former World Bank chief economist and Nobel Laureate, supported the Bangladeshi stand against efforts from the Bretton Woods institution and suggested that retaining Bangladeshi gas would buffer the economy from energy price fluctuations in the future.

This same argument applies to Burma, although Burmese reserves may be somewhat larger. The authoritarian nature of the Burmese regime has meant that the long-term interests of the Burmese people have been subsumed by the short-term interests of the junta's military elites. Despite concerns by environment and human rights groups over cooperation on this pipeline between the Bangladeshi government and the Burmese military junta, the Bangladeshi High Commissioner to Australia insisted to me that governance in Burma was an "internal" issue and that, in attempting to maintain good relations with its neighbors, Bangladesh worked with the "government of the day, whoever that may be" (Ashraf-ud-Doula

2005). Activists from Burma and throughout the region agree with this position, but differ as to who the legitimate government is, arguing that the democratically elected government of Aung San Suu Kyi and the National League for Democracy should be holding any negotiations.

The indigenous Muslim Rohingya people of northern Arakan State are particularly opposed to the pipeline. The Rohingya face perhaps the most severe discrimination in Arakan State. Being effectively denied Burmese citizenship, the detrimental effects of increased militarization due to the pipeline would fall disproportionately on this community (Amnesty International 2004). The main Rohingya group in Arakan, the Arakan Rohingya National Organization (ARNO), has lent its voice to the campaign against the Shwe pipeline (ARNO 2006), and the Second International Convention on the Restoration of Democracy in Burma, held in Delhi, discussed the pipeline as a threat to regional security (Mirante 2004).

The main Arakanese group in exile, the Arakan National Congress (ANC), has also been vocal in its opposition to the pipeline, arguing that it would harm the struggle to reestablish democracy in Burma. Even though the pipeline project is in its infancy, the campaign to halt it has spread even more widely than that of the Yadana project, with significant international involvement of activists. The Internet has revolutionized communications and the dissemination of information for activists both within and outside Burma, and nowhere was this more evident than when the Shwe Gas Movement (SGM) organized three International Days of Action Against the Shwe Gas Project in October 2005 and April and November 2006 (Doyle and Simpson 2006, 757; SGM 2005b). Through email and Internet promotion, Burmese exiles and activists coordinated simultaneous protests outside Daewoo's head office in South Korea and South Korean embassies in 16 countries, resulting, in April 2006, in 99 people being arrested in Thailand and Malaysia (ERI 2006). In December 2006, the indictment of Daewoo International's President Lee Tae-Yong for fabricating export documents and illegally exporting military production facilities and weapons technology to Burma provided further ammunition for activists in the campaign against Daewoo's engagement with Burma (Shin-who 2006).

In Burma, under the current military regime, the Shwe pipeline project is unlikely to provide either environmental or energy security to communities living in the pipeline's vicinity. The earth rights of ethnic minorities in Arakan and Chin States are likely to come under increasing pressure as forced labor and environmental destruction increases throughout the region in the wake of greater militarization and the pipeline project. In Bangladesh and northeast India, ethnic minorities also face increased pressures due to the project, and it is no more likely to alleviate their environmental security issues than it is those of the marginalized and oppressed peoples of Burma.

Conclusion

The three gas pipeline projects discussed above provide compelling case studies demonstrating how human rights abuses can be linked to environmental insecurity. As is often the case with large-scale energy projects, particularly in majority world countries, marginalized local communities bear the brunt of the industrialization dreams of their government elites and colluding transnational corporations. The rationale of energy security continues to be used to undermine dissenting views against these energy projects, but the necessity of these projects remains contested. Thailand currently imports gas from Burma in the west via the Yadana pipeline while exporting gas to Malaysia in the south via the Thai-Malaysian pipeline. Both these projects are causing dislocation in various local communities and their environments while business, government, and military elites reap the dividends.

The Yadana pipeline has been sending gas from Burma to Thailand since 1999 while, throughout Burma, electricity distribution and reliability outside of Rangoon is something of a regional embarrassment. The proposed Shwe pipeline is designed to export gas to India through Arakan and Chin States in western Burma while the capital of Arakan State can only manage four hours of electricity a day. The ruling Burmese regime uses the foreign exchange earned from these projects to prop up the military, on which it spends almost half its budget, while education and health spending barely register.

The motivation behind these projects, despite the dominant discourse of energy security and development, must be seriously questioned. Nowhere in these case studies do we see benefits flowing to local inhabitants, who invariably bare the true costs of the projects. Earth rights are not respected and insecurity results. The top-down hierarchical development model, with its attendant over-dependence on hydrocarbon sources for energy, is unsustainable both in the majority and minority worlds, and it is only by increasing public participation and transparency in decision making and rigorously regulating corporate activity that energy projects can provide sustainable and socially beneficial outcomes for the future.

It is particularly important that the issues raised in these projects are addressed as several other gas pipelines in the Indian Ocean Region, including from Burma to China and from Iran to India, are also being explored. In January 2007, China and Russia, whose corporations both have interests in the Burmese oil and gas industry, stepped in to veto a U.S.-sponsored Security Council resolution calling on the Burmese military to stop persecuting ethnic minorities and political opponents; the first double veto by these countries since 1972. While the lessons learned from the Yadana pipeline could be used to mitigate the suffering of local communities in future projects, it appears that collusion between authoritarian-leaning governments and transnational corporations will ensure the same repression and mistakes are repeated.

In November 1995, the execution of Ken Saro-Wiwa and the rest of the Ogoni Nine in Nigeria became a catalyst for activists throughout the world to investigate the link between oil and gas companies and the abrogation of the environmental and human rights of marginalized communities in energy-rich majority world countries. Over a decade has passed since their deaths, and it is instructive to note that little has changed for the Ogoni and ethnic minorities in the Niger Delta.

The seemingly inextricable link between transnational extractive energy industries, collusive governments, and earth rights violations that momentarily caught the world's attention in 1995 continues to this day in Burma and to a lesser extent in Thailand, India, and Bangladesh. It is only with a paradigm shift from the dominant fossil fuel energy security discourse of nation- states and their elites to a more holistic, small-scale, and localized environmental security agenda that this heinous link will be broken.

NOTES

The author would like to gratefully acknowledge the cooperation of EarthRights International and other NGOs and activists throughout Thailand, India, and Burma during field research for this chapter.

1. For some background on the critical security approach used here, see Barnett 2001, Booth 2005, and Dalby 2002.

2. For a discussion of this situation relating to the Baluchaung (Mawbye) dam in Burma, see KDRG 2006, 27–49, and Simpson 2007.

3. The author made a submission on Thailand to the 84th Session of the UN Human Rights Committee in July 2005 documenting many of the issues discussed in this section.

4. A separate announcement in April 2006 of a parallel oil pipeline to be built from Sittwe in Arakan State to Kunming also raised concerns similar to those relating to the gas pipelines.

REFERENCES

(Thai and Burmese names are listed by first name)

Amnesty International. 2004. "Myanmar: The Rohingya Minority, Fundamental Rights Denied." May 19. http://web.amnesty.org/library/Index/ENGASA160052004?open&of= ENG- MMR (accessed February 10, 2007).

ARNO (Arakan Rohingya National Organisation). 2006. http://www.rohingya.org/index.php (accessed October 20, 2006).

Ashraf-ud-Doula. 2005. Personal Communication: On Bangladesh's Foreign Policy. Bangladeshi High Commissioner to Australia. University of Adelaide. May 10.

Barnett, J. 2001. *The Meaning of Environmental Security: Ecological Politics and Policy in the New Security Era.* New York: Zed Books.

BCUK. 2005. "Total Oil: Fuelling the Oppression in Burma." Burma Campaign UK (BCUK). February. http://www.burmacampaign.org.uk/PDFs/total%20report.pdf (accessed February 10, 2007).

Bello, W., S. Cunningham, and L. K. Poh. 1998. *A Siamese Tragedy: Development and Disintegration in Modern Thailand.* London: Zed Books.

Booth, K., ed. 2005. *Critical Security Studies and World Politics.* Boulder: Lynne Rienner Publishers.

Chaturvedi, S. 2005. "India's Quest for Energy Security: The Geopolitics and Geoeconomics of Pipelines?" In *Energy Security in the Indian Ocean Region,* ed. D. Rumley and S. Chaturvedi, 116–49. New Delhi: South Asian Publishers.

Dalby, S. 2002. *Environmental Security.* Minneapolis: Univ. of Minnesota Press.

Denton, A. 2004. "Interview with Arundhati Roy." *Enough Rope.* October 18. Australian Broadcasting Corporation. http://www.abc.net.au/enoughrope/ (accessed October 18, 2004).

Devraj, R. 2004. "India to Export Diesel to Burma." June 8. http://www.mizzima.com (accessed January 21, 2007).

Doyle, T., and A. Simpson. 2006. "Traversing More Than Speed Bumps: Green Politics under Authoritarian Regimes in Burma and Iran." *Environmental Politics* 15 (5): 750–67.

Dupont, A. 2001. *East Asia Imperilled: Transnational Challenges to Security.* Cambridge: Cambridge Univ. Press.

Eddy, E. 2004. "Environmental Security: Securing What for Whom?" *Social Alternatives* 23 (4): 23–28.

Enerdata. 2004. "Malaysia Profile." November. http://www.enerdata.fr/enerdatauk/ (accessed September 30, 2005).

ERI (EarthRights International). 2004. "Another Yadana: The Shwe Natural Gas Pipeline Project." http://www.earthrights.org/. Updated: August 27 (accessed February 1, 2007).

ERI (EarthRights International). 2005. "Historic Advance for Universal Human Rights: Unocal to Compensate Burmese Villagers." http://www.earthrights.org/. Updated: April 2 (accessed December 20, 2006).

———. 2006. "Worldwide Protests Call for Daewoo International to Withdraw its Gas Investments in Burma." http://www.earthrights.org/. Updated: April 18 (accessed April 20, 2006).

Fahn, J. 2003. A Land on Fire: The Environmental Consequences of the Southeast Asian Boom. Chiang Mai: Silkworm.

Giannini, T., and A. Friedman. 2005. "A Report on Forced Labour in Burma." March. http://earthrights.org/ (accessed August 17, 2005).

Giannini, T., K. Redford, B. Apple, J. Greer, and M. Simons. 2003. Total Denial Continues, 2nd ed. (Washington, D.C., and Chiang Mai: EarthRights International.

Goldsmith, E. 1996. "Development as Colonialism." In The Case Against the Global Economy: And for a Turn Toward the Local, ed. J. Mander and E. Goldsmith, 253–66. San Francisco: Sierra Club Books.

Greer, J., and T. Giannini. 1999. Earth Rights: Linking the Quests for Human Rights and the Environment. Washington, D.C.: EarthRights International.

Hewison, K. 2005. "Neo-Liberalism and Domestic Capital: The Political Outcomes of the Economic Crisis in Thailand." Journal of Development Studies 41 (2): 310–30.

HRC (United Nations Human Rights Committee). 2005. "Concluding Observations of the Human Rights Committee." United Nations Human Rights Committee, 84th Session. July 28. http://www.ohchr.org/english/bodies/hrc/hrcs84.htm (accessed August 12, 2005).

ILAB (Bureau of International Labor Affairs). 2000. "2000 Report on Labor Practices in Burma." Washington D.C.: U.S. Department of Labor. http://www.dol.gov/ILAB/media/reports/ofr/burma2000/burma2.htm (accessed October 16, 2004).

ILO (International Labour Organization). 2004. "92nd Annual Conference of the ILO Concludes Its Work." June 17. http://www.ilo.org/public/english/bureau/inf/pr/2004/32.htm (accessed June 30, 2006).

———. 2006. "ILO Governing Body Concludes 297th Session." November 17. http://www.ilo.org/public/english/bureau/inf/pr/2006/53.htm (accessed November 23, 2006).

KDRG (Karenni Development Research Group). 2006. "Dammed by Burma's Generals." March. http://www.salweenwatch.org/downloads/dammed-eng.pdf (accessed March 17, 2006).

Kline, R., and T. Pinch. 1999. "The Social Construction of Technology." In The Social Shaping of Technology, 2nd ed., ed. D. MacKenzie and J. Wajcman. Buckingham, U.K.: Open Univ. Press.

Luthra, G. 2005. "Conceptualising Energy Security for the Indian Ocean Region." In Energy Security in the Indian Ocean Region, ed. D. Rumley and S. Chaturvedi, 18–33. New Delhi: South Asian Publishers.

Mahn Nay Myo, M. Imamura, J. Foley, N. Robinson, Shwe Maung, Naing Htoo, and T. Giannini. 2003. Entrenched: An Investigative Report on the Systematic Use of Forced Labor by the Burmese Army in a Rural Area. Chiang Mai: EarthRights International.

Mander, J. 1996. "Technologies of Globalization." in The Case Against the Global Economy: And For a Turn Toward the Local, ed. J. Mander and E. Goldsmith, 344–59. San Francisco, Sierra Club Books.

Mirante, E. 2004. "Out of Burma: Cross-Border Resource Extraction." Paper presented at the Second International Convention for the Restoration of Democracy in Burma. October 15–17. Delhi, India.

Mukherjee, S. 2004. "Myanmar: Cheers, Jeers over Giant Gas Find." Asian Times, February 14. http://www.atimes.com/atimes/South_Asia/FB14Df05.html (accessed October 1, 2005).

Naing Htoo, Shwe Maung, Oum Kher, Mahn Nay Myo, K. MacLean, M. Imamaura, and T. Giannini. 2002. *We Are Not Free to Work for Ourselves: Forced Labor and Other Human Rights Abuses in Burma.* Chiang Mai: EarthRights International.

Raju, A. S. 2005. "Energy Cooperation in South Asia: Some Observations." In *Energy Security in the Indian Ocean Region,* ed. D. Rumley and S. Chaturvedi, 190–203. New Delhi: South Asian Publishers.

Ross, M. L. 2003. "Resources and Rebellion in Aceh, Indonesia." Prepared for the Yale-World Bank project on "The Economics of Political Violence". June 5. http://www.polisci.ucla.edu/faculty/ross/ResourcesRebellion.pdf (accessed January 10, 2006).

SGM (Shwe Gas Movement). 2005a. "Issues in the Shwe Natural Gas Project: Human Rights Abuses." http://www.shwe.org/issues/militarisation-and-human-rights-abuses (accessed February 7, 2007).

———. 2005b. "International Actions." October 14. http://www.shwe.org/take-action/international-actions (accessed January 30, 2007).

———. 2006. "Supply and Command: Natural Gas in Western Burma set to Entrench Military Rule." July. http://www.shwe.org/media-releases/publications/file/ (accessed July 26, 2006).

Shin-who, K. 2006. "Daewoo Head Indicted over Illegal Exports." *Korea Times,* December 6. http://www.koreatimes.co.kr/www/index.asp.SUPPLYANDCOMMAND.pdf (accessed December 7, 2006).

Simpson, A. 2004. "Gas Pipelines and Green Politics in South and Southeast Asia." *Social Alternatives* 23 (4): 29–36.

———. 2005. "Energy Security and Earth Rights in Thailand and Burma (Myanmar)." In *Energy Security and the Indian Ocean Region,* ed. D. Rumley and S. Chaturvedi, 253–84. New Delhi: South Asian Publishers.

———. 2006. "Downfall? Capitalism, Dissent and the Media in Thaksin's Thailand." Paper presented at the Oceanic Conference on International Studies. July 5–7. University of Melbourne, Melbourne, Australia. http://www.politics.unimelb.edu.au/ocis/Simpson.pdf (accessed February 7, 2007).

———. 2007. "The Environment-Energy Security Nexus: Critical Analysis of an Energy 'Love Triangle' in Southeast Asia." *Third World Quarterly* 28 (3) (April): 539–54.

Supara Janchitfah. 2004. *The Nets of Resistance.* Bangkok: Campaign for Alternative Industry Network.

UNDESA (United Nations Department of Economic and Social Affairs). 2005. "Report on the World Social Situation 2005: The Inequality Predicament." August. http://www.un.org/esa/socdev/rwss/media%2005/cd-docs/media.htm (accessed November 8, 2006).

U.S. Department of State. 2005. "President Bush and the Asia-Pacific Partnership on Clean Development." July 27. http://www.state.gov/g/oes/rls/fs/50314.htm (accessed September 21, 2005).

Vallette, J., and S. Kretzmann. 2004. "The Energy Tug of War: The Winners and Losers of World Bank Fossil Fuel Finance." Washington, D.C.: Sustainable Energy and Economy Network, Institute for Policy Studies. April. http://www.seen.org/PDFs/Tug_of_war.pdf (accessed August 1, 2005).

Wawryk, A. 2004. "OGEL Special Feature on Renewable Energy—Introduction by the Editor." *OGEL* 2 (4). http://www.gasandoil.com/ogel/members/articles/welcome.asp?key=1207&n_key= (accessed October 22, 2004).

Wawryk, A., and A. Bradbrook. 2002. "Government Initiatives Promoting Renewable Energy for Electricity Generation in Australia." *University of New South Wales Law Journal* 25 (1): 124–59.

World Bank. 2005. "World Development Report 2006: Equity and Development—Overview." September 20. http://siteresources.worldbank.org/INTWDR2006/Resources/477383-1127230817535/WDR2006overview.pdf (accessed September 21, 2006).

Yuthana Praiwan. 2005. "PTT Eyes 15% Stake in Field near Burma." *Bangkok Post,* August 22.

16 The Uranium Trade in the Indian Ocean Region

DENNIS RUMLEY AND TIMOTHY DOYLE

Introduction

It is an interesting irony that, on the one hand, apart from Southwest and South Asia, the Indian Ocean is surrounded by nuclear weapons–free zones (per the Antarctic Treaty, Treaty of Bangkok, Treaty of Pelindaha, and Treaty of Rarotonga) while, on the other hand, it is fast becoming a nuclear ocean (Doyle 2005). Apart from the increasing number of regional nuclear weapons on land, as well as the indeterminate number on and under the ocean itself at any one time, the increasing global and regional demand for nuclear energy is having a significant impact on the structure of the Indian Ocean uranium trade (see table 16.1). These impacts, in turn, raise a host of security questions linked to nuclear safety, uranium flows, flows of nuclear waste, and the security of sea lanes of communication (SLOCs).

Table 16.1   Indian Ocean Region: Nuclear Energy Users, Uranium Suppliers, and Waste

Nuclear Energy Users		
Indian Ocean Region	*Actual*	India, Pakistan, South Africa
	Potential	Indonesia, Iran
Extra-Regional Impact		China, France, Japan, South Korea, UK, USA
Uranium Suppliers		
Indian Ocean Region		Australia, India, Iran, South Africa
Extra-Regional Impact		Namibia
Nuclear Waste		
Indian Ocean Region		"Dumping" nuclear waste in Africa
		Potential Regional Depositories
Extra-Regional Impact		Japan, France

Source: Rumley 2005.

Global and Regional Nuclear Energy Demand and Supply

In 2002, the energy mix of Indian Ocean states indicated the minimal regional use of nuclear energy (see table 16.2). Indeed, most IOR-ARC member states did not produce any nuclear energy, while South Africa and India produced relatively small amounts. By 2005, South Africa produced 6.1 percent of its electricity requirements from nuclear energy, compared with 3.3 percent for India and 2.4 percent for Pakistan (World Nuclear Association 2006).

This relatively rapid increase in the importance of nuclear energy for regional states is part of a broader global trend implicating at least three sometimes overlapping groups of states—those that are energy dependent, those that are industrializing, and those that are interested in maintaining or developing their own nuclear technology. In all three groups, however, the development of nuclear energy has important implications for the spread of nuclear weapons, since, although the nuclear nonproliferation treaty is at pains to emphasize the legitimacy of the development, use, and application of nuclear energy "for peaceful purposes," there is now "a very fine line between the civilian and military applications of the nuclear fuel cycle" (O'Neil 2005). It would therefore be remiss not to make the point that in all of these groups of states, there is an increasing link between nuclear energy and the militarization of the region.

Projected Global Nuclear Energy Consumption

The U.S. Energy Information Administration (USEIA) provides projections for nuclear energy consumption to 2025, and these have been extrapolated for the

Table 16.2   IOR-ARC Energy Mix, 2002 (% primary energy consumption)

	Oil	Natural Gas	Coal	Nuclear	Hydro
Australia	33.7	19.1	43.8	0	3.4
Bangladesh	24.1	71.6	2.8	0	1.4
India	30.1	7.8	55.6	1.4	5.2
Indonesia	50.0	30.6	17.4	0	2.1
Iran	45.8	52.6	0.7	0	0.9
Malaysia	43.4	46.9	6.4	0	3.3
Singapore	95.7	4.3	0	0	0
South Africa	21.6	0	74.9	2.7	0.8
Thailand	51.2	33.8	12.5	0	2.3
UAE	25.9	74.1	0	0	0

Source: Rumley 2005.

Note: Columns do not add up to exactly 100% due to rounding.

world's largest oil consumers. While many industrialized European states currently do not plan significant nuclear energy expansion (for example, Belgium, Netherlands, Spain, Sweden, Switzerland, and the UK), two of these states—Germany and Italy—are projected to consume no nuclear energy by 2025. In addition, nuclear consumption is projected to decline in Canada and Russia. Meanwhile, nuclear energy consumption is projected to increase for the remaining six largest oil consumers. This is especially the case in absolute terms for France (+103 billion kwh), China (+88 billion kwh) and South Korea (+79 billion kwh). However, the largest percentage increases will occur in China (+133 percent), South Korea (+56 percent), and India (+43 percent). France, India, and South Korea have all been described as "energy import dependent states" (Rumley 2005).

As is well known, combating human-induced climate change requires states to reduce the carbon intensity of their economies, and it has been argued that, by 2025, G8 members should generate at least 25 percent of all of their electricity from renewable sources. However, to some commentators, climate change is happening so rapidly that a 2025 deadline will be too late to avoid its most serious implications. They view the rapid expansion of nuclear power as being the only major solution to solving global warming (Rumley, 2005). This argument is especially relevant for the ten states possessing the world's largest absolute volumes of carbon dioxide emissions—the United States, China, Russia, Japan, India, Germany, Canada, South Korea, Italy, and France. As we have seen, of these states, only China, India, and South Korea are projected to have significant increases in nuclear power over the next two decades. However, the 2004–2005 "oil shock" has prompted the United States to seemingly reassess its position on nuclear energy, and, in a speech in April 2005, the U.S. president declared that "a secure energy future for America must include more nuclear power" (Rumley 2005). Whereas the United States had not planned any increase in the number of nuclear reactors, this speech implies a likely increase from its present complement of 104 (World Nuclear Association 2006).

This argument, which is heavily endorsed by the public relations position of the nuclear industry itself, is enjoying wide currency among policy makers in the Indian Ocean Region and beyond. Environmental non-governmental organizations, on the other hand, are also spending a significant amount of time and resources refuting the uranium and nuclear energy industry's "greenhouse friendly" status. In a discussion released simultaneously by Friends of the Earth, the Australian Conservation Foundation and Greenpeace in 2005, the industry argument is refuted on the basis that it is widely accepted that emissions reductions of the order of 60 percent are required by 2050 in order to stabilize concentrations of greenhouse gases to avert significant climate change. The July 2005 report reads: "Because of economic and public accountability problems, and nuclear power's limited potential other than in electricity generation, the potential for nuclear power to contribute to reducing greenhouse emission is limited. A doubling of nuclear power by 2050 would reduce greenhouse emissions by about 5 percent—less than one-tenth of the reductions required to stabilize atmospheric concentrations of greenhouse gases" (FoE, ACF,

GP 2005, unpub.). Whatever the scientific case, the public relations battle between nuclear industry advocates and environmental NGOs is heating up, and will be a common argument occurring within media outlets in the region over the coming decade, ultimately shaping national and regional public policy.

For extra-regional states, however, adopting a "nuclear view" of climate change and its potential impact on the energy mix, coupled with the current structure of the Indian Ocean nuclear energy trade, implies that in future decades the ocean will be increasingly used as a "uranium highway" for Europe (primarily France and the UK), and more especially for Northeast Asia (China, Japan, and South Korea). This latter point is emphasized in the large number of nuclear reactors (47) that are planned or proposed for Northeast Asia, which represents 42 percent of the global total. Estimated uranium demand from these five states in 2005 is 26,342 tonnes of uranium, which is 39 percent of global requirements and 74 percent of global uranium production in 2003 (World Nuclear Association 2006).

Potential Indian Ocean Nuclear Energy Consumption

Apart from the current small amounts of nuclear power generated by India and South Africa, one possible regional scenario from this perspective of climate change is that other Indian Ocean states will also seriously consider the development of nuclear power programs. Iran has already indicated its intention in this regard. Furthermore, Indonesia, even though in favor of increased regional cooperation in the field of renewable energy, continues to debate the development of nuclear power, an option that it shelved in 1997. As it stands, the current plan is for Indonesia to begin the construction of its first nuclear power station in 2010, with a view to commencing nuclear power production in 2016 (Rumley 2005). In addition, Pakistan, which produces a small amount of nuclear energy, plans to increase its number of nuclear reactors to three. There is currently a lively debate within Australia over the prospects and possibilities of nuclear energy.

Uranium Suppliers

The current largest uranium suppliers are not necessarily those with the largest uranium reserves (see table 16.3). For example, Canada, with the third largest global reserves (14.1 percent), was the world's largest uranium producer in 2002, with 29.2 percent (Uranium Information Centre 2006). On the other hand, the two states with the world's largest reserves—Australia and Kazakhstan—together produced 30 percent of the world's uranium in 2002.

In 2002, Australia exported virtually all of its 7,637 tonnes of uranium oxide to the northern hemisphere, with only five states receiving in excess of 500 tonnes— United States (2,790), Japan (2,688), South Korea (756), UK (576), and France (503) (ERA 2006). India, on the other hand, while possessing about 2 percent of world's uranium reserves, has the second largest global reserves of thorium, and produces almost entirely for the domestic market. One of the long-term goals of its nuclear program is to develop an advanced heavy-water thorium cycle (World Nuclear Association 2006).

Table 16.3   Global Uranium Reserves and Production, 2002
(% of global total)

Uranium reserves	Uranium production
Australia (27.8%)	Canada (29.2%)
Kazakhstan (15.2%)	Australia (21.2%)
Canada (14.1%)	Kazakhstan (9.2%)
South Africa (9.6%)	Niger (8.8%)
Namibia (7.6%)	Russia (8.8%)
Brazil (6.3%)	Namibia (5.7%)
Russia (4.2%)	Uzbekistan (4.9%)

Sources: Rumley 2005; Uranium Information Centre 2006.

From a global perspective, both Australia (with 27.8 percent of reserves and 21.2 percent of production) and South Africa (with 9.6 percent of reserves and 2.1 percent of production) could be regarded as "underproducers," and, given their relative political stability, are both likely to be future sources for growing Indian Ocean and Northeast Asian demand.

Consequently, political pressure from various quarters is mounting for Australia to change its current uranium mining policy. While the current Federal Coalition government favors a review and policy debate, the opposition Labor party prefers uranium mining to be restricted to three mines. Constitutionally, the Australian states possess the power over the extraction of minerals resources (so-called minerals power), and uranium mining is currently disallowed in all states and territories except South Australia (which contains Australia's largest deposits at Olympic Dam) and the Northern Territory.

This issue is rapidly developing into an important federal-state conflict in Australia, as states such as Western Australia, with significant uranium deposits and no uranium mines, will become increasingly at odds with a federal government keen to open up new mines and to expand Australia's uranium exports. Political pressure will also be backed up by powerful economic pressure, since, in Western Australia, BHP Billiton holds two of the largest uranium deposits, at Yeelirie and Kintyre.

Transboundary Movements of Nuclear Waste: The Legal Basis

No universal definition exists of "waste," and national definitions vary considerably and are often subjectively based. One legal definition is that waste comprises "substances or materials which are disposed of, or are intended to be disposed of, or are required to be disposed of by the provisions of national law." "Hazardous waste," on the other hand, consists of materials of varying categories and having specific characteristics that are generally considered harmful to human health (Bamako Convention, article I, annex 1 and annex II, African Union web site 2006).

For the most part, the transboundary movement of hazardous waste has followed the "path of least resistance" principle. Furthermore, there is generally an "economic and regulatory imbalance" between the generating and the importing states. Thus, dumping at sea is easier and less costly, and the developing world, and particularly Africa, has been seen as an attractive recipient region on account of relatively inexpensive disposal costs (Krummer 1999, 4–7; Lipman 2002). However, post–Cold War international law, especially in the form of the Basel Convention, has been developed in order to regulate the transboundary movement of hazardous waste.

The Basel Hazardous Waste Convention

The Basel Convention on the Control of Transboundary Movements of Hazardous Wastes and Their Disposal came into force in 1992, and as of April 2005 it had been ratified by nearly all Indian Ocean states. Apart from the United States, notable regional exceptions included Afghanistan, Bhutan, Burma, Iraq, Laos, Somalia, Sudan, Swaziland, and Zimbabwe.

One of the more important concerns lying behind the convention was the fact that, of the more than 400 million tonnes of hazardous waste produced each year, approximately 80 percent came from Organization of Economic Cooperation and Development (OECD) countries and a large proportion was being "dumped" into industrializing states (Greenpeace 1999). The scope of the Basel Convention, however, does not extend to the transboundary movement of radioactive materials, although it does allow some transboundary movement of hazardous waste "only when the transport and the ultimate disposal of such wastes is environmentally sound." This clause has been used as a bargaining position for those states possessing hazardous waste exports since it could imply unlimited external access so long as appropriate local environmental expertise and technology existed. An important amendment to the Basel Convention, however, adopted in 1995, prohibited the export of all hazardous wastes from richer to poorer states from 1998.

The issue of the transboundary movement of nuclear waste was explicitly not inserted within the Basel Convention because its movement was seen as falling within the sphere of competence of the International Atomic Energy Agency (IAEA). The adoption in 1990 by the General Conference of the IAEA of a nonbinding code of practice on the international transboundary movement of radioactive waste, which was proposed by UNEP, however, has in fact resulted in a weakening of the principles underpinning the Basel Convention (Krummer 1999, 85).

The Bamako Convention

While Africa possessed the dubious distinction of being "first choice" for the dumping of European nuclear waste and persistent organic pollutants in the 1980s, it was also the first to respond politically to the threat of "waste colonialism" (Bernstorff and Stairs 2001, 4). Prior to the ratification of the Basel Convention, many African states were especially concerned about the transboundary movement of such hazardous waste into Africa from industrialized countries, and some indeed saw this process as the "dumping" of nuclear waste into Africa (Krummer, 1999, 99). At the May 1988 Organization of African Unity (OAU) Council of Ministers 48th Ordinary Session in Ethiopia, a resolution condemned the importation into Africa of industrial and nuclear waste as a "crime against Africa and the African people" and called upon member states to introduce import bans. The resolution condemned "all transnational corporations and enterprises involved in the introduction, in any form, of nuclear and industrial wastes in Africa; and DEMANDS that they clean up the areas that have already been contaminated by them" (Organization of African Unity Secretariat, CM/Res. 1147–1176, 1988).

As a consequence of this resolution, work began on an African Convention under the auspices of the OAU shortly after the adoption of the Basel Convention, since the latter excluded nuclear waste. There was therefore a concern that certain of the needs of African states were not properly taken into account, and thus, while the Basel Convention was a Convention of the North, there was need for a Convention of the South. The resultant Bamako Convention, which was adopted in Mali in January 1991, entered into force in April 1998.

Clearly, adherence and compliance are major problems, since, of the 53 African Union states, only 28 had signed and only 21 had ratified the Bamako Convention as of April 1, 2006. Furthermore, the convention has been ratified by only 8 of the 21 African Union Indian Ocean members.

Of particular international concern are the five states that have neither signed nor ratified the Bamako Convention, as well as a further seven that have signed but have yet to ratify. It may be that some states have put off either signing or ratifying the agreement in order to participate in the lucrative trade in hazardous waste (UNEP 2000). This may well be true for the six Indian Ocean littoral states of Djibouti, Kenya, Madagascar, Seychelles, Somalia, and South Africa, none of which were in the original convention signatory group of 12 states. Furthermore, of these six littoral states, two have neither signed nor ratified Bamako (Seychelles and South Africa) and a further two (Djibouti and Somalia) have yet to ratify either the Basel or Bamako Conventions.

Dumping Nuclear Waste: The Example of Somalia

The Indian Ocean tsunami of December 2004 resulted in the washing up on Somalian beaches of many containers of nuclear and toxic waste that were illegally dumped during the early 1990s (Clayton 2005). It is alleged that, in at least one case, a lucrative financial agreement had been reached between the interim government headed by Ali Mahdi Muhammed and certain Swiss and Italian companies to import into Somalia from Italy millions of tonnes of nuclear waste. These companies were alleged to be under the control of the Italian mafia, and the Somalian deal was said to be only a part of so-called eco-mafia operations (Grosse-Kettler 2004, 29). For the Europeans, the cost per tonne (US$8) represented a fraction of the likely cost of up to US$1,000 per tonne of appropriate local treatment and disposal in the 1990s (Clayton 2005).

Given Somalia's strategic location and its current statelessness, such illegal or unauthorized movements of nuclear waste have potentially very significant implications, not only for the human security of the Somalian population, but also for the Indian Ocean environment, the Indian Ocean routes along which such flows take place, and the lethal prospects of the potential terrorist use of such nuclear materials. It has been noted that, in fact, Somalia is a "stateless war economy," one of the requirements of which is to engage in international "commercial complicity" since its local economy is unable to meet military expenditures. Funding of the war economy is achieved in various ways, including via trade by local conflict groups with international corporations and institutions in unauthorized commodities, including nuclear waste. Indeed, Somalia currently functions as a transshipment point and a supply route for a wide variety of illegal merchandise for the whole of the Horn of Africa and beyond (Grosse-Kettler 2004).

The Movement of Nuclear Waste Through the Indian Ocean

At the regional level, not only is waste generated within the region, but also there is an ever-increasing amount of waste passing through the region via sea routes. As a consequence, the Indian Ocean Region is currently being used as a key transport route for nuclear waste. Much of this transport revolves around the servicing of the two biggest destinations for the processing of waste: Sellarfield, in England, and La Hague, in France. Most of this waste in the region is produced by Japan. Song writes: "The first question in nuclear waste disposal is reprocessing, which can recover a significant quantity of useable material for nuclear reactors and reduce the amount of high-level waste that must be stored to about 3 percent of the original spent fuel" (Song 2003, 8).

Waste reprocessing breaks down spent fuel, chemically dissolving the rods and separating the plutonium from the other materials. The plutonium is then mixed with uranium (MOX) and re-used in conventional reactors. The Japanese are the biggest proponents of this process. They receive their nuclear fuel shipments from both the British and French reprocessing plants. This MOX fuel is transported through the Indian Ocean on its way back to Japan, though few reliable records are available in the public domain documenting this traffic. The few attempts at monitoring these movements have been embarked upon by international environmental non-government organizations (ENGOs) like Greenpeace, in the absence of efforts made at both the nation-state and international levels. It is impossible, therefore, to know just how many of these shipments are being made, due to the high levels of secrecy which surround them (Doyle 2005). According to Greenpeace, on July 21, 1999, two ships carrying weapons-usable plutonium, left Europe via the Cape of Good Hope, through the Indian Ocean to Japan. Greenpeace reported as follows: "The two British flagged vessels, the Pacific Teal and the Pacific Pintail, left Barrow in Britain and Cherbourg in France carrying the first commercial shipment to Japan of mixed-oxide (MOX) reactor fuel, made from plutonium and uranium. An estimated 446 kilograms of plutonium is contained in the 40 nuclear fuel elements—enough fissile material to construct at least 60 nuclear bombs. . . . The Cape of Good Hope has become the path of least resistance" (Greenpeace 1999).

Only Mauritius, acting alone, made public its opposition to the reprocessed fuel's transport, by refusing to admit the vessels into their Exclusive Economic Zone (African News Service 1999). Of course, this can only be a symbolic position, as the devastation which could occur if the vessel was sunk, or caught fire, would make the 200-kilometer zone, as a zone of protection, look ludicrous. Under existing liability agreements, there is some limited compensation under international conventions; "but no assurances exist whatsoever that the full costs of health, environmental and economic damages would be paid to victims in en route states." (Greenpeace 1999).

Since the turn of the millennium, limited surveillance by ENGOs of Indian and Pacific oceanic nuclear flows has continued in a piecemeal fashion, with Greenpeace Australia concentrating on shipping movements from Albany, Sydney, and Tasmania. But even this limited surveillance provided by ENGOs has now declined. According to Greenpeace Australia's nuclear campaign coordinator, James Courtney, the costs associated with aerial surveillance have proved increasingly prohibitive for the not-for-profit organization (Courtney 2005).

Another key event needs to be mentioned here that may dramatically effect the flows of nuclear waste in the region: the decision by Japan to commission its own reprocessing plant. Japan has now embarked upon a new ten-year energy plan, calling for the expansion of national nuclear energy by approximately 30 percent (IAEA 2004). Not only will this include the construction of up to 12 new nuclear plants on top of its 54 existing reactors, but the construction of a reprocessing unit which will convert spent fuel into mixed oxide plutonium that will be reused, in some cases, in specifically designed reactors. At this stage, it is envisaged that the reprocessing plant will only be used to treat waste produced from the Japanese domestic market. If this is the case, it is likely that shipments to Sellarfield and La Hague may decline in number. On the other hand, if the reprocessing unit opens up its facility to the international market (particularly the emerging facilities in the less affluent Indian Ocean)—converting waste sourced from non-Japanese facilities— this may actually substantially increase waste and reprocessed waste flows within the Indian Ocean Region.

Nuclear Waste Storage in the Indian Ocean Region

At this juncture, the environmental security concerns of waste storage and transport become intermeshed once more with more traditional security concerns of nation-states and their defense. Location of such waste dumps is highly politicized, with the United States increasingly involved in decisions as to who can and who cannot store and reprocess spent nuclear fuel. In fact, recently the United States has decided to store all its own spent fuel at Yucca Mountain in Nevada by 2010, in large part due to its fears that exported waste may find its way into the nuclear defense programs of other states (Doyle 2005).

Australia

Given the Amendment to the Basel Convention and given Australia's apparent reluctance at the time to support it, trade in hazardous wastes to and from Australia with other OECD states is likely to be a real possibility. A well-publicized report, which surfaced first in December 1998, showed that the Swiss-based multinational mining company Pangea Resources, following a global site survey and on the basis of a "high isolation" concept, had already targeted inland Australia for the global dumping of nuclear waste. Most of the funding for this endeavor had been provided by British Nuclear Fuels Limited. However, the Australian industry, science, and resources minister at the time stated in federal parliament that no ministerial discussions had taken place on this issue. The Western Australia state deputy premier, however, admitted that discussions had taken place with Pangea "about two years ago" and that Pangea believed that the "Centralian Superbasin" in Western Australia was "the perfect storage facility" on account of its "stable political scene and geography."

It was argued that since this sedimentary formation had been stable for 500 million years, it could potentially take nuclear waste from the more than 400 nuclear power stations around the world. It was also suggested that, to a significant degree, the global nuclear waste problem would therefore be solved since this facility could take in over 75,000 metric tonnes of waste over a forty-year period. Furthermore, storage costs and infrastructure development would generate an enormous economic dividend to Australia, in the order of about 1 percent of GNP per annum. The ensuing public and political opposition to this proposal and the subsequent closure of Pangea's Australian office led many commentators to feel that, by 2002, the Pangea concept was a non-starter (IAEA 2004, 13). In fact, "Pangea ceased operations in 2001 when the owners decided that the commercial prospects for an international repository were too far into the future to justify the investment required" (IAEA 2004).

During the last two years, differing signals regarding the development of nuclear power and the creation of nuclear storage facilities in Australia have been emerging from Australian politicians. For example, in July 2004 the Australian prime minister announced that the Australian government is examining options for the siting of a facility for nuclear waste, "with a preference for an offshore site." Furthermore, in September 2004, the Australian environment minister, Western Australian senator Ian Campbell, stated that the only locations being considered by the Australian government for nuclear waste storage were on "offshore islands." However, on June 6, 2005, the minister did not rule out Western Australia as a possibility, since New South Wales, South Australia, and the Northern Territory "had been given assurances already that nuclear waste would not be buried there" (Dortch and Mason 2005). However, while the New South Wales premier appears to favor nuclear power, the NSW government is still reviewing the findings of its Joint Select Committee on the Transportation and Storage of Nuclear Waste, which reported in February 2004. On the other hand, Western Australia (2004), South Australia (2003), and the Northern Territory (2004) have all legislated against the construction and operation of any facility designed for nuclear waste storage. The Queensland state government, however, prefers to seek clean coal technology for its 300-year supply of coal.

Nonetheless, Pangea Resources, which reformed itself in Switzerland in February 2002 into the Association for Regional and International Underground Storage (ARIUS), still believes that Western Australia is "the best location in the world for nuclear waste storage" (Law 2005). Clearly, such a global repository, if it came into being, would have very significant long-term implications for the environmental security of the Indian Ocean itself and for the security of sea- lanes terminating at their Western Australian destination. In the 2005 budget, the Australian government allocated around A$140 million to protect offshore oil and gas platforms in the North-West Shelf against a potential medium-level terrorist threat. This would allow for two extra patrol boats and trials of unpersonned flights. However, a much more comprehensive security strategy would be needed if a global nuclear waste repository were located in Western Australia.

Other Indian Ocean States

Two other Indian Ocean countries—India and Pakistan—store their own waste. In the increasingly controversial case of Iran, there appears to be some tension as to whether the waste from the newly constructed Bushehr nuclear power plant will be transported to Russia, or will remain on home soil (Kerr 2002, 29). Sections of the Iranian government want to store their own waste (to potentially utilize the enriched uranium as part of a possible weapons program), while powerful elements in the international community—particularly the United States—have made it clear that if the enriched waste is not returned to Russia, then the nuclear program within Iran should be terminated.

In South Africa, high-level waste from the country's two nuclear reactors at Koeberg (which generates about 95 percent of the waste) and Pelindaba is stored on site because it is considered too dangerous to move. Critics of South Africa's nuclear waste policy argue that there is "no real plan" for its disposal despite the release for a brief month-long public comment in 2003 of its radioactive waste-management strategy (Roelf 2005). Apparently, the policy document identifies three main options for South Africa's waste—above-ground interim storage, deep geological disposal, and reprocessing. Although deep storage was favored, there were problems locating a suitable site. Reprocessing, on the other hand, would require shipments to the UK, Japan, or France. South Africa has indicated that it would never consider accepting nuclear waste for storage from another state, however.

Conclusion

The Indian Ocean is fast becoming the nuclear ocean. Because of its status as the Ocean of the South, the environmental security focus on nuclear power has not been sufficiently explored, as the possibilities of nuclear accidents—whether in the mining of uranium, power generation, reprocessing, transport, or storage—are seen as risks which those who are less affluent are expected to take. With the Indian Ocean's increased nuclear profile, it is critical that environmental security concerns are included alongside the more traditional concerns of weapons proliferation and possible nuclear war.

REFERENCES

ABC News Online. 2006. "WA Dump." May 24. http://www.abc.net.au/news.

African News Service. 1999. "Mauritius-Nuclear Mauritius Opposes Nuclear Waste Transfer." *African News Service,* August 2.

African Union. 2006. http://www.africa-union.org/.

Albright, D., and M. Hibbs. 1993. "South Africa: The ANC and the Atom Bomb." *Bulletin of the Atomic Scientists* 49 (3): 32–37.

Association for Regional and International Underground Storage (ARIUS). http://www.arius-world.org/.

Bernstorff, A., and K. Stairs. 2001. *POPs in Africa: Hazardous Waste Trade, 1980–2000.* Amsterdam: Greenpeace International.

Clayton, J. 2005. "Somalia's Secret Dumps of Toxic Waste Washed Ashore by Tsunami." http://www.timesonline.co.uk/.

Courtney, J. Interview with author, personal communications. October 2005.

De Villiers, J. W., R. Jardine, and M. Reiss. 1993. "Why South Africa Gave up the Bomb." *Foreign Affairs* 72 (5) (Nov./Dec.): 98–109.

Dortch, E., and G. Mason. 2005. "WA Nuclear Waste Dump Fear Revived." *The West Australian,* June 7, page 1.

Doyle, T. 2005. "The Indian Ocean as the *Nuclear Ocean*: Environmental Security Dimensions of Nuclear Power." In *Energy Security and the Indian Ocean Region,* ed. D. Rumley and S. Chaturvedi, 230–52. Delhi: South Asian Publishers.

Editorial. 2006. "Australia Has No Waste Obligation." *The West Australian.* May 16, page 16.

Energy Resources of Australia. 2006. http://www.energyres.com.au.

Friends of the Earth, Australian Conservation Foundation, and Greenpeace. 2005. "A Nuclear Future 2005." Unpublished report. Melbourne, Australia.

Greenpeace. 1999. "Japanese Plans to Make Carribean the Toxic Throughway for Clandestine Shipments of Nuclear Waste and Plutonium." Unpublished briefing paper, April.

Grosse-Kettler, S. 2004. "External Actors in Stateless Somalia: A War Economy and Its Promoters." Paper 39. Bonn, Germany: Bonn International Center for Conversion (BICC).

IAEA (International Atomic Energy Agency). 2004. *Developing Multinational Radioactive Waste Repositories: Infrastructure Framework and Scenarios of Cooperation.* IAEA-TECDOC-1413. Vienna: IAEA.

Jognson, C. 2006. "Inquiry Set to Back Uranium Enrichment." *The West Australian,* October 6, page 6.

Kerr, P. 2002. "U.S. Reportedly Offers Russia Deal on Bushehr." *Arms Control Today,* November, 29.

Krummer, K. 1999. *International Management of Hazardous Wastes.* Oxford: Oxford Univ. Press.

Law, P. 2005. "New Bid for WA N-Dump." *Sunday Times,* June 12.

Lipman, Z. 2002. "A Dirty Dilemma: The Hazardous Waste Trade." *Harvard International Review* 23 (4) (winter): 67–71.

Michelmore, A. 2004. "Olympic Dam's Position in the World Uranium Industry." Address to the Citigroup Global Markets, uranium information session, Sydney, December 14.

O'Neil, A. 2005. "Nuclear Nightmares." Comment in the Transcript of Australian Broadcasting Corporation (ABC), Radio National, Background Briefing program, May 22.

Organization of African Unity, Secretariat, CM/Res. 1147–1176, 1988.

Roelf, W. 2005. "SA Has 'No Real Plan' for Nuclear Waste." *Mail and Guardian on line,* May 25.

Rumley, D. 1999. *The Geopolitics of Australia's Regional Relations.* Dordrecht: Kluwer.

Rumley, D. 2005. "The Geopolitics of Global and Indian Ocean Energy Security." In *Energy Security and the Indian Ocean Region,* ed. D. Rumley and S. Chaturvedi, 34–53. Delhi: South Asian Publishers.

Shanahan, D. 2006. "We Could Be Energy Superpower: Howard." *The Australian,* July 18, page 1.

Smith, L. 2006. "Smuggles Nuclear Waste Cases Double." *The Weekend Australian,* October 7–8, page 12.

Song, F. 2003. "Currently Indisposed: Managing Radioactive Waste." *Harvard International Review* (summer): 8–9.

UNEP (United Nations Environment Program). 2000. *Global Environment Outlook,* chapter 3: Policy Responses—Africa.

USEIA (United States Energy Information Administration). 2004. *International Energy Outlook 2004.*

Uranium Information Centre. 2006. http://www.uic.com.au/.

World Nuclear Association. 2006. http://www.world-nuclear.org/.

PART V

WIND

17   *Wind*

AIR SECURITY IN THE INDIAN OCEAN
REGION

TIMOTHY DOYLE

In 2000, we were in New Delhi taking part in initial meetings leading to the formation of the Indian Ocean Research Group. Moving about Delhi can be a hazardous
process. The air was thick with pollution. Many buses and auto-rickshaws ran on
diesel, or a heady mixture of petrol and kerosene. To make matters worse, the
sheer number of these vehicles admitted into the heart of Delhi acted as a multi-
plier to the massive amounts of carbon monoxide, hydrocarbons, and lead being
emitted into the atmosphere.

Apart from vehicle emissions, coal, animal dung, and vegetable-based fuels are
still commonly used in the cooking and heating processes of many living in the
metropolis. On top of all this is a problem common to all of the emerging parts of
the IOR: rapid and unrestricted industrialization. In India, entire cities are forming
outside of established infrastructure. In these areas there is no polite divide
between residential areas and industrial areas. In addition, these industries rarely
have in place the environmental safeguards that would be compulsory in the affluent world. In fact, in order to compete in globalized markets, many industrial
enterprises have to deliberately cut environmental corners to ensure competitive
advantage in the marketplace.

So the air in Delhi at the turn of the millennium was a pungent and toxic soup.
After the first day of moving around in an open-air auto rickshaw, our party—
many of whom were Westerners—complained of stinging eyes and shortness of
breath. On the second day, we watched in amazement as a single man pedaled a
rickshaw, stacked with four fully grown, well-fed, Western men. The lightly built
rickshaw operators of Delhi struggle and gasp for breath just to get their over-
loaded rickshaws moving, as most bicycles are not equipped with gears. But what
was even more incredible to witness were the superhuman efforts of the "transport
haulers." These men pushed and pulled motorless transports, piled high with the
many assorted ingredients and products of commerce, up hills and steeply inclined
overpasses through the crowded streets of Old and New Delhi. These are rickshaws on a massive scale. Basically, instead of oxen, humans are used to pull the
colossal loads. Others are not strapped to these transport carts, but wait at the bottom of hills for overburdened haulers. These men, for the price of one rupee from

the "driver" (equal to a few U.S. cents), put their shoulders and backs to each cart, gradually nudging it up the incline. Once they have successfully maneuvered the cart up the hill, they return to the bottom and perform the task all over again. This backbreaking and lung-bursting work begins before sunrise, and finishes long after the sunsets.

What makes these tasks all the more Herculean is that they are performed within a poisonous atmosphere. As each man's lungs clutch for much needed oxygen, he must inhale, instead, from a poisonous soup.

On the third day of meetings, one of our party—with a history of asthma— was simply walking the streets near the market when he collapsed and went into febrile convulsions. In the land beyond medical insurance (which is the case in much of the IOR), even the most basic things, like ringing for an ambulance, are problematic for Westerners. Many people who collapse due to either direct, contributing, or associated effects of respiratory conditions simply don't make it to hospitals, and as a consequence their illnesses or subsequent deaths do not register in official records. When a vehicle did arrive, we did our best to squeeze our unconscious colleague into the back of the van and were taken to the nearest hospital.

After negotiating lengthy bureaucratic procedures at the front desk while our colleague was still fitting in our arms, we were admitted to the emergency room. Westerners often enjoy watching popular television series set in the emergency rooms of affluent world hospitals, but no television series would be filmed here. One of our colleagues described it as close to what he could imagine Dante's Hell to be, here on earth. The room was simply a rectangular space of 30 meters by 10 meters, packed with beds on castor wheels. Basic triage was being administered by doctors and nurses, akin to what might take place in a battlefield. On first count, there were 65 beds pinched into that confined space. The noise of the screams—the pain and suffering—in that room, and the multitude of others like it spread around India, is something that will never leave those who have experienced it.

After what seemed an inordinate amount of time, our patient was attended to. On hearing protests about the lengthy delay, a young, quietly spoken doctor reminded us that many in the room were far more seriously ill than our colleague. He then checked over our sufficiently humbled patient and began writing something on a scrap piece of paper. "This is a list of the medicine you will need," he said.

Thinking that he wanted us to endorse the medicine's usage, we replied, "Of course, give it to him."

"No," he replied. "You must go and buy it first. We have no medicine in the hospital. . . . You must get it from a pharmacy." Shocked that basic medicines like paracetamol, glucose, and ventilin were unavailable in hospitals, one of our group left to search out a supplier.

Eventually, some pattern emerged within the room. The beds moved anticlockwise around the walls of the room (though many remained jumbled in the middle). As initial treatment was provided, the beds were moved around the wall, to make way for the constant stream of incoming casualties. In one corner of the room, however, half a dozen beds had fallen away from the constantly moving stream. During treatment of our colleague, I asked the young intern who these people were, and he relied: "Those are the unlucky ones . . . they have not responded to triage . . . they cannot afford medicines." As our own patient continued in the swirl of beds around the room, we drew close to these unfortunates. One young man of no more than thirty lay on his back, his hands folded neatly on his stomach, the light of life visibly draining from his eyes. He was encircled by his family, quietly standing vigil, their heads hung low, whispering words only fit for the ears of loved ones. After a time, we knew firsthand the sound of "the death rattle," as the young man fought with all his fast dwindling strength to do what many of us take for granted: breathe. Finally, the pain visible in his eyes dissipated, and they took on a look of nothingness as his lungs eventually failed. Two things stuck us as we witnessed his passing: first, the dignity of his family during the moments of his death; and second, how most of us in the affluent world are shielded from experiencing the death of a stranger.

Much later that evening, when our friend had been moved into a recovery room, we again met the remarkable young doctor who, at the end of an 18-hour shift, was preparing to leave the hospital. One of our group asked him directly what the young man had died of. His response chilled us. He replied, "heart attack, preceded by respiratory failure. . . . He was a rickshaw driver."

According to a study put together by the Chittaranjan National Cancer Institute, two out of every five New Delhi residents suffer from health problems associated with poor air quality, while residents of Bombay deal on a daily basis with air that has been likened to smoking 2.5 packs of cigarettes per day (Walsh et al. 2004, 16).

The World Health Organization reports that two-thirds of the 800,000 premature deaths caused by air pollution occur in Asia. Walsh et al. write of the long-term daily impacts as follows: "Long-term exposure to air pollution can raise the risk of pulmonary and heart disease, irritate underlying respiratory problems and potentially take months or more off a healthy life-span. . . . This is a systematic problem, not an occasional problem" (Walsh et al. 2004, 17).

What happens to those who live and work in these conditions does lead to death, as we discovered firsthand. But more often it leads to a shortening of life, coupled with chronic illness. This is an issue of environmental justice and security of the first degree.

Why are we writing this first-person piece in the past tense? Because since this experience in Delhi, measures have been instigated by environmental activists and put in place by governments that have had a significant, positive impact on the air in the capital. When we returned to Delhi in 2002, already the air was noticeably cleaner and easier to breathe. Although moves to restrict buses, taxis, and other vehicles from using diesel and kerosene as fuel have existed since 1998, much opposition from the drivers themselves had been mounted, quashing the reforms on the basis that new fuels—such as natural gas—would be far more costly for the transport operators. It took the Supreme Court to establish a series of fines to inflict on law-breakers before real improvements to ambient air quality took place. But the atmosphere responded rapidly. Between 1996 and 2003 recorded sulfur dioxide levels have decreased by 63 percent; while respirable suspended particulates have been reduced by 30 percent (Walsh et al. 2004, 16).

Despite these positive gains, air pollution problems in many cities across the IOR are still critical. Much of the problem still emanates from dirty industries that swiftly multiply due to the region's rapid and unremediated transition from largely agricultural to industrial economies, in part due to the dominance of corporate-led globalization. Air in many parts of the IOR, from Johannesburg to Tehran to Delhi to Jakarta, isn't about aesthetics, or even possible climate change at some time in the future: it's about life and death now.

Air—and most particularly hydrogen and oxygen—is a basic element of life. People, animals, and plants need to breathe to live.

Since the birth of the modern environmental movement in the West in the mid-1960s in North America, Europe, and Australasia, some of the earliest environmental issues have centered around air quality and pollution. In 1970, when Earth Day was first celebrated in the United States, air pollution issues were among those at the top of the new environmental agenda. These early environmentalists were concerned specifically with two forms of air pollution: industrial pollution and pollution from automobiles. Opposition to industrial air pollution, of course, predates the modern environmental movement, with its roots in public dissatisfaction during the industrial revolution in Europe in the 19th century, most aptly and beautifully captured by William Blake's celebrated poem "Jerusalem," with his reference to the "dark satanic mills" despoiling England's "green and pleasant land." Of course, what made the consequences of industrial pollution even greater during this earlier period was the mass movement of people from rural areas to urban centers that were, in themselves, the new centers of industrial production, placing new migrants in direct proximity to heavy air pollution.

In the developed world, excessive industrial air pollution has not only been linked to human health, but also to the vigor of nonhuman ecosystems. The issue of acid rain has been central to this debate. Also, at the time of Earth Day, the United States was releasing 28 million tons of sulphur dioxide into the air annually. Most of this was coming from coal-fired power plants. These pollutants, when mixed with moisture and sunlight, convert to sulphuric and nitric acids (Easterbrook 1995, 164), which in turn fall to the earth's surface as rain. This acid rain became a central environmental issue when it was discovered that its impact upon ecosystems could be devastating, leading to massive die-offs of forests and other plant species, as well as populations of fish and other water-borne populations.

The second most celebrated issue during the first flush of modern environmentalism—automobile emissions—usually concentrated on the quantities of lead released into the atmosphere. Lead directly impacted upon the health of humans, being toxic to all mammals. During the 1970s, Los Angeles, for example, infringed on the federal standards for carbon monoxide emissions on over 40 occasions. These emissions were directly related to respiratory illnesses and headaches (Easterbrook 1995, 182).

As far as the IOR was concerned, Australia, reminiscent of events in North America and Europe, experienced early environmental movements positioned in direct opposition with governments and corporations in a bid to alter industrial and automobile pollution. There can be no doubt that some substantive, early gains were made by the environmental movement on these issues, with the real improvements achieved in addressing such pollutants as strontium 90, mercury, airborne lead (through restricting lead-based vehicle emissions), and polychlorinated biphenyls (PCBs). Despite these gains in air quality, these activist movements were unsuccessful in challenging advanced industrialism's over-reliance on coal, oil, and gas. End-of-pipe approaches and technologies may have improved the quality of the air for human health, but key issues are unanswered in relation to the globe's continued over-reliance on fossil fuels. In the last decade in the more affluent parts of the world, environmentalists have now shifted their focus, reconstructing air quality issues to fall under the broad issue banner of climate change.

In most parts of the Indian Ocean, as mentioned at the outset of this book, environmental movements did not emerge until two decades later, during the 1980s. Since that time, many environmental concerns have related directly to issues of resource maldistribution: that is, environmentalists in the South have been largely concerned with gaining control of resources and production from the North, rather than being concerned about environmental problems associated with industrial production, or those problems connected to excessive urbanization. Indeed, the key solution for most nations in the IOR has been to industrialize, to develop, to "catch up" with the rest of the industrialized world. Any voices that have questioned the limits of this development have been sidelined.

Thus, it has only been in the last decade or so that we have seen issues of air pollution emerging forcefully onto environmental justice and security agendas. These issues are eerily similar to those of early industrial Europe, but on a far grander scale. On the political level, many of these problems are the result of many years of colonial imperialism on behalf of the North. Much of the stress on cities in the IOR, as aforesaid, comes from the huge migration of people from the country into these urban areas (see Graeme Hugo's chapter in this volume). These cities are increasing in population 80,000 to 200,000 people per annum (Douglas et al. 1994, ix–xv). One of the causational factors of this migration is the globalization of trade, which has destroyed the opportunities of small landholders and workers to make a subsistence living, while at the same time increasing the profits of large corporations that can enter and leave markets almost at will. Multi- and transnational corporations can produce commodities far more "efficiently," utilizing cheap labor markets and the less stringent environmental demands of local legislation (Doyle and McEachern 2001, 79). Furthermore, "damage is partly the result of local industries necessarily producing 'dirty' products in a bid to maintain competitiveness in the 'new global economy'" (Doyle and McEachern 2001).

Again, like Europe in the industrial and agrarian revolutions, "in many cities in Asia (like Bandung in Indonesia, Bombay in India, or Bangkok in Thailand) where there is a massive population explosion, entire cities are forming outside of the established city limits" (Douglas et al. 1994, ix–xv). These new residential settlements are also the sites of major industrial expansion in the IOR.

In India, this rapid transition from an agricultural to an industrial economy has had a profound impact upon the air. In a 2004 study of the connections between air pollution and chronic respiratory morbidity in a industrial town in northern India, Kumar et al. list the three main contributors to chronic air pollution as being industrial pollution, vehicle emissions, and household pollution. In the study it is clear that higher risks of respiratory diseases exist "among residents living in areas of poor ambient air quality" (Kumar et al. 2004, 471).

Special mention must be made here of a non-littoral state of the IOR— China—in this context. Although a non-littoral state, China's current rapid industrialization is having, and will continue to have, a profound impact upon the environmental security of the region for decades to come. The earth has never seen such magnitude of industrial expansion, or such a shocking jolt (movement is too gentle a word) from a peasant-based society to an urban one. What makes the Chinese experience so deeply disturbing from an environmental perspective is fourfold: (1) within its one-party state, it is difficult for environmental dissidents to question the primacy of these industrial goals; (2) environmental safeguards are often considered luxury items that are not even thought valid in relation to expansion; (3) the willingness of the affluent world to feed this insatiable giant with the resources and technological necessities for expansion is unrestrained, and (4) the sheer size of this transition is without precedent. The truth of the matter is that acid rain, once thought to be relegated to history books, has again reared it ugly head, destroying ecosystems and striking at the heart of the China's civilization. The World Bank has listed China as possessing 16 of the top 20 most polluted cities on earth. China's ministry for science and technology has released figures attributing the deaths of 50,000 newborn babies per annum to air pollution (Walsh et al. 2004). Who knows what the unofficial figures are?

In the IOR, air is a classic environmental security issue in that it knows no nation-state boundaries. Whereas water in rivers can be dammed in a manner that matches the borderlines of human polities, air is borderless—transnational in the true sense of the word. Due largely to the Chinese environment disaster, as well as other hastily industrializing parts of the Indian Ocean, including much of South Asia, Southeast Asia and China have formed a massive "brown cloud" for as long as four months a year, particularly during the winter months. A UN report documented in the *British Medical Journal* describes the cloud as a blanket nearly 3 kilometers deep, leading to the premature deaths of "several hundreds of thousands" as a consequence of higher levels of respiratory illnesses (S. Kumar 2002, 513).

And then, on the western side of the IOR is South Africa, nicknamed "the dirty man of Africa." Ford writes: "Based on 2002 figures, South Africa alone is responsible for 90.6% of Africa's energy emissions. This astonishing figure is the result of two factors: South Africa is by far the biggest power generator in Africa; and the country's dependence on coal-fired plants . . . respiratory diseases caused by air pollution are still the fourth biggest cause of infant death in South Africa" (Ford 2005, 44–45).

Although sharing air pollution problems of industrialization and automobile dominance, the IOR's air security issues are exacerbated from a source not experienced in the affluent world: in Africa and South Asia, as well as other parts of the Indian Ocean, there is also an enormous problem associated with air pollution indoors. For example, in many parts of the IOR, cooking and heating in houses is carried out in the traditional way: a fire burns inside the house, often fuelled by animal dung and vegetable waste, with inadequate ventilation. In the *World Health* journal, the World Health Organization is quoted as saying that "morbidity and mortality from respiratory disease in children under five is a serious problem" (de Koning 1990, 8), and "exposure of pregnant women to indoor air pollution is one of the risk factors that contributes to lower birth weight."

In a study of environmental rights in urban South Africa, Wisner also tells of the effects of open air burning of heating fuels that are no longer used on a widespread basis in the minority world. Concentrating on the urban settlement of Alexandria, he writes: "Many residents burn coal in open braziers for heat in the winter. A pall of smoke settles in the river valley in the evening and in the early morning. Density, poverty, lack of accessible and affordable electricity, and topography combine to create a major risk to the respiratory health of Alexandra's residents, especially those living in the valley (who tend to be the poorest), and especially for the very young, the very old, and those, such as retired miners, who may already suffer from lung disorders or those suffering tuberculosis (very common in South Africa)" (Wisner 1995, 274). Connections to issues of environmental justice are obvious here.

In Indonesia, another source of air pollution continues to create serious health risks: the mass burning of forests. Due largely to human use, enormous tracts of forest in Indonesia have been degraded. Aiken writes of the link between the trend toward forest fragmentation and ever- increasing forest fires: "Expanding road networks are a major cause of forest fragmentation, and they also open up intact forests to the depredations of pioneer farmers, loggers, hunters, invasive plant and animal species, and drought and fire. . . . Nowhere is this trend more evident than in Indonesia. . . . In addition to their destructive impact on forest resources, biodiversity, and indigenous peoples' homelands, out-of-control fires yield huge quantities of smoke. In 1997 and 1998, smoke from fires on Sumatra and Kalimantan blanketed most of insular Southeast Asia, periodically disrupting transportation, hindering economic activity, and creating serious health risks" (Aiken 2004, 55).

In his study of the 1997–1998 fires, Aiken goes on to make the point that some 70 million Southeast Asians were exposed to smoke-haze. Of the 12 million exposed in eight Indonesian provinces between September and November of 1997, 527 died, 16,000 were hospitalized, and 36,000 received outpatient care. Symptoms ranged from mild to fatal, depending on the amount of particulate matter in the ambient air and the duration of exposure to the pollutants. Children, the elderly, and the chronically infirm were among those most at risk from the toxic effects of the polluted air. Of course, those who sought help and were recorded by authorities as doing so were only the tip of the iceberg. Aiken writes: "Much about the public health effects of the smoke- haze, however, will probably never be known because, among other things, many ailing people probably chose not to or were unable to obtain medical care, and the long-term health effects of prolonged exposure to high levels of particulate pollution are difficult to predict" (Aiken 2004, 71).

To most in the IOR, essential environmental issues pertaining to the atmosphere have nothing to do with barely perceptible changes to climate that might eventually lead to global warming and rising sea levels. Instead, they revolve around issues of air pollution and their direct impacts upon human health. These issues are more reminiscent of those that evolved in the North during the 1970s, though in the case of the South these issues are exacerbated due to the size and rapidity of industrialization, coupled with a profound lack of environmental infrastructure.

As touched upon, many air pollution problems in the affluent world are now gathered together under the catchall of climate change. Climate change is an important, global problem, and despite the existence of factions of scientists still denying the problem, it seems one side—the side advocating global climate change—is now gaining a firm upper hand. The ascendancy has been gained by a combination of factors, including: (1) the results of most forms of scientific experimentation in relation to, for example, the melting of ice caps and the rising sea level; and (2) the increasing championing of the pro-climate position—after an initial period of rejection—by powerful political and business interests at both the national and international levels, most particularly in the North. This recent embrace by parts of the business community, in part, can be linked to the ease with which climate change arguments can justify business-as-usual approaches, as well as their propensity to be mustered to promote the growth of the nuclear industry across the globe (see chapter 16).

Most environmental commentators accept, therefore, dominant science's paradigmatic shift, now almost irrefutably demanding the conclusion that current levels of carbon dioxide and methane in the atmosphere are higher at the moment than at anytime in the last half million years, and pointing to disastrous outcomes that face the earth and its people if, in the long term, we continue to ignore our part in it. Even if still skeptical, simply on the basis of advocating the precautionary principle (when in doubt, better to err on the side of caution), it remains prudent to seriously address these issues.

Despite this dominant position in the affluent world, many environmentalists in the IOR regard climate as a non-issue—a matter constructed by affluent Western science. They argue that it was only during the 1980s that the North came to comprehend that it had to share the same atmosphere and oceans with the South and that a continued policy of laissez-faire in relation to the third world would be detrimental for the more affluent minority. The North then constructed green concerns as environmental security issues to control the less affluent from pursuing the very path of development that the minority world has pursued without restraint since the industrial revolution.

A critical view of climate change is that it takes much of the politics—the conflict—out of environmental resource issues, providing a polite filter between human action and human consequence, taking the direct and instrumental power relationships out of the equation. It is no longer people against people: the exploiters versus the exploited, or in this case, the polluters versus the polluted. Rather, although people are still the initiators, they are cast in a far more oblique light, often unwittingly setting off a calamitous, climactic punishment for all. A force of nature is, in the end, the nemesis, whereas the initiators, the environmental degraders, are in relative safety, at a convenient one-step removed from the atrocities inflicted upon the many. Also, by constructing the concept of an environmental "day of judgment" for all, all humans (all creation) are cast as victims, not differentiating between the perpetrators and fatalities. As the first half of this chapter bears witness, there are environmental winners and losers in the politics of air: climate change advocates usually forget this fact.

Tensions over the climate position between minority and majority world environmentalists have been most evident in the world's largest environmental organization: Friends of the Earth (FoE). FoEInternational is a confederation of branches in over 70 countries. In recent years, for example, FoEEquador took the issue so seriously that it has withdrawn from the confederation over a range of issues, including the minority world FoE branches' obsession with climate issues, which they perceived as an elitist, first world view of environmental concerns (Doherty and Doyle 2006). These critical third world voices saw the issue of climate change as a form of green imperialism: Northern groups capturing the environmental agenda of the South and repackaging it in a way which did not sufficiently call to order the direct and environmentally degrading practices of the affluent, corporatized world.

Cam Walker, a contributor in this section on air, currently serves as co-coordinator of FoEAustralia. Walker was extremely concerned about the split between third and first world environmentalists within FoEInternational, and was one of those who worked assiduously to mend the split. Rather than rejecting climate change as a focus, Walker and others decided that the narrative had become too powerful and, in turn, have sought to co-opt it for their own purposes, recasting it as climate justice. This argument tries to introduce the previously missing political dimension: issues of inequality. It promotes the concept that all people of the earth must have access to a fair share of carbon and atmospheric resources. Walker argues the weaker, less affluent people of the planet will suffer most when the inevitable happens, and that people living on the periphery of the global economy will be the first to suffer, creating an enormous wave of climate refugees across the region.

This more enlightened view of climate issues has started to take hold in the IOR. In part it has assumed greater prominence among majority world environmentalists, due to the fact that some of the world's biggest polluters and/or reliers on fossil fuels have not signed the climate change protocols in Kyoto and Johannesburg. At the end of October 2002, 5,000 people from communities in India, including international NGOs, gathered in a Rally for Climate Justice in New Delhi. This rally was organized to coincide with the UN meeting on climate change (Conference of Parties 8—COP8), and was organized by the India Climate Justice Forum, including the National Alliance of People's Movements, the National Fishworkers Forum, Third World Network, and CorpWatch. In a press release, Friends of the Earth International (FoEI) wrote of the current frustration with climate change negotiations from a climate justice angle: "But climate negotiations show no progress and communities are calling for urgent action to address climate change and to protect their livelihoods in a manner that is consistent with human rights, worker's rights, and environmental justice. . . . Given the entrenched opposition to action from the fossil fuel industry and governments like the US and Saudi Arabia, environmental organizations joined forces with social movements in order to progress this most urgent agenda. The window of opportunity to prevent dangerous climate change is closing fast and, for many communities, the impacts are already alarmingly present" (FOEI 2004).

Further tensions have emerged due to the fact that both island states in the Indian Ocean and poorer dwellers and coastal fishworkers on coastlines will be the principal victims in global climate change. In this manner, climate change is metamorphosing from an elite, scientific, Northern issue into one that can usefully fit into the environmental justice agenda of the South. It is important to stress, however, that this justice interpretation remains subservient to the more traditional, business-friendly elucidation discussed earlier.

In turn, this leads us directly to the work of Christian Bouchard, the other contributing author in this section, as he concentrates on the climate change implications of small island states in the IOR. For the sake of discussion, let us now just pick one group of islands that Bouchard addresses: the Maldives. Eighty percent of the Maldives is, in fact, less than one meter above sea level, and yet 350,000 people live there (Bouchard 2006). What would happen if the earth's air was warmed to a point where, in turn, water temperatures rose, leading to a melting of the polar ice caps? What would happen when the number of extreme weather events increase due to these changes in the earth's atmosphere? What would happen if the worst predictions of scientists in relation to global climate change were realized (whether it be the result of a long-term "natural" cycle and/or human-induced). These hypothetical questions, not so long ago, would have been flights of fancy. But in the early years of the 21st century they are central questions in environmental security management. Since the concept of global climate change first rose to prominence in the 1980s, similar hypothetical questions have led to predictions of mass devastation.

The highest island in the Maldivian archipelago is Villingili Island in the Addu Atoll, standing at only 2.4 meters. This statistic is vital when trying to understand the impact of the tsunami that devastated this island chain on December 26, 2004. The massive tidal waves washed over the 1,192 low-lying coralline islands that make up the Maldives, sitting on the equator, south of the Bay of Bengal. Less dramatic erosion of Maldives's coastlines has been in progress since the inception of the settlement, but accurate measurements are difficult to come by. The capital city of the Maldives, Malé, houses over 70,000 people on an island of only 192 hectares. Forty-five percent of this land has been reclaimed from the sea. The island has been extended by the building of a series of protective seawalls.

Erosion creates enormous problems for dwellers of the littoral zones, from fisher folk, to farmers, through to the tourist industry. It not only demands the construction of protective infrastructure, but also impacts directly upon water quality, as saline sea water increasingly impregnates the sands and soils that sit precariously upon the atolls. Apart from directly threatening the quality and safety of drinking water, these natural processes have enormous repercussions for the long-term sustainability of agriculture.

Erosion aside, scientists are looking at other key indicators, such as the warming of the seas which envelop the 8,920 square kilometers of reef area that make up the Maldives. The warming of the seas in recent times, for example, has had a dramatic impact upon the bleaching of the coral. In 1998, in a huge "bleaching event," 90 percent of living corals were totally or partially bleached, leading to the increased incidence of coral mortality. In places such as Australia, coral bleaching means a loss of biodiverse marine ecosystems and a loss of tourism, which is focused on coralline phenomena. In the Maldives, tourism is also a concern, but more so, reef resilience is the basis upon which these civilizations are built.

What makes this issue doubly perplexing for Maldivians is that the concept of climate change is an ecological catastrophe that is not of their own doing. Whether climate change is simply due to the incremental processes of the time-worn forces of wind and sea, or whether it is human-induced due to excessive industrialization and its concomitant reliance on the burning of fossil fuels, this "calamity-in-waiting" is impossible to comprehend within the scale of human lifetimes. Its very conceptualization is totally outside of their experience.

The magnitude of the event makes it difficult to digest on a day-to-day basis. Climate change for Maldivians is an interesting phenomenon. It is their version of ecological Armageddon; their Year Zero. With the melting of icecaps, whether it be from natural cycles of the earth, human-induced effects, or a combination of both, Maldivians, like many living on coastal plans and other low-lying areas of the Indian Ocean Region, are confronted, quite simply, with nonexistence. This is the story of the ancient flood, with no Mount Ararat to rest on. This concept is annihilation of culture, history, and future. Nothingness.

So, when considering climate change from an environmental justice perspective, we are forced to imagine human displacement on a massive scale. This is also an important focus of Cam Walker's chapter. Norman Myers, regarded by many to be a leading researcher on environmental refugees, argues that by the middle of the 21st century, 150 million people will be displaced if the worst-case scenarios of climate scientists are realized. The questions is then asked, "Where will these people go?"

But we must reiterate that these environmental justice interpretations of climate change do not dominate policy considerations of nation-states in the IOR. In Australia's case, again cast as the minority world partner in the IOR, both government and business have, in the 1990s, worked assiduously to dismantle environmental opposition based on concerns over climate change. The example of greenhouse research is an excellent example of this approach. Although climate change was accepted in most nations of the earth as a crucial shared concern, Environment Minister Robert Hill's performance at Kyoto at the Greenhouse Summit in the late 1990s, despite being testament to his diplomatic skills, was evidence of increased government pandering to corporate interests in most areas of environmental policy development. In fact, so corrupted was this process by the pressures of vested business interests that Alan Powell, a key technical adviser to the Australian Bureau of Agricultural and Resource Economics (ABARE), resigned due to these compromising pressures (Lunn 1998, 2). ABARE had placed a price tag of $50,000 on joining the policy defining committee. Effectively, this promoted business input and denied entry to most NGOs. To make matters worse, these sources of funding were kept secret. The Commonwealth Ombudsman, Philippa Smith states: "By not allowing adequate and balanced community input, and by not accurately declaring the sources of its funding in its climate change report, the bureau has compromised the credibility of its work" (Smith, quoted in Lunn 1997, 2).

Since the turn of the millennium, business has worked less directly against climate change agendas, moving to a position of co-option. This "climate co-option" repositioning by the ultra-right has taken two main forms: first, by accepting climate change but remaining against the Kyoto Protocol as the "right way" of addressing the problem; and second, by advocating that nuclear energy is the answer to provide the earth with greenhouse-friendly fuel. Let us address the argumentation of the right against Kyoto first. At the heart of this rhetoric lies the inaugural meeting of the Asia-Pacific Partnership on Clean Development and Climate in Australia in January 2006. As well as bringing together the two noncompliant nations—Australia and the United States—to the climate change table, it also managed to secure the participation of China, India, Japan, and Korea. The major theme of the conference was that it is with business, and not with nation-states (or Kyoto), in which the salvation to a reduction in global climate change lies.

The Weekend Australian reports: "The reactionary response to the Asia-Pacific Partnership meeting this week demonstrates that support for Kyoto cloaks the green movement's real desire—to see capitalism stop succeeding. Extreme greens cannot bear to accept that our best chance of reducing greenhouse gas emissions will occur when free enterprise has incentives to implement solutions" (*The Weekend Australian,* January 14–15: 16).

So, in this vein, "extreme greens" are created who support Kyoto as a communist model, while right-wing think tanks paint themselves as moderate greens, now accepting the current climate crisis, but offering a different solution: a roundtable built by business, not the nation- state. Climate change will be resolved by the very perpetuators of the crisis out of some sense of corporate moral responsibility. In fact, this model is so attractive to big business industries, such as transnational extractive industries, because it will lead not quite to business-as-usual, but to business better-than-usual. Cate Faehrmann of the New South Wales Nature Conservation Council argues that the APPCDC's six nations voluntary approach was a "license for government and business to do nothing. . . . Without any incentives or penalties there is no reason for industry to move away from burning coal and fuel" (Faehmann, quoted in Wikinews, January 12, 2006).

This is not an ideological battle between socialism and capitalism, as the "opinion piece" suggests, but one between two ideological strands of the right: liberalism and neoliberalism. Like neoliberals, the classical liberal position argues for the primacy of the individual, and upholds the basic tenets of the capitalist economic system. But liberalism differs from its neoliberal or radical libertarian cousins, as it maintains that the state has a role to intervene in human affairs when the will of the anti-social minority (in this case environmentally degrading companies) interferes with the wishes of the majority. In this light, the Kyoto Protocol is firmly entrenched in the liberal tradition, as it sees a role for responsible, democratic governments coming together to provide sticks as well as carrots to alter poor, environmentally degrading, national and corporate practices.

The neoliberals, on the other hand, see any state intervention in the marketplace as anathema. Rather than championing democracy, the neoliberals actually champion plutocracy: the wealthy should decide. Further, the earth itself is simply a large corporation, and nature is the market—for the market is deemed natural, per se. All environmental issues would resolve themselves if only left to the free hand of the market principles. In both Australia and the United States, this current ideology is rampant, whereas in Europe—the champions of Kyoto—a less virulent strand of liberalism is dominant. But Tony Blair's "Third Way" can hardly be interpreted as a socialist conspiracy to overthrow capitalism.

But even the more state-centered approaches championed within the Kyoto Protocol are fraught with difficulties within a third world, IOR context. As most nations—excluding Australia—within the region are developing nations (classified as Annex Two nations), they are not required under the Protocol to accept any emission reduction or stabilization targets. Although carbon emissions trading programs are emerging, allowing developed nations to buy emissions quotas from under-developed nations in exchange for supporting projects that are more greenhouse friendly, national attempts within the IOR to cut down on carbon emissions in real terms are controversial. Lindow documents this line of criticism as follows:

> In its earliest phases, the Kyoto Protocol commits industrialized signatory countries to cut their greenhouse gas emissions by 2012 to an average of 5.2 percent below 1990 levels. It allows the rich world to meet part of its obligations by financing projects in developing countries that achieve reductions in greenhouse gas emissions, and then claiming the certified emissions reduction credits (CERs) generated by these projects as their own. . . . But its critics point to the wider debate over whether carbon trading serves the needs of the global

poor, or forces them to bear the brunt of reducing greenhouse gas emissions while the west carries on with business as usual. They argue that such projects undermine the integrity of the Protocol by creating perverse incentives for countries and companies to keep polluting in order to attract investment. (Lindow 2005, 22)

To summarize, then, climate change appears to be a threat to the livelihoods of many in the IOR. Whether this threat is immediate or whether, in fact, it will ever eventuate is open for debate. Accepting the precautionary principle as an important environmental management mantra, however, means taking the climate change argument seriously, though not to the point where it obfuscates other more pressing environmental justice and security issues in the IOR. Of more immediate concern for most who dwell in the region is the lack of secure access to healthy air, whether it be produced by excesses of industrialization, by the handing over of cities to the rampages of automobile culture, or whether it pertains to the continued burning of unsafe fuels for the purposes of domestic cooking and heating.

In final conclusion, depicting all major issues relating to air security as climate security is a flawed position on two counts: first, air-based catastrophe for the many in the IOR is a daily reality, not a calamity-in-waiting. Second, the ultimate day-of-judgment, a future day when the earth's climate change will lead to another great flood, imagines an environmental punishment being dished out, ultimately by forces of nature. Projecting a force-of-nature as the ultimate source of retribution conveniently provides cover for the key perpetrator of air pollution. Corporate-controlled globalization has, and continues to deliver, massive profits to the few, decimating the many: people against people.

REFERENCES

Aiken, S. Robert. 2004. "Runaway Fires, Smoke-Haze Pollution, and Unnatural Disasters in Indonesia." *The Geographical Review, Journal of the American Geographical Society of New York* 94 (1): 55–79.

Bouchard , C. 2005. "The Energy Challenge in Small Island States and Territories: The Case of the Southwest Indian Ocean Small Islands." In *Energy Security and the Indian Ocean Region,* ed. D. Rumley and S. Chaturvedi, 204–29. New Delhi: South Asian Publishers.

de Koning, W. 1990. "Air Pollution in Africa." *World Health* (January–February): 8–9.

Doherty, B., and T. Doyle. 2006. "Beyond Borders: Transnational Politics, Social Movements and Modern Environmentalisms." *Environmental Politics* 15, no. 5 (special issue, ed. B. Doherty and T. Doyle): 697–712.

Douglas, M., Y. S. F. Lee, and K. Lowry. 1994. "Introduction to the Special Issue on Community Based Urban Environmental Management in Asia." *Asian Journal of Environmental Management* 2 (1): ix–xv.

Doyle, T., and D. McEachern. 2001. *Environment and Politics,* 2nd ed. London: Routledge.

Easterbrook, G. 1995. *A Moment on the Earth: The Coming of Age of Environmental Optimism.* New York: Viking Penguin.

Ford, N. 2005. "The Dirty Man of Africa." *African Business,* March, 44–45.

Friends of the Earth. 2004. Climate Justice Collection. *Chain Reaction: The National Magazine of Friends of the Earth Australia* 90: 18.

Kumar, R., M. Sharma, A. Srivastva, J. S. Thakur, S. K. Jindal. 2004. "Association of Outdoor Pollution with Chronic Respiratory Morbidity in an Industrial Town in Northern India." *Archives of Environmental Health* 59 (9) (September): 471–77.

Kumar, S. 2002. "Indian Government Denies Health Impact of Brown Cloud." *British Medical Journal* 325 (7363) (September 7): 513.

Lindow, M. 2005. "Green House, Back Door." *New Internationalist*, December 22.

Lunn, H. 1998. "Greenhouse Influence Easily Bought." *The Australian Newspaper*, February 5, 2.

Walsh, B., S. Jakes, C. Estulin, A. Adiga, and T. Sekiguchi. 2004. "Choking on Growth: Rapid Economic Development Has Led to Filthy Air." *Time International* (Asia edition) 164 (24) (December 13): 16.

Wikinews. 2006. "World's Biggest Polluters Won't Cut Back on Fossil Fuel." http:// en.wikinews.org/wiki (accessed May 1, 2006).

Wisner, B. 1995. "The Reconstruction of Environmental Rights in Urban South Africa." *Human Ecology* 23 (2): 259–84.

The Weekend Australian. 2006. "Climate Change Facts," opinion piece. *The Weekend Australian*, January 14–15, p. 16.

18

Climate Change, Sea Level Rise, and Development in Small Island States and Territories of the Indian Ocean

CHRISTIAN BOUCHARD

Introduction

Small island states and territories (SISTs) are of limited size, possess small populations and vulnerable economies, rely on limited local resource bases, and are environmentally fragile. Cumulating smallness (small land mass, small population, and small economy) and insularity (which implies geographical isolation and even spatial fragmentation in the case of archipelagos), SISTs are widely recognized as singular cases both in terms of environment and development.[1] However, even if all these islands share many common development constraints deriving from their small size and insularity, they all possess their own identities in regard to human and physical environments. In the Indian Ocean, seven small island developing states (SIDS) and eight small inhabited island territories qualify as SISTs (see map 18.1). This chapter focuses on the cases of the Union of Comoros, Maldives, Mauritius, and Seychelles, as well as on the French islands territories of Mayotte (part of the Comoros Archipelago) and Réunion (part of the Mascarene Archipelago), which together cover a wide range of specific small island situations.

In the global context of SISTs, climate change and sea level rise are classically pinpointed as one of the most serious challenges that these island systems will be facing in the 21st century. It is commonly said that SISTs stand to be very negatively impacted by coastal erosion and land loss, flooding, soil salinization, intrusion of saltwater in groundwater aquifers, lower coral resilience, and more severe weather events. In addition, the gravity of these impacts may well be enhanced by their cumulative interactions as well as by human factors. Thus, even given the lowest climate change and sea level rise projections, it is highly probable that their outcome will be quite significant in small islands. Collectively, climate change impacts are expected to particularly affect human health and well-being, coastal environments, agriculture, fisheries, and tourism, and thus the general sustainability of the island communities.

As the climate change phenomenon emerges as a reality, the main concern becomes how the small islands will cope with its predicted manifestations and impacts. Even though the fears in the 1980s of a 2 to 3 meter rise in sea level for the 21st century have been discarded, the issue remains of great significance, as we now know that even a rise of twenty or more centimeters will have drastic effects on some coastal environments as well as on vulnerable coastal infrastructures and communities.

Overall, the final outcome of climate change and sea level rise on the small island systems will depend on the nature of the climate change itself (what will really happen?), the feedback mechanisms (interactions between humans and the environment), the human adaptive capacity, and the resilience of biophysical and human systems (IPCC 2001, 868). Given the great variability of the local geographical settings; including environmental, socio-cultural, economical, and political aspects, the overall outcome of climate change is likely to vary considerably from one SIST to another and even between islands of the same SIST. Thus, the specific impacts of climate change on each of the Indian Ocean small islands have to be addressed by giving strong attention to their individual human and physical attributes.

The Indian Ocean Small Island States and Territories

Small island states and territories can be defined as island entities that are less than 30,000 square kilometers (with no individual island being more than 17,000 square kilometers), that have a permanent population (and thus a real native island society), and that, in the case of territories, are at a distance exceeding several hundred kilometers from the continental state to which they belong (Bouchard 2006). There are formally seven small island states and eight small island territories[2] in the Indian Ocean Region (see map 18.1). East Timor, Bahrain, and Singapore represent atypical small island states cases that will not be addressed here;[3] neither will the cases of the small island territories of Andaman and Nicobar (India), British Indian Ocean Territory (UK), Christmas Island and Cocos Islands (Australia), Lakshadweep (India), and Socotra (Yemen) be discussed.

Out of the six studied Indian Ocean SISTs, the Maldives are the most vulnerable to climate change and sea level rise. The Maldivian archipelago is made up of 1,192 low-lying small coralline islands grouped into 26 atolls situated on top of a volcanic ridge 960 kilometers in length (orientated north-south). About 80 percent of its 298 square kilometers of land are located at less than 1 meter above sea level, while its highest point is only at an altitude of 2.4 meters (Villingili Island in Addu Atoll). Straddling the equator, the archipelago lies outside the cyclone area of the Bay of Bengal but does not escape bad weather events (storms, showers, and heavy winds) and rough sea conditions, especially in the southwest monsoon (May to October).

Maldives' population of approximately 350,000 people is spread across 199 islands, most of which are smaller than 50 hectares (Gan is the largest one at 517 hectares). With a human development index of 0.752 (UNDP 2004), the island nation is a middle-ranked developing country that is very heavily dependent on tourism and fisheries for its economy. In regard to national development and security, among the

SMALL ISLAND STATES
Small Island Territories

- Exclusive Economic Zones (EEZ)
— Delimited boundaries
--- Virtual boundaries

0   1000   2000
                      Km

Indian Ocean

CHINA

VIETNAM

LAOS

THAILAND

CAMBODIA

BURMA

BHUTAN

NEPAL

BANGLADESH

INDIA

SRI LANKA

PAKISTAN

IRAN

IRAQ

QATAR

OMAN

UNITED ARAB EMIRATES

SAUDI ARABIA

YEMEN

BAHRAIN

PHILIPPINES

BRUNEI

MALAYSIA

SINGAPORE

INDONESIA

AUSTRALIA

TIMOR-LESTE

Ashmore and Cartier (Austr.)

Christmas (Austr.)

Cocos [Keeling] (Austr.)

Andaman and Nicobar (India)

British Indian Ocean Territory (U.K.)

Lakshadweep [Laccadives] (India)

MALDIVES

Socotra (Yemen)

St. Paul & Amsterdam (Fr.)

Mahé

SEYCHELLES

Mayotte (Fr.)

COMOROS

Rodrigues

MAURITIUS

Réunion (Fr.)

MADAGASCAR

MOZAMBIQUE

SOMALIA

ETHIOPIA

DJIBOUTI

KENYA

TANZANIA

UGANDA

RWANDA

BURUNDI

SUDAN

MALAWI

ZAMBIA

ZIMBABWE

BOTSWANA

SWAZILAND

LESOTHO

SOUTH AFRICA

French Indian Ocean Scattered Islands (Fr.)
A - Tromelin
B - Glorioso Islands
C - Juan de Nova
D - Bassas da India
E - Europa

BAHRAIN

SAUDI ARABIA

QATAR

Persian Gulf

UNION OF THE COMOROS
Grande Comore (Ngazidja)
Anjouan (Nzwani)
Mohéli (Mwali)
Mayotte (Fr.)

Aldabra

Glorioso Is. (Fr.)

SEYCHELLES

MADAGASCAR

MOZAMBIQUE

MALAYSIA

State of Johor

Straits of Singapore

SINGAPORE

INDONESIA Pulau Bintan

20°E   30°E   40°E   50°E   60°E   70°E   80°E   90°E   100°E   110°E   120°E   130°E   140°E

10°N

0°

10°S

most serious concerns is high population growth, environmental degradation, flooding, and limited water resources. The nation is also experiencing a social crisis in unemployment and poverty, with many of the population impatient to see tangible improvements in their living standards.

Unlike the Maldivian archipelago that is made of a single unique island type, the Seychelles are comprised of two very different groups. The largest islands of the archipelago, and best suited for human settlement, are the granitic islands (Inner Islands). Located around latitude 4°30' south, a position that protects them from cyclones, these islands are mountainous and well forested. The coralline islands are either atolls (like Aldabra and Farquhar in the south) or unique and isolated small cays (like Bird and Denis islands in the north). In terms of socioeconomic development, the Seychelles rank highly in the world group of small island developing states. Its economy is based on the development of tourism since the 1970s and of large-scale industrial fisheries in the 1990s, while offshore financial and commercial activities are now also in place.

Recognized for the beauty of its landscape and its environmental richness, both inland and at sea, the Seychelles have been a leader in the Indian Ocean Region in regard to environmental protection and conservation. The early creation of marine and terrestrial national parks attests to this strong interest in their natural capital.[4] Nevertheless, human activities are impacting very negatively on the marine environment in front of Victoria (the national capital and port as well as the largest city of the country). Outside of Mahé (the largest and most populated island), and especially in the resort islands, human activities are less intensive and often occur at a scale that is more respectful of the island's size and carrying capacity.

Réunion is the largest and highest small island in the Southwest Indian Ocean. It is formed by two distinct volcanic cores, the Piton des Neiges, which is extinct and culminates at an altitude of 3,069 meters, and the Piton de la Fournaise, which is a Hawaiian style (basaltic, fluid lava) very active volcano that culminates at 2,612 meters. Because of its high and mountainous interior, as well as its intense volcanic activity, human occupation is limited to only about 40 percent of the island, mostly on the small coastal plains and the lower part of the external slopes that run from the summits of the island to the littoral zone. Réunion enjoys the highest socioeconomic development of the studied islands, due to the tremendous help and support given to the island by France since the 1960s and now by the European Union. Environmental issues (lagoon, soil, biodiversity, cyclones, etc.), very intense resources consumption (energy and water), a huge trade deficit, a relatively fast-growing population, and a high rate of unemployment (more than 30 percent) constitute the most noteworthy sustainability challenges facing Réunion.

Mauritius, Réunion's sister island (both are related to the same geologic feature and share a lot in regard to history and population), is also volcanic and relatively large. Nevertheless, its extinct volcanoes have been extensively eroded and only a small number of peaks culminate over 500 meters in altitude. Unlike Réunion (which only possesses a small number of fringing reefs), Mauritius is entirely surrounded by an extensive coral reef, and features a lagoon and white sand beaches. This coastal setting is largely exploited by the tourism industry, and the island economy also relies on a large sugar cane sector, well-developed commercial and industrial sectors, and developing financial and new technologies sectors. Even though the human development index is quite high (0.785 in 2002), living conditions remain difficult for a large number of people, and environmental and local resource degradation is significant. Like Réunion, Mauritius is also affected by cyclones, a recurrent problem to which it remains quite vulnerable both in terms of human security (especially because of poor housing) and economy (especially in regard to the tourism and agriculture sectors).

The four islands of the Comoros Archipelago are also sister islands, as they are geologically related to the same hot spot and are inhabited by a common traditional Swahili population. Mayotte, the oldest island, possesses a relatively low volcanic residual relief and sits at the center of a very large lagoon (more than 1,000 square kilometers). Grande Comore, the youngest island, possesses the only active volcano and the highest altitude, but less developed coral reefs. Anjouan and Mohéli represent intermediate situations. The low human development conditions (Comoros's HDI was only of 0.530 in 2002) are shared by all the islands even though Mayotte has remained French-administered since the Union of the Comoros independence (1975). This is because France did not invest much in the development of the island before the middle of the 1990s. (This was related to the political uncertainty created by the Comoros claim over Mayotte.) Now that France and Mahorais have agreed on the status of Mayotte inside the French Republic, the island is entering into a rapid development phase (mostly due to the development of state institutions and public services). On the other hand, although the Comorians are slowly recovering from the dramatic global crisis that erupted in 1997, when Mohéli and Anjouan claimed independence, human development conditions will remain low for a long time in the three islands of the Union. Thus, in regard to socioeconomic development, the gap is now widening rapidly between the French island of Mayotte and its three Comorian sister islands. Nevertheless, all four islands are facing serious development problems, especially in relation to rapid population growth, high poverty levels, and resultant environmental degradation.

Overall, this rapid overview shows the great diversity of situations found in the Indian Ocean SISTs. Everywhere, climate change and sea level rise only represent one of the numerous challenges faced by these islands in their quest for sustainable development. Taken as a whole, there are other serious issues in the fields of demography (population growth), sociology (poverty, unemployment, education, health), culture (modernization, cohabitation), economy (diversification, growth, imports/exports ratio, etc.), environment (forests, coral reefs, soils, water, etc.), politics (institutions, social peace), and even in science and technologies (knowledge, capacity, availability). Nevertheless, climate change and sea level rise are very likely to have significant adverse impacts on all of the studied island systems, and those that are more vulnerable and less resilient will inevitably be more affected than the others.

Predicted Climate Change Manifestations and Impacts

Table 18.1 gives an overview of the predicted specific climate change impacts for SISTs as well as of their most vulnerable environments and assets. Although there is still some uncertainty remaining about the magnitude of the climate change manifestations and their local variations, some air and sea surface temperature warming will occur, as will an increase in air and ocean carbon dioxide content. Because of the former, tropical storms are likely to be more intense, and perhaps more numerous, but this remains debated. Because of the cumulative effects of both, coral reefs appear to be very vulnerable to climate change. This threatens the islands' systems in many ways, as degradation of the reefs means less natural protection against the waves, lower biological productivity in the coastal waters, and adverse effects on tourism and coastal fisheries. All of this is without consideration of the sea level rise that is said to be already occurring at a fast rate and may even be accelerating.

Table 18.1   Main Predicted Climate Change Manifestations and Impacts for the Small Island States and Territories

Predicted climate change manifestations	Most probable impacts	Most vulnerable environments/ assets/localities
Sea level rise	– coastal erosion and land loss	– beaches, coastal settlements, and infrastructures
	– increased flooding in very high tides and storm surges	– flat, low-lying islands and littoral plains
Warming air surface temperature	– increased evapotranspiration (increased plant moisture stress)	– crops, plantations, and natural vegetation
	– adverse effects on human health and comfort	– low altitude areas
Warming ocean surface temperature	– coral bleaching and mortality	– coral reefs
	– degradation of coastal water quality (especially in lagoons)	– lagoons
	– higher energy for cyclones	– all islands submitted to cyclones
Heavier rainfall events	– increased runoff	– steady slopes
	– flash floods	– easily flooded zones
	– soil erosion	– agricultural lands

(Continued)

Table 18.1   *(Continued)*

Predicted climate change manifestations	*Most probable impacts*	*Most vulnerable environments/ assets/localities*
	– landslides	– unstable slopes and cliffs
Drier dry season	– lower water resources	– flat, low-lying islands, leeward side of high islands
	– lower agricultural yield	– crops and plantations
More intense tropical storms and cyclones	– coastal erosion and land loss	– coastal environments
	– flooding (due to rainfall and/or storm surge)	– easily flooded zones
	– landslides	– unstable slopes and cliffs
	– wind damage	– settlements and infrastructures
		– crops, plantations, forests, and other natural vegetation
Higher atmospheric carbon dioxide content	– increased productivity of some plants (especially C_3 crops) in ideal conditions (but increased water and heat stresses can easily overwhelm this positive effect)	– crops, plantations, forests, and other natural vegetation
Higher oceanic carbon dioxide content	– lower coral resilience (reduced coral development)	– coral reefs

Source: Bouchard 2007.

For the Indian Ocean, the 2001 IPCC report projects an annual mean tempera-ture change between 1990 and 2080 ranging from 2.61° Celsius [Å0.65] to 3.16° Cel-sius [Å0.89] depending on the scenario (GHG+A or GHG).[5] Considering that the numbers in brackets show standard deviation between model projections, the warming for that period should be between 2° and 4° Celsius (consistent with the 2007 IPCC best estimates for the global temperature change ranging from 1.8 to 4.0° Celsius). There is practically no seasonal effect on the temperature predicted. It is for precipitation that a perceptible seasonal effect is predicted, with a decrease in the dry season (June to August) and an increase in the wet season (December to February). Overall, these precipitation changes are projected to be around 6 per-cent for both seasons [Å10 percent], which means that the annual mean precipita-tion is projected to increase around 4.3 percent [Å4.9] to 5.1 percent [Å4.3], depending on the scenario (GHG+A or GHG). According to the 2007 IPCC report, and excluding future rapid dynamical changes in ice flow that could increase the projection by as much as 10 to 20 centimeters, the magnitude of the global sea level rise for the period 1980–1999 to 2090–2099 should be in the range of 18 to 59 centimeters. Other very significant, but still quite uncertain, issues in the Indian Ocean are the climate change impacts on monsoon and trade wind patterns, and thus on surface ocean currents, heave, and upwelling. It is possible that even tides could be affected, at least slightly.

Before addressing the vulnerability of the studied small islands in regard to these climate change manifestations, it is useful and meaningful to compare the actual observed trends to the IPCC projections. In the Maldives (Maldives 2001, chapter 1), measured annual maximum and minimum temperatures for the period of 1969–1999 showed a rising trend (Malé station), while the total annual rainfall data showed a decrease (Malé and Gan stations). With an annual maximum temperature increase of 0.17° Celsius every 10 years, and an annual minimum temperature increase of 0.07° Celsius every 10 years, the annual temperature change has been about 0.12° Celsius every 10 years over the period (which is consistent with the global warming scenario). For precipitation over the same period, the observed trend shows a decrease of 2.7 millimeters in rainfall every year in Malé (at the center of the archipelago) and of 7.6 millimeters a year in Gan (south of the archipelago). This decreasing trend does not match with the overall Indian Ocean projections, but this might well be attributed to a regional effect.

Still in the Maldives, the situation becomes much more interesting when we tackle the issue of sea level rise. Two very opposed positions have been debated in the last few years: some argue that the rise is occurring, accelerating, and will have dramatic impacts on the whole nation (Maldives officials' documents, IPCC discourse, and other international SIDS documents), while others contend that there have been no sea level changes since the end of the 1970s and thus that the supposed already ongoing "quasi inevitable" flooding of the country has simply not happened yet. Unfortunately, there is nothing on observed sea levels in the *First National Communication of the Republic of Maldives to the United Nations Framework Convention on Climate Change* (Maldives 2001). According to Nils-Axel Mörner (Mörner 2003, 2004a, 2004b), who started a Maldives Project in 2000 while he was president of the INQUA Commission on Sea Level Changes and Coastal Evolution (1999–2003), sea level has not been rising in the Maldives in the last few centuries (remaining at 30 centimeters over the actual for the period 1790–1970), and at around 1970 it even experienced a significant decline (−30 centimeters to reach the actual level).[6] In the Seychelles, a very comprehensive coastal geomorphology work on the small cay of Bird Island showed the great natural mobility of the shores and concluded that an accretion of the island by some 14 percent occurred between 1960 and 1999 (a unique case for the Seychelles cays), and did not consider sea level variation as a determinant factor for the period (Cazes-Duvat and Magnan 2004a).[7]

However, and even if the complete explanation for that rise is not yet agreed upon (Miller and Douglas 2004), the total 20th-century rise is estimated to be 17 centimeters [Å 5] (IPCC 2007). Satellite imagery suggests that the rate of global mean sea level rise over the last decade (1993–2003) was of 3.1 millimeters per year [Å 0.7] (Cazenave and Nerem 2004; IPCC 2007). As the debate continues over the actual magnitude of global sea level rise and its possible acceleration, it seems more and more inevitable that this rise will have adverse impacts on many vulnerable coastal areas. If the sea level rise is limited to the actual minimum projections of 18 to 26 centimeters by 2100, the rise alone might not be such a dramatic problem even in the most vulnerable low-lying islands (made of sand, coral, or limestone), but coastal erosion and land loss can be accelerated by reef degradation (of either natural or human origin) and more intense storms. If the sea level rise is around the maximum projection of 38 to 59 centimeters by 2100, then the rise itself will pose a dramatic problem that could be further exacerbated by other factors lowering the resilience of the coastal areas and low-lying island systems.

In the Maldives, the tsunami of December 26, 2004, came as a reminder of the fragile equilibrium between the nation and the sea as well as the very real vulnerability of every single island to any important sea level rise. In the worst-case scenario, atolls could totally and definitively disappear. However, today in the Indian Ocean, this seems to be more a small possibility rather than a strong probability, at least for the present century. But the 2007 IPCC report now affirms that "anthropogenic warming and sea level rise would continue for centuries due to the timescales associated with climate processes and feedbacks, even if greenhouse gas concentration were to be stabilized." Thus, the sea level rise could have to be considered over a millennia timescale, with the possibility that the mean sea level reaches as much as 4 to 6 meters over it actual level (which was the case in the last interglacial period about 125,000 years ago). For the SISTs, as well as for all the other coastal communities in the world, this would represent a huge challenge to cope with. In any case, there is strong confidence that the phenomena of the sea level rise will last for centuries, and thus that the 21st-century rise will only be a share of the total sea level rise related to the ongoing climate change.

Vulnerability to Sea Level Rise and Other Climate Change Manifestations

In terms of global vulnerability to sea level rise, the smaller, flat, low-lying coralline islands are much more vulnerable than the larger and higher volcanic or granitic islands. However, all SISTs stand to be affected by coastal erosion, coral reef degradation, and flooding. In addition, human factors are very likely to intensify the negative effects of sea level rise. Among these factors are pollution from inland sources (urban, industrial, and agricultural), excessive sedimentation in the lagoons (due to soil erosion), pollution from maritime activities, overexploitation of living resources, destructive fishing practices, mangrove deforestation, dredging and mining of reefs, badly conceived coastal infrastructure, and overly intensive sport and leisure activities.

In Réunion, for example, where white sand beaches (of coralline origin) only represent 11 percent of the total island coastline, rapid coastal urbanization and intense beach frequentation (by both locals and tourists) are threatening the very survival of the limited fringing reefs (some 25 kilometers in total). In the long term, if the situation is not addressed urgently and properly, the small reef flats and the white sand beaches could vanish, an evolution that would be accelerated by climate change and by sea level rise impacts.

Like Mahé's lagoon in front of Victoria (in the Seychelles), some areas of the Mauritian lagoon seem to be under great threat, especially from pollution at Pointe Roche Noire and Tombeau Bay (just north of the capital city and nation port of Port Louis) and even at Grand Baie (the nation's well-known seaside tourist station). In Rodrigues, where coral flats are still trampled and broken on a day-to-day basis, octopus over-harvesting is severely damaging both the resource stock and the overall health of the lagoon. In Mayotte, the large lagoon appears to be in much better condition, but the island's very rapid population growth (over 3 percent per year) and coastal urbanization are sources of concern. In Comoros, over fishing, poaching, destructive fishing practices (trampling, small grid nets, dynamite, etc.), sand dredging, and coral mining have all contributed to serious lagoon degradation.[8]

In the case of Maldives, which possesses about 8,920 square kilometers of reef area, more than 90 percent of the living corals were wholly or partially bleached in the dramatic 1998 coral bleaching event. As periods of sustained high temperatures could become more frequent, there is increased probability of a recurrence of the phenomena of mass bleaching, thus raising the likelihood of mass mortality. Locally, especially around inhabited islands and resort islands, human stresses can weaken coral resilience, limiting their ability to adapt to climate change. Furthermore, as ocean warming coincides with sea level rise and perhaps more frequent tropical storms and El Niños, reefs are likely to experience greater coastal erosion, sedimentation, and turbidity, which would add to their demise (UCSUSA 2005). In all, in the Maldivian archipelago, the spatial (beach erosion and land loss) and economic (tourism, fisheries) outcomes of predicted climate change and sea level rise will depend greatly on reef resilience, a dimension over which there is still much scientific debate and which is also very susceptible to anthropogenic disturbances.

Regarding coastal erosion in the Maldives, an estimated 50 percent of all inhabited islands and 45 percent of the resort islands are already experiencing varying degrees of beach erosion (Maldives 2001, 53). For example, the North Malé Atoll islands of Thulusdhoo, Huraa, and Viligili are on the national list of 86 inhabited islands that have reported severe beach erosion since 1990. In the wake of the tsunami of December 26, 2004, all the inhabited islands of this particular atoll reported beach erosion or damage to coastal infrastructure, while several resorts have experienced severe damage, forcing closure for renovation and reconstruction (e.g., Club Med Farukolhufushi, Club Med Kanifinolhu, Four Seasons, Soneva Gili, Taj Coral).

Coastal erosion is generally attributed to natural factors, but an environmental assessment in eight resort islands of Malé Atoll (and four in the Seychelles) has clearly shown that poor land use and environmental management has greatly affected the sustainability of these small island systems (Cazes-Duvat and Magnan 2004b). This assessment pinpointed bad practices that led to excessive vulnerability to coastal erosion and land loss, especially identifying Kurumba, Paradise, Full Moon, and Lohifushi in North Malé Atoll as being particularly vulnerable. On the other hand, Ihuru appears to be in a much better situation, even if not totally ideal, while Banyan Three and Thulhagiri are in an intermediate situation. Also, according to these authors, hard solutions like breakwaters and protective seawalls, especially used to protect inhabited coastlines, are not necessarily the best solutions to safeguard beaches, reefs, and thus the land. But where important management mistakes and rapid coastal erosion accumulate, there appears to be no alternative to hard solutions to safeguard people, goods, and infrastructure from the assault of the waves (Cazes-Duvat and Magnan 2004a, 186).[9]

When it comes to fresh water resources, it is again the flat, low-lying coralline islands that are the most vulnerable, as their limited stock can easily be degraded either by saline water intrusion or pollution infiltration. In addition, their small fresh water lenses will diminish as the sea level rises. Seasonal shortages in the dry season are also projected to increase as precipitation is reduced (even slightly) and needs rise (for human consumption and agriculture). Better rainfall harvesting and consumption habits will be helpful, but sea water desalinization may need to be used where the resource does not meet the need on a persistent basis (like is already the case in Malé). As water stresses can affect crops yields very negatively, some agricultural activities could suffer productivity losses. This is of great concern for the largest agricultural activity in the studied Indian Ocean SISTs, which is the sugar cane industry of Mauritius and Réunion. Thus, irrigation will become even more of a necessity in order to sustain yields in the context of increased temperature and evapotranspiration.

A further significant risk faced by some small islands is that of cyclones. This is a recurrent phenomenon that affects Réunion and Mauritius in particular,[10] but can also occur in Mayotte and Comoros. As there is no way to avoid these huge storm systems, their projected increased intensity represents a potentially very serious climate change impact. Heavy precipitation, storm surges, and fierce winds can bring dramatic devastation on shores as well as on inland areas. Nevertheless, damage, fatalities, and economic loses do not only depend on the intensity of the storms, but also very much on the quality of the land-use planning, the quality of the buildings and infrastructures, and the degree of preparedness (including early warning and anticipatory actions). Because of the small island systems' size, the relative costs of a cyclone are usually much more significant there than in larger systems, where the damages are geographically restricted to only one part of the system area and where some costs can be assumed at the entire system level (and thus, not only by those directly impacted).

As climate change occurs and its manifestations are observed, there is now no other choice for the small island states and territories than to develop global strategies that will allow them to cope with their general socio-economic development needs and the new challenges brought by climate change and sea level rise. These strategies are to include mitigation measures, adaptation measures, and efficient management systems (e.g., integrated marine and coastal management). Globally, the best way to lower the small islands' vulnerability to climate change, as well as the future costs generated by its adverse impacts, will be that of anticipation instead of reaction to the events. As resources (human, financial, and technological) on a global scale are quite limited in SISTs, there are concerns that most of them might not be able to take all the necessary actions and develop all the needed management capacities rapidly enough. Unfortunately, lack of anticipation, planning, and preparedness can leave the small islands more vulnerable to climate change impacts and thus less resilient as global geographical systems.

Conclusion

Climate change and sea level rise represent great challenges for the 21st century in all of the Indian Ocean small island states and territories. Nevertheless, our survey of the specific island situations in respect to the global environment (human and physical) and development (conditions and needs) shows that it is only one of the very numerous difficulties that the SISTs are presently facing. Overall, the final outcome of climate change is likely to vary quite a lot from one island to another in relation to the intensity of its manifestations, their vulnerability to each of its impacts, and their capacities to adapt to the new conditions.

The specific outcomes of climate change will be very much related to human factors. These must be urgently addressed to safeguard the very valuable ecosystems and the great biodiversity of the small islands, both inland and at sea. On the one hand, there are the negative anthropogenic disturbances to the environment and natural systems that are too often, either directly or indirectly, more or less rapidly, destroyed or degraded. As a result, the most affected ecosystems and species will potentially be less capable, or even not capable, to adapt to the climate change manifestations. There is also the management aspect to consider. Where efficient management systems are put in place and adequate resources are available for anticipatory and adaptive measures, climate change and sea level rise should have much less severe impacts.

Overall, the reef environment can be identified as the most vulnerable environment, as it will be adversely affected by the warming of the sea, the rising sea level, and the intensification of storms. Its vulnerability is further amplified by anthropogenic stresses that have increased rapidly almost everywhere in the last few decades. If the reefs vanish, this could lead to the disappearance of the small, low-lying coralline islands (Maldives atolls, Seychelles Outer Islands), to major environmental and economical losses for the higher islands that possess well- developed barrier reefs and large lagoons (Mayotte, Rodrigues in Mauritius) or extensive fringing reefs (Mauritius, Seychelles granitic islands, Mohéli and even Anjouan in the Comoros), and to the loss of important coastal assets in the other high volcanic islands where the fringing reefs are more limited (Réunion and Grande Comore).

Finally, in terms of dealing with climate change manifestations and impacts, the Maldives seems to be in a much more difficult situation than the other studied islands. Its vulnerability is especially high (because of its particular physical settings and also several human factors), the pillars of the nation are at great risk (the land, the people, and the economy), and its resources for both anticipatory and adaptive measures are not matching the needs. Despite the fact that the Seychelles Outer Islands are also flat, small, low-lying coralline islands (just like the Maldives islands), the nation appears to be in a better position, as all the people and most of its economical assets are located on the granitic islands (Inner Islands).

However, in addition to coral reef, human health, and fresh water issues, no studied islands will escape the challenges brought by more severe weather events (storms in general, tropical cyclones in the Mascarene and Comoros archipelagoes), along with increased coastal erosion and flooding. Thus, the larger and higher volcanic and granitic islands are also going to be significantly affected by climate change and sea level rise, even if the final outcome should not be as dramatic as the case in the more vulnerable low-lying coralline islands.

NOTES

Special thanks to Mr. Léo L. Larivière, technologist for the Department of Geography at Laurentian University. Thanks also to the Laurentian University Research Fund (LURF) for financing a field mission to Mauritius, Réunion, and Seychelles in June 2004.

1. On the international scene, this recognition has led to the Barbados Program of Action for the Sustainable Development of Small Island Developing States (1994) and the Mauritius Strategy for the further implementation of the Barbados Program of Action (2005). In the European Union, this recognition has been formalized through the creation of the Ultraperipheric Region status and the evolution of the Overseas Countries and Territories status.

2. This includes the Chagos Archipelago (known as the British Indian Ocean Territory) as the Chagossians claim their right to return and settle back (the entire local population was expelled between 1967 and 1973 to allow the construction and the operation of the U.S. military base of Diego Garcia).

3. Occupying about 53 percent of the Timor Island, East Timor is not really small (about 6 times Réunion Island), while Bahrain and Singapore are coastal islands well integrated with their neighboring environment and thus possessing a very relative insular isolation.

4. The first protective measures taken in Seychelles were in the mid-19th century, when two areas on Praslin were purchased as Coco-de-Mer reserves. Today, about 50 percent of Seychelles land has been designated as protected areas, including two World Heritage sites: Aldabra Atoll (1982) and Vallée de Mai Nature Reserve on Praslin (1983). In addition, Seychelles was the first country in the Indian Ocean to set up Marine Protected Areas, beginning with the Ste Anne Marine Park (1973).

5. For more details about these projections, see chapter 17, "Small Island States," in IPCC 2001.

6. Interestingly enough, even those who are very critical of Mörner's work and conclusions admit that the region's sea level history remains uncertain and do not bring tangible proof of any significant recent rise or increasing rate of sea level rise in the Maldives region (Kench et al. 2005).

7. Recognizing that a general trend of coastal erosion and land loss in sandy coastlines and low-lying coralline islands is noticeable worldwide, Cazes-Duvat and Magnan insist on the role of storms in the evolution of these coastlines in general and in Bird Island's coastline in particular. Nevertheless, all other parameters being the same (storm intensity, coastline settings,

etc.), coastal erosion peaks (land losses) and flooding will definitively be accentuated if the sea level is higher. These two phenomena should be accentuated even more by the projected intensification of the storms. Thus, rare extreme land loss and flooding events could finally become much more usual.

8. Because of the extraction of sand, coral, sandstone, and beach rock for construction purposes, it has been reported that some beaches have already completely vanished in all of the three Comorian islands (Lilette 2004).

9. In the case of the city island of Malé, which is now totally encircled by protective seawalls, this solution has been engineered to protect the city under present climatic conditions and so does not consider climate change and accelerated sea level rise (Maldives 2001, 54). At Hulhulé International Airport, the runway is only 1.2 meters above mean sea level (0.5 meters above highest high water level), while the surface of the new reclaimed land of Hulhumalé is only about 2 meters higher than the actual mean sea level. This means that these infrastructures will be increasingly vulnerable to wave action, storm surge, and tsunami as the sea level rises.

10. As an average in the last few decades, Mauritius and Reunion have been directly hit by a cyclone every four to five years, and almost all of the cyclones were of category 1 or 2.

REFERENCES

Bouchard C. 2006. "La Géographie et le Développement: Le Cas des Petits États et Territoires Insulaires du Sud-Ouest de l'Océan Indien." *Cahiers de Géographie du Québec* 50 (141) (December 2006).

Cazenave, A., and R. S. Nerem. 2004. "Present-Day Sea Level Change: Observations and Causes." *Reviews of Geophysics* 42, RG3001.

Cazes-Duvat, V., and A. Magnan. 2004a. *L'Île de Bird aux Seychelles: Un Exemple de Développement Durable?* Paris: L'Harmattan.

———. 2004b. "Les Îles-Hôtels, Terrain d'Application Privilégié des Préceptes du Développement Durable: L'Exemple des Seychelles et des Maldives." *Les Cahiers d'Outre-Mer*, no. 225, pp. 75–100.

IPCC (Intergovernmental Panel on Climate Change). 2001. *Climate Change 2001*: Impacts, Adaptation and Vulnerability. IPCC Third Assessment Report—Climate Change 2001. Geneva: The Intergovernmental Panel on Climate Change. http://www.ipcc.ch/ (accessed August 11, 2005).

———. 2007. *Climate Change 2007*: The Physical Basis, Summary for Policymakers. Geneva: The Intergovernmental Panel on Climate Change, Contribution of Working Group I to the Fourth Assessment Report of the IPCC. http://www.ipcc.ch/ (accessed February 11, 2007).

Kench, P. S., et al. 2005. Comment on "New Perspectives for the Maldives," by N.-A. Mörner et al. *Global and Planetary Change* 47 (1) (May 2005): 67–69.

Lilette, V. 2004. "L'or Vert de Cendrillon: Environnement, Espace et Protection des Tortues Marines à Mohéli." In Le Territoire Littoral: Tourisme, Pêche et Environnement dans l'Océan Indien, ed. B. Cherubini, 267–88. Paris/Saint-Denis: L'Harmattan/Université de la Réunion.

Maldives. 2001. *First National Communication of the Republic of Maldives to the United Nations Framework Convention on Climate Change.* Malé: Ministry of Home Affairs, Housing and Environment. http://www.mv.undp.org/projects/environment/fnc/ (accessed August 11, 2005).

———. 2004. *Statistical Yearbook of Maldives 2004.* Malé: Ministry of Planning and National Development. http://www.planning.gov.mv/yrb2004/intro.htm (accessed September 10, 2005).

Miller, L., and B. C. Douglas. 2004. "Mass and Volume Contributions to Twentieth-Century Global Sea Level Rise." *Nature* 428 (March 25, 2004): 406–9.

UNDP (United Nations Development Programme). 2004. *Human Development Report 2004*. New York and Oxford: United Nations Development Programme and Oxford Univ. Press. http://hdr.undp.org/reports/global/2004/ (accessed August 20, 2004).

UCSUSA (Union of concerned scientists). 2005. "Climate Impacts, Early Warning Signs: Coral Reef Bleaching." Cambridge, Mass.: Union of Concerned Scientists. http://www.ucsusa.org/global_warming/science/early-warning-signs-of-global-warming.html (accessed September 9, 2005).

19   Climate Security

AN AUSTRALIAN PERSPECTIVE

CAMPBELL WALKER

Wind, as one of the four elements, is an apt metaphor to discuss the concept of security in the Indian Ocean Region (IOR). While security often refers to military or economic concerns, climate security is, and will be, a matter of growing concern in the IOR in coming years. Regionally, "wind," in its various forms as part of the phenomena of weather, is playing ever greater havoc with the lives of people through extreme weather events, and, with the phenomena of global warming, it is anticipated that this will continue. "Weather" is the "general name for processes in the atmosphere—winds, rain, thunderstorms, etc.—driven by the heating of the Earth by sunshine. That heat has to be returned to space, and weather processes are the result" (O-SIE). On a simple level, the extreme weather connected with global warming is just a case of "what you do comes back to you." But this simple fact has a double resonance for the people of the IOR: first, because it is a region essentially defined by ocean rather than land, and second, because of the sheer human poverty evident in much of the region.

First, to the matter of the IOR being a region defined by water rather than land. Most other geographical or political groupings or places are focused on land mass: Europe, the Americas, Asia, and so on. The Atlantic Ocean is largely an adjunct to Europe or South America rather than having its own "life" in human politics and economy. The Pacific is an exception to this rule, and like the IOR, it is currently being adversely affected by human-induced global warming, arguably far beyond that being felt by people on the larger land masses. This focus on water is significant when considering climate security, for "weather" as experienced by humans is often created where water and land masses intersect; hence, the Indian Ocean generates much of the weather that affects, sustains, and devastates the nations surrounding it. The significance of this should not be lost on anyone concerned about environmental security in an era of climate change. The oceans, long a source of food and inspiration, become, in a post–global warming world, a source of devastation, fear, loss, and dislocation.

Second, when we take into account that the IOR is essentially a majority world region characterized by human populations living at or below the poverty level, another dimension comes into play when we consider the idea of wind or weather and the "payback" of nature. The people of the IOR have, by and large, contributed very little to the phenomena called anthropogenic climate change or human-induced global warming, yet like the poor elsewhere, they are bearing the greatest burdens associated with it. According to the UN Environment Program (1993), "the predicted impacts of climate change would probably exacerbate hunger and poverty around the world. The poor would suffer the most because they have fewer options for responding to climate change." The inequity between cause (driven by the North) and impact (felt by the South) must be at the heart of our attempts to establish climate security within the IOR.

Global warming is "an increase in the average temperature of the earth's atmosphere, especially a sustained increase sufficient to cause climatic change. Most scientists believe that a rise in carbon dioxide levels (caused by automobile, power plant, and other emissions) will lead to further global warming" (Hubbard). Average global air temperatures have already increased by 0.7° Celsius over the last century, and the hottest decade of recorded history was the 1990s. While the greenhouse effect, which traps warmth near the earth's surface, created the conditions that enabled life to evolve and flourish on the planet, global warming threatens most natural processes and will impact on people in a multitude of mostly negative ways. The ecological costs of this warming are reasonably well understood and increasingly well documented. However, lost in the detail of the scientific literature, almost like fine print that is easy to miss, much of the current modeling on climate change suggests that along with these enormous ecological impacts will be unprecedented human catastrophe as well. Physical displacement, possibly of huge numbers of people, is looking ever more likely. For those concerned about climate security and the impacts of global warming in the IOR, key factors that will need to be considered in developing a response include: the fact that it will be the poor who suffer the most; the fact that most countries within the IOR have contributed very little to global warming; the fact that large numbers of people could be forced to leave their homes because of global warming (becoming "climate refugees"); and the fact that changes in weather patterns could adversely affect agriculture and infrastructure, and, more broadly, the development of human society in countries throughout the IOR. Accordingly, global warming may fuel or create conflict at a number of levels, both within and between nations.

Thus, global warming should really be seen as being essentially a human rights issue rather than just an ecological concern. If it is a case of "nature coming back to bite us," it is tragic that it is those least to blame who will probably suffer the most.

The backdrop to any planning for global warming is the fact that humanity is having an ever greater impact on the natural systems that we rely on for our food, water, fiber, and other resource needs. In 2005, the environmental organization WWF, in its *Living Planet Report* (Halls 2005), described an increasing "budget deficit" with nature, noting that people were consuming resources 20 percent faster than they can be renewed. The *UN Millennium Assessment* report (UN 2005), launched in early 2005 and described by its authors as a "stark warning" to humanity, is perhaps the most thorough snapshot yet of the health of local and global ecosystems. It was based on the work of around 1,300 scientists in 95 countries and reaffirmed the basic message of earlier WWF reports—that humanity is living beyond its means when it comes to use of natural resources and causing, among other problems, climate change. Natural systems have become simplified, fragmented, and overused and are now also facing dramatic impacts from global warming. Rapid population growth, intensive agriculture, overgrazing, and industrial pollution are all placing unprecedented pressure on natural ecosystems.

In spite of this overuse of natural systems for human needs, many people in the IOR live without access to the means of a dignified and fulfilling life. Many nations are still struggling to achieve a form of development that will benefit all people in that country. Previously described as the third or "developing" world, much of the Global South still lacks robust economic systems that allow for the creation of physical infrastructure and economic opportunity that the North takes for granted.

Any contemporary discussion about development occurs in a very different political climate to previous decades. While concepts of "development" have gone through many phases and been based on various approaches, especially since the end of the Second World War, there is now growing awareness of the intimate link between ecological health and the ability of a society to "develop." In spite of this, most Southern nations continue to pursue a development model based on high consumption patterns and individually focused lifestyles, as exemplified by nations like the United States and Australia. With the knowledge that we now have regarding humanity's overuse of resources, it is becoming increasingly clear that these types of high-impact lifestyles are simply unavailable for the 6.5 billion people currently living on the planet, let alone the 10 billion expected by the middle of the century. Before the practice of development can change, it will be necessary to substantially modify the concepts we use and our vision of what might constitute a "sustainable development." The Universal Declaration of Human Rights, adopted by the United Nations in 1948, was both a historic document and a milestone in the development of a common concept of humanity, recognizing as it did the "inherent dignity and the equal and inalienable rights of all members of the human family." Increased understanding of ecology since then, as well as the rise of new threats to the dignity of humankind, has meant that this document should now be extended to include concepts of environmental and climate security, environmental rights, and the reality of climate refugees and the need to protect their rights.

Yet this changed reality has not yet been incorporated into the work or priorities of national governments or international institutions, such as the UN or World Bank. For example, the UN Development Program only refers briefly to the idea of broadened concepts of security, saying that: "Environmental threats countries are facing are a combination of the degradation of local ecosystems and that of the global system. These comprise threats to environmental security" (UNEP 1994). And the UN High Commissioner for Refugees (UNHCR), the body responsible for caring for refugees, those displaced by war and repression, does not, as yet, recognize those people displaced by global warming as being refugees. Even the Red Cross, which has arguably been one of the most forward thinking international institutions with regards to climate change, feels it is "difficult" to recognize environmental refugees as a separate category. In Australia, the current government refuses to accept the reality of climate refugees, although the leadership in a number of IOR nations, such as Bangladesh, are now raising the issue of human displacement due to global warming and the need for the North to respond with action and a keen sense of justice.

Climate Refugees

According to the 1951 Convention Relating to the Status of Refugees, a refugee is a person who: "owing to a well-founded fear of being persecuted for reasons of race, religion, nationality, membership in a particular social group, or political opinion, is outside the country of his nationality, and is unable to or, owing to such fear, is unwilling to avail himself of the protection of that country."

In recent years, there has also been a growing public awareness that many people are being forced to flee their homes because of environmental factors. As early as 1948, writer William Voight used the term "ecological displaced persons" in his book *Road to Survival* to identify this category of people, but it was a report written by Essam El-Hinnawi in 1985 for the UN Environment Program that began to popularize the term. The terms "environmental migrants," "ecologically displaced people" (EDPs), "resource refugees," "natural refugees," "climate change exiles," and "eco refugees" have also sometimes been used to describe these people. A simple definition of an environmental refugee put forward by the researcher Norman Myers (1994) is a "person who no longer gains a secure livelihood in their traditional homelands because of what are primarily environmental factors of unusual scope."

Building on El-Hannawi's definitional work, it appears that there are now three categories of ecologically displaced people (or environmental refugees): those fleeing non-human-created natural disasters, such as earthquakes; those fleeing direct human-induced causes (for instance, desertification, as well as externally funded projects that displace communities, such as large-scale hydro dams that flood agricultural areas, projects that convert primary forest or agricultural land into plantations, resulting in displacement of indigenous peoples or traditional farming communities, or those impacted by the Chernobyl or Bhopal disasters, etc.); and those fleeing indirect human-induced causes (in particular, the enhanced greenhouse effect which is leading to global warming, with corresponding impacts on ecosystems and the human communities that depend on them). It is this last category, sometimes known as "climate refugees," who appear to be the largest and most rapidly growing in number.

The Swedish-based World Foundation for Environment and Development has further elaborated on the fact that displacement is caused by "acute environmental degradation" with a number of different causes: natural disasters, degradation of land resources, involuntary resettlement, industrial accidents, aftermath of war, and climate change.

Although there is no international body like the UNHCR that looks after the needs of these people (and hence no single tally kept of their numbers), it is clear there are already many millions of ecologically displaced people. According to the International Federation of Red Cross and Red Crescent Societies in their *World Disasters Report 2001*, more people are now forced to leave their homes because of environmental disaster than because of war. According to this source, it appears that by 2000 there were already around 25 million people who could be classified as being environmental refugees—58 percent of the world's total refugee population at that time. The *State of the World Report* (UNPF 2001), published by the UN Population Fund, and quoting World Bank sources, concurs with this figure. While the World Watch Institute (WWI) reports that the number of recognized international refugees had declined to 9.7 million by the end of 2003—the lowest figure since 1980—the plight of many internally displaced people (which includes many environmental refugees) is "often far worse than that of recognized refugees" (Renner 2005). The WWI says that, in contrast to declining numbers of recognized refugees, there are now "perhaps 30 million" environmental refugees and that "these numbers are likely to go up sharply in coming years."

The nations of the IOR seem to be "over represented" in terms of the global numbers of EDPs. There are already many millions of people displaced in the region by causes such as desertification, flooding, storm surge, and so on, and some nations such as Iran have enormous numbers of displaced people within their borders who have fled ecological breakdown. However, without immediate action on global warming, especially by the minority or industrialized world, it does appear that there will be many more such refugees to come.

Norman Myers, a researcher based at Oxford University, is commonly acknowledged as the foremost author on the topic of environmental refugees. In his groundbreaking research of the early 1990s he made what he called a conservative estimate that climate change would increase the number of environmental refugees six-fold over the next fifty years to 150 million (1994). According to his research, the IOR will experience much of this displacement (see Table 19.1):

Table 19.1   Total Refugees Foreseen by 2050 (millions of people)

China	30
India	30
Bangladesh	15
Egypt	14
Other delta areas and coastal zones	10
Island states	1
Agriculturally dislocated areas	50
Total	150

Source: Myers 1994.

Many of those people identified by Myer as being "agriculturally dislocated" will come from sub-Saharan Africa. According to Wulf Killman, the chair of the UN Food and Agricultural Organization Climate Change group, much of Africa has experienced increased periods of extended drought since the 1970s (FAO 2005). As mentioned previously, displacement will come from a multiplicity of (often inter-connected) sources and factors, including sea level rise, increased desertification, increased incidence of extreme weather events, the spread of vector-borne disease into new areas, loss of water supplies for domestic and agricultural purposes, and so on. Africa is seen as being especially at risk from droughts that may become "semi permanent under climate change," according to Killman. In Central Asia and India, dropping water tables constitute a great threat to many agricultural communities. Many poor and subsistence economies are finely attuned to the ecological realities of their local place, and relatively minor changes could cause great suffering before displacement is forced on communities.

As shown in the table above, India and Bangladesh, as important IOR nations, are expected to shed large numbers of people due to changed ecological conditions. This has already been happening. As with most examples of environmentally influenced movement, there are various factors at play, including the desire for a better life and economic advancement. This is borne out in the case of these two nations, for example, where more than 10 million Bangladeshis have moved to neighboring Indian states over the last decade (IPCC 2001). The reasons for this include population growth and land scarcity, but these factors have been exacerbated by a series of droughts, devastating floods, and loss of land in coastal regions. As noted by the Intergovernmental Panel on Climate Change, "climate change will act in parallel with a complex array of social, cultural and economic motivations for and impacts on migration" (IPCC 2001).

Australia's Role in Creating Climate Security

Within this unfolding scenario, Australia sits in a strange place; being one of the few minority world or Northern nations in the region and, after Saudi Arabia, the world's highest per capita greenhouse gas emitter. Taking the understanding that global warming is a result of historical use of fossil fuels since the time of the industrial revolution, the people currently alive in Australia find themselves doubly burdened, not only with the fact that their current consumption rates are globally unsustainable and hugely inequitable, but also that this has happened for generations, giving rise to a "carbon debt" to the poorer nations for overuse of the atmosphere, a global commons.

And yet the national response of the current Australian government to the issue of displacement by global warming has been skepticism and inaction. This is in spite of the fact that an assessment of the causes behind the movement of these refugees will identify that Australia has a disproportionate responsibility for creating them, and hence an onus to officially recognize them as a separate category of refugee as well to take immediate action to do what it can to reduce the forces driving this displacement and help communities adversely affected by climate change.

Apart from environmental refugees, Australia's recent track record on tackling global warming has been less than inspirational. While the current federal environment minister, Ian Campbell, has been increasingly vocal on the issue of global warming, taking a more proactive stance than his recent predecessors, the Howard government still refuses to ratify the Kyoto Protocol, currently the "main game" in global attempts to take action on the looming crisis of global warming. The Australian government has now developed an alliance on global warming with the United States, South Korea, China, and India specifically outside the UN framework and without any binding agreements to reduce greenhouse gas (GHG) emissions, as well as advocating for nuclear power as a solution to global warming (Campbell 2005). In addition, there has been consistent resistance on the part of the government when it comes to grappling with the historical dimensions of global warming.

The New Economics Foundation, in the book *Environmental Refugees: The Case for Recognition* (Conisbee and Simms 2003), states that "western Europe and the US cannot continue to consume with impunity, without regard to their impact on the global environment. This means an historic act of facing up to the real cost of our lifestyle." This is equally true of Australia. Despite the increasing rates of industrialization currently occurring in the global South, the Northern countries continue to be the major cause of greenhouse pollution. And when historical emissions are added to current activity, the Northern debt to the other peoples of the planet becomes even more apparent. More than 80 percent of human induced warming so far has been caused by emissions from the North and it is still producing more than 60 percent of human-created greenhouse gases being released into the atmosphere, despite only having roughly 25 percent of the world's human population. In contrast, the poorest 20 percent on the planet only produce 2 percent of emissions (Lammi and Tynkkynen 2003).

The Centre for Science and the Environment (CSE 1998) in India says that industrialized countries will still be contributing 79 percent of the temperature increase by 2020 under current use patterns (this is down from 88 percent in 1990). Under the CSE's figures, the South will pass the North in terms of contribution to changed climate in 2150. The key point here is that the historical contribution of greenhouse gases has come from the industrialization that allowed the North to develop their economies and therefore allow high-consumption lifestyles. This development also provides the resources and infrastructure that will help it cope with the impacts of global warming in coming years.

The UN Framework Convention on Climate Change (UNFCCC), which was signed into existence by 154 nations in 1992, represents the best advance as yet by the global community in tackling global warming. Its main implementation process is the Kyoto Protocol. The Australian prime minister, John Howard, and some others blame their unwillingness to sign the Protocol on the belief that it unfairly targets industrialized countries because it sets emissions targets for them. The United States, the world's largest polluter, has similar views on this issue. In 1997, the U.S. Senate adopted the so-called Byrd-Hagel resolution, which commits the United States to "limit" or "reduce" GHG emissions only if Southern nations are also involved in a similar process (Simms 2004). This position goes to the heart of the question of carbon debt and the legacy of colonialism. In effect, the Berlin Mandate adopted at the UNFCCC meeting in Germany in 1995, and which marked the direction of climate change negotiations over the next half decade, was a profound acknowledgment of history because it declares, in effect, that the "rich should go first" and accept binding greenhouse gas emission reductions, while the South would be initially exempt from such measures. This meeting led, in turn, to the creation of the Kyoto Protocol in 1997, which finally came into force in 2005, and a key element of this is the fact that it contains legally binding greenhouse gas emission targets for industrialized or Annex 1 countries that would aim to reduce emissions by 5.2 percent compared to 1990 levels in what is called the first implementation period. Binding targets for reduction of greenhouse gases in developing (Annex 2) countries would not be put in place until the end of this period. An unwillingness to accept historical fact is the genesis of the Howard argument on Kyoto, which is doubly shameful because of the preferential treatment accorded Australia under the Protocol, which was actually allowed to increase its emissions by 8 percent.

The IOR as we know it in the early 21st century is a product of several centuries of European colonialism. Nations and economies were created and broken according to the will of British, German, and other imperial nations and their companies. As Mike Davis highlights in his book *Late Victorian Holocausts: El Niño Famines and the Making of the Third World* (2001), drought and the resulting famines were used for centuries as effective tools for breaking local resistance to the colonization process. This era left many nations with limited social infrastructure like hospitals and water and sewerage systems because wealth from local labor and resources was channeled to Europe and later North America. This "side note" of history may seem like an irrelevance, yet it sets the scene for the 21st century, having created the far-from-level playing field that different nations will have to contend with in dealing with the changes associated with global warming over the coming years.

No one would argue that the enacting of the Kyoto Protocol is the end of the climate change debate. It will only lead to cuts of between 1 and 3 percent of current GHGs compared with the 60–80 percent that many scientists say may be required to stabilize the atmosphere (Lambert 2002), and so it will be the most tentative of first steps in a coordinated global response to climate change and, specifically, to halt global warming. But there is a deeper dimension to the issue of setting targets for the Annex 1 (or wealthy) countries. That is, how do we, as a global community, finally balance the benefits that have accrued to the peoples of the North, in this instance, Australia, through the many centuries of industrialization and colonialism, with the needs and rights of people of the South to develop in such a way that would ensure a dignified existence for all. The waiving of targets for developing nations is but a first and tentative step in this process.

To talk about meeting all humanity's needs (including of those not yet born), we, as a global community, will need to accept that all of us, regardless of race, class, ethnicity, or gender, have an equal right to a "fair share" of resources that will allow for a life of dignity. This means that justice (or equity) must be at the core of our response to global warming. To be effective in a world with enormous and growing gaps between rich and poor and a limit to the overall levels of greenhouse gases that can be created, an international treaty on climate must therefore enshrine a rights-based approach and be focused on per capita emissions targets—this is sometimes called the environmental space with equity approach. This is at odds with the "business as usual" approach to tackling global warming favored by many governments and corporations, who tend to assume that current production and consumption rates can continue, albeit with reduced emissions through improved technology, whereby, as long as they can afford it, richer nations (or enclaves of wealth in the South) can keep their current lifestyles through buying "cleaner" products or services or off-setting emissions by "buying" carbon credit in international trading markets, as exemplified by the Kyoto Protocol.

In contrast, the equity approach of setting targets for individual emission levels has been denounced by some as "carbon socialism," and it will be an immense task to get popular support among consumers and governments in the affluent nations. But consider the question of ecological limits for a minute. Many ecologists have been arguing for an end to overconsumption for decades, yet we have not yet reached, on a global level, the ecological collapse foreseen by many of these people. However, as outlined in documents like the UN Millennium Report, it is now clear that, as a whole, humanity is living beyond the ability of the planet's ecosystems to renew resources or absorb our wastes into the indefinite future. But global warming, barely mentioned in scientific literature only 30 years ago, has rapidly become arguably the single most pressing reason for people to put their foot on the brake when it comes to resource consumption. While previous "limits to growth" arguments were sometimes seen as being the preserve of eco-nuts and doomsayers, the current need to limit resource use (and hence the release of carbon into the atmosphere) is becoming increasingly accepted as fact. Perhaps in the next decade or so, we will reach the point in our history where we reach a "tipping point" where enough governments and other decision makers or influencers accept this fact. Acceptance of the need for a per-capita allocation of carbon production will surely follow rapidly, as unlikely as it may seem at present.

When talking about per capita levels, there is the obvious question of "how much per person is sustainable." Like climate modeling, much of this is in the realm of scientific theory, but there are still various models that can be used to try and answer this question. In an era of global warming we must accept that resource consumption and contribution to climate change are intimately linked. Any targets must therefore consider both. For example, some have argued that the starting point for setting targets is to define the level of climate change that is acceptable, and then develop a global "emissions budget" in accordance with it, based on emission trajectories. This would then be used to develop per capita targets, based on existing or projected global population levels. When compiled at the national level, this gives a sense of how much over or under the average global level or "allowance" a specific country is.

In reflecting on why so many nations have joined together through instruments like the UNFCCC to tackle global warming, we are presented with a remarkable opportunity. This global cooperation is indicative of a trend that has only been noticeable, or, for that matter, possible, for roughly the last century and a half. As flawed and limited as international institutions such as the UN or the hundreds of international conventions may be, the sentiment behind them—of joining together across national boundaries to tackle shared problems—marks a wonderful and visionary development in the history of humankind's time on this planet. Developments in communications technologies, ease of travel, globalization, and evolving political systems at the national and international level have allowed the development of global cooperation. But there is a danger that, as lofty ideals are lost in intensely political negotiations and haggling over emission levels and carbon trading regimes, we may lose sight of an incontestable fact. That is, that the atmosphere is, in the words of the Centre for Science and the Environment (CSE) in India, a "global common property shared by all human beings." It delivers benefits to all, as do the oceanic and terrestrial "sinks," such as forests that absorb carbon and help stabilize the atmosphere. The environmental space with equity approach recognizes this fact and seeks to define a way to understand and deal with it. The CSE (1998) proposes three options to achieve equitable emissions entitlements for all people.

First, they propose agreeing to share the world's common sinks (that is, the processes that absorb the gases that cause global warming) equally. This would require substantial cooperation, because nations may assert that their terrestrial sinks (a large area of natural forest system, like the Amazon, for instance) are their national rather than global property. However, as oceans belong to all humanity, it can be argued that the oceanic sinks (estimated at be able to offset carbon of the order of 2 billion tonnes of carbon per year—or roughly 0.38t/year per person with a global population of 5.3 billion) are the common heritage of all people. This carbon offset could act as the basis of a carbon "budget" that all people can take without fuelling global warming (CSE 1998). Second, they propose sharing the world's future emissions "budget" (that is, the levels of emissions that are sustainable) equally; this type of entitlement comes from the Contraction and Convergence model. Under this approach, the world would have to agree on what would be the upper level of atmospheric carbon concentration which can be considered acceptable, and by which year this concentration should be achieved, then distribute the resulting carbon budget equally between all people. And third, establishing a per capita emissions target, or entitlement, which all countries will agree to converge on.

This system for distributing carbon allocations is a little simpler than the process described above in that the entitlement would be based on an "ad hoc" amount, which all countries would agree to. The key issue, of course, would be what target would be chosen, for if it were too high, then global warming would continue, just with a more equitable distribution of the benefits that come with that (meaning higher consumption for those who are currently the poorest and, possibly, an acceleration of global warming compared with current trends).

Regardless of what model we eventually adopt, it seems only fair for the over-consuming nations to take the lead, and reduce their per capita and hence national GHG emission levels, thereby "freeing up" resources for the Southern nations to increase their consumption levels. As the main Northern nation in the IOR, there is a particular onus on Australia to act. But given recent history, such as the 2001 federal election campaign based on fear of "boat people" and the resulting "Pacific Solution" of mandatory detention of asylum seekers, there is the significant question of whether Australia will ever have a government brave enough to articulate this vision.

As discussed earlier in this chapter, it is clear that humanity is already being affected by global warming, and it will be the poorest who will suffer the most. The acknowledgment of the advantage that has accrued because of history, and a commitment to share these benefits with our neighbors, will be the foundation stone of an honorable response by Australia to the question of global warming. This, of necessity, would lead to Australia's adopting a number of measures, including the following:

- the creation of a quota system for climate refugees;
- the increasing and modifying of foreign aid to account for changed climatic conditions and growing displacement;
- the cessation of funding projects that fuel global warming;
- the Australian government's advocating internationally for recognition of environmental refugees;
- the committing of funds beyond the formal aid budget to support adaptation in affected communities;
- as part of their recognition of the ecological debt, all Northern nations', including Australia's, canceling of all foreign debt owed by Southern nations.

Recognize Climate Refugees

> By recognizing environmental refugees you recognize the problem. By recognizing the problem you start on the road to accepting responsibility and implementing solutions.
>
> —Jean Lambert, Greens MEP (Lambert 2002).

Australia will need to develop an official program allowing for an annual intake of climate refugees. Given the simple human imperative of assisting those in need, this program should be created without any reduction in the other current Australian refugee programs. This is said with full acknowledgment that there are substantial definitional questions that need to be clarified about how these people would be classified, as well as the question of where the category of economic migrants "ends" and environmental refugees "begins." We would also need to resolve the question of what would constitute a "fair" share of refugees. One suggestion put forward by Senator Andrew Bartlett of the Australian Democrats (AAP 2002) was that Australia should accept the percentage of people displaced by global warming commensurate with the percentage of global emissions we are responsible for. In 2004, this would be around 1.3 percent of climate refugees.

Modify Aid to Allow Adaptation

As part of a strategic response, Australia should consider the levels of foreign aid it provides, and investigate whether there needs to be increased funding made available for communities who are impacted by changed climate and weather patterns. All donor governments, including Australia, should integrate, as a matter of urgency, climate risk factors into all their Overseas Development Assistance (ODA) program planning, implementation, and evaluation.

Our ODA is 0.25 percent of Australia's Gross National Income (GNI), slightly better than recent budgets but near the lowest level ever in Australia, and well below the OECD countries' average and the United Nations target of 0.7 percent of GNI that was agreed on in 1970 (Buckman 2004).

Any increase in aid levels should occur with a thorough review of how Australia's aid program is currently delivered. This is because Australia's ODA is, like that of a number of Western nations, increasingly used as an economic and political tool or point of leverage. The tendency to impose ideological or economic agendas on recipient countries will need to be addressed, and, ultimately, foreign aid will need to be applied strategically at the points of greatest human need and where it can be most effective rather than as a means of gaining benefit for the donor country.

Some specific existing programs may need to be adjusted to account for the different environmental conditions and social issues that will arise under human-induced climate change. A fundamental reason for reviewing ODA would be to find ways to provide funding to community-controlled adaptation programs, which would allow affected communities to remain in their homelands, where possible, and where this is the choice of that community. Adaptation will be far preferable for most impacted peoples to the alternative of either suffering ever more dismal lives without support in changed conditions, or becoming environmental refugees. Noted Samoan environmentalist Fiu Mata'ese Elisara-Laulu (2004) believes that indigenous communities have the right to maintain their sovereign status in their own homelands rather than being displaced because of global warming. With displacement being likely throughout the IOR, but with different forces at work in different areas, it will be necessary to continually fine tune both public and private aid to best serve local adaptation strategies. Often the means to stay will require low-tech solutions that will allow communities to modify their interactions with the surrounding environment to take advantage of, or adapt to, changed conditions. Small-scale farming in containers may allow continued food production in areas where saltwater inundation is affecting yields. Iron roofing and water tanks may allow the harvesting of enough water to make up for lowered soil moisture in dry land regions to maintain crops. While adaptation must form the core of a renewed and restructured aid program by wealthy countries, appropriate post disaster relief and in some instances internal resettlement will also be necessary.

With the impacts of global warming becoming more pronounced, and more individual communities coming under ever greater stress from economic and social losses, the delivery of post-disaster aid also needs to be modified. As noted by the International Red Cross (2002), "post disaster recovery efforts will increasingly be judged not by how quickly structures are rebuilt—only to be destroyed again the next time disaster strikes—but by how reconstruction contributes to the long-term disaster resilience of communities." The Red Cross says that post disaster aid should be delivered in a way that meets two targets; alleviating immediate suffering, and helping to strengthen local economies (IRC 2001). In practical terms, this will mean considerations like ensuring that local labor is used, with resources bought locally wherever possible rather than bringing in ready-made replacement infrastructure or services. Sourcing of materials from sustainable sources was a matter of considerable concern in Aceh and other IOR nations after the tsunami in December 2004. "Plans for disaster recovery need to be employment rich and locally rooted, rather than flying in aid from abroad. Small, locally based enterprises will be at the heart of rebuilding infrastructure and services." In a broader sense, this is also significant in terms of food aid and food security. Most nations suffering food crises will have at least some regions within the country with a surplus of food. Flying in excess food from elsewhere rather than providing cash to purchase food locally can effectively undermine food security in recipient countries. Accordingly, donor nations should commit to providing cash for local purchase of foods wherever possible.

Stop Funding the Displacement Process

In addition, it is clear that the current Australian ODA program, public sector funding, and trade programs are, in a number of instances, increasing funding for climate change through support for specific projects that cause or increase production of greenhouse gases. In Australia, the Export Credit Agency (EFIC) consistently funds fossil fuel projects rather than those based on renewable technologies. The Sydney-based NGO AID/Watch estimates that the ratio of funding is 100:1 and has been for the 11 years to 2004. EFIC has provided almost $7.6 billion for the fossil fuel industry compared with $67 million for renewables during this period (AID/Watch 2004).

The inconsistency of spending money to alleviate the impacts of global warming while continuing to fuel the process that leads to the problem should be obvious. Australia, like all countries with an ODA program, needs to ensure that all its international interventions, be they delivery of aid programs, involvement in international forums, bilateral relations and diplomacy, and investment in other nations are linked to a broad vision that seeks to reduce human suffering and ensure sustainable development. The Millennium Development Goals should act as a framework in this regard. There is, however, a fundamental problem for Australia in regard to the specific point of fueling global warming—that of its reliance on the export of coal. Australia is the world's largest exporter of coal, including to a number of nations in the IOR, and this fact influences domestic energy and climate policies as well as the well documented history of funding "clean coal" developments in other parts of the world. The current Australian government has firmly attached itself to coal as the principal future source of energy (Campbell 2005). This link will need to be broken before Australia can play a truly responsible part in aiding other IOR nations to shift to renewable energy sources. A responsible Australian government would greatly increase support for renewables in the IOR.

Advocate Internationally for Recognition of Environmental Refugees

As noted previously, environmental refugees are currently not recognized under UN structures. Australia should advocate for UN recognition of environmental refugees as a new form of refugee under the Geneva Convention through all appropriate domestic and international channels.

Australia Should Cancel All Foreign Debt

External debt keeps many countries in a "holding pattern" of meeting repayments on debt, and hence they are unable to move forward with developing their own resources for their own benefit. In the context of global warming, a "side note" on this disadvantage means that their social infrastructure remains limited and therefore the buffer to cope with disasters is less than in the North. Many nations need to liquidate or otherwise overexploit their natural resources in order to maintain payments. The UN Development Program states that while US$50 billion is provided to Southern nations as aid each year, these same nations lose about US$500 billion in interest payments and reduced prices for raw materials (Shiva 2001).

Poverty Alleviation and Climate Security

It is widely acknowledged by a great number of bodies and organizations that, in the words of the World Commission on Environment and Development (WCED 1987), "poverty is a major cause and effect of global environmental problems. It is therefore futile to attempt to deal with environmental problems without a broader perspective that encompasses the factors underlying world poverty and international equality" (and hence the right to a "development" that will meet the basic needs of all people). Therefore, to adequately respond to simultaneous and interlinked trends and underlying causes, any response to global warming and environmental displacement must equally address and fund the means of ensuring all communities around the world are truly able to achieve a "sustainable" development. In a global warming and human rights context, this must focus on a profound reassessment of the concept of what development is and how nations will achieve it. It must also focus on balancing needs with the availability of resources, developing nonmonetary indicators of economic well-being, and carefully assessing the impacts of market deregulation and integration, as well as the impacts of economic globalization. Even among many organizations advocating and working for poverty alleviation there is a fundamental belief that economic rationalism or neoliberalism will provide solutions through access to global markets: the "rising tide lifts all boats" approach. As Tasmanian author Greg Buckman (2004) notes, there is a low-level debate within the aid and development NGOs at present, between what he calls the "Fair Trade/Bretton Woods" school, which argues for immediate reform of the world's trading system, capital markets, and global institutions, and the "Localization" school, which "takes a more radical . . . position that argues for the abolition of these institutions and an outright winding back of economic globalization." Regardless of whether free trade was ever going to deliver a dignified life for all, this belief certainly needs to be reassessed in light of our awareness of the threats posed to humanity by climate change.

Returning to the need to develop a framework for ensuring climate security in the IOR, it must be remembered that without food security, it can be expected that social, economic, and political problems and, potentially, military conflict will continue. In mid-2005, the Food and Agricultural Organization warned that climate change "threatens to increase the number of the world's hungry by reducing the area of land available for farming in developing nations." Production losses could threaten around 40 countries, with a combined population of 2 billion, "severely hindering progress in combating poverty and food insecurity." As one example, it cites the case of India, which risks losing around 18 percent of its current gross agricultural product (equivalent to around 125 million tonnes of cereal production).

Current development models and lending policy, driven by neoliberal economics, encourage nations to specialize and focus on increasing exports, yet this will often put nations at risk in a time of disaster (the example of the collapse of the Honduran banana industry after Hurricane Mitch in 1998 highlights the danger of this approach). In contrast to this simplification/specialization approach, it is becoming accepted that a better option is to encourage local communities to diversify economic activity. The International Federation of Red Cross and Red Crescent Societies suggest "diversification, not specialization, production for consumption not export, and re-distribution of good-quality land" as mechanisms for increasing food and economic security (IRC 2001). The IRC also notes that strong health and education systems strengthen resilience and aid recovery after disaster. This approach, of encouraging diversification, will also require opposition to any further privatization, and should become the core basis of further ODA provided by the North to the South. It is at odds with the bilateral trade agreements being negotiated between Australia and other nations, all of which focus solely on reducing barriers to trade rather than encouraging healthy and diversified local economies. Australia, as one of the richest nations in the IOR, must take the lead on all these issues.

Summary

As a regional community focused on the Indian Ocean, there is great potential for better cooperation, mutual aid, and shared benefits between all nations of the IOR. A key contemporary challenge is how we would overcome the differences of opportunity because of the legacy of the colonial era. The recent emergence of global warming as a great threat to humankind adds a new dimension to the need to collaborate for shared beneficial outcomes, offering as it does new threats and opportunities. Given its unique status as a highly developed and wealthy nation with grossly disproportionate historical and contemporary greenhouse gas emission levels, there is a double onus on Australia to take a proactive role in creating the mechanisms that would lead to climate security for all people living in the Indian Ocean Region.

If Australia did recognize, and act on, its historical responsibilities through developing a climate refugee program, increasing and modifying its ODA, and engaging in far more transfer of appropriate technology, its reputation in the IOR would be greatly enhanced. A proactive response to the looming crisis would also help avert potentially massive levels of human disruption, in one of the regions most likely to be adversely affected by global warming.

REFERENCES

Aid/Watch. 2004. "Aiding and Abetting Climate Change." Sydney: Aid/Watch.

AAP (Australian Associated Press). 2002. "Hill Avoids Issue of Environmental Refugees," August 28, 2002.

Australian Council for International Development (ACFID). 2004. "Our Fair Share: Submission to the 2004–5 Federal Budget." Canberra, Australia.

Buckman, G. 2004. *Globalization. Tame It or Scrap It?* London: Zed Books.

Campbell, I. 2005. "Technology Key to Cutting Greenhouse Gas Levels." Press release, Minister for the Environment and Heritage, March 16, 2005, Canberra, Australia.

Conisbee, M., and A. Simms. 2003. *Environmental Refugees: The Case for Recognition.* London: New Economics Foundation.

CSE (Centre for Science and Environment). 1998. Definitions of "Equal Entitlements." CSE dossier, factsheet #5, New Delhi, India.

Davis, M. 2001. *Late Victorian Holocausts: El Niño Famines and the Making of the Third World.* London: Verso.

El-Hinnawi, E. 1985. *Environmental Refugees.* Nairobi: United Nations Environment Program.

Elisara-Laulu, F. M. 2004. Speech given during climate justice tour organized by Friends of the Earth Australia, April–May 2004.

FAO (Food and Agriculture Organization). 2005. "Climate Change and Agriculture." Background document.

Francis, D., and H. Hengeveld. 1998. *Extreme Weather and Climate Change.* Downsview, Ontario: Environment Canada.

Hubbard Brook Ecosystem Study. 2007. http://www.hubbardbrook.org/6-12_education/HBEducationHomepage.htm.

Halls, C., editor in chief. 2006. *Living Planet Report, 2006.* Gland, Switzerland: WWF International.

IPCC (Intergovernmental Panel on Climate Change). 2001. "Climate Extremes and Migration." *Climate Change 2001: Working Group II: Impacts, Adaptation and Vulnerability, Section 11.2.6.1.* Geneva: The Intergovernmental Panel on Climate Change.

IRC (International Red Cross/Red Crescent Society). 2001. *World Disasters Report 2001.* Geneva: International Red Cross/Red Crescent Society.

———. 2002. *World Disasters Report 2002.* Geneva: International Red Cross/Red Crescent Society.

Lambert, J. 2002. *Refugees and the Environment: The Forgotten Element of Sustainability.* Brussels: The Greens/European Free Alliance in the European Parliament.

Lammi, H., and O. Tynkkynen. 2001. *The Whole Climate: Climate Equity and Its Implications for the North.* Tampere, Finland: Friends of the Earth Finland.

McGirk, T. 2000. "Environmental Refugees, Latin America." *Time Magazine,* February 7, 2000.

Myers, N. 1994. "Environmental Refugees: A Crisis in the Making." *People and the Planet* 3 (4).

O-SIE (Open-Site Internet Encyclopedia). 2007. http://open-site.org/Science/Astronomy/Terminology/W.

Renner, M. 2005. "Numbers of Refugees Declines." *Vital Signs* 2005. Washington, D.C.: Worldwatch Institute, 66.

Shiva, V. 2001. *Protect or Plunder? Understanding Intellectual Property Rights.* London: Zed Books.

Simms, A. 2004. *An Environmental War Economy. The Lessons of Ecological Debt and Global Warming.* NEF pocketbook 4. London: New Economics Foundation.

United Nations. 1948. "Universal Declaration of Human Rights." United Nations General Assembly.

———. 2005. Millennium Ecosystem Assessment Series. www.millenniumassessment.org.

UNEP (United Nations Environment Program). 1993. *Climate Change Scenarios: Why the Poor Are the Most Vulnerable.* Nairobi: UNEP Information Unit on Climate Change.

———. 1994. *Annual Report on Human Development.* Nairobi: UNEP Information Unit on Climate Change, 28.

UNPF (United Nations Population Fund). 2001. *State of the Environment Report 2001: Footprints and Milestones: Population and Environmental Change.* New York: United Nations Population Fund.

Vidal, J., and T. Radford. 2005. "Drought Soon a Way of Life in More Countries." *The Guardian,* July 1.

WCED (World Commission on Environment and Development). 1987. *Our Common Future.* Oxford: Oxford Univ. Press.

20

Environmental Cooperation in the Indian Ocean Basin

A COMPARATIVE ANALYSIS OF THE
INDUS BASIN TREATY AND THE MALÉ
DECLARATION

SALEEM H. ALI

Among the four elements of survival, air is the most mobile and difficult to physically constrain. The security of airsheds is thus acutely dependent on regional cooperation. This chapter will explore the emergence of a regional cooperation regime around air quality by comparing it to a more familiar water management agreement. Through this comparison, the relative challenges and merits of managing air quality at a regional level will be accentuated.

The Indian Ocean basin has a highly complex meteorology due to seasonal monsoonal conditions that prevail in the summer, which are inextricably linked to the water availability in much of South Asia. Exploring the physical and figurative confluence of air and water management regimes is thus important. The chapter also considers the structural pathways to cooperation that exist when evaluating these cases. By considering the broader structural elements of cooperation that can emerge from regional air and water management regimes, the instrumental value of such agreements to larger security imperatives can be evaluated.

Models of Environmental Cooperation

While recognizing that distribution of environmental resources may contribute to conflict, recent research has instead begun to focus on the potential for using environmental threats as a common aversion to stimulate conflict resolution (Graeger 2000; Conca and Dabelko 2002; Ali 2003). For policy makers, such an approach is perhaps more useful since it is aimed at problem-solving rather than a diagnostic analysis. What is most significant for government decision makers to consider is that even if the diagnosis of a conflict is not found to be environmental in nature, the remedy may well be achieved through environmental means. The key to appreciating environmental cooperation is to dispense with linear causality and instead consider conflict de-escalation processes as a dynamic, nonlinear process, often constituting a complex series of feedback loops (Ali 2003). Positive exchanges and trust-building gestures are a consequence of realizing common environmental threats. Often a focus on common environmental harms (or aversions) is psycho-logically more successful in leading to cooperative outcomes than focusing on common benefits, which may lead to competitive behavior over the distribution of the gains generated (Stein 1993).

It may be argued that cooperation on environmental issues among adversaries would be relegated to low politics and might not translate into a larger resolution of the high politics of conflicts, such as national security from military threats. In this view, environmental conservation would at best be a means of diplomatic maneuvering between mid-level bureaucrats, and at worst be a tool of co-optation by the influential members of a polity. Such critics give examples of cooperation on water resources between adversarial states like India and Pakistan or Jordan and Israel without subsequent translation into broader reconciliation or peace (Lowi 1995). Thus it could be argued that resource and environmental issues are not important enough in world politics to play an instrumental role. However, a more pos-itive framing of the case might reveal that water resources in this context are so impor-tant that even adversaries must show some semblance of cooperation over them even if they do not spillover to broader peace (Ali 2003; Conca and Dabelko 2002).

Furthermore, the generative use of environmental issues in building peace must be considered in an evolutionary way over longer time horizons and repeated interactions, premised empirically on the following conditions:

- Development of a joint information base on a common environmental threat;
- Recognition that cooperation is essential to alleviate that threat;
- A cognitive connection and trust-building from initial environmental cooperation;
- Continued interactions over time due to environmental necessity;
- Clarification of misunderstandings and de-escalation of connected conflicts;
- Increased cooperation and resultant peace-building. (Axelrod 1997)

Given the necessity for certain environmental resources and a growing realiza-tion that environmental issues require integrated solutions across (and within) bor-ders, the likelihood for their instrumental use in conflict resolution has increased in recent years (UNEP 2004).

One of the earliest contributions to the study of environmental peace-building was Peter Haas's work in the context of the Mediterranean Action Plan (Haas 1992). In his work, Haas focused on ways by which knowledge exchange promotes environmental cooperation through the formation of what he termed "epistemic communities." Often such exchange of knowledge and the networks that provide the means of environmental information exchange comprise civil society groups that are facilitated through development donors.

There is also a growing commitment from donors to "bioregionalism," or the realization that ecological management must be defined by natural delineations, such as watersheds and biomes, rather than by national or other borders (Pirages and Cousins 2005). Numerous joint environmental commissions between countries and jurisdictions have taken root all over the world in this regard. This has played out in various ways at international forums where bioregionalism and

Table 20.1   Key Pathways to Environmental Cooperation and Case Attributes

Pathway	Environmental factors	Relevant case and policy issues
Distributional cooperation over a necessary resource	Water as an essential rivalrous, mobile resource. However, some uses may be choice-driven and demand may be exaggerated by lack of conservation.	Indus Basin Treaty: – Acceptability of technical solutions – Robustness of agreement in absence of trust – Peace dividends for existing conflicts – Role of external agent (World Bank)
Cooperation over common aversion of diminished environmental quality	Air as a mobile non-rivalrous public resource whose diminished quality can impact health but whose regulation may lead to economic pressure on industry and urban centers.	Malé Declaration on Air Quality: – Application of research policy coordination – Ongoing monitoring and self-enforcement – Exchanging best practices – Role of external agent (UNEP and SIDA)
Cooperation in crisis as catalyst of lasting cooperation	Environmental vulnerability of coastal populations. Early warning system for stochastic ecological disturbances is only possible through rapid information sharing.	December 2004 Indian Ocean Tsunami: – Rapid data exchange and trust-building – Collective crisis management prospects – Peace dividends for existing conflicts – Aid allocation and relief management

Source: Ali 2007.

common environmental sensitivities have sometimes transcended traditional notions of state sovereignty.

In this chapter, two cases where environmental cooperation occurred on water and air policy, either bilaterally or multilaterally, are explored. A third case of cooperation in crisis, following the Asian tsunami, is briefly considered but has been explored in more detail by other scholars (Renner 2006). It is also important to consider that the tsunami response prompted very different outcomes for larger peace-building in Aceh versus Sri Lanka—in the former, the tsunami catalyzed a peace accord between the rebels and the Indonesian government, while in the latter case the crisis further strengthened the Tamil tigers and destabilized the country. Each case has its own peculiarities and exemplifies three facets of environmental cooperation as well as some key attributes shown in Table 20.1. This delineation brings forth some key policy concerns that will be addressed as part of the case analysis. These cases were chosen to exemplify multiple pathways to environmental cooperation and to address salient questions relevant to policy makers.

While there may be other pathways to environmental cooperation, I have chosen the most empirically observed causal mechanisms, following a collective review by policy analysts at a workshop organized by the UN Environment Program in March 2005.

The Indus Waters Treaty: Enduring Cooperation Despite Armed Conflict

The Indus Waters Treaty is often cited as a success story of international riparian engagement that has endured numerous conflicts between India and Pakistan. Since 1960, the agreement between these two nuclear rivals has withstood major wars (1965 and 1971) and also several skirmishes over water distribution, as well as derivative territorial concerns (Alam 2002). The agreement is also heralded as a success story for the World Bank, which played an instrumental role in its negotiation during the height of the Cold War. The role of the World Bank in this region was particularly remarkable since India was a vanguard of the nonaligned movement and wanted to disavow any pressure from international institutions. The emergence of the agreement is thus particularly striking since the impetus came from foreign quarters.

Indeed, the technical advisor and initiator of the agreement was the former head of America's Tennessee Valley Authority, David Lilienthal, who suggested that an engineering perspective could contribute to resolving this political stalemate. After a visit to India and Pakistan in 1951, he advised that India and Pakistan first divide the Indus basin geographically. India would have unrestricted use of the three eastern rivers (Ravi, Sutlej, and Bias), while Pakistan would completely control the three western rivers (Jhelum, Chenab, and Indus). The World Bank played a significant role by providing mediation, support staff, funding, and proposals. Under the leadership of President David Black (who was a personal friend of Lilienthal) the World Bank was able to persuade the international community to contribute nearly US$900 million in support for impoundment construction. Nine years after Lilienthal's initial visit, both countries were finally convinced to sign the agreement in 1960. The Indus Waters Treaty obligated Pakistan to build a canal system, decreasing its dependence on Indus tributaries given to India by utilizing previously less developed rivers. The treaty also asks India and Pakistan to exchange information and establish joint monitoring mechanisms to ensure enforcement. The key provisions of the agreement are as follows:

- an agreement that Pakistan would receive unrestricted use of the western rivers, which India would allow to flow unimpeded, with minor exceptions;
- provisions for three dams, eight link canals, three barrages, and 2,500 tube wells to be built in Pakistan;
- a ten-year transition period, from April 1, 1960, to March 31, 1970, during which water would continue to be supplied to Pakistan according to a detailed schedule;

- a schedule for India to provide its fixed financial contribution of $62 million, in ten annual installments, during the transition period;
- additional provisions for data exchange and future cooperation.[1]

As is often the case with riparian agreements, the treaty also established the Permanent Indus Commission, made up of one Commissioner of Indus Waters from each country. The two commissioners would meet annually in order to:

- establish and promote cooperative arrangements for the treaty implementation;
- promote cooperation between the Parties in the development of the waters of the Indus system;
- examine and resolve by agreement any question that may arise between the Parties concerning interpretation or implementation of the Treaty;
- submit an annual report to the two governments.

The dispute resolution provisions of the agreement subjects parties to binding arbitration of technical questions through the appointment of a neutral expert chosen by the World Bank (and acceptable to both parties). If conflicts rise to the level of a dispute, the permanent Indus River Commission will agree to mediation or arbitration. One representative from each country comprises the Indus River Commission. In the technocratic spirit of the agreement, these representatives are often engineers rather than politicians. India and Pakistan constructed and carried out this agreement amidst skirmishes, threats, and full-scale war and amazingly enough neither country sabotaged water projects even during armed conflict.

For the purposes of this study, it is interesting to note that since 1960 no projects have been submitted under the treaty's provisions for "future cooperation," nor have any issues of water quality been submitted at all. There have, however, been several other disputes that have arisen over the years. The first issues arose from Indian non-delivery of some waters during 1965–1966, but became instead a question of procedure and the legality of commission decisions. Negotiators resolved that each commissioner acted as government representatives and that their decisions were legally binding. Another dispute surrounding the design and construction of the Salal dam was resolved through bilateral negotiations between the two governments.

As noted in a recent study of Pakistan's water policy (World Bank 2005), there were conflicting principles put on the table— "no appreciable harm" versus "equitable utilization." Both sides continued to foster misgivings about the treaty but accepted it as the best option in a time of conflict. From the Indian side, the fact that Pakistan got 75 percent of the water represented a fundamental violation of the principle of "equitable utilization." From the Pakistani side, the fact that they were allocated "only" 75 percent of the water when they had 90 percent of the irrigated land represented a violation of the principle of "appreciable harm." As a mark of how leadership can lead to reconciliation despite an elusive "perfect agreement," the erstwhile president of Pakistan, Ayub Khan, is quoted in the aforementioned study as saying: "We have been able to get the best that was possible. . . . Very often the best is the enemy of the good and in this case we have accepted the good after careful and realistic appreciation of our entire overall situation. . . . The basis of this agreement is realism and pragmatism" (World Bank 2005, 8).

As part of a study of Tarbela and Mangla dams (the two impoundments constructed on the Pakistani side as a result of the treaty), the World Commission on Dams concluded that: "The Indus Waters Treaty represents the only ongoing agreement between India and Pakistan that has not been disrupted by wars or periods of high tension. Cooperation that builds on this treaty could not only present opportunities for better water management between those two countries, but also serve as a model for water-sharing arrangements between India, Bangladesh, and Nepal" (Siddiqui 2004).

Most recently, the Indus basin treaty is being tested once again as new dam projects are considered by both Pakistan and India to meet rising energy demands. The Baglihar Hydropower Project (BHP) is being undertaken on the Chenab River in India, 160 kilometers north of Jammu, under severe opposition from Pakistan. Apart from objecting to the project design of the BHP, Pakistan has expressed opposition to the Tulbul navigation project, the Sawalkote Hydroelectric Project, and the Kishanganga Hydroelectric Project, all located in Jammu and Kashmir. The Baglihar dispute was taken to the World Bank, and a neutral technical expert, Raymond Lefitte (a Swiss engineer), was appointed by the Bank in August 2005 to make a binding decision on the case. There are also a series of dams that Pakistan has proposed in its strategic plan. The most significant of these are the Basha and Kalabagh dams (along with the two existing Indus basin dams, Tarbela and Mangla).

So far the Indus basin treaty has served its specific purpose very well but has not led to any major spillover effects toward greater peace-building. However, these most recent dam projects in Kashmir raise some potential prospects for using the agreement more instrumentally in resolving the Kashmir dispute. Increasingly, Kashmiri politicians are also arguing that since the status of the territory is uncertain and so many of the disputes are in Kashmiri territory, they should be part of the Indus basin negotiations as well.[2] Whether such integrative solutions to the conflict would be found through cooperation on water remains to be seen. Table 20.2 summarizes some of the key lessons from this case.

Malé Declaration: Air Pollution as a Dilemma of Common Aversion

Air quality has often been considered the most truly global environmental problem because of the relative mobility of pollutants and the inability of technology to confine pollution within borders, as is possible with water by constructing impoundments. It is thus not surprising that some of the major success stories in environmental management tend to be those focused on air quality, particularly when linked to human health concerns, such as the Montreal Protocol on ozone depletion. There is, however, considerable policy debate on how to handle point-source air pollution, such as what emanates from large industrial establishments, and non-point-source pollution, where the number of emissions sources is dispersed

Table 20.2   Policy Lessons from the Indus Basin Case

Key policy issue	Outcome thus far	Future prospects
Acceptability of technical solutions	Very effective in providing civil engineering solutions to dam siting and scale issues	Joint hydrological studies between Indian and Pakistani scientists to promote trust
Robustness of agreement in absence of trust	Withstood conflicts through regular mandated meetings and Indus Basin Commission formed of technocrats	Agreement likely to be a model for other bilateral agreements on fisheries, trade, and oil and gas pipelines
Role of external agent (World Bank)	Continuing support of dispute resolution system and water resource assistance strategies	Make such agreements part of regional development strategy for South Asia
Peace dividends for existing conflicts	Relatively few visible impacts on peace-building. Agreement relegated to mid-level technical management	Since river headwaters are in Kashmir, the agreement could be used as a conduit for the Kashmir dispute resolution process

Source: Ali 2007.

widely within the population. In some cases, countries may be resistant to curtail pollution from large industrial point sources, particularly when they are a source of energy, such as coal-fueled power plants. In other cases, enforcement of non-point and "fugitive" emissions remains the most perplexing challenge for governments.

Air pollution has been a growing concern across South Asia due to rapid urbanization and concomitant deforestation in rural areas that has led to massive erosion and dust development. To address these concerns, on March 20, 1998, representatives of South Asian governments, including India, Pakistan, Bangladesh, Nepal, Sri Lanka, Bhutan, and Maldives met for a policy dialogue meeting held at the Asian Institute of Technology (AIT) in Bangkok, Thailand, and agreed in principle to a draft South Asian Declaration on Control and Prevention of Air Pollution. The policy dialogue meeting was organized by the UN Environment Program/Environment Assessment Program for Asia and Pacific (UNEP/EAP-AP), based at AIT, and the Stockholm Environment Institute (SEI), based in Stockholm, Sweden, as part of the Regional Air Pollution Program in Developing Countries, funded by the Swedish International Development Cooperation Agency (SIDA) and managed by SEI.[3]

The draft declaration was put before the South Asian environmental ministers for the official declaration at the seventh meeting of the Governing Council of the

South Asia Cooperative Environment Program (SACEP), held on April 22, 1998, in Malé, the Republic of Maldives—hence the name of the initiative. SACEP is an intergovernmental sub-regional organization, whose aims and objectives are:

- to promote and support the protection and enhancement of the environment of South Asia individually, collectively and co-operatively
- to encourage the judicious use of the resources of the environment with a view to alleviating poverty, reducing socio-economic disparities, and improving the quality of life of the people.

Among the key functions of SACEP are promoting cooperative activities in environmental protection and management that are beneficial to the member states, and providing resources for project implementation through donor assistance and project support. The implementation of the agreement is coordinated by the UN Environment Program (UNEP) Regional Resource Centre for Asia and the Pacific (RRC-AP).

The declaration aims to achieve intergovernmental cooperation to address the increasing threat of transboundary air pollution and consequential impacts due to concentrations of pollutant gases and acid deposition on human health, ecosystem function, and corrosion of materials. Apart from delineating the general principles of intergovernmental cooperation for air pollution abatement, the declaration sets up an institutional framework linking scientific research and policy formulation. The document also calls for the continuation of this process in stages, with mutual consultation, to draw up and implement national and regional action plans and protocols based on a fuller understanding of transboundary air pollution issues.

Some of the tasks that would be accomplished within this mandate would be: (1) the evolving of an institutional structure at the national level both for policy response and the technical requirements; (2) the strengthening of monitoring arrangements; (3) the completion of baseline studies to assess and analyze the air pollution issue; and (4) the development and/or adoption of national action plans.

In the long-term, it could serve as a forum for exchange between different political systems and as a factor of some stability in times of political change. It could lead to the development of international environmental law and also create the essential framework for controlling and reducing the damage to human health and the environment caused by localized and transboundary air pollution.

In addition to the declaration, a follow-up action plan has also been agreed upon. Follow-up activities will be implemented in three levels, national, sub-regional, and regional. In addition to the baseline studies and national action plans, a network of researchers and policy makers has been established at the national level. Details about these policy experts are publicly available through the UNEP Web site established for this purpose.[4] At the sub-regional level, national level activities will be aggregated through SACEP. Dissemination of tools, methodologies, and data will be done at the regional level through a regional resource center. The follow-up program will be implemented by UNEP/EAP-AP in collaboration with SEI and SACEP and with SIDA support. The countries are providing national resources for the implementation of the declaration. The Stockholm Environment Institute (SEI) provides technical support to the declaration. The implementation is currently divided into three phases:

The first phase of the effort involved the establishment of the National Focal Points (NFP) in ministries of environment and the designation of National Implementing Agencies (NIAs) by the NFPs and was completed by 1999. The NIAs developed baseline studies and national action plans for each country. The baseline studies were developed to ascertain the status of air pollution knowledge and research in the countries and identified gaps. The action plans outlined activities to fill the gaps in order to build a firm basis for future agreements on air pollution emissions.

The second phase of the initiative includes the following activities:

- further development of the NFP/NIA network, including the development of National Advisory Committees;
- initial development of a monitoring network across the region;
- carrying out parallel studies on integrated assessment modeling and emission inventory methodologies.

The final phase will use information and knowledge concerning air pollution problems in South Asian countries as a basis for the further development of the policy cycle in the region. Studies informing the policy process will continue into pollutant emission inventories; modeling atmospheric transfer of air pollutants; monitoring pollutant depositions and concentrations; assessing the risk of impacts to health, crops, materials, and ecosystems; mitigation options; and developing/using integrated assessment models.

The decision-making body of the Malé Declaration is the Steering Committee, made up of the NFPs, UNEP, and SACEP. Technical implementation is carried out under the auspices of the Technical Committee, comprised of the NIAs, the Monitoring Committee (MoC), UNEP, SACEP, and SEI. There is further collaboration with other institutions in South Asia, such as the Indian Ocean Experiment (INDOEX). At a regional level, close links will be forged with other major players in the Asia-Pacific region, such as the East-Asia Network on Acid Deposition (EANET), the Integrated Monitoring Program on Acidification of Chinese Terrestrial Systems (IMPACTS), and the Composition of Asian Deposition activity (CAD).

A growing network of monitoring stations is being developed to provide the cooperating governments with information about the level of regional-scale air pollution. The monitoring sites will be located in rural areas remote from point sources of pollution and will be able to provide information about long-distance transport of air pollutants. The activities are being technically supported by the Monitoring Committees (MoC), who are responsible for advising national monitoring institutions, creating manuals, and ensuring the quality and sustained development of the monitoring network. At each station, rainwater, particulate matter, and certain gaseous pollutants will be sampled.

It is important to note that since this agreement was of a multilateral nature, the opportunities for peace dividends between conflicting countries within the region were minimal. Hence a separate "peace dividend" category is absent from this analysis. While there could still be some potential opportunities for leveraging cooperation here toward larger peace-building, the multilateral scale of the agreement largely precludes such efforts. Another factor that reduces such a potential is the lack of direct flow connections between the players, unlike the riparian case. More detailed air flow models and tracing of pollutants from sources may augment such opportunities for direct bilateral agreements as well. Such opportunities have arisen in the past in cases where identifiable pollutants from point sources have traveled across borders—for example, sulfur emissions from smelters in Ontario, Canada, that were linked to acid rain in northern New England, in the United States. Indeed, there is another UNEP-supported program from which some lessons might be applied to the Malé Declaration, namely the Atmospheric/Asian Brown Cloud (ABC) monitoring system, which was developed in collaboration with the University of California, San Diego. Greater analysis has gone into this case since the cloud is a mobile yearly phenomenon and has relevance to particulate pollution scientists as well as climate change researchers (the cloud diminishes the warming effect of greenhouse gases by 30 percent).[5] However, the Malé Declaration thus far has not bound countries to measure or analyze pollutant fate and transport regimes across borders, despite the fact that transboundary pollution concerns are part of its mandate of inquiry. Table 20.3 summarizes some of the key policy lessons from this case, with the proviso that this is a far newer agreement than the Indus basin case and the implementation program is still in early stages of development.

While the security implications of air pollution are perhaps not as starkly visible to countries as those of water scarcity, the lack of control that countries have on airsheds necessitates cooperation if the issue is to be adequately addressed. The Malé Declaration is a first step in forming an epistemic community around the threat posed by poor air quality to regional health. Framing the matter in terms of diminished tourism revenues and reduced work productivity due to time lost in days coping with respiratory ailments might also bring the issue within more mainstream economic security concerns. Thus far, the cooperation resulting from the Malé Declaration has been primarily technical in nature, though ecological data-sharing can itself raise sensitivities of military security. In that respect, perhaps the willingness of countries to share information about emissions that would reveal the quality of coal being used for power generation and other related matters indicates a strengthening of ties. However, in order for the full potential of environmental cooperation on air quality to be achieved, all countries in the region will need to perceive the matter with as much immediacy as water is perceived for food production.

Conclusions

Countries in South Asia are increasingly constrained by the quantity of usable water available and the quality of their air resources. By framing pollution of both air and water as a common aversion, we may be able to foster cooperation between

Table 20.3   Policy Lessons from the Malé Declaration Case

Key policy issue	Outcome thus far	Future prospects
Application of research to policy coordination	Individual studies of air quality completed in all countries with public dissemination of findings	Fate and transport models and joint research prospects following the UNEP-ABC model
Ongoing monitoring and self-enforcement	Monitoring centers are being set up, but their location is largely determined by national governments. Local laws for compliance are applied rather than regional standards	Independent monitoring of emissions from point sources as well as a potential treaty for regional air quality (especially for highly mobile toxic pollutants)
Exchanging best practices	Limited technology transfer thus far or sharing of information on specific abatement procedures	Joint technology development of pollution control devices and exchange of expert technicians
Role of external agent (UNEP and SIDA)	Provided financial support for initial air quality data and monitoring and information exchange via Web site maintenance	Providing support to draft a treaty on regional air quality and provide means of third-party auditing and compliance assurance

Source: Ali 2007.

otherwise antagonistic players. Doing so would ameliorate regional security and reduce the threat of armed conflict while also improving the environmental conditions that could lead to endemic vulnerability and scarcity- induced disputes. The Indus basin treaty is a useful example of how environmental cooperation can exist even during times of intense suspicion and armed confrontation between two nations. While the instrumental use of such cooperation in resolving larger territorial disputes remains questionable, there is no doubt that cooperation on environmental issues can improve the relations between scientists and form epistemic communities. Sharing of knowledge on environmental issues through initiatives such as the Malé Declaration are indeed positive signs that the countries in the Indian Ocean basin are beginning to transcend the paranoia of old security discourses that had prevented sharing of technical information. Instead we are beginning to see signs of an emerging ecoregional approach to resource management that augers well for improving security for the SADC countries.

NOTES

The author wishes to thank UNEP and the Woodrow Wilson Center in Washington, D.C., for their support of this project.

1. Descriptive details about the Indus Basin Treaty are derived from textual information on the Transboundary Freshwater Dispute Database at Oregon State University: http://www.trans-boundarywaters.orst.edu/projects/casestudies/indus.html (accessed July 2006).

2. Personal communication with Siraj Wahid, Vice Chancellor of the Islamic University of Kashmir, Toronto, United Nations mandated University for Peace meeting, May 16, 2006.

3. Descriptive material for this case is derived from the Regional Air Pollution Program in Developing Countries Web site, based at York University (UK): http://www.york.ac.uk/inst/sei/rapidc2/rapidc.html (accessed July 2006).

4. UN Environment Program, Regional Resource Centre for Asia and Pacific (Bangkok, Thailand): http://www.rrcap.unep.org/issues/air/Maledec/ (accessed July 2006).

5. Details about the ABC collaborative research led by Dr. V. Ramanathan can be found at the University of California, San Diego Web site: http://www-abc-asia.ucsd.edu/ (accessed July 2006).

REFERENCES

Alam, Undala. 2002. "Questioning the Water Wars Rationale: A Case Study of the Indus Waters Treaty." *Geographical Journal* 168: 341–53.

Ali, Saleem H. 2003. "Environmental Planning and Cooperative Behavior." *Journal of Planning Education and Research* 23: 165–76.

Axelrod, R. 1997. *The Complexity of Cooperation.* Princeton. N.J.: Princeton Univ. Press.

———. *The Evolution of Cooperation.* New York: Basic Books.

Bose, Sugata. 2006. *A Hundred Horizons: The Indian Ocean in the Age of Global Empire.* Cambridge, Mass.: Harvard Univ. Press.

Conca, Ken. 2005. *Governing Water: Contentious Transnational Politics and Global Institution-Building.* Cambridge, Mass.: MIT Press.

Conca, Ken, and Geoffrey D. Dabelko. 2002. *Environmental Peacemaking.* Baltimore, Md.: Johns Hopkins Univ. Press.

Crisis Management Initiative. 2006. "The Aceh Negotiations: Online Resource Compendium." Helsinki, Finland. http://www.cmi.fi/?content=aceh_project.

De Boer, Jelle Zeilinga. 2004. *Earthquakes in Human History : The Far-Reaching Effects of Seismic Disruption.* Princeton, N.J.: Princeton Univ. Press.

Fuwa, Yoshitaro. 2003. "Natural Resource Management from a Conflict Resolution Perspective." *Japan Bank for International Cooperation Review* 8 (November), special issue.

Graeger, N. 2000. "Environmental Security." *Journal of Peace Research* 33 (1): 109–16.

Haas, Peter. 1992. Saving the Mediterranean: The Politics of International Environmental Cooperation. New York: Columbia Univ. Press.

Hakim, Iftikhar A. 2005. "The Indus Waters Treaty: An Institutional Mechanism for Addressing Regional Disparity." Master's thesis, Department of Urban Planning, UCLA.

Hicks, W. K., et al. 2001. "Development of the Regional Policy Process for Air Pollution in South Asia, Southern Africa and Latin America." *Water Air and Soil Pollution* 130 (1–4): 211–16.

Homer-Dixon, Thomas. 1998. *The Environment, Scarcity and Violence.* Princeton, N.J.: Princeton Univ. Press.

International Crisis Group. 2006. "Aceh: Now for the Hard Part." Briefing, Area Briefing No. 48. March 26.

Jha, Raghbindera. 2005. "Alleviating Environmental Degradation in the Asia-Pacific Region: International Cooperation and the Role of Issue-Linkage." Australian National University Working Paper, Canberra.

Kelman, I. 2005. "Tsunami Diplomacy." *Sociological Research Online* 10 (1) (April). http://www.socresonline.org.uk/10/1/Kelman.htm (accessed August 2006).

Lowi, Miriam. 1995. *Water and Power: The Politics of a Scarce Resource in the Jordan Basin.* Cambridge: Cambridge Univ. Press.

Malik, Bashir A. 2005. *The Indus Waters Treaty in Retrospect.* Lahore, Pakistan: Brite Books.

Najam, Adil. 2003. "The Human Dimensions of Environmental Security: Some Insights from South Asia." *Environmental Change and Security Project Report* 9:59–73.

Pirages, D. and K. Cousins, eds. 2005. *From Resource Scarcity to Ecological Security: Exploring New Limits to Growth.* Cambridge, Mass.: MIT Press.

Park, Jeffrey, et al. 2005. "Performance Review of the Global Seismographic Network for the Andaman-Sumatran Megathrust Earthquake." *Seismological Research Letter* 76 (3).

Renner, Michael. 2006. "Turing Disasters into Peacemaking Opportunities." *State of the World 2006.* New York: Norton.

Samaddara, Ranabira, and Helmut Reifeld. 2001. *Peace as Process: Reconciliation and Conflict Resolution in South Asia.* New Delhi: Manohar Publishers.

Schiff, Maurice, and L. Alan Winters. 2002. "Regional Cooperation, and the Role of International Organizations and Regional Integration." Policy Research Paper 2872. Washington, D.C.: World Bank.

Shand, Ric, and K. P. Kalirajan. 1997. "Yamazawa's Open Economic Association: An Indian Ocean Grouping for Economic Cooperation." *The Developing Economies* 35 (1): 3–27.

Siddiqui, Toufiq. 2004. "An India-Pakistan Détente." Analysis Report No. 75. Honolulu, Hawaii: East-West Center.

Stein, Arthur. 1993. *Why Nations Cooperate?* Ithaca, N.Y.: Cornell Univ. Press.

United Nations Environment Programme. 2004. "Understanding Environment, Cooperation and Conflict." Washington, D.C.: Woodrow Wilson Center, and Nairobi, Kenya: UNEP. http://www.unep.org/pdf/ECC.pdf (accessed July 2006).

World Bank. 2005. "Pakistan's Water Resource Assistance Strategy." Report PK-34081. Washington, D.C.: World Bank.

PART VI

CONCLUSION

21

The Politics of Hope

UNDERSTANDING ENVIRONMENTAL
JUSTICE AND SECURITY IN THE
INDIAN OCEAN REGION WITHIN A
POST-COLONIALIST FRAME

TIMOTHY DOYLE

Introduction

This book's strength has been to bring together disparate voices across this vast region defined by its proximity to the Indian Ocean: the Ocean of the South. Obviously, there have been many different emphases which have emerged in the telling of the stories that litter the previous pages. In this final conclusion, however, let us revisit certain common themes, flagged in Part One, which provide the strands tying this oceanic tapestry together. First, let us again make mention of recent trends toward market-driven models of governance across the region. By focusing on models of management for the ocean itself, we stress the necessity of both nation-state responsibility and community action, rather than divesting citizens' powers wholly to the private sector as the market models of advanced Northern capitalism dictate, thrust on the inhabitants of the poorest ocean as essential parts of economic restructuring programs. Any sustainable and environmentally just oceanic future in the region must include a strong role for nation-states (and part-nerships between states), as well as partnerships with nonstate partners, while stressing the limits of neoliberal natural resource economic management models.

In celebrating the emancipatory role of citizens' groups and environmental justice movements within this collection, another key point has emerged. This relates to the appropriateness of specific interpretations of environmental security in given contexts: environmentalisms in minority world parts of the IOR are essen-tially different from those as interpreted by the majority. Most simply, the domi-nant notion of environmental justice is anthropocentric in the IOR, rather than being about the rights and privileges of nonhuman nature (but not always). It is crucial to understand that discussions of environmental security will never reach an informed and shared conclusion, if the profound differences in the diverse and culturally rich interpretations of what the "environment" actually entails are not discussed, understood, and respected. These differences, often historical by nature, are usually discussed in terms of a simple dichotomy between North and South.

In this instance, we address the differences in a slightly more complex division of three: post-materialism, post-industrialism, and post-colonialism. It is within a more post-colonial frame that movements for environmental security and justice, across the IOR, can be understood in a more powerful and emancipatory fashion.

In Search of Genuinely Cooperative Oceanic Governance: In Defense of the Role of the State

In chapter 4 of the introductory part of this book, Marcus Haward explained the international, regional, and national approaches to marine and coastal management in the region. He emphasized the importance of international conventions and national laws, but stressed the importance of the development of an integrated regional approach to oceanic governance. He also commented on management trends toward more market-based approaches. The outcomes of the UN Conference on Environment and Development (UNCED) in 1992, most notably the Rio Declaration and Agenda 21 (particularly Chapter 17) as well as the Biodiversity Convention and the agenda established by the World Summit on Sustainable Development (WSSD) in 2002, have had significant impacts in the development of oceans governance. A decade and a half later, key post-Rio principles—sustainable development, integration, the precautionary principle/approach, and intergenerational equity—have introduced these new approaches to the management of marine living resources. Since this time we have seen increasing use of economic instruments in the management of marine resources. These developments highlight new areas of governance where "market" approaches shape policies and practices. These tools and approaches have developed at a time when traditional, regulatory-based management arrangements have been seen to have "failed."

Let us discuss this move toward governance using market instruments. The Australian case is salient here. There is no doubt that a nation's capacity to govern—that is, to collate baseline data, to legislate, and to moderate—are undoubtedly important. In recent times, however, the Australian government has moved away from these traditional liberal democratic roles, to more neoliberal, purchaser-provider models of public service which, though cost efficient, often lead to exclusively industry-friendly outcomes. And the case of marine management has provided some particularly pertinent examples as to what happens when states hand over basic responsibilities to markets. Australia adopted free market economic principles in the mid-1980s. It is a small, (largely resource) export-based economy. Australia is firmly embedded in the international economic system. Bührs and Barlett write: "Keeping (export) prices down, and maintaining conditions favorable to overseas investment, are the foremost political-economic priorities. Getting these key economic indicators right is more important than the level of unemployment, the distribution of income, and the social and environmental effects of development. . . . People and the environment are looked upon more as 'resources' for 'the economy': than as ends in themselves" (Bührs and Bartlett 1997).

But understanding a nation as part of an economic system is different from operating from a premise that the market is in itself natural, and that nature is a marketplace. The move from multiple-use models of marine management to wise-use models, shows the move of Australia from a position in the 1970s where it was at the vanguard of good environmental governance (where the state played an active and responsible role), to a current position where basic responsibilities are handed almost exclusively to the corporate sector.

Gifford Pinchet championed the earlier, more state-centric "multiple use" as a way of resolving land-use conflicts. These models were firmly rooted in notions of nature as constituting a series of resources for human use. Nature itself was not of value outside of these utilitarian notions. Multiple use has been dominant as a resource allocation model in many parts of the world, including Australia. It emerged most vociferously in the language that framed the establishment of the Great Barrier Reef Marine Park in the 1970s. It was during the second period, however, when it became the key resource management strategy within the ideology of sustainable use. Multiple-use planning imagines nature divided into a pie. All possible uses of nature (as pie to be consumed) are known and explored, as all of nature is a commodity. In the same way as nature is construed as a series of pie segments, so too is society itself. Multiple use is very much reliant on pluralist and corporatist concepts of power and the state. The roundtable is a symbolic representation of the pie, the table itself being provided by the state. People, or the now more fashionable "stakeholders,"[1] are physical manifestations of possible resource use and conflict. Environmental managers using this multiple-use model argue that most environmental processes are reversible, and that all sectors can pursue diverse goals for resource use without unnecessary conflict. All that it takes to succeed is that conflicting sectors produce end positions based on compromise and negotiation (Doyle 1999).

Multiple-use decision-making has weaknesses. In true pluralist terms, all interest groups are perceived as equal stakeholders, while the state perceives and portrays itself as an objective middle person, attempting to provide a working compromise between conflicting sets of "values." Values, of course, are important, but by concentrating solely on reconciling values, power differentials between conflicting positions are almost totally denied and neglected. To be fair to multiple-use resource allocation and decision-making, however, when genuinely interpreted as a conservation regime it can achieve results. What is essential to good multiple-use decision-making is the open recognition that some interests, some values, are more paramount than others. Also, depending on context, sometimes not all resource equations are "win-win" situations. In fact, on many occasions, certain interests are more successful than others, resulting in zero-sum outcomes. Australia's Great Barrier Reef is an excellent example. Central to the reef's management is the existence of marine national parks, or no-take areas (Prideaux et al. 1998, 15). The benefits of no-take areas are widely recognized by scientists attempting to maintain some "control" areas, which allow the development of successful management strategies. The majority of the Great Barrier Reef is not so exclusively protected. Most of its Marine Protected Areas (MPAs) allow commercial interests to enter into the Reserve. Multiple use can only work from a conservation perspective, when these multiple access areas are coupled with a strong sample of representative habitats that are "no go zones" for commercial interests, such as mining. Frameworks that do not explicitly provide any exclusiveness to any interests are at best ecologically useless, and at worst, promoters of commercial, anti-ecological interests. These systems cease to be the more favorable multiple use and take on the more neoliberal tag wise use.

Under wise-use decision-making, these areas are now renamed resource "lock-ups." "No-take areas," exclusion zones, scientific control zones, and ecological buffer zones are now increasingly obsolete. Any ecological "use" is only considered after business interests have deemed it appropriate insofar as they have no further utilization for the areas in question. Other wise-use jargon refers to this as sequential use, which promotes a strict hierarchy in the order of access to the "resources." The biosphere, in this view, can be used over and over again, fulfilling all the demands placed on it by the multitude of stakeholders, with no long-term negative consequences. Also, the state, in this view, hands over its role as moderator of the roundtable: it is now seen simply as another interest.

An excellent example of this absence of "no takes zones" in wise-use natural resource management occurs in the conservative government's declaration of the Great Australian Bight Marine Park (GABMP) in 1998. A map of this park consists of a great number of different lines, specifying different uses. Aquatic environments are often seen under wise use as three- dimensional domains: to provide resource extraction industries with unlimited access. In the Great Australian Bight Marine Park (GABMP), the park is divided using sets of latitudinal and longitudinal lines, as well as horizontal and vertical ones. Two key management zones are proposed: the Marine Mammal Zone, and the Benthic (sea floor) Zone. Basically this translates into certain practices being pursued in different surfaces areas, as well as at different depths. This means that activities such as mid-water trawling, demersal shark netting, and petroleum/gas extraction are allowed above and below the benthos, although these practices have obvious and significant impacts on the seabed. To add to this industry-friendly regime, there are zero no-take zones in the overall "park." Grady writes: "Without any 'no-take' sanctuary zones in the Commonwealth waters, there are no control sites by which to access the effects of trawling, fishing (shark and lobster), mineral and petroleum extraction. Hence, the proposed research and monitoring program for the park will not be able to demonstrate the effects/benefits of the zones—as the zones do not actually prohibit any activities" (Grady 1998, 130).

The then-minister for environment under the Howard Ministry, Robert Hill, argued that "no-take zones" will no longer appear in his government's resource management strategies. In an ABC radio broadcast from Port Lincoln in September 1998, Hill addressed the management of the Great Australian Bight. He stated that "MPAs (Marine Protected Areas) which exclude use are an old-fashioned view" (Hill 1998). GABMP is not a park at all, but an industry free-for-all, using the language of conservation as window dressing. This "park" will prove virtually useless in protecting endangered species such as whales, dogfish, and Southern Ocean tuna, and equally useless in providing Australia with a genuinely sustainable fishing industry. This complex map of smoke and mirrors promotes all and denounces nothing: it is wise use at it destructive best.

The Marine Stewardship Council (MSC) is another example of neoliberal principles governing fisheries management. Initially established through the joint efforts of the World Wide Fund for Nature (WWF) and the major food group Unilever in 1997, it is now an "independent" authority that has established a set of "principles and criteria" for the certification of sustainable fisheries. Its mission is to become a global accreditation board that, through its label, will let consumers know which products are sourced from "sustainable" fisheries.

The MSC initially presented itself as a nonprofit group that provided accreditation of certain fisheries. "Certification," the MSC argues, "uses market incentives to influence the way fisheries are managed in favor of environmental standards. . . . Consumers know that by buying products with the MSC Label, they are supporting healthier oceans and healthier environment" (Burton 2001). Consumer sentiment in Europe cannot exclusively be used as an adequate governance tool in the IOR. Just because this model has emerged from the markets of the affluent world does not mean it is more advanced, or even appropriate to an Indian Ocean context. It is too often imagined that more affluent countries have more resources to spend on good governance; but too often good governance has been interpreted as handing over basic marine management responsibilities to the market.

Wise use and overly neoliberal sustainable development work hand in hand with free market economics. As the market is deemed "natural," the ecology of the ecosphere becomes "the market." All inputs and outputs are given value in monetary terms and then, so it is argued, the "natural," "real," and "essentialist" economy of ecology shall emerge, unfettered by the constraints of science and governmentality. The trickle-down effect, we are told, will benefit those species living on the lower rungs of the natural hierarchy, promoting widespread ecological health and doing away with, forever, any notions of science-generated ecological safety nets thrown over the most disadvantaged, those species and habitats, those resources, most at risk. Nothing is irreversible; everyone and everything will win. This line of argument, of course, also fits neatly into the parameters of neo-Spencerism, promoting the notion that those human and nonhuman communities most likely to survive unfettered "natural" systems will be all the better for doing so, having weeded out those less able to survive.

The reality is, however, that almost exclusively relying on consumer sentiment and other such global market instruments in the affluent world is not sufficient to develop long-term environmental governance for the IOR region itself. Ultimately, such models will deliver ecological wealth to the minority, robbing the people of the South of any semblance of environmental justice. Successful governance must embrace ecological, democratic—as well as, but not only—market factors that emerge from within the region itself. But, more importantly, environmental security for the region demands that nation-states retain the key responsibilities of moderator and overseer, honoring a clear line between their market-based and public duties.

The Three Green Posts

The contributors in this work have used the terms North/South, first world/third world, developed world/developing world, and minority world/majority world interchangeably. Most of these dualistic divisions are oriented around poverty and development issues. We acknowledge that all these terms are imperfect categories. Most of the IOR can be classified as majority world, but obviously there are also more affluent, minority world countries and enclaves of power within the region (Doherty and Doyle 2006).

It is problematic to define entire hemispheres as being rich and poor. There is huge variance in levels of poverty in countries classified as part of the South. Sometimes, the World Bank uses the term "fourth world" to differentiate between the poorest nations and the simply poor nations of the third world. On other occasions, it has taken out the oil-rich nations of the Middle East from its "South" categorization. There are also classification problems when considering recently industrializing countries versus those who are yet to undergo significant industrialization. In some ways, one can follow the advice of the Calverts in their text devoted to discussions of the environment and North-South and simply say that the South is "taken to mean all the countries of the world not defined as Advanced Industrial Countries (AICs)" (Calvert and Calvert 1999, 6). The problem with this approach, as Calvert et al. accept, is that enormous discrepancies of wealth exist within nation-states. In the Australian aboriginal situation, for example, with indigenous peoples living a fourth world existence within a first world nation-state, it becomes obvious that the South can exist within the North. Of course, the opposite is also true: elites in the South can enjoy wealthy lives akin to what is generically expected in the North. In any study of social movements, terminology must be employed that is not wholly based on a discourse relating to nation-states, for, as aforementioned, social movements often traverse nation-state boundaries.

Of course, as already stated, this is an overly dualistic and simplistic, but useful broad-brush technique of highlighting differences. It is reminiscent of Guha and Martinez-Alier's construction of the "environmentalism of the poor" (Guha and Martinez-Alier 1997) as distinct from that of the wealthy. On the one hand, the environmental justice of the minority world is constructed as largely post-materialist: more interested in the rights of "other nature," which are implicit in conservation, threatened species, and wilderness campaigns. Contrarily, the issues we have described above, far from being post-materialist, are issues for survival. Elsewhere, Doyle (2005) uses this simple dichotomy of the minority world and the majority world. Unlike some forms of post-modern and post-positivist analysis, then, we still find the binary mega-division between majority and minority worlds—though imperfect—a useful one, as it continues to match and describe the "empirical reality" as we have encountered it, as long as it is understood that these great divisions are neither necessarily geographically oriented nor nation-state specific. Rather, there is an immense gulf in the context of comparative environmental movements between the experiences of the majority of the earth's people (the South), when contrasted with those encountered by a small minority (the North). A rather simple, often quoted equation needs to be reinforced here. Approximately 80 percent of the earth's resources are either consumed or owned by approximately 15 percent of the earth's people. On the other hand, 85 percent of the earth's people have access to only 20 percent of the earth's resources (Doyle and McEachern 1998).

One criticism leveled at this work, as well as that of Guha and Martinez-Alier, is that it unfairly and inaccurately represents green concerns in many parts of the industrialized world. Building on this North-South dualism, then, it may be more accurate to construct a tripartite system of characterization for contemporary environmentalism: post-industrialism—depicting the European traditions of political ecology; post-materialism—depicting the largely non-anthropocentric concerns of nature conservation that have dominated in the New World; and post-colonialism—descriptive of the experience of the majority of the earth: the South (Doherty and Doyle 2006).

In the minority countries of the New World—particularly the United States (which we have to acknowledge as a major presence in the IOR) and Australia—there can be no doubt that post-materialist issues have dominated environmental agendas over the past generation. Environmental justice and security, then, can be understood in a post-materialist frame through championing the politics of "other nature," the protection of wilderness areas, and the saving of threatened species. In this vein, environment movements pursuing environmental justice and security are seen as possessing post-materialist values that directly contest—in a paradigmatic battle—the dominant materialist values of modern society (Doyle and Kellow 1995, 34–35). This thesis is commonly identified with the writings of Inglehart (Inglehart 1977, 1990; see Papadakis 1993). Strongly premised by Maslow's "hierarchy of needs" (1954), post-materialists argue that having largely fulfilled its more basic needs of safety and security, parts of advanced industrial society are able to pursue the "higher," more luxuriant causes of a world—such as love and a sense of belonging—beyond the old politics of material existence (Doyle and McEachern 1998, 2001, 2008). Inglehart states: "A process of intergenerational value change is gradually transforming the politics and cultural norms of advanced industrial societies. A shift from Materialist to Post-Materialist value priorities has bought new political issues to the center of the stage and provided much of the impetus for new political movements . . . from giving top priority to physical sustenance and safety toward heavier emphasis on belonging, self-expression, and the quality of life" (Inglehart 1990, 66).

Arguments relating to the aesthetic values of nature, nonhuman rights, the spirituality of place, and those with an emphasis on holism and ecology can be explained by the post-materialist hypothesis, though not all first world movements are predicated on post-material values (Doyle and McEachern 2001).

The political ecology movements of western Europe, which combined post-materialism with a broader New Left-derived analysis of power developed a significantly different green ideology, and, alongside traditional nature conservation issues, wrestled with questions of structural change and multiple forms of social inequality (gender, race, sexuality, class, and bureaucracy) from their inception. In the United States and Australia these issues were in a subservient position to post-material environmental issues, which have been interpreted in a particularly apolitical manner by the largest environmental organizations (Dowie 1995; Brulle and Jenkins 2006).

Through a post-industrialist lens, environmentalism challenges the excesses of the industrialist project, the rights of corporations to pollute and degrade, and the dwindling of the earth's resources as they are fed into the advanced industrial machines. An alternative account of the origins of environment movements emerging all over the globe is based on the thesis of post-industrialism.[2] Advocates of this position argue that advanced industrialism, championed by both the market systems of latter-day capitalism and the state-centered models of socialism, has pushed the earth, its habitats, and all its species (including people) to the brink of extinction. This industrial/development paradigm has promoted economic growth at all costs. Initially this pursuit of growth was rooted deeply in the Enlightenment project of the scientific and industrial revolutions, and the pursuit of progress. Hence the environment (and nature) was presented as an eternal cornucopia, where resources were unlimited.

In more recent times, industrialism has been globalized and homogenized. Now there is widespread and partial acceptance of natural constraints to growth—or a finite carrying capacity—but the Enlightenment project continues, as it now advocates increased growth through improvements to environmental efficiency and management, the promotion of the global "free market," and the advocacy of homogenous "democratic," pluralist systems. Most recently this has been pursued under the key terms sustainable development and ecologically sustainable development. Carl Boggs writes from the post-industrialist perspective: "to the degree that the radicalism of new social movements tends to flow from the deep crisis of industrial society, its roots are generally indigenous and organic, making it naturally resistant to totalistic ideologies that galvanized the Second and Third Internationals . . . the eclipse of the industrial growth model, the threat of nuclear catastrophe, bureaucratization, destruction of natural habitat, social anomie—cannot be expected to disappear simply through the good intentions of political leaders" (Boggs 1986, 23).

Nonetheless, the post-industrialist thesis has numerous, extremely apt uses, especially since the emergence of global ecology in the latter part of the 1980s (Chatterjee and Finger 1994, 8). In the IOR it is particularly salient in those parts of the regions that are undergoing rapid industrialization. But in even poorer and dominantly rural parts of the region, movements for environmental justice and security are motivated by basic issues of survival that are often the result of extreme environmental degradation and hundreds of years of colonial exploitation. So as an all-encompassing theory capable of explaining a global phenomenon, both the post-materialist and post-industrialist theses are found wanting (Doyle and McEachern 2001).

Using post-colonialism as the narrative frame, green concerns are cast in the light of the colonizer versus the colonized, the dichotomous world of affluence and poverty. There are obvious crossovers with the previous post-industrialist thesis, recognizing structuralist lines between the haves and the have-nots. In different parts of the world, these frames, or story lines—and combinations of them and others—are used more often to explain the causes and effects of environmental issues and problems. In the "Ocean of the South," the frames of post-colonialism and structuralism usually dominate.

Traditional social movement models based on Marxist—and most particularly structuralist—accounts of power enjoy enormous currency in the South. A large number of environmental activists in the developing world identify themselves as Marxists, seeing the key cause of environmental degradation being that resources and production are in the hands of a ruling class (Routledge et al. 2006). Solving these problems does not lie necessarily in better management or developing more efficient and sustainable practices. Rather, the first part of the answer lies in local people gaining control over their own resources, their own lives.

Indeed, one of the critical traits that Calvert et al. list as a characteristic of the South is the fact that almost all states are former colonies. This element of colonization is taken up by Doug Torgerson (2006). He agrees that an image of a "divided planet" in terms of rich and poor, or "Eurocentric planet," is a needed correction to the concept espoused by Ward and Dubos's *Only One Earth,* commissioned for the UNCED Conference in 1972. Torgerson goes further, arguing that the divisions of the planet bear the "unmistakeable mark of the legacy of colonialization," and "as concerns are voiced from formerly colonized regions of the divided planet, the many environmentalisms tend to converge in the focus with the Global Justice Movement, a 'movement of movements.'"

Although wilderness-oriented movements exist, they are largely overshadowed in many national agendas by the environment/development nexus.[3] Much of the movement in the South is involved in human-centered environmental causes of basic survival. Obviously, the post- materialist thesis is largely meaningless here. There is little about "higher values" (in Western terms) when considering the South's environmental crisis: and crisis it is. There is also little credence given to post-industrialist arguments, as most people in the South see the key problem being lack of ownership of their own resources. Chatterjee and Finger comment on this point: "[Whether it be] the Third World Network in Malaysia or the Centre for Science and the Environment in India, it is no longer industrial development per se which is considered destructive of the environment. Rather it is the fact that development remains controlled by the North instead of the South. The weakness of this argument, of course, stems from the fact that it mixes together Southern peoples and Southern Elites" (Chatterjee and Finger 1994, 77).

The dominant view of the North is that the poverty of the South has caused and continues to create environmental degradation.[4] This environmental degradation is of grave concern to the North, now advocating global ecology and, as a consequence, seeing itself as inevitably having to share the earth's essential survival mechanisms with the South. Along these lines, the North portrays the major problems of the South as species extinction, global climate change, desertification, and population control.[5]

The unwritten assumption here is that the South is the main environmental offender, while the North is a model of environmental controls and reforms. In this view, the North sees itself as bringing its environmental message (including that of sustainable development and management) to the South, to save the latter from itself. With increased growth and democratization, "civil society" will emerge—the North argues—allowing conditions where people will help themselves.[6] It is true that Northern environmental activists, mostly through the vehicles of international NGOs, are active in the South. The reality is, however, that many successful networks—both non-institutional and institutional—of the Southern environment movement are inspired by local activists, many of whom would be construed as "poor" by Northern standards. They are not degraders, not sustainers, but actors.

In the Philippines, for example, there is a vibrant and vast local environment movement that is fighting environmental degradation head-on across a range of fronts (Broad 1994, 813). "From the Naam movement in Burkina Faso to women's tree-planting cooperatives in Kenya, grass-roots organizations across Africa have taken a leading role against environmental degradation" (Ekins 1992, 114). In India, the movement against the Narmada dam (Ekins 1992, 88) (which threatened to dispossess entire communities of their traditional lands) and the Chipko movement were mostly driven by local activists. The case of the Chipko movement illustrated how a group of local people, with only the power of their own solidarity, were able to curtail logging in Uttar Pradesh in April 1973 by hugging trees—using the Gandian method of satyagraha (nonviolent resistance). This spontaneous movement spread to many parts of the Himilayas over the next five years (Ekins 1992, 143).

In Thailand, local people fought the Nam Choan dam project in the 1980s. Few Western and Japanese investments had been popularly resisted since the 1950s. The construction of dams in Thailand had previously led to deforestation and changes to local climatic conditions, soil fertility, and water and fishery resources (Hirsch and Lohmann 1989, 445). In Indonesia, China, and Iran, the local environment movements are one of the few dissenting voices allowed under authoritarian regimes (MacAndrews 1994, 369–80; Doyle and Simpson 2006). In fact, the list is endless. Poor people are those most affected by environmental degradation in the South, and they are also the motor of emancipatory movements that fight to secure justice and security for all. Broad writes: "A reader need only flip through any issue of the British journal *The Ecologist* or the Malaysian *Third World Resurgence* journal to find numerous case studies of the poor being involved in protecting the environment—replanting trees, struggling against the enclosure of ancestral lands, fighting for indigenous and community resource management" (Broad 1994, 813).

It can be proven that the jeopardization of the right to subsist—not growth or increased democratization—leads to environmental activism (Doyle 1998). Despite this reality, the North continues to tout its sustainable development vision.

Along with its economic growth policies comes the other half of the neo-Malthusian equation: those policies revolving around the reduction in number of the world's poorest populations. There can be no doubt that there are eventual limits to the earth's carrying capacity. But by not overtly considering issues like the overconsumption of resources by the North (coupled with these resources' maldistribution worldwide), this limits to population growth argument reeks of eugenics and not so subtle forms of genocide (Pepper 1984, 204–14).[7] The fact is that the United States and Japan together represent 40 percent of the world's gross national product (Imura 1994, 355). Although some forms of continued poverty do often have a negative impact on local environs,[8] both the degradation and the poverty are generally caused by ancient land-use and ecological histories (such as deforestation, desertification, etc.) coupled with the more recent (in human terms) exploitation of the South by the North, and a complex interplay between these factors.

So, on the political level, many of these problems are the result of many years of colonial imperialism on behalf of the North. The nations of the South were seen as—and still are—a treasure trove for Northern traders for hundreds of years. With many of these nations having now achieved "independence," they have embarked on their own development projects since the 1960s. One of the trends to emerge from green globalization has been for Northern groups to attempt to incorporate those very different concerns expressed by their Southern compatriots into their own agendas.

There is no doubt that increasingly, diverse interpretations of green identity are under pressures to homogenize. This issue will be developed more fully later, when we address the concept of the emergence of the green governance state. But we must accept that, despite these recent trends at conceptualizing and sharing grand green narratives, the actual environmental issues on the ground are profoundly different in the South than the North. Movements, therefore, that surface in countries like India, Bangladesh, or Somalia—in the majority world of the IOR—will be more oriented around issues of basic environmental security that have littered this collection: that is, the rights of people to gain access to the fundamental resources for survival: air, water, earth, and fire. As aforesaid, the most pressing environmental issues in the Indian Ocean Region, for example, comprising one-third of all the peoples on the earth, are almost always anthropocentric: people fighting for food and water security, struggling for adequate admission to a market that provides basic health care and adequate shelter, providing a society to live in that is not consistently ravaged by wars—such as Afghanistan, Palestine, or Angola. Wave after wave of colonialism, in all its forms, has created catastrophic tsunamis of human-making. Whereas in many parts of the North these issues, however compassionately understood, are literally worlds apart from the lives of the wealthy minority, most of whom will only ever experience the lives of the majority—what Toffler (1970) calls the Living Dead—through the vicarious experiences offered by travel and lifestyle programs on television and the Internet.

After more than thirty years of new environmentalisms, we are still only at the beginning of first discovering and then addressing the fundamental environmental problems in the Indian Ocean Region, which are just as rooted in transnational structures of power as they were three decades ago. The key difference is that new transnational structures of governance have split environmental movements into two main categories. First, there are those parts of a green public space that can be understood in emancipatory terms, building regional and global networks in a manner that increases the power resources of the poor and the environmentally

Box 21-1   Three Stages of Development in IOR Environment
and Development Movements

Stage 1: 1960s

First emergence of environmental movements in minority world countries, such as Australia. But for the majority, the first development decade in the South brought optimism. Northern-style growth and development were the goals. So much so, that there was little movement opposition within the countries of the South. The movements from outside the South—mainly in the form of large NGOs—occasionally entered the political sphere.

Stage 2: 1970s

During this period environment movements emerged in the South—again, dominated by some key NGOs (e.g., the Green Belt Movement in Kenya, the Environment Liaison Centre International, Environment and Development Action in the Third World, and Sahabat Alam Malaysia). Few movement participants opposed the Northern development ideology. But they fought for "people's development"—"another development"—not governments' or multinationals' development. This type of development shares many similarities with the political ecology movements in the North, particularly western Europe.

Stage 3: 1980s to current day

During this period movements split into two categories. After a period of emphasizing local and grassroots development in the 1970s, many networks in these movements began to collaborate with the governments, multi-national corporations, and international agencies again, as in the 1960s. We refer to these here as the green governance state. Many of these coalitions of grassroots groups and local NGOs formed umbrella coalitions (e.g., Asia Pacific People's Environmental Network, African NGOs Environmental Network, the Asian NGO Coalition, etc.). Many of these powerful coalitions bypass government, on occasions, and negotiate directly with corporations and international aid agencies. Other parts of the green public space maintained their activist, emancipatory stance, leading to the development of environmental protest movements, very similar to the political ecology movements of the North. These networks criticized Northern development schemes. They criticized Northern science, technology, industrial practices of transnational corporations, national governments, Northern governments, and international aid agencies (Chatterjee and Finger 1994; Doyle and McEachern 2001).

degraded. In the following analysis, these transnational players will be referred to as emancipatory groups (EGs). These emancipatory groups have a strong social movement dimension. Often, but not always, they construct themselves as separate from any notion of the state, whether it be national or transnational—including green governance states—and often in rugged opposition to what they perceive to be a global neoliberal project. These EGs, often through grassroots networking, develop shared techniques, strategies, and repertoires of action alongside more localized networks and groups and they celebrate more noninstitutional forms of organization. It is in this manner that the aforementioned national repertoires of resistance are shared and transmuted across borders throughout the IOR and beyond. These organizations see a clear divide between the concepts of a global green public sphere and an environmentalized governance state, seeing themselves as part of the former, but remaining outside the latter.

Other groups—particularly powerful and well-resourced environmental NGOs— are denoted here as part of the environmental governance state (EGS). They position themselves as part of the neoliberal project of the global governance state, using lim- ited—usually post- materialist—interpretations of green concerns to continue to dis- cipline societies that do not mirror their own constructions of nature, or what, in their minds, constitutes a productive and democratic civil society. These large transnational organizations, usually based in the North, construct grand narratives and systems of meaning, while giving some voice to the local, also often herding diverse forms of environmental opposition into one omnipresent story—such as climate change (as argued in the section on Air in this collection)—gutting the stories of the local.

Many emancipatory environmental movements are seen as key antagonists to corporate globalization, constantly attacking neoliberal market strategies and the largely ungoverned rampages of transnational corporations. Routledge et al. have produced a detailed analysis of the workings of a global justice network: the People's Global Action Asia (PGA). Its foremost "collective visions" directly attack corporate control, and embrace "a very clear rejection of capitalism" and a "confrontational attitude, since . . . transnational capital is the only real policy maker" (Routledge et al. 2006). There are a multitude of such groups and NGOs across the IOR—outside of the funding structures of the World Bank and wealthy nation-states—who continue to mobilize in largely structuralist fashion against the maneuvering of global capital.

Of course, structuralist and other more radical responses targeted at the global "other," though very apparent in many parts of the neo-colonial South, are not so appropriate in other parts of the world. In nondemocratic regimes, such as Iran (Doyle and Simpson 2006), newly emerging green NGOs provide access to the national political process for the first time to younger Iranians eager to communicate their dissatisfaction with the all-powerful regime that governs them. This process, through far from being revolutionary, is potentially emancipatory, in that it has seen the emergence of a green public sphere in Iran, which could in time be a har- binger of increasing democracy, ultimately leading to the ultimate overthrow of the ruling theocratic regime.

Of course, even emancipatory environmental justice groups operating at the transnational level can be accused, on occasions, of not going far enough in addressing inequities and, in doing so, becoming part of the problem rather than the solution. Doherty's research is of particular interest here in relation to EGs (Doherty 2006). By focusing on one international environmental NGO, Friends of the Earth International, with groups in 70 countries, Doherty addresses the basic issues that create friction between Northern and Southern branches in the same confederation. In an attempt to address the "divided planet" issue mentioned in the introduction of this edition, the European FoE groups were very proud of their concept of ecological space, which was used to show the gross inequities of consumption patterns between North and South.

But some Indian Ocean groups, and others from the South, felt that it did not go far enough, for it did not recognize the ecological debts imposed on the South by centuries of colonial exploitation. This failure to address past exploitation patterns and an inability to focus on issues of redistributive justice and basic environmental security drove a shard of ice into the very heart of the FoE confederation, which, to its credit, is currently seeking to address this profound difference in interpretation—in global political economy terms—between Northern groups and those in the South. These tensions in EGs are constant, as they openly wrestle with their capacities to liberate, on the one hand, and to denigrate on the other. These moral dilemmas are not so evident in those large green transnational organizations we refer to here as the global green governance state.

Rosaleen Duffy's research on transnational environmental management in the IOR island of Madagascar is of particular relevance here (Duffy 2006). She argues that in the case of the South, increasingly close relationships between states, global environmental NGOs, private companies, and the World Bank make it more appropriate to talk of the production of governance states, rather than the creation of a separate global civil society. NGOs like WWF and Conservation International work so closely with the interests of transnational capital and nation-states that they often become part of the same donor consortiums. In Madagascar, the donor consortium is comprised of USAID, the German government, the Japanese government, the French government, the Swiss government, Conservation International, WWF, Wildlife Conservation Society, and the World Bank.

In this picture, sovereignty is not a delimitation of one geographical space over another (nation-states), but is a space "formed through a series of practices which are defined by an interaction of forces" (Duffy 2006), including some powerful environmental NGOs. In this model, NGOs are just as much part of sovereign, global governance states as national governments.

In these cases, environmental concerns rarely reflect the needs and aspirations of local people. Associated with the aid and donorship programs are attached conditionalities. These conditions for "rebuilding societies"—whether it be after a war, after communism, after terrorism, or after colonialism—most usually include a pluralist, democratic system of governance, coupled with a neoliberal interpretation of the marketplace. In this vein, NGOs are constructed as vehicles that can recreate and reconfigure societal relationships, replacing and ignoring social systems of the "old order." The old, intra-national relationships are constructed as the problem: the West or the North (whatever the construction of the polarity) is the solution. This is synonymous with "the objective of colonial discourse," as Torgerson (2006) would have it. According to Homi Bhabba, the objective is "to construe the colonized as a population of degenerate types on the basis of racial origin, in order to justify conquest and to establish systems of administration and instruction" (Bhabba 2002). But, with a lack of continuous funding, one set of top-down NGOs is replaced by others better positioned to achieve success under the latest round of funding, creating an orientation toward external funders and away from representing local people. There is no support offered to lasting administrative and social structures that would allow citizens to decide and implement appropriate management structures, as indigenous networks are shunned.

In a controversial article published in *World Watch* by Mac Chapin, the funding of three of the largest of these environmental governance organizations—WWF, Conservation International (CI), and The Nature Conservancy (TNC)—was explored in some detail (Chapin 2004). Chapin concludes that the funding arrangements of "the big three" are intermeshed with the vested interests of transnational capital. This funding has made these organizations more dependent on large amounts of cash emanating from other parts of the governance state, leading to strong market competition between them. More importantly, this funding regime has led to the decimation of local organizations. He writes: "In dealing with smaller organizations, either they tend to use their sheer heft to press their agendas unilaterally or they exclude the smaller groups altogether. A common tactic is to create new organizations out of whole cloth in foreign countries, implanting local bodies as extensions of themselves" (Chapin 2004, 25).

The dominance of these large organizations is without precedence since the first emergence of the modern environmental movements in the 1960s, and its impacts are far-reaching. Along with a particularly apolitical version of democracy, which sees ENGOs as service providers rather than mass mobilizers and endorsing profit-based, market solutions, a particular type of environmentalism is also constructed as a central plank of this global sovereign conditionality. It is here that the politics of neocolonialism continues, using environmental concerns as a stick to beat local people into submission. One way in which environmentalism is used as a continued plank of imperialism is the narrow, post-materialist way in which it is defined. In this vein, Duffy, in her study of Madagascar, takes issue with Conservation International and the Wildlife Conservation Society as "fortress conservation" organizations, meaning that they support policies that would exclude people from designated wildlife zones in order to protect nonhuman nature. This version of environmental security is actually a continued but reoriented form of neocolonialism. This is probably the clearest indicator that separates the earlier mentioned emancipatory environmental justice groups from those who are part of the green governance state. Emancipatory environmentalists argue that only by engaging with the subjective voices of the local, traditional, and indigenous peoples can adequate ecological management strategies be assembled; whereas organizations like CI prefer the guidance of an objective, Western science, masking as apolitical and technical what is in fact a profoundly ideological position. This post-materialist "fortress" approach, again, sees poor people of the IOR as the main environmental degraders, and seeks wilderness parks devoid of human imprints: "a romanticized view of a stunning wilderness and an aura of extraordinary biodiversity" (Duffy 2006). The three green NGOs in the Madagascar donor consortium are all wildlife oriented, though incredibly, they direct much national policy making in Madagascar, both environmental and non-environmental, including the national poverty reduction strategy. Central to this approach are the "the debt-for-nature swaps" and the establishment of wildlife corridors. The green voices of the IOR are deafeningly silent here.

The emergence of this EGS—with its tightly controlled post-materialist focus— may not actually denote trends toward democratic change at all, but, rather, the construction of a state- controlled civil society, or worse, a hollow construction with civil society only marked by the clever use of nomenclature and imitation. In the cases of Iran or Burma (Doyle and Simpson 2006), this public mobilization may actually be an indicator of authoritarianism, or even totalitarianism, rather than an indicator toward democratic change. Or, alternatively, the emergence of these kinds of EGS can be seen as an indicator of free markets taking root in a given society. Even in an authoritarian regime such as Iran, the language of corporate globalization is never far away: the reinvigoration of the third or "civil society" sector is not really about empowering citizens, but rather is seen as a convenient way to "downsize government" and reduce its direct responsibilities in environmental policy making.

These environmental governance organizations, with their increasing dominance of the green political space, are increasingly building and selling grand environmental narratives with global reach. Climate change is the current theme used most often in the ecopolitical marketplace. These stories are the songlines of ecological conditionality, mapping out the coordinates that determine which groups shall be included in agenda-setting and decision-making, determining those who will be funded, selecting those who shall be corporatized into the global governance state, and relegating those who shall remain on the noninstitutionalized periphery.

Conclusion

This book has investigated the rapidly burgeoning academic and activist fields devoted to concepts and practices of environmental security. As we have discovered through the contributions to this volume, the concept of environmental security is equally diverse in its meaning: it includes the traditional, conflict-based, statist frameworks that view environmental stress as an additional threat to peace and stability; the securitization of the environment by nation-states; and, then, more innovative interpretations that envision it as a lynchpin of cooperative models of regional and global security, with the potential to secure access for all people to fulfill their basic needs for survival—a security to practice a diverse range of livelihoods (Barnett 2001; Dalby 2002; Dodds and Pippard 2005). But underwriting more liberal and critical interpretations of environmental security is a definition of human and environmental justice that is reflective of the post-colonial historical and cultural reality of the Indian Ocean.

In the early years of this new millennium, it is hoped that nation-states can continue to provide regional leadership across the Indian Ocean, rather than handing over their basic democratic responsibilities to transnational corporate interests. Currently, however, it is social movements that are the most visible players fighting for the basic rights of all people to secure access to the fundaments of human survival. Issues of access to adequate resources, in most parts of the IOR, are not the subject of polite politics operating within a forum of business-as-usual. The politics of environmental justice and security in the IOR is more often about direct resistance led by emancipatory people's movements, fuelled by their only true source of power—their own solidarity. It is within these struggles of resistance and emancipation where the crucible for survival can be found.

NOTES

1. Of course, "stakeholders" cannot be confused with "people" or "the public." The concept of the stakeholder is often used to fully excuse any further dealings with "the public." The choice of the appropriate stakeholders is an intensely political process that is rarely democratic or representative of broader interests.

2. These two bodies of theory are not mutually exclusive, and share several propositions.

3. As aforesaid, there are numerous exceptions. There are active wilderness-oriented movements, for example, in parts of Africa.

4. In 1990, the UN Human Development Report stated: "poverty is one of the greatest threats to the environment." In 1993, an International Monetary Fund article read: "Poverty and the environment are linked in that the poor are more likely to resort to activities that can degrade the environment" (Broad 1994, 812).

5. For an excellent example of this line of reasoning, read Hartshorn 1999.

6. In many well-meaning works prior to the UNCED "summit" in Rio in 1992, it was constantly argued that the South (and the Eastern parts of the North, for that matter) had to become more like the United States in its political system if environmental degradation was to be brought under control. In this vein, the development of "civil society" (a U.S. term) is central to discussion. Underlying this "civil society" is an unquestioned acceptance of the apolitical American form of democracy based on capitalism and global free-market places. An excellent example of this mode of reasoning is a central plank of the book *Grassroots Environmental Action,* by Ghai and Vivian (1992). They write: "The existence of a democratic space allowing the expression and defense of community rights and claims has proven to be a crucial factor influencing successful grass-roots environmental action. . . . The essence of these activities is to persuade or pressure the state to intervene on behalf of the communities through adoption of new legislation" (18–19).

7. China, for example, has over 1 billion people in its population. India has a little under this number. These two combined populations use less resources than the 250 million citizens of the United States.

8. In an article by Robin Broad on the Philippine's environment movement, "The Poor and the Environment: Friends or Foe" (1994), an important distinction is made on the connections between types of poverty and environmental degradation. Broad separates between the "merely poor" and the "very, very poor." Fundamentally, the former category are those still operating subsistence lifestyles (though under threat) and those who have been recently removed from this lifestyle. The latter category are the "landless and rootless." These have no security of tenure and little connectedness to place. This category includes those peasants and squatters who survive by cutting forest cover, by consuming wildlife, and by planting crops on soils that will erode.

REFERENCES

Anheier, H., and N. Themudo. 2002. "Organisational Forms of Global Civil Society: Implications of Going Global." In *Global Civil Society 2002,* ed. H. Anheier, M. Glasius, and M. Kaldor. Oxford: Oxford Univ. Press.

Bandy, J., and J. Smith. 2005. "Introduction: Cooperation and Conflict in Transnational Protest." In *Coalitions Across Borders: Transnational Protest and the Neoliberal Order,* ed. J. Bandy and J. Smith, 1–20. Oxford: Rowman and Littlefield.

Barnett, J. 2001. *The Meaning of Environmental Security: Ecological Politics and Policy in the New Security Era.* New York: Zed Books.

Bhabba, H. 1990. "The Other Question: Difference, Discrimination and the Discourse of Colonialism." In *Out There: Marginalization and Contemporary Cultures,* ed. R. Ferguson, M. Gever, T. Minh-Ha, and C. West, 71–87. Cambridge, Mass.: MIT. Press.

Bob, C. 2001. "Marketing Rebellion: Insurgent Groups, International Media, and NGO Support." *International Politics* 38 (3): 311–34.

Boggs, C. 1986. *Social Movements and Political Power: Emerging Forms of Radicalism in the West.* Philadelphia, Pa.: Temple Univ. Press.

Broad, R. 1994. "The Poor and the Environment: Friends or Foe." *World Development* 22 (6): 812–22.

Brulle, R., and J. Craig Jenkins. 2006. "Spinning Our Way to Sustainability." *Organization and Environment* 19 (1): 82–87.

Bührs, T. and R. V. Bartlett. 1997. "Strategic Thinking and the Government: Planning the Future in New Zealand?" *Environmental Politics* 6 (2): 72–100.

Burton, B. 2001. Interview with the author, May.

Calvert, P., and S. Calvert. 1999. *The South, The North and the Environment.* London: Pinter.

Castells, M. 1997. *The Power of Identity.* Oxford: Blackwell.

Chapin, M. . 2004. "A Challenge to Conservationists." *World Watch* (November/December): 17–31.

Chatterjee, P., and M. Finder. 1994. *The Earth Brokers: Power, Politics and World Development.* London: Routledge.

Dahl, R. 1969. "The Concept of Power." In *Political Power: A Reader in Theory and Research,* ed. R. Bell, D. Edwards, R. Harrison Wagner, 201–15. New York: Free Press.

Dalby, S. 2002. *Environmental Security.* Minneapolis: Univ. of Minnesota Press.

Dodds, F., and T. Pippard, ed. 2005. *Human and Environmental Security: An Agenda for Change.* London: Earthscan.

Doherty, B. 2002. *Ideas and Actions in the Green Movement.* London: Routledge.

———. 2006. "Friends of the Earth International: Negotiating a Transnational Identity." *Environmental Politics* 15 (5): 860–80.

Doherty, B., and T. Doyle. 2006. "Beyond Borders: Transnational Politics, Social Movements and Modern Environmentalisms." *Environmental Politics* 15 (5): 697–712.

Dowie, M. 1995. *Losing Ground: American Environmentalism at the Close of the Twentieth Century.* Cambridge, Mass.: MIT Press.

Doyle, T. 1998. "Sustainable Development and Agenda 21: The Secular Bible of Global Free Markets and Pluralist Democracy," *Third World Quarterly* 19 (4): 771–86.

———. 1999. "Research Decision-Making in Arid Lands: The Consequences of Wise Use." In *Environmental Policy 2,* ed. K. Walker and K. Crowley. Sydney: Univ. of NSW Press.

———. 2005. *Environmental Movements in Majority and Minority Worlds: A Global Perspective.* New Brunswick, N.J.: Rutgers Univ. Press.

Doyle, T., and A. Kellow, A. 1995. *Environmental Politics and Policy-Making in Australia.* Sydney: Macmillan.

Doyle, T., and D. McEachern. 1998, 2001, 2008. *Environment and Politics.* London: Routledge.

Doyle, T., and A. Simpson. 2006. "Traversing More than Speed Bumps: Green Politics Under Authoritarian Regimes in Burma and Iran." *Environmental Politics* 15 (5): 750–67.

Duffey, R. 2006. "New Governmental Organisations and Governance States: The Impact of Transnational Environmental Management Networks in Madagascar." *Environmental Politics* 15 (5): 731–49.

Edwards, M., and J. Gaventa. 2001. *Global Citizen Action.* London: Earthscan.

Ekins, P. 1992. *A New World Order: Grassroots Movement for Local Change.* London: Routledge.

Fraser, N. 1990. "Rethinking the Public Sphere: A Contribution to the Critique of Actually Existing Democracy." *Social Text* (25/26): 56–80.

Ghai, D., and J. Vivian, eds. 1992. *Grassroots Environmental Action: People's Participation in Sustainable Development.* London: Routledge.

Grady, M. 1998. "SA's Biggest Park—Juggernaut in Low Gear." *Environment South Australia* 7 (3): 13.

Grove, R. 1995. *Green Imperialism: Colonial Expansion, Tropical Island Edens, and the Origins of Environmentalism, 1600–1860.* Cambridge: Cambridge Univ. Press.

Guha, R., and J. Martinez-Alier. 1997. *Varieties of Environmentalism: Essays North and South.* London: Earthscan.

Hartshorn, G.S. 1991. "Key Environmental Issues for Developing Countries." *Journal of International Affairs* 3: 393–401.

Hill, R. 1998. Quoted in ABC Radio interview, Port Lincoln, August 5.

Hirsch, P., and L. Lohmann. 1989. "Contemporary Politics of Environment in Thailand." Asian Survey 29 (4): 439–51.

Imura, H. 1994. "Japan's Balancing Act." *Asian Survey* 34 (4): 355–68.

Inglehart, R. 1977. *The Silent Revolution: Changing Values and Political Styles Among Western Publics.* Princeton, N.J.: Princeton Univ. Press.

Keane, J. 2003. *Global Civil Society.* Cambridge: Cambridge Univ. Press.

Keck, M. E., and V. Sikkink. 1998. *Activists Beyond Borders: Advocacy Networks in International Politics.* Ithaca, N.Y.: Cornell Univ. Press.

Lukes, S. 1974. *Power: A Radical View.* London: Macmillan.

MacAndrews, C. 1994. "Politics and the Environment in Indonesia." *Asian Survey* 34 (4): 69–80.

Martinez-Alier, J. 2004. "Ecological Distribution Conflict and Indicators of Sustainability," English translation. *Revista Ibero-Americana de Economia Ecologica* (1): 21–31.

Maslow, A. M. 1954. *Motivation and Personality.* New York: Harper.

Matthews, K., and M. Paterson. 2005. "Boom or Bust?: The Economic Engine Behind the Drive for Climate Change Policy." *Global Change, Peace and Security* 17 (1): 59.

Melucci, A. 1996. *Challenging Codes: Collective Action in the Information Age.* Cambridge: Cambridge Univ. Press.

Mignolo, W. 2000. "The Many Faces of Cosmo-Polis: Border Thinking and Critical Cosmopolitanism." *Public Culture* 12 (3): 721–48.

Papadakis, E. 1993. *Politics and the Environment: The Australian Experience.* Sydney: Allen and Unwin.

Pepper, D. 1984. *The Roots of Modern Environmentalism.* London: Groom Helm.

Prideaux, M., M. Horstman, and J. Emmett. 1998. "Sustainable Use or Multiple Abuse." *Habitat,* Melbourne 26 (2) (April): 15.

Princen, T., and M. Finger, eds. 1994. *Environmental NGOs in World Politics.* London: Routledge.

Rootes, C. 2004. "Environmental Movements." In *The Blackwell Companion to Social Movement,* ed. D. Snow, S. Soule, and H. P. Kriesi, 608–40. Oxford: Blackwell.

Routledge, P., C. Nativel, and A. Cumbers. 2006. "Entangled Logics and Grassroots Imaginaries of Global Justice Networks." *Environmental Politics* 15 (5): 697–712.

Smith, J. 2005. "Building Bridges or Building Walls? Explaining Regionalization Among Transnational Social Movement Organisations." *Mobilization* 10 (2): 251–69.

Tarrow, S. 1998. *Power in Movement.* Cambridge: Cambridge Univ. Press.

Tarrow, S., and D. Della Porta. 2005. "Transnational Protest and Social Activism." In *Transnational Protest and Global Activism,* ed. S. Tarrow and D. Della Porta, 1–17. Oxford: Rowman and Littlefield.

Toffler, A. 1970. *Future Shock.* London: Pan.

Torgerson, D. 1999. *The Promise of Green Politics.* Durham, N.C.: Duke Univ. Press.

———. 2006. "Expanding the Green Public Sphere: Post-Colonialism Corrections." *Environmental Politics* 15 (5): 713–30.

Touraine, A. 1980. *The Voice and the Eye: An Analysis of Social Movements.* Cambridge: Cambridge Univ. Press.

Thörn, H. 2006. *Anti-Apartheid and the Emergence of a Global Civil Society.* Basingstoke: Palgrave.

Ward, B., and R. Dubos. 1972. *Only One Earth: The Care and Maintenance of a Small Planet.* New York: Norton.

Whatmore, Sarah. 2002. *Hybrid Geographies: Natures, Cultures, Spaces.* London: Sage.

Wood, L. J. 2005. "Bridging the Chasms: The Case of People's Global Action." In *Coalitions Across Borders: Transnational Protest and the Neoliberal Order,* ed. J. Bandy and J. Smith, 95–117. Oxford: Rowman and Littlefield.

Young, I. M. 2001. *Inclusion and Democracy.* Oxford: Oxford Univ. Press.

Notes on the Contributors

SALEEM H. ALI is associate professor of environmental planning at the University of Vermont, and holds adjunct appointments at Brown University and the United Nations mandated University for Peace (Costa Rica). He received his doctorate in environmental planning from MIT, a master's in environmental studies from Yale University, and his bachelor's in chemistry from Tufts University. His latest book is the edited volume *Peace Parks: Conservation and Conflict Resolution* (MIT Press, 2007).

APARAJITA BISWAS completed her M.A. in international relations from Jadavpur University, Kolkata (erstwhile Calcutta). She did her Ph.D. in African studies from University of Mumbai and presently is a professor at the Centre for African Studies, University of Mumbai, India. She is associated with many universities, research institutes, and research groups in India and abroad. She has written extensively on African affairs in reputed Indian and foreign journals. Apart from a number of chapters in books published in India and abroad, she also has a publication, *Indo-Kenyan Economic and Political Relations* (Delhi, 1992). Her book on *Post-Apartheid South Africa's Relations with the SADC Countries* is scheduled for publication toward October–November 2007.

DR. CHRISTIAN BOUCHARD is currently teaching at the Department of Geography at Laurentian University (Sudbury, Canada). He has developed interest and works in two main research areas, which are Indian Ocean geopolitics and development in small island states and territories. Over time, he has developed particular expertise in the fields of maritime political geography and energy issues in small islands. Dr. Bouchard is a member of the Committee of Management of the Indian Ocean Research Group (IORG), in which he is also responsible for a research program on development in the small island states and territories of the Indian Ocean.

DR. SANJAY CHATURVEDI is a Reader in political science at Panjab University (Chandigarh, India) and vice- chairman of the Indian Ocean Research Group, Inc. He is co-chair of Research Committee 15 (Political and Cultural Geography) of the International Political Science Association and a member of the Steering Committee of the IGU Commission of Political Geography. Chaturvedi serves on the editorial board of *Geopolitics* (Routledge) and *Cooperation and Conflict* (Sage). He is the author of *Polar Regions: A Political Geography* (John Wiley and Sons) and co-author of *Partitions: Reshaping Minds and States* (Routledge), and the co-editor (with Dennis Rumley) of *Security of the Sea Lanes of Communication in the Indian Ocean* (Maritime Institute of Malaysia).

PROFESSOR TIMOTHY DOYLE is chair of politics and international relations in SPIRE at Keele University, United Kingdom, and chair of politics and international studies at the University of Adelaide, Australia. His most recent works include the books: *Environment and Politics* (Routledge, 1998, 2001, 2008); *Green Power: The Environment Movement in Australia* (Univ. of New South Wales Press, 2001); *Environmental Movements in Minority and Majority Worlds: A Global Perspective* (Rutgers Univ. Press, 2005); and *Beyond Borders: Transnational Environmental Politics,* with Brian Doherty (Routledge, 2008). At Keele, he teaches global political economy and environmental politics. In his academic capacity, he has taught and contributed to university courses in the United Kingdom, the United States, Malaysia, India, and Australia. He has been a dedicated environmental and human rights activist since the late 1970s. He is currently serving as Founding Convenor of Human and Environmental Security for the Indian Ocean Research Group.

DR. RADHA D'SOUZA is a Reader in law at the University of Westminster, London. Her research interests include water conflicts, law and development, colonialism and imperialism, socio-legal studies in the "third world," and global social justice. She teaches law and development and has previously taught in sociology, development studies, and human geography, besides public law and legal theory.

MARCUS HAWARD is an associate professor at the School of Government at the University of Tasmania, and is program leader of the Policy Program, Antarctic Climate and Ecosystems Cooperative Research Centre (ACE CRC). His research interests include Antarctic and Southern Ocean law and policy, fisheries management, and coastal and oceans governance, and he has published widely in these areas.

RICHARD HINDMARSH is a senior lecturer in biopolitics and environmental policy at the Griffith School of Environment, and is also a member of the Centre for Governance and Public Policy, Griffith University, Brisbane. He was awarded a Ph.D. from Griffith University (1995) and an Australian Research Council Postdoctoral Research Fellowship (1995–98). His latest book is *Edging Towards BioUtopia: A New Politics of Reordering Life and the Democratic Challenge* (University of Western Australia Press, 2008).

JONATHAN RIGG is a professor in the Department of Geography at Durham University, United Kingdom. His research interests lie in agrarian and livelihood change in Asia, and particularly in mainland Southeast Asia. His publications include: *Southeast Asia: The Human Landscape of Modernisation and Development* (Routledge, 2003), *Living with Transition in Laos* (RoutledgeCurzon, 2005), and *An Everyday Geography of the Global South* (Routledge, 2007).

MELISSA RISELY is an environmental consultant and researcher. Awarded a Ph.D. from the University of Adelaide in 2003, much of her early research focused on the rapidly emerging biotechnology industry (see *The Politics of Precaution: An Ecopolitical Investigation of Australia's Biotechnology Policy, 1992–2000*). More recently she has been involved in environmental and social impact assessment in the mining sector. With deep-seated environmental justice concerns, Risely has become very much involved in the IORG Human and Environmental Security Project, and for the past three years has worked tirelessly on pursuing its objectives.

DENNIS RUMLEY is currently an adjunct professor at Edith Cowan University (Perth, Western Australia) and an Honorary Senior Research Fellow at the University of Western Australia. He has been an editorial board member of various international journals and has published widely in many areas of political geography and international relations, including electoral geography, local government, federalism, Australia's regional relations, geopolitics, India-Australia relations, and the Indian Ocean Region. He is currently chairperson of the Indian Ocean Research Group (http://www.iorgroup.org).

EVA SAROCH received her Ph.D. from Panjab University (Chandigarh, India). Her areas of research are resource geopolitics, climate change, variability and disaster risk reduction. Some of her publications include *Turning Ecological Spaces into Geopolitical Spaces: Views from South Asia* and "Water Nepal, Kathmandu, Representing (hydro)borders in South Asia," *Encyclopedia of Water* (John Wiley and Sons). Currently she is a research associate with the Institute for Social and Environmental Transition in Boulder, Colorado, and involved in their projects in South Asia.

DR. CLIVE SCHOFIELD is a QEII Research Fellow based at the Australian Centre for Ocean Resource and Security (ANCORS), at the University of Wollongong, Australia. He is a political geographer specializing in the study of maritime boundaries. Previously he has served as a Vice-Chancellor's Research Fellow, University of New South Wales, and as director of research for the International Boundaries Research Unit, University of Durham, United Kingdom.

ADAM SIMPSON is a lecturer in international politics in the School of International Studies at the University of South Australia. He was previously an analyst with several British and U.S. investment banks in London. His current research focuses on South and Southeast Asia and includes green activism under authoritarian regimes and the nexus between human rights and environmental protection. Recent publications have appeared in *Third World Quarterly* and *Environmental Politics*.

DR. MAY TAN-MULLINS is a research associate in the Department of Geography at Durham University. She is currently working on the politics of Chinese engagement with African development relations. As well as her work on the geographies of rehabilitation of tsunami-affected communities, May is involved in ethnographic research in Southern Thailand and methods of conflict resolution.

CAMPBELL WALKER is campaigns coordinator with Friends of the Earth (FoE) Australia and has been active in the environmental and social justice movements for many years. He has traveled and worked extensively with community organizations in Latin America, Europe, and, most recently, Africa. He lectures part-time in the School of Social Science at RMIT in Melbourne. Prior to working with FoE he was a secondary teacher.

CARL GRUNDY-WARR is a senior lecturer in the Department of Geography at the Singapore National University. His research interests span political geography, borderland geographies, and environmental security. He has been working on mainland Southeast Asia for many years.

Index